GE:
GENETIC ENGINEERING
AND YOU

GE:
Genetic Engineering and You

MOYRA BREMNER

HarperCollins*Publishers*

HarperCollins*Publishers*
77−85 Fulham Palace Road,
Hammersmith, London W6 8JB

Published by HarperCollins*Publishers* 1999
1 3 5 7 9 10 8 6 4 2

ISBN 0 00 653190 3

Set in Linotype PostScript Meridien by
Rowland Phototypesetting Ltd,
Bury St Edmunds, Suffolk

Printed and bound in Great Britain by
Clays Ltd, St Ives plc

To my dear friends
Anne Baring and Sarida Brown
who have understood the dangers of genetic engineering
misuse for so long. Their support and encouragement has
made a huge contribution to this book.

Contents

Acknowledgements

In writing on this subject I have been brought into contact with so many people who have inspired me with their integrity and dedication: scientists from all over the world who have risked their careers by denying the false reassurances of big business and governments, and many others who have invested enormous time, energy and money in opposing the misuse of genetic engineering. Their generosity and kindness to me have been extraordinary. To thank them adequately, or fully do justice to such a wealth of help and information, would be impossible. I simply hope this book makes a contribution to the debate about which they care so passionately.

It is impossible to name all those who have helped me. But I owe a particular debt to Professor John Fagan, Dr Ricarda Steinbrecher, Mark Griffiths, Dr Mae-Wan Ho, Dr Michael Antoniou, John Verrall, Professor Ronald Cummins, Hope Shand, Professor Sheldon Krimsky, Dr Sue Meyer, Joyce D'Silva, Dr Vandana Shiva, Patti Rundall, Hartmut Meyer, Bob Phelps, Professor Philip Regal, Professor George Monbiot and Dr Michael Hansen. Special thanks go to RAFI, which has been so generous with its material.

I am also greatly indebted to all the individuals and organisations listed below, not in order of priority, to all the government and company press officers who helped me and to many others too numerous to list (I apologise for any titles, accidentally omitted): Professor Barry Law, the Gaia Foundation, Norman Baker MP, Kathy Heaton, Professor Stuart Newman, Peter Warburton, Compassion in World Farming, Jose MacDonald, GeneWatch, Michael Mansfield QC, Professor Miguel Altieri, Charles Colville, the Soil Association, Professor David Latchman, Dr Ben Mepham, Professor Colin Blakemore, The Corner House, Professor Sir Joseph Rotblat, Professor Brian Wynne, The Marchioness of Worcester, Bridget Gillman, Beth Burrows, Professor Ingrid Williams, Professor Erik Millstone, Helena Paul, Professor Jean Golding, Dr Desirée Cox-Maksimov, Dr Majid Katme, Dr Pauline Lane, the Women's Environmental Network, Dr Paul Rumsby, Dr Alex Hankey, Professor Marion Nestle, Professor Elaine Ingham, Viola Sampson, Tom Wakeford, The Infant Feeding Coalition Canada, Elisabeth Sterken, Robert Vint, John Whiting, Sue Dibbs, Tim Lobstein, the Food Commission, Action Aid, PANNA, Bill Wadsworth, Christine Orr, the British Union for the Abolition of Vivisection, the Pure Food Campaign USA, Patrick Holden, Emma Parkin, Bridges Weekly, Neil Thomas at Stevens Hewlett, Patti Rundall, Baby Milk Action, Dr Vernon Barber, *The Ecologist* Magazine, the GMO Campaign Oxford, the European Network on Genetic Engineering, David Buffin, the Pesticides Trust, the Council for Responsible Genetics, Richard Wolfson, the Roslin Institute, Jane Akre and Steve Wilson, Mary Whiting, the Australian Gene Ethics Network, the Consumer Policy Institute (New York), Ellen Hickey, Dr Matthew Kiln, the Insulin Dependent Diabetes Trust, Greenpeace, York Nutritional Laboratories, Boots Plc, Dr Julia Wrathall, RSPCA, Alan Simpson MP, Jan Rietema, Sandra Bell, Friends of the Earth, the BMA, Adrian Arbib, Lesley Buckett, the Genetics Forum, GEN, the British Diabetic Association, the World Health Organisation, Rowan Tilly. My thanks also go to those in so many other organisations whom I have not been able to name, to my publishers, to my family for their support, and especially to my daughter for her invaluable help.

Introduction

My editor at HarperCollins said to me, 'The trouble with genetic engineering is that it's like a soap opera – if you've got a life you keep missing bits of the plot.'

This book is for everyone who feels they know it all and want something new. For those who have missed some of the plot, for those who have missed the plot entirely, or have found it too confusing and given up. It's also for those who want to check out their own knowledge against an overview; those who know the facts but want to put them in context, or who'd like to know what's coming next.

To tell you absolutely everything about genetic engineering (GE) would take several encyclopaedias. However, this book will tell you the background to the issues, the latest issues, and the key issues. Because GE food is a big concern a large section of it is devoted to food and food safety but it also covers almost every aspect of GE from medicine to work on animals. It has a list of useful addresses and books, ideas for action you might take if you're incensed by any aspect of GE, plus a glossary and list of acronyms in this area. In fact this book is designed to cover all the major current issues, and coming issues, in genetic engineering that most affect you, your life, the world around you, and those you care about.

Here, I have a confession to make. I adore science. So, originally, I approached genetic engineering as eagerly as a child spying a new sweet shop. I was so enchanted with claims of living organisms cleaning up oil spills and detoxifying poison dumps that I didn't immediately see the extraordinary dangers GE also poses. Even today I'd like nothing better than for genetic engineering to be used only for good; for all the vast corporations, which drive it, to be humanitarian and environmentally responsible; for it to involve no violation of nature, no lack of ethics, no threat to democracy, no reduction in freedom, no danger to wildlife, no threat to crops and gardens, no damage to the soil, no cruelty to animals, no increase in poverty and no risk of starvation, new diseases, or harm to children.

Unfortunately, aspects of biotechnology bring all these dangers, and it took me a while to remove my rose-tinted spectacles and begin writing articles about how it really is. Would it have made a difference if I'd rung warning bells in the early days of GE, when I was broadcasting on science for the BBC? Of course not. All the same, I wish I could claim the long-range foresight of Jeremy Rifkin who, more than twenty years ago, wrote the book *Who Should Play God?* in which he and his co-author Ted Howard warned of the practical dangers and moral dilemmas which genetic engineering would create.

On the other hand, there couldn't be a better time for writing a book on this topic. At this very moment biotechnology is on a make-or-break course. Scientifically it is – in key areas – set out on what may well be a track to new and virulent diseases; ethically it is dabbling in very murky waters; ecologically it may be setting light to a time bomb which could destroy aspects of the environment without which humanity cannot survive; commercially, it is being exploited with a ruthlessness and a greed which make some film plots seem tame. And it is doing all this in ways that reach deep into the personal lives of every one of us – in ways few people realise, despite all the media attention.

This is a branch of science which governments are following, rather than controlling and which is failing to set itself ethical boundaries and make rogue practitioners behave responsibly. As a result it may be heading for repercussions which will discredit the whole of biotechnology and wrongly foster public distrust of science itself.

As any of you who have read my articles on the topic might expect, I am concerned with facts. If there are benefits to any aspect of genetic engineering I say so. I'm not anti-science, anti-big business, anti-progress, or radical in any other way – I would not have written on business and science for the *Sunday Times*, or presented BBC Television's *Money Programme*, if I had been. Where I criticise it is because the facts over-whelmingly merit criticism. My aim is to clearly and simply outline these facts and put you, the reader, in a stronger position to judge when politicians, partisan scientists, or PR officers from the agro-chemical companies try to peddle half-truths, disinformation and lies.

This book is about you and me – about the nuts and bolts of how genetic engineering is changing our lives, and how it may affect the lives of all generations to come. It is also about what we can do to prevent the harm, if we choose. At the same time I wanted to take you inside the subject, show you a little of what is going on behind the scenes and tell you some of the secrets which make sense of the extraordinary biotech scene – secrets which some companies don't want you to know. In doing all this I have looked at biotechnology from a wider perspective than that of GE itself: the perspective of a world which is invisibly interconnected and interactive.

Using This Book

This book has been designed not only to be read from cover to cover, but also to be cherry-picked, dipped into for reference, nibbled by the paragraph – or whatever suits you. Having filled it with as many fascinating and vital facts as possible, I hope you'll enjoy all of it. But you may want to dive straight into a particular aspect of genetic engineering that concerns you – perhaps food safety, or research on animals. If so, the detailed contents list at the front of the book is there to make it easy for you to find what you want. The frequent headings let you narrow your search still further.

I wanted to bring you the views of as many people as possible. So, threaded between my paragraphs, you'll find comments from people and organisations from all over the world. Reading their words, you may be surprised to see how many scientists, doctors and other experts are profoundly concerned about many aspects of genetic engineering. You'll notice I talk about 'genetic engineering' and 'GE', rather than GMOs (genetically modified organisms). The main reason is because this book is about all aspects of this topic, not simply about food, and GE can be used for all of them. It is also because 'modified' is a weasel word which the companies use to make the process seem less mechanical, and more natural. Modified starches have been on ingredients lists for ages – and have nothing to do with biotechnology. So using the word 'modified' put GE food cosily into the sheepfold of familiar starches. But it is a wolf dressed up as a sheep. Genetic modification uses invasive, complicated and risky processes that nobody would apply to crops if they respected wildlife, or human life.

Now that GMOs have got a bad name, the biotech companies want us to call them LMOs – Living Modified Organisms – which they will doubtless try to change to Less Modified Organisms. Before long they will be trying to persuade us that GE is more natural than nature. When the nuclear power station Windscale leaked they applied the same verbal cosmetic surgery and renamed it Sellafield. It didn't change the facts there, and it won't change them with GE.

Another reason for using the term GE is that GMO doesn't always fit the many ways in which genetic engineering affects our food. There are about half a dozen ways in which our food could have had a close encounter of the genetic kind. For example, some foods are from crops which are themselves changed (or modified) genetically. Others are substances produced by organisms which have been genetically engineered – produced in the sense that bees produce honey. Others might be meat from animals injected with genetically engineered substances, or which have eaten GE crops. In most of these cases the food itself hasn't been genetically modified – yet, in every one of them, genetic engineering has affected their nature and/or their safety. So, to simplify matters, I use GE to mean both 'genetically engineered' and 'genetic engineering'. I use 'GE food' in situations in which the food would not have existed in that form if genetic engineering hadn't got in on the act somewhere, at some time. But if you prefer to think 'GM' every time you see 'GE' it will still make sense.

I hope you'll find the book as fascinating to read as I've found it to write.

One World

In 1854, the authorities in Washington made an offer for a large area of Indian land and promised a 'reservation' for the Indian people. Their reply, sometimes attributed to Chief Seattle, has been described as the most beautiful and profound statement on the environment ever made. He wrote:

How can you buy or sell the sky, the warmth of the land? The idea is strange to us. If we do not own the freshness of the air and the sparkle of the water, how can you buy then? Every part of this earth is sacred to my people. Every shrinking pine needle, every sandy shore, every mist in the dark woods, every clearing and humming insect is holy in the memory and experience of my people . . .

We are part of the earth and the earth is part of us. The perfumed flowers are our sisters. The deer, the horse, the great eagle, these are our brothers. The rocky crests, the juices of the meadow, the body heat of the pony, and man – all belong to the same family.

We know that the white man does not understand our ways . . . The earth is not his brother, but his enemy, and when he has conquered he moves on . . . His appetite will devour the earth and leave only a desert . . . Teach your children what we have taught our children, that the earth is our mother . . . Whatever befalls the earth befalls the sons of the earth.

If men spit upon the ground they spit upon themselves.

This we know, the earth does not belong to man; man belongs to the earth.

This we know.

All things are connected like the blood which unites one family. All things are connected. For whatever happens to the beasts soon happens to man. All things are connected. Whatever befalls the earth befalls the sons of the earth. Man did not weave the web of life; he is merely a strand in it. Whatever he does to the web, he does to himself.

Even the white man, whose God walks and talks with him as friend to friend, cannot be exempt from the common destiny.

One thing we know, which the white man may one day discover – our God is the same God. You may think now that you own Him as you wish to own our land, but you cannot. He is the God of man, and His compassion is equal to the red man and the white. This earth is precious to Him, and to harm the earth is to heap contempt on its Creator. Contaminate your bed, and you will one night suffocate in your own way.

That destiny is a mystery to us, for we do not understand when the buffalo are all slaughtered, the wild horses are tamed, the secret corners of the forest heavy with the scent of many men, and the view of the ripe hills blotted by talking wires.

Where is the thicket? Gone.

Where is the eagle? Gone.

The end of living and the beginning of survival.

1

Sowing the Storm

Three Myths

Everything is separate.
Genetic engineering is well regulated.
If GE food is rejected biotechnology will fail.

The late twentieth century has witnessed a scientific gold rush of astonishing proportions: the headlong and furious haste to commercialize genetic engineering. This enterprise has proceeded so rapidly – with so little outside commentary – that its dimensions and implications are hardly understood at all . . . The work is uncontrolled. No one supervises it . . . There is no coherent government policy, in America, or anywhere else in the world.

The most disturbing fact is that no watchdogs are to be found among the scientists themselves. It is a remarkable fact that nearly every scientist in genetic research is also engaged in the commerce of biotechnology. There are no detached observers. Everybody has a stake.

Michael Crichton, introduction to *Jurassic Park*[1]

Michael Crichton's book *Jurassic Park* wasn't just entertainment – it was a warning of the dangers of biotechnology over-reaching itself. The book ends with the main characters admitting that some of the creatures have escaped beyond recall. They are left wondering if the earth will ever be the same again. If GE continues on its present course we ourselves may one day be left with the same uncertainty. But the creatures running amok will be far harder than dinosaurs to contain and to trace – for they will be invisible, and deadly microbes.

Preparing for Disaster

The European Commission is already preparing for such an emergency. It has issued a five-point plan – as if for a nuclear disaster – to be used in the event of a genetic accident in which genetically modified plants cause widespread illness, or the death of wildlife. The plans say that before planting GE crops, companies must have a detailed strategy for coping with disaster, which must include:

- plans to protect human health and the environment in a disaster
- ways of isolating the affected area
- methods of decontaminating the affected area
- methods of decontaminating the affected plants, animals, soil, etc.
- procedures for controlling the genetically engineered material in the event of an unexpected spread

Clearly the Commission feels that genetically engineered material from crops may very seriously infect the area around them, and may have to be contained. All scientifically correct. Yet these plans are extraordinary.

In everyday life, someone who decided to innovate by lighting a fire in the middle of a wooden floor, while preparing to control the fire if it spread, would be thought insane. He would be asked, 'Why light a fire on a wooden floor if you know it's likely to spread? What if you can't control it and it burns the house down? Is it worth it, just to do something different?'

Of course, these arguments wouldn't cut much ice with anyone insane. In theory, however, the European Commission, and the governments of Europe, aren't insane. Yet these plans show that the Commission *knows* that GE crops are no more safe than a fire on a wooden floor, that the danger is likely to spread, and that GE crops might:

- create or spread serious human diseases
- infect animals so dangerously that the corpses need special disposal
- blight plants so gravely that they need special handling
- cause soil to become gravely infected and contaminated
- infect and contaminate whole areas

and that all this can be so serious as to need quarantine. Yet the authorities have not only allowed GE crops to be grown in the open air, but continue to fuel the fire with every new GE crop approved. While they denied the dangers their folly was explained by ignorance. Now they have shown that they know the dangers, the questions they should be answering are 'Why was the fire lit? And why continue to stoke it?'

Experiments with Life

Genetic engineering (GE) is being sold to us as a great benefit to mankind. Yet there is probably no field of science in which there has been more secrecy, more disinformation, less regard for ethics, less respect for life, such a lack of monitoring, or such irresponsible legislation. Nor is there any field of human endeavour which has greater implications for us, the planet and the world's children.

What is extraordinary is that genetic engineering is being talked about as if it was quite normal. And that genetically engineered crops are being grown in the open, and their products put into shops, as if there was no difference between manufacturing goods and restructuring life itself.

Having come to genetic engineering as a science lover, it took me a while to fully appreciate its dangers – dangers which become more and more evident as research progresses. Now I am gravely concerned at the growing irresponsibility of much that is being done for commercial gain – and by the claims of its benefit to humanity. In some fields, such as medicine, there are benefits, but in many areas it is becoming more unethical and uncaring with each new step.

People in the Third World are being exploited. There is work on animals, and planned work on humans, which violates the very basis of respect for life. Much work on crops is likely to increase the use of chemicals, not reduce it, and may devastate the environment. Far from feeding the hungry, it may damage crops and could cause famine. Yet all this is being done with the support of governments and without any effective regulation.

A potent force

Short of atomic or germ warfare nothing human beings can do is likely to have more far-reaching consequences than what is being done now. For in genetic engineering genes are usually taken from one species and inserted into a totally different one. And a central fact in the whole genetic engineering debate is that *genes aren't inserted by themselves*. They have to be combined with living sections of viruses and bacteria to help them work. These extraordinary parcels of genes, spliced together, could be the most potent force for change the world has ever seen. Yet they are totally invisible and are designed to be invasive. Having been created to invade a particular plant or animal, and alter the way in which its cells function, that need not be the limit of their activity.

It is possible for any gene of any species to spread to any other species, especially if the gene is carried on genetically engineered gene-transfer vectors.

Dr Mae-Wan Ho 1998, Genetic Engineering: Dream or Nightmare[2]

A predicted hazard

The initial approval of GE crops might have been understandable if warnings about the hazards of biotechnology were a new phenomenon. They aren't. As long ago as 1977, an American report on legislative control of micro-organisms said:

Foreign DNA in a micro-organism may alter it in unpredictable and undesirable ways. Should the altered micro-organism escape from containment, it might affect human beings, animals or plants causing disease and modifying the environment.[3]

So, some twenty years before the EU's disaster plan, or the launch of GE crops, American officials warned of unpredictable consequences to every aspect of the natural world – and perhaps especially to us. In saying that the risk comes from the altered micro-organism escaping 'from containment' the report highlights the most extraordinary aspect of genetic engineering today – and the biggest danger.

What GE seems to have overlooked is that it is using bacteria and that there are bacteria everywhere around us and within us. The danger comes from their nature. As ecologist James Lovelock puts it:

'So efficient is communication among the bacteria that for many purposes the whole world of bacteria can be thought of as a single organ.'[4]

This extraordinary system means that bacteria combine and swap bits of themselves as easily as children swap Lego bricks. So when genetic engineers change bacteria the changes aren't confined to the ones they modify. The generous nature of bacteria means that they will share changes with others, spreading them anywhere and everywhere in the bacterial world.

Creating diseases?

That sharing has always happened. What is new is the way genetic engineering now cuts and splices infectious material to make it more powerful – then releases it into the open air in the cells of crops. Once out of the laboratory, this new, more powerful form is available to combine with any passing bacteria – handing on its power. Viruses too may evolve and become more powerful, aided and abetted by genetic engineering.

Normally viruses and bacteria have chosen hosts. We don't get distemper and dogs don't get flu. But in most genetic engineering the spliced material from bacteria and viruses is specially engineered to be able to cross species barriers – an ability which can be transferred to passing relatives. When this happens there is a danger of perhaps creating new, more virulent, diseases which could infect people, animals, plants – even the organisms of the soil itself.

Despite its high-flown claims, genetics is still in its infancy and largely working in the dark. Science hasn't even identified – let alone understood – all natural genes of the plants and animals which are now being engineered. Moreover, biotechnology began in the 1970s and grew out of a simplistic and mechanistic idea of genes which is long outdated. In reality, the natural genes within any living thing are mobile and interactive, with harmonious patterns of interdependence. They

---

＊ Fast bacteria can divide every twenty minutes, creating several billion a day.

also respond to conditions within and beyond their 'home' organism. This ability to change and react, means that those who tamper with genes should expect the unexpected. On top of that, the nature of key genetic engineering techniques means that the dangers of applying GE to crops go far beyond whether the food is safe to eat, and threaten every aspect of our lives. This means that while a case can be made for GE in the containment of a laboratory applying it to crops is gravely irresponsible.

> Genetic engineers make use of recombined versions of precisely those causing diseases including cancers, and others that carry virulence genes and antibiotic resistance genes. Thus the technology will contribute to the transfer of those genes that are responsible for virulence and anti-biotic resistance, allowing them to generate new pathogens [infectious organisms]
>
> Dr Mae-Wan Ho, molecular biologist, OU

Such organisms are being put into the air at this moment. They are alive, and evolving, and can never be recalled. They may change not only our lives but our planet itself.

A natural world

At least thirty new diseases have surfaced since 1978 – of which AIDS is only one. So far as we know none of them is connected with genetic engineering. However, GE also took off in the mid-1970s. Recently a government adviser warned that GE could create more serious forms of infections like meningitis. Is it pure coincidence that we have recently had the worst outbreak of meningitis for half a century? Perhaps it is. But next time it may not be. Is it a coincidence that a number of new, and newly virulent diseases are cropping up in America – where there are millions of acres of GE crops? Perhaps, but, at the very least, GE could fan the flames.

The vulnerability of crops

This isn't simply a matter of human diseases. Since crops are the main source of genetic material being put into the environment plant diseases are equally likely to be empowered by contact with GE organisms, becoming more potent and attacking a wider range of crops. This could be a recipe for disaster. For, while creating the potential for more virulent plant diseases GE is also narrowing the range of crop varieties. Huge swathes of the same GE varieties are being grown. And the more that any one variety is grown the greater the risk of devastation by any one disease. You would have thought that America, with its large Irish population, would have learnt from Ireland's potato famine: but seemingly it has not.

Transnational corporations aim to sell GE seeds worldwide. So we are looking at the possibility of a new, or newly virulent, crop disease, made powerful by traits it has gained from engineered organisms, devastating a particular GE crop not just in one country but perhaps in many. Since GE is focusing on core crops – soya, maize, potatoes, wheat, rice – the human and economic consequences could be immense.

In the spread of AIDS worldwide we have seen the huge impact of one new virus. With GE it is a matter of innumerable viruses and bacteria in the environment and in engineered crops – and a game of Russian roulette in terms of what combines with what.

Russian roulette

Some scientists see the prospect of powerful engineered genes transferring to disease-causing organisms as the greatest single threat posed by the technology. Yet the EU emergency precautions seem to be the first public acknowledgement of this. Unfortunately, genetic engineering is a technology which has been applied, and put into the market place, long before scien-

---

∗ Genes have been found to transfer between species and organisms in fresh and salt water, and in the soil.

tists had the knowledge to predict its effects, or regulators had the understanding, and foresight, to guard against them.

When the American report quoted on page 5 talks about micro-organisms 'modifying the environment' it is referring to the potential for momentous and unpredictable changes. Unseen – and unforeseeable – harm which could affect every aspect of the natural world. Perhaps harm to the invisible allies of plants – the beneficial insects and birds without which pests would be rampant and many crops would fail. Perhaps changes to the bacteria which cause dead leaves to crumble and enrich the earth, or to the delicate balance of river life, or to the world of the seas and oceans without which we would have no fish – perhaps even changes to the weather.

We don't yet know which genetically engineered combinations are likely to be most hazardous. All we know is that every single release of GE organisms into the open air risks creating more hazardous bacteria and viruses. Saying 'It's just a field trial' is no more reassuring than saying 'Don't worry, it's only a *small* bomb'. Yet discussion of the ethics of using biotechnology in ways which create a human and ecological time-bomb doesn't seem to be on any government's agenda.

Rain-free ice prevention

At the same time there is always the chance that some well-intentioned scientist will forget about the interactions of the natural world and create some seemingly small change which could have a massive impact on our ability to survive. A beautiful example of this is the story of 'ice-minus' bacteria. Ice on crops causes billions of pounds of damage each year. The ice forms round minute particles of protein on a crop bacterium. So someone had the bright idea of modifying the bacteria to get rid of the protein particles. The plan was to remove the bacteria's 'appendix', so to speak, then spray this 'ice-minus'

* From 1986–97 some 25,000 field trials were conducted on 60 engineered crops in 45 countries for 10 traits.

strain on crops and hope it would replace the natural form. A harmless enough change, you might think.

There was just one small drawback. Rainfall depends on tiny particles of ice forming in the upper atmosphere to make clouds. Nobody knows whether the bacteria which form ice crystals on crops also help clouds to form crystals. So what if the 'ice-minus' strain not only ousted normal bacteria on plants but in the atmosphere as well – with catastrophic effects on rainfall?

After a court case, which divided the scientific community, and authorised and unauthorised field trials, the issue died. The weather in California, where the trials took place, didn't appear to change. But they were small trials and there's a lot of sky over California. The point is that, as so often in all aspects of genetic engineering, nobody knew enough about the role of this bacteria, or about ecology, to say for sure that the modified bacteria were harmless. Nor could those who believed they were dangerous quantify the danger. That is typical. The whole essence of the danger from genetic engineering is that biotechnology is sailing in uncharted waters with no compass, and we are all aboard.

Less control, not more

In a world that was saner, and less obsessed with quick profits, the onus would be on researchers to prove that their work was safe. And the more leading edge the work, the more thought would have to be given to unexpected effects. In our world the opposite is so. The more GE has developed the more casual people have become. Controls in most countries have been gradually relaxed, violations of the rules by companies are either ignored or punished so lightly as to be laughable.

In America, researchers no longer have to tell the authorities if they are carrying out 'low risk' trials.[5] But are researchers

---

＊ News stories on genetic engineering are among the least reported in America – no matter how important the issue.

the best people to judge if their work is 'low risk'? This isn't simply a matter of personal involvement but of breadth of knowledge and experience. The scope of modern science is so huge and the average scientist so specialised that tunnel vision is normal, breadth of vision exceptional. Moreover, few scientists know much, if anything, about the natural world which could be so profoundly disrupted by their work. That suggests that only a panel of experts with a wide range of knowledge can judge the potential safety of any trial which might disrupt the balance of nature.

Learning from history

Michael Crichton lamented the lack of 'detached observers'. As nine out of ten scientists, worldwide, are funded by, or have links with, industry he was right. But happily there are still some independent scientists and around the world more and more of them have been expressing their concern at the misuse of biotechnology and calling for greater caution. This book owes much to them.

You would think that when scientists want to put a brake on science they should be listened to. In the past they have not been – yet they were proved right. Before nuclear power stations were built scientists and environmental groups urged caution, just as they do today over GE. Instead of listening to their warnings about radioactive pollution, governments and those who stood to gain from nuclear power compared its 'clean' energy with the dirt of coal – just as today the promise of 'chemical-free' insecticide-bearing plants is compared with the pollution of chemical spraying. With nuclear power, high-sounding claims and big promises brought huge investment and deep government commitment. The same has happened with genetic engineering.

✳ FDA records show US experts warned that GE foodstuffs could be hazardous – yet the FDA declare them safe.

Agricultural biotechnology will be the greatest disaster of modern capitalism.

Jeremy Rifkin

As nuclear power stations became established, the propaganda machine continued to roll, as it has done with genetic engineering. Organisations like Greenpeace and Friends of the Earth warned about unstable, ill-maintained power stations. Governments ignored them. For years independent scientists and environmental organisations have given similar warnings about biotechnology – warned of the dangers attendant upon the unregulated use of a potent and fledgling science which changes not only life itself but uses the very techniques employed to create the weapons of germ warfare. Once again governments and officials have ignored them.

A lesson from Chernobyl

My daughter was near Chernobyl when it blew up. It took that terrible nuclear disaster to awaken the authorities to the danger of nuclear power. Today we all live in the shadow of the latest technological 'miracle' – technology just as capable of 'trickle' effects as a nuclear power plant, just as unpredictable and unstable, and with its unseen harm borne just as easily on the wind across continents.

Some responsible scientists say that, without far better regulation, the question is not *if* biotechnology will cause a disaster comparable to Chernobyl, but *when*. Almost every day research is published somewhere in the world showing that some aspect of genetic engineering is more hazardous or unpredictable than had been thought. Today children within many miles of Chernobyl are 1000 times more likely to get thyroid cancer than they were before the explosion. Unlike a power station, biotechnology is not limited to one place. Its presence and its exports are global. Everybody's children could be within range.

Self-regulation

Some scientists, such as Professor Sir Joseph Rotblat, the Nobel Prize-winning atomic physicist, having seen all that can happen with the atom, say that science must realise that just because something new can be done does not mean that it should be done.

> Genetic engineering raises the issue of the social responsibility of scientists. For a long time scientists have held the precepts that 'science is neutral' and 'science is not responsible'. All that was an illusion. The Hiroshima bomb finally demolished that ivory tower.
>
> Professor Sir Joseph Rotblat, speaking at London University, 1999

People often talk as if science should not be held back. As if it is some kind of god which must be allowed to do as it will. Science is not a god. It is, however, in this case, in danger of being a puppet.

Economic Driving Forces

Biotechnology is driven not, on the whole, by impassioned scientists seeking truth. It is driven by impassioned executives seeking profits – and power. The industry is dominated by companies which know more about two inanimate substances – chemicals and money – than they do about the constant, subtle yet powerful interactions of living things. There is nothing wrong with profits. But, in this instance, profits may come at the price of grave damage to the rest of the world, damage which may not always be accidental, to judge by some extraordinary patents which could threaten both our food supply and democracy itself.

Genetic engineering is being driven forward by companies of quite extraordinary wealth and influence. This field is dominated by a handful of multinational corporations, most of which originally made their billions in farm chemicals, pharmaceuticals, or both. Some of these new-made gene giants can swallow competitors as easily as a whale scoops up plankton, have budgets larger than New Zealand's, and a worldwide web of influence at every level. They are companies which can contribute telling sums to political parties, and wine and dine officials like kings. They laid on so many public relations officers when a vital law was going through the EU Parliament that one MEP said it felt as if there was one PR to every two of them. For these companies are experts in persuasion.

The agro-giants would have us believe their contradictory claims that genetic engineering is so normal that it presents no dangers and needs no special testing yet so high-tech and different that it deserves patents and special privileges and funding. In relation to crops, they have tried to sell us the fable that genetic engineering improves food, reduces chemical use, and is needed by the Third World. Even if all these claims were justified – and they aren't – the risks of growing or eating GE food would far outweigh the benefits. In reality, the world has a food surplus. But many are too poor to buy food. That poverty would be increased, not reduced, by GE crops. And, of course, the emergency for which the EU has made preparations could happen anywhere.

The United States Department of Agriculture reports that, for food related patents, 98 percent of genetic alterations are done to make food production easier and more profitable for the companies doing it. Only 2 percent are aimed at improved taste or nutrition.

The Council for Responsible Genetics, USA, 'Consumer Alert'

✳ In 1997 at least 78 per cent of malnourished children lived in countries with surplus food.

The World Trade Organisation rides again

A disturbing feature of the GE debate is the long shadow cast by the World Trade Organisation (WTO) and its allied bodies. Deputed to oil the wheels of worldwide trade, the WTO has been doing so with all the intelligence, subtlety and finesse of a punchy nightclub bouncer in one of the sleazier quarters of New York. Writ large across the front of the WTO's T-shirt are the words 'Trade at all costs!' The back simply reads 'What ethics?'

That is not a slur: the rules of the WTO commit it to further-ing trade and it tends to ignore caveats about not doing so if it causes people to starve, or damages the natural world. Ethics seem no part of its operation. So the WTO has made it plain that GE products must be treated like any others, and accepted for import, even if they bring us risks without benefits. One of the GE industry's feats of disinformation has been persuading governments that the future of the entire bio-tech industry rests on GE food being accepted. That is no more true than believing that the future of flying depended on the early planes which failed. No technology ever rests on one type of applica-tion, least of all on one as dangerous, unethical and inappropri-ate as engineering crops and farm animals.

Yet the false belief that the success of GE food is vital to economic progress has meant that we have been subjected to an extraordinary propaganda campaign and that governments the world over have fostered corporate agro-chemical interests at the expense of the public. In doing so, they have turned every one of us into human guinea-pigs in a vast unplanned and unsupervised experiment.

Power politics

To an extraordinary extent politicians of almost all political parties, the world over, have let multinational companies lead them by the nose. Often the reassurances of ministers could have been taken from a company press release. As a result, laws have consistently lagged far behind the science they, ostensibly, seek to control.

There is no way of knowing whether politicians genuinely believe the shabby reasoning and inaccurate science on which so many of them have consistently based arguments uncritically favouring this technology. Whether they are so limited in their concept of progress that they believe any forward movement is a good forward movement – even for lemmings. Or whether, knowing that political life is short, some hope for a lucrative seat on a board when their political day is done. Whatever the reasons, they have done a grave disservice to their voters.

They have done that disservice not merely by word but by deed. We had a right to expect that governments would evaluate genetic engineering impartially, permitting only what benefited the long-term welfare of the people of their country and of the world. We also had a right to be told the truth, yet instead of balanced evaluation we have consistently been offered propaganda.

The aim of at least one government body includes 'promoting' biotechnology – and the government used market research to determine what to say about GE to persuade us to accept it.

In Britain even school children may not be given balanced facts. The biotechnology sections of some school textbooks for GCSE and A-level are so devoid of any hint that genetic engineering could ever be harmful that they could have been written by a gene giant's mother. Clearly the official syllabus is such that children can pass their exams without ever knowing that GE has any negative effects whatsoever – and some of those in key government ministries will have been educated by such textbooks.

∗ Nine US scientists have joined forces in a lawsuit against America's FDA for failing to safety test and label GE foods.

A Great Con Trick

The British government's portrayal of GE has been a marketing ploy – not an attempt to tell us the facts. In 1997 the Ministry of Agriculture commissioned a survey of public attitudes to GE food and crops. It found the climate 'inhospitable'. It recommended that modern biotechnology should be portrayed to us as 'not tampering or interfering with nature', but as 'adopting existing natural processes under controlled conditions, to create stronger, higher yields and disease resistant agricultural products, in turn giving rise to more nutritious, safer food'. We've all heard that advice being acted upon – heard those very claims become the public mantra of officials and politicians alike. Never mind the truth, here's the soft soap. An interesting concept of democracy.

Should We Blame Science?

Yet perhaps the biggest tragedy in all this is the misuse of science itself. As science has developed it has given us the tools with which to see and appreciate the wonders of the microscopic world. A world which makes possible our existence and is so extraordinary, so miraculous in its beautiful, interactive complexity, that it makes the most advanced computer miniaturisation look like child's play. Yet instead of wondering at, and learning to understand, the boundless subtle interactions between all living things, from the most microscopic to the most immense, biotechnology has largely behaved like a curious and destructive child.

Instead of respecting the miracles of life laid before it, the child has, for over twenty years, been cutting and pasting the very stuff of life itself, as if DNA were just words on a computer screen. Ruthlessly used pieces of our oldest living ancestors, of plants, animals and humans, as mere tools with which to reshape the world in a money-spinning mode.

Fair evaluation

There is, however, an enormous difference between use and misuse. Radiation in the right place can be a blessing. Which of us would want to be without X-rays after a serious accident? But such limited, specific and essential use of radiation, in the controlled conditions of a hospital, is very different from constant, unlimited use in a power station or a bomb. So, it is important not to demonise genetic engineering. Demonising the whole technology will blind us both to what is really wrong with it and to how it may best be used.

You may question whether it is ever right to violate the nature of an organism as genetic engineering does. In many ways that is the most natural and logical viewpoint. At the same time, in medicine engineered micro-organisms can save lives. And we cannot predict whether some aspects of genetic engineering may not be vital to the world's future. It is the inappropriate, dangerous, unethical and premature uses which we have every right to oppose. The question which confronts us all is where and when to draw the line?

A time to rethink

For over 300 years science and medicine have increasingly taken their justification from numbers. Decisions on human life have been number-crunched till the heart went out of them. At the same time science and the understanding of science has become fragmented, mechanised and dehumanised. Perhaps the most exciting and heartening aspect of the rise of biotechnology is that, paradoxically, it confronts us all, from road sweepers to presidents, with questions which numbers cannot answer and with issues which force us to remember that everything is one, that the world is an interconnected living system which has cradled us for millennia.

Again and again, in writing this book I have felt that humankind has been brought, or has brought itself, full circle. Everything alive on this planet, including ourselves, evolved from invisible organisms – bacteria, yeasts, algae and microbes of every sort. And the richness of our planet's plants and creatures is a testimony to the power, as well as the promiscuity, of these under-estimated allies. By its exploitation of them genetic engineering creates moral, practical and economic dilemmas which may force us to review our attitude to the world around us, and the relationships between key aspects of our lives.

Every aspect of genetic engineering raises issues of relationship. The relationship between profits and ethics, politics and democracy, between law and justice, and between consumers and companies. GE calls in question our relationship with our own bodies, with the natural world, with the generations which come after us, and with the very nature of life itself. In doing so, it challenges us to reconsider the relationship between our actions and our personal sense of justice, humanity and compassion.

Genetic engineering is so sweeping in its scope, embraces topics of such moral importance, and is so immense in its potential for harm, that it brings us face to face with the most ancient questions of all. What is life? What is it to be human? What is our role on this planet? What boundaries should limit our actions? What are our rights, and our duties – to those alive today and to those who come after us, if not to any concept of the divine? Do we own the world – or are we stewards cherishing it for coming generations?

2

Safety: Trust Me, I'm a Chemical Company

Three Myths

GE uses a precise, predictable technology.
GE food has undergone rigorous safety testing.
GE crops are an extension of normal plant breeding.

> Monsanto should not have to vouchsafe the safety of our
> biotech food. Our interest is in selling as much as possible.
> Assuring its safety is the FDA's job.
>
> Phil Angell, Monsanto's Director of Corporate Communications[1]

The aspect of genetic engineering which affects us most
immediately, and over which we have the greatest control, is
its use in food. So food is the main focus of this chapter. The
safety of the environment and of medicines are mainly covered
later.

The biotech industry has made out that criticism of genetically engineered food is exaggerated, irrational and inappropriate. It seeks to portray all opposition as Luddite or a mere
knee-jerk reaction. Some comments have indeed been ill
informed – on both sides – but the fact that science is sometimes feared doesn't mean that those who oppose the use
of GE in food are irrational. Nor does it mean that they are

anti-science. There are many rational and scientific reasons for opposing GE food.

Many of GE's strongest opponents are not just scientists but scientists experienced in genetic engineering. They urge caution not out of ignorance, but precisely because they fully understand what is involved – and know its dangers. For there is strong evidence that applying this technology to food may be not only unnecessary and inappropriate: it may create serious threats to human health.

The Risks – from GE Food

Anthropologists say that even the tribes of early man, which might be considered primitive by computer-age man, had food-testing rituals to prevent the whole tribe being poisoned. New food would be carefully prepared to minimise any suspected risks. Then minute quantities of it would be given to selected strong young men. If no harm came to them the dose would be raised, the preparation varied. Only when its safety seemed proven would other adults eat it. And only when they were unharmed would it be given to children. The tribes which did that thrived on an ever-growing diet. The ones which did not may have been less lucky. Survival of the wisest, you might call it.

Today we are not so wise. Although Monsanto has repeatedly boasted of 25,000 trials of GE crops they are *field trials*. Food safety isn't tested in fields. There have been *no scientific long-term human trials to test the safety of GE food*. And the animal trials are usually brief and conducted by the companies which created the products. So governments worldwide have allowed companies to sell inadequately tested foods which have never

---

✷ To deter insects, companies plan to build into GE crops poisons from scorpions, wasps, and deadly funnel web spiders and patents are pending.

before been in the human diet. Unlike tribal man they have even allowed such food to be given to babies, pregnant women, the sick and the elderly. And they have done this even without even setting up appropriate post-approval monitoring to ensure that no ill effects go unnoticed.

> In a therapeutic situation you've got maybe 4% of the population taking a drug, on average for about 10 days, under supervision. With GE food you've got billions of people eating or drinking it for a lifetime with no supervision at all. Yet the conditions by which they're judging GE food are more lax than for any drug.
>
> John Verrall, medical pharmacologist

Dangers on the Plate

The potential dangers from eating genetically engineered foods come directly from the processes involved. Factors creating risks in GE food include:

- the unpredictability of interactions between genes
- the stress created in an organism which is engineered
- such stress making it over-react to other stresses
- the unfamiliar substances created by the inserted genes
- using DNA from viruses and bacteria as tools

Any of those, alone or in combination could alter the composition of food enough to make it harmful. That doesn't mean that GE food will necessarily harm you. Far too little is known about it for anyone to be sure where the risks lie. What is certain is that, without long-term human testing, nobody can guarantee it is safe. Moreover, the dangers on the plate could be more numerous than you may think. (The potential hazards marked with a star below are from foodstuffs which haven't yet reached European tables – but are in the pipeline.)

Allergy and sensitivity
- allergens could occur in foods which were never allergenic
- new levels of known allergens could be created
- this could happen unexpectedly if crops are stressed.

Poisons
- new poisons could be created in formerly safe crops
- new poisons could be created in foodstuffs from GE micro-organisms
- the levels of natural poisons in crops could be increased
- GE crops under stress could unexpectedly create poisons
- food may contain increased levels of poisons from weed-killers
- the doses of certain weedkillers we receive from food may be larger, through more crops using the same weedkillers.

Diseases & damage
- unborn babies may be harmed by unexpected substances in food, or by changed levels of expected substances
- meat and other products from animals fed on GE crops may carry engineered DNA which could perhaps be harmful
- the risk of breast, prostate and other cancers may perhaps be increased by milk from cows injected with BST*
- the risk of childhood bone cancer may perhaps be increased by milk from cows injected with BST*
- the immune systems of unborn babies, children and adults may be harmed by some GE foods
- bacteria used in GE can spread resistance to antibiotics
- meat and products from animals engineered to have human genes may encourage animal diseases to spread to humans*
- GE makes it easier for viruses to create new diseases

✳ Worldwide 10 million people a year are affected by tuberculosis which resists most antibiotics.

- GE makes it easier for bacteria material to combine to create new diseases
- GE may enable existing diseases to become more virulent.

One reason why GE food introduces a totally new degree of risk into our food is that it will never be possible to say that all GE food is safe. Every time a new crop variety or organism is engineered, or a new technique used, something could go wrong. Our food could contain 100 different versions of GE maize – and be perfectly safe, until they introduced the 101st. The snag is, we wouldn't know they'd introduced it. The danger is that people may come to feel GE foods are totally safe just because there is no evidence of harm – yet.

You will have noticed that none of the risks involved means that you or I will take a bite of food, keel over and die. Paradoxically, that may be a pity. If any harm was immediate we'd know the dangers at once and fewer people would be harmed. The fact that any harm is likely to be slow-acting and gradual means it will be very difficult to lay at the door of genetic engineering.

Chemical blinkers

It's easy to see why GE was rushed into food with so little concern for such risks if you look at the type of companies involved. They are some of the world's biggest chemical and drug companies. It's a sector of industry which has, in the past, assured us of the safety of thalidomide, DDT, PCBs and many farm, garden, and industrial chemicals and medicines which have later proved dangerous and even fatal. Scores of such chemicals have been withdrawn because they proved to be more harmful than they once seemed.

This means that GE food – by which I mean crops, animal products and food from micro-organisms – is largely being produced by an industry with a mind-set utterly unsuited to food. Most chemicals are dangerous, in sufficient quantities,

Casual Errors

Forethought isn't always a strong point of some of these companies either. Having spent tens of millions creating a tomato to be picked ripe, yet last for weeks, one company harvested mashed tomatoes. Tomatoes are normally picked green and hard, to ripen later. Nobody had stopped to think that ripe tomatoes wouldn't suit mechanical picking.

The seed company Pioneer Hi-bred decided to improve on nature by engineering soya beans to achieve a balance of amino acids. Having spent a fortune inserting genes from Brazil nuts to alter that balance, it had to scrap the project. The chosen genes weren't those thought to cause nut allergy – yet tests showed that this GE soya could trigger nut allergy. Despite that, other companies are now inserting Brazil nut genes into several crops. When companies show such a limited ability to think ahead – even when their own money is at stake – what confidence can we have that they have thought about how their products will affect human health in the long term?

so the chemical and drug industries don't think in terms of safety but in terms of degrees of risk

Any company that thinks risks are normal isn't well suited to creating food. Most of us don't want risks on our plates. We want safe food. Of course there are those who say there are so many dangers from the chemicals already on food that to worry about GE is pointless. We do have chemical-laden food. But to add the dangers of GE food (which will not reduce chemical use, as has been promised) is surely to pour petrol on a burning house.

So, before we believe their marketing it may be wise to look at the track record of these companies. Some have shown scant concern for human and environmental safety and allowed serious chemical pollution of land, air and waterways. Some have reputations for poor safety tests, concealed and dubious results, back-room deals, and a disregard for the law. Merely in the course of normal business, Monsanto has made DDT, Agent Orange (the defoliant that devastated Vietnam and was alleged to have serious side-effects on the American military), and brought the world highly toxic PCBs.

The Broad Safety Issues

In thinking about the safety of GE crops there is one overwhelming fact to consider:

> At present GE crops are of no benefit to consumers whatsoever.
>
> Richard Powell, Novartis, 1999

Yet, despite that and the clear evidence of potential dangers, governments have allowed an infant science to experiment on crops and farm animals, and release totally new organisms into the environment and into our diet, *without*:

- adequate scrutiny of claims made by GE companies
- proof that they offer any benefits to the consumer
- long-term tests to see if they harm those who eat them
- thinking of the suffering GE might bring to animals
- looking at the risks of creating new diseases
- considering how uniformity and disease result
- first checking for harm to wildlife
- considering the risk of creating superweeds
- first checking for harm to beneficial insects

✳ Glyphosate, the main herbicide for GE crops, is California's third most reported cause of pesticide-related illness.

- first checking for harm to the insects needed for pollination
- considering that honey would be contaminated
- first checking for harm to soil fertility
- first checking the potential for damaging organic farming
- investigating the dangers created by the procedures used
- first proving long-term benefits to farmers
- establishing suitable monitoring systems
- making the manufacturers legally liable for any harm done
- considering the special harm in the Third World
- checking whether yields really increase
- asking us if we wanted GE food
- listening to the warnings of scientists
- considering if the risks outweigh any benefits
- considering the unwisdom of tampering with the essence of life.

In anyone's book that is a pretty hefty list of things undone that should have been done. Yet there is more to come – in other chapters.

Engineering Micro-organisms

Oddly, the least controversial area of genetic engineering is the one with the greatest evidence of harm. However, engineering micro-organisms – yeasts, bacteria and cells – is one of the most long-standing uses of GE. It is used, for example, to manufacture vegetarian rennet, which is in much of the world's cheese. So far it seems harmless enough. And in Britain the food industry uses about a dozen other GE enzymes. Cultured in a controlled environment, and involving no cruelty to animals, they seem beyond reproach. GE functional foods and so-called nutraceuticals – genetically engineered 'health foods' and food

✳ GE insect sprays are being developed using viruses and toxins from mites, beetles and scorpions.

supplements which claim to offer something a normal diet doesn't provide, are now set to be one of the big growth areas for GE. However, small doesn't always mean beautiful. A food supplement from micro-organisms was involved in the worst-ever GE accident.

Death by food supplement?

In the 1980s a US-based Japanese company, Showa Denko, made and sold the food supplement tryptophan. Harmless bacteria were fermented in vats, from which tryptophan was extracted and purified. All went well until the company decided to speed things up by engineering new genes into the bacteria.

The new GE tryptophan was introduced onto the US market in 1988. Within months 37 people who used it were dead, and some 1,500 permanently disabled. They became paralysed, had neurological and heart problems, painful swellings, cracked skin, memory loss, headaches, extreme light sensitivity, and fatigue – all symptoms of a disease with the pithy name *eosinophilia myalgia syndrome* (EMS). As the GE tryptophan had the same label as non-GE tryptophan, it took months to link it to the illness.

Independent research showed that tryptophan produced by genetically engineered bacteria contained several highly poisonous substances, one of which could kill, even at less than one part in a thousand. It was suggested that the filtration, not GE should be blamed. But the filtration system hadn't changed and no illness had ever been associated with non-GE tryptophan. So several reputable independent scientists think GE was to blame. The manufacturer then denied liability when lawsuits, said to total $2 billion, were filed against it. However, it has made undisclosed, out of court, settlements with those who claimed compensation.

Genetically altered micro-organisms pose risks to human health and to the environment. Scientists and regulators promise to keep that risk to a minimum, but our own history warns of the 'whoops' theory of risk assessment (something can go wrong – or perhaps already has – and those affected are left with the apology, 'whoops, sorry, we made a mistake').[3]

P. Spallone, Generation Games, 1992

The implications for our food

This case is important because foodstuffs from micro-organisms can slip into the food supply unobserved and perhaps without appropriate levels of control. In 1996 the marketing of ribo-flavin (vitamin B2) from GE bacteria was approved. Despite the fact that contaminants at *less than* 0.1 per cent in trypto-phan had *already* killed and crippled, only contaminants at *greater than* 0.1 per cent in riboflavin had to be identified. This vitamin seems to have done no harm. But, however safe today's products seem, if low levels of contamination aren't looked for when GE products are approved for sale, a disaster like that with tryptophan may be on the cards. For tryptophan is not the only micro-organism to have behaved oddly, yeast has too.

A Surprising Little Yeast

Yeasts for bread and brewing are relatively simple organ-isms. So people didn't expect great problems with GE yeasts. But they have proved unpredictable.

One engineered yeast produced high levels of a very nasty substance called methylglyoxal, a poison which can deform unborn children.[4] Luckily the researchers dis-covered that genetic engineering had created this poison in the yeast. So this is one GE hazard which was nipped in the bud.

Engineered Crops

One of the most striking aspects of GE crops has been the extent to which there has been a concerted attempt to brainwash us. When GE ingredients began filtering into every kind of manufactured food there was a flurry of propaganda – propaganda that was often scientifically incorrect. Government and supermarket leaflets were glossy and reassuring. Biotech men, appearing on TV in white coats, held up traditional tomatoes and GE tomatoes, showing that they both looked the same, hoping that naïvely we'd think that whatever looked the same was the same. And, curiously, retailers, walk-on scientists and government officials all seemed to sing from the same song sheet – the gene giant song sheet, while the opposite case, from eminent scientists, remained unheard. The propaganda continues – but it's more subtle now.

No extension of normal plant-breeding

A key plank of the disinformation campaign has been the claim that GE food is just an extension of cross-breeding. This is absurd. Genetic engineering is a natural extension of previous plant-breeding only in the way the atom bomb was a natural extension of all previous bombs. Being one of a long line of bombs didn't stop the atom bomb from being distinctly different and having different and greater dangers.

Nature only allows cross-breeding within species: you can't mate a cat with a dog or cross an apple tree with a rose, still less a dog with a rose. Genetic engineering, of course, breaks down nature's boundaries and allows scientists to do just that. Comparing GE with normal cross-breeding is like saying there is no difference between grafting one apple tree onto another and grafting an animal's ear onto an apple tree.

Genetic engineering makes it possible to put genes from any species into any other. The techniques are still very hit and miss but they allow scientists to introduce into food crops and farm animals genes from bacteria and viruses, flowers, fish, insects and even people. That is not a misprint. Human genes are being put into farm animals. Not all those combinations are on your table – yet – but they're in the pipeline.

> One key problem that keeps coming back time and again is that regulation of food is nothing like as strict as the regulation of drugs. And when you start tinkering around with the genetic structure of food you have to move towards thinking of food products as pharmaceuticals.
>
> Jonathan Rhodes, Professor of Medicine, Liverpool University

A Crop of Surprises

Disrupted genes

As alien genes disrupt both individual cells and the entire system, anything can happen. Some normal activities may slow down or halt. Others may speed up. Others may have their timing altered. New substances may be produced, or existing ones increased or decreased. These unintended and unpredictable changes could cause plants and other organisms to:

- reduce their levels of vitamins and other beneficial substances
- be less healthy and/or have lower yields
- boost existing substances to toxic or allergenic levels
- produce new, unexpected, poisons or allergens

This means that food from a plant or organism could become less nutritious, or become unsafe. In one experiment, researchers were trying to convert an existing plant oil into a more beneficial one. They achieved this but also produced a totally unexpected poisonous plant oil – which may now be used in the chemical industry. That may sound like a happy ending but one potential hazard is that genes may move from GE crops to non-GE ones – making such changes in normal crops without anyone being aware of it. For engineered genes can 'move house' spontaneously.

Petunias See Red

Some experiments illustrate how unpredictable GE can be. A gene for redness was put into white petunias, along with a gene for antibiotic resistance.

The petunias did turn red, but suddenly they also grew differently, were less fertile and more resistant to fungi.

Salmon engineered to grow faster developed green skin and, during research, GE tobacco produced a highly toxic acid known as OTA. These are just some examples of a mass of strange unexpected effects which have occurred when genes were inserted. Nobody knew why.

The hit-and-miss basis of GE and the resulting unpredictability also mean that every single case is different. If one GE variety of transgenic maize or soya is safe, it no more guarantees the safety of the rest than drawing a red playing card from a pack guarantees that all future cards will be red.

Splicing a gene for human growth hormone into mice produces very large mice; splicing the same gene into pigs produced skinny, cross-eyed, arthritic animals. The FDA warns that splicing a single gene into any organism for a single desired effect may unintentionally cause other harmful reactions within that organism which are not detectable.

The Council for Responsible Genetics (USA)

Stress reactions

To add to the unpredictability any ill effects may not show at once. GE is stressful to all organisms, but any ill effects may not develop until outside stress, such as a heat wave, proves the last straw.

Plants react to every aspect of their environment. So extreme heat or cold, drought or any other form of stress can affect their chemistry – and the way crops respond to alien genes.

The weedkillers which the vast majority of GE plants are engineered to survive, are stressful for plants and resisting them takes energy away from other activities. So sometimes the plants are weaker, less productive, or more vulnerable to other stresses. Here again GE opens the door to unexpected toxins being produced.

As stress reactions in all living things are unpredictable, this means a crop, or other GE organism, could be safely eaten for years. Then, during a heat wave, or some other cause of stress, it could suddenly become poisonous, allergenic or unexpectedly fail. In one experiment with flowers a totally unexpected change took place after more than a year. As a result:

It is impossible to guarantee that GE food is safe.

Risks from weedkillers

Before GE was introduced, lots of different toxic chemicals were sprayed onto crops. That risked a multi-chemical response. With GE the risk is that our food will contain a narrow range of chemicals each of which we will eat in greater amounts. As 'the poison is the dose', this could make food more toxic than it has ever been. The greatest risk is likely to be to the unborn, as they are the most vulnerable. Yet over 80 per cent of the world's GE crops are now engineered to withstand a specific all-purpose weedkiller being sprayed

---

∗ Swedish research has linked non-Hodgkin lymphoma with exposure to glyphosate.

directly onto them. The vast majority are engineered to with-stand Monsanto's glyphosate-based weedkiller Roundup. Another large group resist weedkillers based on glufosinate. And some have even been genetically engineered to withstand bromoxynil. According to Professor Joe Cummins of the University of Ontario, bromoxynil poisons fish and has been shown to cause birth defects in rats and mice – so raising worries that it might do so in humans. Pesticide Action Network in America says companies are not required to test the effects of these chemicals in repeated small doses – such as a foetus might receive if a mother was eating pesticide-loaded crops at intervals. Yet the foetus may have no defence against such chemicals.

Soya: the first signs of trouble?

Another risk is that conflicts between the host plant and the inserted gene, or interactions with the weedkiller it is engineered to survive, will alter its chemistry – making it poisonous or allergenic.

It took decades to collect enough evidence to prove that cigarettes caused lung cancer, heart disease and other serious illnesses. Any harm done by GE foods may be equally difficult to prove. But the first signs may be emerging.

In 1998 the York Nutritional Laboratory, which tests people for food allergies, found signs that reactions to soya may be rising rapidly. In 1999 soya became, for the first time, one of the top ten foods most likely to cause an allergic reaction. In a random sample, 15 per cent of those they tested reacted to soya in 1999, as against only 10 per cent in 1998.

As allergies and food intolerances usually develop gradually this is about the time any allergen in GE soya might start to affect people. And the laboratory thinks the figures may show a growing intolerance to GE soya.

Birth defects and oestrogens

One of the many unpredictable aspects of GE crops engineered to withstand weedkillers, is how the plant's own chemistry will react to the chemicals applied to it. They may well cause it to alter its own chemical balance in ways that may make the plants less nourishing or more hazardous.

Does GE Soya Harm Babies?

This heading is sensational because it's a question regulators should be asking – and they aren't. Millions of acres of glyphosate-resistant soya are being grown. Yet no one knows how glyphosate is affecting the chemistry of soya beans. Plants in the pea and bean family, including soya, naturally make plant hormones similar to female sex hormones. The levels of these may alter either way, creating special risks when such plants have to withstand glyphosate-based weedkillers – as with soya.

Herbicide tolerant members of the bean family are known to produce higher levels of plant oestrogens. If GE soya responds in the same way when exposed to glyphosate, the active ingredient in Monsanto's Roundup, excessive concentrations of these oestrogens could present a potentially severe risk to children, as these plant oestrogens mimic the role of female sex hormones and may cause severe dysfunction of the reproductive system, especially of boys. Without rigorous testing, after exposure to herbicide, such beans should not be allowed in food.

Dr Ricarda Steinbrecher,[6] biologist and geneticist

Increased plant oestrogen in sprayed GE soya may explain the increased fat content in milk from cows fed on such soya. The seriousness of a possible increase in female hormones in GE soya is underlined by research by Professor Jean Golding in Avon. In a study of 14,000 children she found that vegetarians give birth to significantly more babies with penis abnormalities than do other mothers. Though careful not to blame any particular food, Dr Golding said they would need to investigate whether plant oestrogens were linked to the abnormalities. For, of course, vegetarians eat far more soya than most meat-eaters. Moreover, if plant oestrogens are affecting children, the potential harm may be far greater than it appears. Oestrogens don't simply affect the reproductive system. They play an important part in a whole range of body functions, from how we metabolise calcium to the functioning of our immune system – and the delicate balance of body systems means that more isn't better. If the amount of oestrogen in GE soya is higher it could affect all those eating GE soya, not just babies. (See also Baby Foods in Labelling)

> Exposure to additional hormones during critical periods before birth, or in infancy, can harm far more than the reproductive system. Hormones are intimately bound up with every aspect of our body-mind system. They affect our brain, our feelings, and how we resist diseases. And the levels are critical too. A little too much oestrogen can make a boy more feminine. Much too much and he could become too masculine – and so could a girl baby.
>
> Candace Pert, Professor of Physiology, Georgetown University

New proteins and allergens

Many plants naturally produce compounds that may be toxic to humans or alter food qualities. Examples include neurotoxins, enzyme inhibitors, and hemolytic substances. Generally, these compounds are present in today's food at levels that do not cause acute toxicity. However, the FDA notes that such toxicants may be produced at unusually high levels as a result of genetic engineering.

> The Council for Responsible Genetics (USA)

The hit-and-miss nature of GE means that a successful combination of genes will be used again and again on different crops. For example, many crops are being engineered with genes from the soil organism *Bacillus thuringiensis* (Bt), which kills the grubs of moths and butterflies. But there's no precedent for us eating significant amounts of the compounds which Bt produces, or causes plants to produce. So maybe, as more and more plants contain them, many tiny doses will add up to an amount which is harmful. The American Food and Drugs Administration (FDA) has warned that new proteins created in food by GE may cause allergic reactions in some people. That is not surprising – even minute traces of certain allergens can induce powerful allergic reactions.

> Bt toxin that has a powerful biological activity against one class of organisms might have some biological activity even in . . . vertebrates. Such activity might become apparent if the toxin is consumed in large amounts.
>
> Because individuals will probably not have been previously sensitized to these new allergens, these substances will probably not elicit a powerful allergenic response at first exposure. However, if such an allergen becomes a common component of the food supply, allergenicity will develop as exposure continues.
>
> Professor John Fagan, Assessing the Safety of GE Food, 1998[7]

Why more nutrition may mean less

There are promises that GE food will be more nutritious. But making food more nourishing will be neither easy nor safe. Either new genes must be inserted, or existing genes boosted. As inserting genes is risky, it's not the safest way to get nourishment. Unfortunately, plants may not respond well to having

---

* To deter insects, companies plan to build into GE crops poisons from scorpions, wasps, and deadly funnel web spiders.

their functions boosted either. In one experiment the red gene in petunias was amplified and multiplied to make them even redder. The result? Assorted flowers – white, pink and red. However, in subsequent flowerings plants which had produced red flowers produced white ones. It seems almost as if plants sense the imbalance of over-boosted genes and just switch them off.

This is called gene silencing and could be serious if anyone tried to boost the genes for vitamins and other nutrients. For crops which seem more nourishing when first tested and approved could later on become less nourishing than before they were engineered.

Antibiotic Resistance

The BMA believes the use of resistance marker genes in GM foodstuffs is a completely unacceptable risk, however slight, to humans.

British Medical Association Interim Statement on GM,
Agriculture, Food and Health, 1999

Sections of bacteria which carry antibiotic resistance are being used as tools in genetic engineering as casually as if they were screwdrivers. Yet genes from antibiotic-resistant bacteria can pass this resistance on to whole bacteria in the air, so increasing the already alarming spread of antibiotic resistance. This risk is increased by the use of plasmids – parts of bacteria which are extremely adept at moving home and well able to carry antibiotic resistance with them.

In addition to any transfer through the environment, genes from antibiotic-resistant bacteria which are in the food itself can also be taken up by the gut bacteria of people and animals

✳ In Britain the number of cases of antibiotic-resistant salmonella have risen more than ten-fold since 1990.

Inserted Genes Evolve

As genes have evolved for millennia they continue to do so after being engineered. And inserted genes seem especially changeable. In GE rice succeeding generations may have more or fewer copies of the alien genes than the first generation of GE plants. Nobody knows how this happens – but it adds a whole new uncertainty to gene–host interactions, and to the levels of nourishment and any oestrogens, toxins or allergens which are produced from one year to the next.

eating GE crops containing resistant bacteria. Once in the gut they can pass their antibiotic resistance to other gut bacteria. Until recently this was only a theory, but research in Holland has now shown it can happen.

> The experiment showed each [antibiotic-resistant bacterium] had a 1 in 10 million chance of passing DNA containing antibiotic resistance genes to ... gut bacterium when they came in contact. There are normally a thousand billion gut bacteria, suggesting many would be transformed.
>
> Debora MacKenzie, New Scientist, 30 January 1999[10]

This report added that if microbes in the gut were weakened through use of antibiotics the risk of transfer would be ten times greater. Which means that those who are already sick and on antibiotic treatment are the most vulnerable to acquiring resistant bacteria.

Concern about antibiotic resistance has led a number of organisations, including the National Farmers' Union (NFU), to oppose the use of crops carrying antibiotic-resistance. And some organisations would like a total ban on the use of such genetic material. Despite this, the EU and the British government have approved the growing of such crops, and Zeneca's tomato paste carries a marker for resistance to the antibiotic kanamycin. This antibiotic is little used, but resistance to kanamycin can encourage resistance to other valuable antibiotics.

Growing Antibiotic Resistance

Antibiotic resistance is growing at an unprecedented rate. In one hospital the incidence of vancomycin resistance rose from 3 per cent in 1993 to 95 per cent in 1997. A form of Staphylococcus is resistant to 31 drugs, and many types of venereal disease resist most antibiotics. This pattern is repeated globally for such a wide range of antibiotics and bacteria that diseases such as tuberculosis, formerly thought controllable, are now out of control.

Antibiotic resistance is also reviving the old risk which used to attend surgery. In one Cambridgeshire hospital *E. coli* (much used in GE) resists all but one antibiotic.

New Diseases

In the first chapter I mentioned the dangers of using material from viruses and bacteria in genetic engineering. Some people would say there is no danger because only a DNA fragment and a single gene are used. In theory, they may be harmless. But anyone who has even a nodding acquaintance with microorganisms knows they're the Houdinis of the natural world, adept escapologists and quick-change artists, impossible to restrain and amazingly resilient. The reality is that disarmed viruses can re-arm and fragments of bacteria combine with others.

You also need to cook them to over 80°C before you can knock them out. And even then they may survive. They're in every cell, so whenever a part of their host moves around, they go with it. These partial viruses and bacteria will be in dead leaves from GE plants, in the roots which rot into the soil, in flakes of animal skin, fish scales, pollen, and so on, all of which can flow into waterways, drift on the wind and travel long distances. On their travels they are bound to encounter whole bacteria and viruses, and, as I explained in Chapter 1, these organisms have the knack of exchanging information with relatives.

Microscopic movement, huge effect

In healthy soil every plant is supported by a 'food web' of about 100 billion tiny organisms, from insects to bacteria, which surround its roots and help its development. The vast majority are beneficial bacteria and fungi. As yet, science knows very little about the life of the soil and the activities of these organisms. But Dr Mae-Wan Ho, a leading expert on genetic engineering, says there is a risk of bacterial genes in GE plants combining with soil bacteria to produce a new, different and perhaps dangerous organism. The greatest risk of this is when genetic engineering links bacterial genes to a forceful promoter, such as CaMV, which can make the genes it accompanies highly active in any organism they choose to enter.

In farming one danger is that this would create a new soil microbe which would disrupt the balance of soil organisms and seriously damage soil fertility. Such a bacterium could spread rapidly through soil, water and air, and would not be limited to the area where the GE crop was grown. Such damage to soil fertility might be impossible to repair and could spread irreversibly across vast tracts of land. But GE genes could equally well combine with a disease infecting plants or other hosts with equally serious results.

✱ Spain is making all GE crop producers contribute to US$100 million insurance against environmental accidents.

Engineered fragments of bacteria in GE plants can interact with any bacteria, with unpredictable results. Being unstable, such engineered genes can insert themselves in the cells of other species randomly, resulting in a range of harmful effects, including cancer.

Viruses mate after dinner

Few scientists worried about parts of viruses and bacteria being incorporated into GE food because they assumed that any harmful DNA in the food would be destroyed in the gut. However, in science, what is gospel one year is disproved the next. The gut's supposed ability to destroy viruses is no exception. When mice were fed food containing viral DNA, the viral DNA got into their livers, spleens and white blood cells. It did so in considerable numbers – occurring in one cell in a thousand. Clearly it is not destroyed in the gut.

This means that any viral or bacterial DNA in GE food crops may be incorporated into our bodies. Moreover, when we eat meat from animals which have fed on GE crops – as most do – we can assume that such DNA is in the flesh of those animals.

New diseases from combined viruses

One of the greatest threats to humanity is of genetic material from two different viruses, used in GE, combining with whole viruses to create a major new viral disease which could infect human beings. As an example of a plant virus which could harmfully combine with plant, human or animal viruses, Dr Ho cites the Cauliflower Mosaic Virus.

A potentially major source of new viruses arising from recombination . . . is the powerful promoter gene from cauliflower mosaic virus (CaMV) which is routinely used

* Soil bacteria are some of the closest relatives of bacteria causing human diseases.

... in transgenic crop plants for herbicide and disease resistance.

The CaMV promoter can drive the synthesis of related viruses. It is functional in most plants, in yeast, insects and *E. Coli*. Two kinds of potential hazards exist: reactivation of dormant viruses within the plant itself, and recombination between the CaMV promoter and other viruses ... to generate new, super infectious viruses or viruses with a broadened host range.

Dr Mae-Wan Ho, in a briefing for the Minister for the
Environment[12]

Pointing out that it closely resembles the AIDS, human leukaemic and human hepatitis B viruses, she says, 'the promoter gene can drive the synthesis of these viruses as well. There is therefore a possibility for the CaMV promoter to combine with human viruses when ingested in food.'

Dr Ho is not the only distinguished biologist to be concerned at the risk of viruses in GE food creating or spreading human diseases. The Australian molecular geneticist Professor Cummins has also been warning of this for some time: as large numbers of humans consume CaMV modified tomatoes recombination between CaMV and hepatitis B viruses will take place creating a supervirus propagated in plants, insects and humans.[13]

This ties in with dangers from GE foods which were highlighted in the research by Dr Pusztai (in the next chapter).

* The insect virus, baculovirus, can invade mammalian cells yet it is being engineered into toxic crop sprays as an insecticide.

Unauthorised Releases

One of the dangers of GE is that anyone with the right skills and a lab the size of a kitchen can change the very essence of life itself. And because GE is done on a minute scale they could modify bubonic plague without anyone knowing. In fact, someone tried to do just that.

However, it doesn't take a mad scientist to create serious risks; a careless lab technician can do it. In Australia there have been nine detected unauthorised releases of GE organisms, and five other breaches of government guidelines in relation to GE. All have been by respectable establishments – hospitals, universities and companies. Amazingly they include:

- a GE human virus in a defective container
- three years of field trials without permits
- work with a plant disease which broke quarantine and containment laws
- the illegal release of transgenic animals and plants
- the unauthorised use of an experimental GE vaccine on a cancer patient
- unauthorised GE experiments with HIV
- sixty-seven transgenic pigs being sent to an abattoir for human consumption

The pigs had been created through collaboration between a meat company and the University of Adelaide. Only a whistle-blower prevented the pigs, which contained a human promoter sequence, from being eaten. As so often, the world over, none of these breaches of protocol has been taken seriously. According to the report of the Genetic Manipulation Advisory

✴ In 1997 Monsanto withdrew two varieties of GE oil seed rape because of an 'unexpected gene': but 60,000 bags had been sold.

Committee (Annual Report, 1988–9), no penalties were applied. What happens in Australia is probably happening in every country in which GE is undertaken.

> Biotech companies are not behaving responsibly, considering the irreversible nature of any accident which may occur. There should be a moratorium on the introduction of genetically engineered foods until the science can be independently proven safe, and we believe that companies with an invested interest cannot be trusted to do this.
>
> Quentin Gargan, Genetics Concern, Ireland

The Food on Your Plate

There are a whole range of ways in which GE affects your diet. Nobody can say that one of them is more dangerous than another but identifying each of them may clarify the ways in which GE organisms may reach your plate. As there are absolutely no consumer benefits in eating GE food just now, you may feel there's no point in taking risks, however small. But if you can't get non-GE food you may find it useful to have some idea of what risks lie where.

As GE involves putting genes from one organism into another, I shall call the one that receives them the 'host' and the inserted genes the 'alien'. As GE is moving rapidly, I shall also include (but mark with a *) some foods not yet on sale but in the pipeline. The chapter on labelling details what is currently on sale.

* For a potential insect spray an Oxford scientist combined a virus alien to Britain with scorpion toxins – and tested it in the open.

Organisms which have been changed by GE

This covers GE meat*, fish*, fruit*, vegetables*, yeast (if used as yeast) and products which use any of these, or use flour or other 'solids' from GE crops. As the alien genes get into every cell in the host organism, every cell you eat will contain the engineered genes. These foods will also be capable of carrying any poisons or allergens which have been increased or created by GE, plus unfamiliar proteins created by GE, viral and bacterial DNA used as tools in GE, and maybe weedkiller.

Derivatives of a genetically engineered organisms

The term derivatives includes a mass of ingredients used in food manufacturing. These are all the oils, sweeteners, syrups, emulsifiers like lecithin, colorants and other substances which can be extracted from plants – or made from what has been extracted from them. Under EU and British law, none of them need be labelled. The argument is that no protein or DNA gets through into by-products, so there's no detectable difference between GE and non-GE anyway, and no danger exists. Several experts in this field say that the government is wrong, and that:

- filtration varies and protein *often* gets into the extracted oils
- mere *contact* with an allergen can make oil allergenic
- protein *isn't* the only potential source of harm
- tests *can* detect differences between GE and non-GE oils and other derived foodstuffs
- these substances could carry toxins

Substances that aren't themselves genetically engineered, but were created by a GE micro-organism

More and more yeast, bacteria, fungi and other micro-organisms are being engineered to become miniature factories producing substances, such as enzymes, for the food industry. They are so widely used in food and drink manufacturing that any manufactured, non-organic food could contain them.

So far there have been no problems with any of the British foodstuffs created by micro-organisms. But the processes used to make them can be similar to those used to make tryptophan. So their safety cannot be assumed. Despite that those classed as 'food additives' or 'flavourings', by the ministry don't even have to go through the approvals procedure used for GE food.

Meat, dairy products and eggs from creatures fed on genetically engineered crops and other GE substances

GE crops now constitute a large proportion of non-organic animal feed. This is likely to mean feed with a higher load of certain weedkillers. Such feed may also contain soya with higher than usual levels of female sex hormones (plant oestrogens) and crops with DNA from bacteria carrying antibiotic resistance which can be transferred to the animals, making them reservoirs of antibiotic-resistant bacteria. There is also evidence that the DNA from the engineered genes in animal feed gets into the body and white blood cells of the animal and into any young it is carrying. The same would be true of farmed fish*.

With bovine spongiform encephalopathy (BSE) we have already seen how what animals eat can affect not only their health but ours. Even farmers who favour GE are concerned about GE crops in animal feed – yet the government is doing nothing about it. Any non-organic animal may have had such feed. There is a risk of antibiotic-resistant organisms and modified genes being transferred from foodstuffs into livestock, and thence to man.

The truth is that no one has any idea whether the GM organisms fed to animals pose dangers to human health. But surely the very least consumers should have is the right to choose whether they buy these products or not.

Patrick Holden, Director, the Soil Association

Dairy products and meat from animals which have been injected with GE hormones

These entail all the safety problems covered in the section on BST*.

It must be safe – Americans eat it

Opposing all this evidence, agro-giants like to claim that since Americans have had GE foods for years it must be safe. That is no proof at all, for four reasons:

- many of the possible ill effects could take years to show
- many symptoms could be attributed to other things
- many American doctors aren't keen to report serious reactions to drugs, so why would they bother to speculate about reactions to GE food?
- America's laws discourage journalists from alerting the public to the risks from food lest they are prosecuted

For example, serious reactions to GE insulin have been reported in Britain and other parts of Europe, but in America it isn't an issue – not enough doctors have reported reactions. The same can be expected for GE food.

> Be thankful that we don't live in the USA . . . In the USA, journalists are gagged from writing about the dangers of genetic engineering by America's 'agricultural slander' laws. (The same ones that landed Oprah Winfrey in court over her beef comments.) So much for free speech.
>
> Josephine Fairley, founder, Green & Black's Organic Chocolate

3

The How & the Who: Science & Regulations

Three Myths

They only put in one gene
Nobody would ever put viruses in our food
We have the best regulations in the world

The Failure of Government

In December 1996 Dr Pusztai suddenly became aware of the inadequate levels of existing scientific trials on GM maize, when a member of the . . . ACNFP [Advisory Committee on Novel Food and Processes] asked him to assess the validity of a licence application from one of the industry's leading companies. He faxed a two page assessment to the Ministry of Agriculture warning that the tests into nutritional performance, toxicology or allergenicity were insufficient and inadequate.

The *Guardian*, 12 February 1999

For a long time it was thought that genes worked like parts in a machine. So 'one part, one function' led people to think 'one gene, one function'. That isn't so. Genes are subtle, interdependent, multi-tasking and work as a harmonious community. Naming the main role of a gene no more defines it, and its relationships with other genes, than saying your job is X describes you. If one forgets the other potentials in a person, or a gene, one is in for surprises – which is precisely what can happen with GE crops and other foodstuffs. This complexity has been known for decades but biotechnology has ignored it and science is only just beginning to understand it.

Even those at the leading edge know little more of the language of genes than you would know of Russian if you simply learnt to read a few hundred words – out of hundreds of thousands – without understanding the grammar, the nuances, structure and intonations of the language. They haven't even identified the basics of all the genes in the plants, animals and microorganisms they are modifying.

With such limited knowledge you might feel unable to 'improve' a work by Tolstoy. Unfortunately, those involved with genetic engineering aren't so modest. When new genes are inserted into an organism, be it plant, animal or yeast, these genes go into the instruction manual of every cell. It's like instructing a computer to insert a particular word, say 'green', randomly into every single sentence in *War and Peace*. Not a clever way of improving *War and Peace*, even though it might work in the occasional sentence, and no way to improve life-forms either. But this science is so new it's the best they can do.

How Genetic Engineering is Done

Politicians, officials and the GE industry tell us that GE food is safe. Yet in government or EU documents, the word 'risk' occurs again and again. That isn't surprising, for applying GE to food creates four interactive types of risk:

- risks created by the techniques

- risks created by the responses of the engineered organism
- risks caused by releases into the environment
- risks from individual human responses to the new substances created

In looking at these risks I don't want to give the impression that the issue is the *size* of the risk, or whether one risk is acceptable and another not. Far from it. With food the central issue is whether it's an appropriate use of this technology at all.

GE techniques

One of the great claims of genetic engineering is that it's a precise science. TV science programmes sometimes make it look as if inserting alien genes into a plant is as easy as taking one Polo mint out of a pack and slipping in another. Not so. Violating nature is done with difficulty and at a price. If you want to know *why* there may be a price, keep reading, but to skip straight to the consequences find the heading 'A harmonious city invaded'.

The easiest way to understand anything is to do it. Suppose you wanted to stop the water in cacti freezing by creating plants with an anti-freeze gene(s) from a fish. You might:

1 Prepare some plant tissue to receive the gene(s).
2 Isolate and perhaps modify the fish gene(s).
3 Splice the fish gene(s) with a *promoter* – usually a fragment taken from a virus – which will kick the fish genes into action in the plant.
4 Splice both these with a *marker* – often a gene for antibiotic resistance from a bacterium – so you can know if the genes have got into the plant tissue.
5 Splice all this into a *vector* – such as a plasmid from a

bacterium which will invade the plant, like a Trojan horse carrying the 'team' of genes with it

6 Hope the *vector* will carry the spliced genes into the plant.
7 Check for the presence of the *marker* gene.
8 Grow pieces of the plant on to make whole plants from which breeding can begin.

That's vastly simplified and leaves out some variations. The host needn't be a plant, it could be anything from a micro-organism, such as a yeast, virus or bacterium, through to an insect, rodent, pig, sheep, cow, or person.

The key point, as I mentioned in Chapter 1, is that the antifreeze genes aren't inserted by themselves, they have to be combined with the others and inserted as a team. And this use of fragments of infectious agents is probably the biggest – and least talked about – threat to human health and the natural world. For it could lead to the creation of new and virulent diseases threatening plants, animals and people. How serious that is depends on the organisms which contribute to the gene team.

Gene team roles

The main gene (e.g. from a fish) doesn't have to be used solo. They can insert genes for several different characteristics. But the more there are the greater the risk of conflicts with the host genes.

The marker is there because getting genes into a plant is so random that they need a way to check that the genes got into the host. Anything it's easy to test for, or check, will do. So one poor GE mouse had a marker which turned it a bright green. But as strange colours aren't very reassuring in food,

---

∗ When engineered genes are inserted in any organism where they end up, in relation to other genes, is pure chance.

antibiotic resistance is often used in crops. Antibiotic markers can be removed before a crop is grown, but companies seldom bother.

> Transgene-constructs and marker genes [gene-teams] will be able to spread to bacteria and viruses with the potential of creating new diseases and spreading antibiotic resistance among them. The bacteria and viruses in all environments essentially act as a reservoir for the genes and gene constructs, allowing them to multiply, recombine and further spread to all species.
>
> Dr Mae-Wan Ho, in a briefing for the Minister for the Environment

The promoter is chosen for its power. It ensures that the main inserted genes do their job in every cell. Without one they don't work. One of the most widely used promoters is from the Cauliflower Mosaic Virus (CaMV). (Especially the DNA sequence from the gene with the catchy name of 35S.) Some plant viruses are like human and animal viruses. And CaMV is very similar to hepatitis B and to AIDS. Common in GE crops, it was also used in Dr Arpad Pusztai's much-discussed research.

The vector which smuggles the genes in is chosen for its invasive skills. It could be a virus, a bacterium or a plasmid. The vector most used for crops is the Ti-plasmid of *Agrobacterium*. But sometimes, instead of using a vector they shoot the genes, promoter and marker into the plant on minuscule bullets, or use an electric field (electroporation) to 'shock' the plant into opening up and letting the genes in. If you wanted to get the 'gene team' into an animal, you could micro-inject them into the nucleus of a fertilised egg or use a vector from a virus. Whatever the method, where they end up in relation to the tens of thousands of existing genes is haphazard. It can take hundreds of attempts before the desired result is achieved.

The Gene Invaders

In autumn 1998 the prestigious science journal *Nature* carried telling research on gene movement. It showed that genes engineered into a plant are twenty times more likely to escape from the plant than its own genes. This is just one example of the new mobility being found in genes – mobility which should make us think carefully about what characteristics we confer on genes which may be unstable through being engineered.

Movement also seems to be occurring between unrelated species. In December 1998 the proceedings of the National Academy of Sciences in the USA reported that a genetic parasite had suddenly jumped species. In 1995 this parasite had been found only on yeast and on one type of plant. Three years later it was found on forty-eight types of plant.

There is a need to develop more effective and appropriate screening methods to alert companies and government agencies to the unexpected consequences of the often random insertion of genetic traits into plants.

Professor Philip James. Director, the Rowett Institute

A harmonious city invaded

Although I've said that genes are interactive and unpredictable, you might think that if the host organism was just a plant or a yeast, all would be plain sailing. Far from it. Even the simplest organisms have a huge number of complex components, which constantly interact to create all the 'behaviour' of a living thing. Even a single cell is an incredibly active, dynamic entity. And a whole plant or animal is almost like a town, with many specialised areas, a constant hum of interaction with cells as its living houses. But it's a beautifully organised community, in which every part is in harmony with every other part.

That is interrupted when a 'gene team' invades it. The arrival of alien genes in such a community is like having a flying saucer arrive in your home town, then having one of the Martians, plus his henchmen, billeted in every home. The disharmony can cut both ways. The inserted genes may not work properly because they lack the genes with which they normally collaborate. Equally, genes in the host may find their partnerships disrupted and behave abnormally.

The Pusztai Research

> I believe in technology. But it is too new for us to be absolutely sure what we are doing is right.
>
> Dr Arpad Pusztai in a press statement

One of the most controversial pieces of research ever done on GE food was conducted by Dr Arpad Pusztai. The story is a fascinating one. Here was a highly respected scientist, working in a prestigious government-funded laboratory – the Rowett Institute – a man who was a world expert on lectins, substances plants often use to deter insect pests. As part of a government project, he set out to devise ways to test food for safety – and ended up exposing the dangers of GE food.

'I was totally taken aback. I was absolutely confident that I wouldn't find anything, but the longer I spent on the experiment the more uneasy I became', Dr Pusztai said afterwards.

A lot of inaccurate reports and criticisms of Dr Pusztai's work

∗ Roundup Ready crops contain gene sequences from a petunia, a bacterium – and the cauliflower mosaic virus used by Dr Pusztai.

have been aired, but the experiment was very simple and very significant. Three different groups of rats ate three different diets:

- the first group ate plain potatoes
- the second group ate potatoes with lectin sprinkled on top
- the third ate potatoes engineered to contain the same lectin

Dr Pusztai wasn't against GE and – as a world expert on lectins – he carefully used snowdrop lectin, which is harmless to mammals and was already being engineered into crops such as rice and oil seed rape. So he expected the rats to stay healthy. Unfortunately, the rats which had eaten the GE potatoes quite rapidly became unwell. On post-mortem examination they were shown to have undergone significant damage to their immune systems, brains, kidneys, spleens and thymuses; their stomach linings were thickened and their guts looked as if they had suffered a viral infection. The two other groups did not show these symptoms. So Dr Pusztai concluded that the harm had been inflicted by some aspect of GE itself. Within days of making this public, he lost his job at the institute and was denied access to his own research – even though he hadn't set out to attack GE. Yet his findings were important by any standards – and especially so in a field where so little is known.

> If this was generated by a cancer drug then people would certainly need to be worried about the effects on their health and digestive organs. It would be interesting to know if the basic cause of these observations is the increased division of cells, as happens in cancer.
>
> Dr Ian Gibson, MP, Dean of Biological Sciences, Sussex University

✳ Feeding ladybirds with aphids which had eaten potatoes engineered with snowdrop lectin halved their life span.

During the confused comment on Dr Pusztai's work, some said that the lectin itself was poisonous – the one he used isn't – others that raw potatoes are harmful. All that missed the point that *all* the rats ate raw potato, and two groups ate the *same* lectin – but the only ones to become ill were those which ate the GE potato. Dr Stanley Ewan did the post-mortem.

> We didn't expect the result. We expected it would show no difference. But there are differences which cause me concern. We need to know what happens in the mammalian [human] gut with GM food.
>
> Dr Stanley Ewan, senior pathologist, Aberdeen Medical School

When Dr Pusztai was ousted from the Rowett Institute, Dr Ian Gibson, a Labour MP, said that he felt 'there had been some interference with the openness of the scientific process from either industrial or political avenues'. A significant comment.

Why Pusztai's work affects us all

> The geneticist Dr Arpad Pusztai is a dangerous man. He has released into the environment a virulent self-replicating organism, which is already running riot across Britain. It's called the truth.
>
> George Monbiot, *Guardian*, 13 February 1999

When Dr Pusztai came under attack, twenty-two eminent scientists, worldwide, publicly supported his work. It affects all of us because Dr Pusztai's experiment suggests that GE can dramatically affect health. Even if repeating the experiment does not give the same results Dr Pusztai's work shows that, in some circumstances, with some creatures, GE foods can be gravely damaging. That alone should be a strong argument for discontinuing GE food. The changes to the intestinal wall suggest that some GE foods could harm the digestion, making food less well absorbed. This, in turn, would cause a slow decline in health which nobody would put down to GE foods. One possibility on safety is that the damage was inflicted by the CaMV promoter – which is widely used in GE crops – activating a dormant virus in the guts of the rats.

> Dr Pusztai's results, at the very least, raise the suspicion that genetically modified food may damage the immune system.
>
> Dr Ronald Fagan, past president of the British Society of Allergy
> and Environmental Medicine

The British government likes to boast of the 'thorough, rigorous, safety assessment' of novel foods. Yet I've heard it described as 'out of date' and 'wholly inadequate'. The system of assessment of novel foods wasn't set up by the present government. However, it could have modernised it to meet the challenge of GE foods – and it hasn't. In fact, a leaked Cabinet Office memo of February 1999 shows that the government is out of its depth on this issue.

The memo asks:

> 'Why don't we require pharmaceutical type analysis of the safety of these foods with proper trials?
>
> In relation to the voluntary deal with industry to delay commercial planting till the year 2000 it asks.

> 'How can we be sure that deal will not unravel?'

And,

> 'How can we be sure that our line that a moratorium would be illegal is accurate? If this proves to be untrue, the pressure could increase even further.'

It is interesting the way this memo shows more concern for covering the government's back than for protecting the public. This is not surprising, for successive governments have been in love with technology and have believed the object of their love could do no wrong. So they ignore the fact that the criteria by which the safety of GE food is judged are seriously inappropriate.

Substantial equivalence: a licence to kill?

> Genetically engineered foods classified as substantially equivalent are spared extensive safety testing on the assumption that they are no more dangerous than the corresponding non-genetically engineered food. The effect has been to allow [them] to enter the market place without sufficient testing to assure safety . . . The health of the population of Europe is thus being put at risk.
>
> Professor John Fagan, geneticist, head of Genetic ID

Before GE food can be imported into Britain it goes before the Advisory Committee on Novel Food and Processes (ACNFP) for a safety check. It is hard to imagine a process less suited to the very considerable dangers which GE food may present.

The ACNFP is only an advisory committee. It cannot ban a GE food, however dangerous it is, and must judge it by the rules of 'substantial equivalence'. This means a company must present the committee with evidence that its GE version of a foodstuff is substantially equivalent to a non-GE version. So it would, for example, check a GE tomato to see whether it has much the same look, feel, taste, smell, food value and general composition as a normal tomato. Then present the

---

✱ The British Government's Chief Scientific Officer has said a panel should see if GE food can cause birth defects, new cancers or damage to the immune system.

data to the ACNFP, together with figures for a non-GE tomato as a benchmark.

The committee may ask for other tests to be done, or for advice from other advisory committees, but there is no legal requirement for any independent tests to be carried out on GE food. The company's own data is enough. If the figures for the two tomatoes (or whatever) are similar they're considered substantially equivalent and the GE one approved. Yet companies have been known to use out-of-date research in order to show that their GE plant is 'normal'.

By such a test scientists could have examined Jack the Ripper, prior to his crimes, and announced him to be substantially equivalent to a vicar – and fit to walk young women home. With safe food, as with safe human beings, it isn't the substantially equivalent 99 per cent which creates the danger. It's the aberrant, normally invisible 1 per cent, or less.

Will the rules on substantial equivalence find any hazard lurking in that tiny remaining percentage? No, say some experts.

As the criterion by which foodstuffs are deemed fit for import and/or sale substantial equivalence *fails to*:

- look for changes which are *un*expected
- investigate toxins present on levels below 0.1 per cent – though lower levels can kill
- consider stress-related changes in plants
- consider the danger of viral or bacterial DNA in GE food
- test crops *after* weedkiller has been applied to them
- compel independent testing
- compel long-term testing for specific risks

✳ Novartis engineered a maize using DNA from a virus, maize and two different types of bacteria.

- allow for the cumulative effect of tiny doses of any harmful substance
- investigate the effects of eating animals fed on GE crops
- consider moral issues such as human genes in animals
- consider the morality of food which may involve harm to animals

Speaking at a meeting on genetic engineering, Dr Vyvyan Howard, President of the Royal Microscopical Society and head of research on foetal toxicology at the University of Liverpool, said he believed the first evidence of harm from GE foodstuffs would be seen 'in damage to unborn children'. For GE could create totally unexpected substances which could remain undetected for years – slow or subtle poisons which doctors might not even link with the food concerned. Such substances might slowly undermine the immune system, or interact with body chemicals to make people more sensitive to other food or environmental stresses.

Dangerously Un-equivalent

I mentioned earlier that some strains of yeast, intended for use in beer and bread-making, accumulated the highly toxic substance methylglyoxal – which can deform unborn children. Luckily, the researchers working on the yeast accidentally discovered the poison before the yeast went for approval. But they warned that, although methylglyoxal could damage babies in the womb, tests for substantial equivalence would have been *unlikely to have identified* the poison had they put the yeast up for approval.

As an international authority on food testing, Professor John Fagan believes that the tests usually performed to establish substantial equivalence are unlikely to detect such substances:

> Such tests are completely incapable of detecting unsuspected or unanticipated health risks that are generated by the process of genetic engineering itself. It is a scientific fact that the process of genetic engineering often gives rise to unanticipated side-effects. These can – and have been shown to – introduce unforeseen allergens and toxins into foods . . . Not every genetically engineered food will have these problems, but there is a finite probability that any given genetic modification will lead to unanticipated side-effects that result in food characteristics that threaten the health of consumers.
>
> Professor John Fagan

The Advisory Committees

How GE Crops Reach a Field Near You

A company wanting to grow GE crops experimentally in an EU country, or sell the seed for commercial use, must apply first to the country in question. Having been approved there, it must also be accepted by the EU. At this stage countries can object to crops being approved by others, putting their case in a committee of member states. In theory the decision rests on a committee vote. In practice, the EU Commission – which is pro-GE crops – sometimes ignores the vote. How long consent should last, and whether it should be possible to revoke it, is a matter of debate.

In Britain the UK Advisory Committee on Releases to the Environment (ACRE) advises the government on whether to approve applications to grow GE crops, but the process is oddly secretive. There seems to be no public list of applications pending – I was told that 'commercial confidentiality' prevented such a list being made public. Evidently, the Ministry is prepared to consider companies, not taxpayers. An interesting example of 'open government'.

The regulation of GE is also bedevilled by the fact that several ministries and assorted committees advise the British government on issues which may include genetic engineering. Unfortunately, many of these committees may be no more appropriate, as guardians of our welfare, than the criteria of substantial equivalence. It is almost impossible to find a committee containing the range of expertise, experience, and lack of vested interests, which common sense would suggest was wise for such a complex and controversial topic.

Incredibly members of multinational corporations, such as Nestlé, Mars and biotech companies, sit on such committees or on related ones, which put them on intimate terms with relevant officials.

The composition of these committees is beginning to change, but by how much? To date apart from a consumer representative there are often few women, few professionals who aren't professors and usually no one from any Non-Governmental Organisation (NGO). Some years ago, government funding for university research dried to a trickle. So academics have been forced to turn to big business for funding. It is now extremely hard to find academics whose personal research, universities, departments, close colleagues and students are not indebted to industry. Naturally, GE companies fund research on GE and food companies fund research on food. Then those researching food or GE get on food committees. This direct and indirect

---

✳ Since ACRE was set up to control GE crop trials it has not refused a single one.

involvement of industry means that those who have most to
gain from GE may crucially influence the approvals process.
This could explain why risks to human health, the environment, and organic farming were largely ignored for so long.

> One by one the assumptions on which geneticists and
> regulatory committees have based their assessment of
> genetically engineered products as 'safe' have fallen by
> the wayside, especially in the light of the evidence emer-
> ging in the past three years. However there is very little
> evidence of these findings being taken on board.
>
> Dr Mae-Wan Ho, Genetic Engineering, Dream or Nightmare?

In other countries there have been allegations of direct industry
influence on vital decisions on the use of GE in food production.
These include bribery, corruption and executives from the GE
industry being appointed as key government regulators of GE
use. And even without such direct industry influence, it took the
ACNFP more than a year to declare that food crops containing
antibiotic-resistant markers risk creating antibiotic-resistant
strains of fatal diseases such as meningitis: a fact which some
independent scientists have been pointing out for several years.
The lesson is not only that such committees need fresh 'recruit-
ment' policies but that nations cut back science funding at their
peril – though government funding might be no less biased.

> The days of impartiality and independent scientific debate
> are past. So many places in academia depend on com-
> panies for finance. Not just to finance the department
> but them. In the old days there'd be government funded
> post-grads who could do independent trials. You don't
> get that nowadays. Funding is predominantly industry
> and you don't bite the hand that feeds you. Their whole

✳ More than 100 meetings have taken place between GE companies and the government since Labour was elected.

future career depends on publishing papers, and research is industry funded.

John Verrall, Director, Food and Farm Society

A Warning Ignored

The ACNFP actually expressed concern about the safety of Novartis's GM maize because of the antibiotic resistance gene it contained. They recommended that this gene should be removed before the crop was given marketing consent. Despite these concerns, which were shared by 13 of the 15 member states, the maize was still given the go-ahead by the European Commission – and we are eating it, as are farm animals.

Friends of the Earth briefing to MPs

The Need for Safety Tests

The data submitted to the Advisory Committee on Novel Foods and Processes shows that testing is limited to short-term animal feeding trials almost always carried out by the companies themselves. If these products were drugs they would be tested for far longer and would include tests on human volunteers.

Friends of the Earth briefing to MPs

Perhaps the most extraordinary fact of all in relation to GE food is that it is put onto the market without any long-term safety tests. When genetic engineering is used to make medicines it is recognised that those medicines could entail unexpected dangers. To be approved for sale they must undergo stringent laboratory tests, then extensive safety trials on animals – trials which check separately whether the drug might cause cancer, trigger allergies, harm unborn babies, and so on. These tests and trials alone can take up to ten years. And only if a drug passes those tests will it even be allowed to be tested on human volunteers.

The techniques for making a GE drug are essentially the same as for making some GE foodstuffs. The risk of creating an unexpected hazard need be no less great. So why shouldn't the procedures to check their safety be equally strict? If such long-term tests are needed before GE medicines can be sold, logically they are even more necessary for GE food. We take drugs because we have a problem, and may willingly accept a degree of risk to cure that problem. Risks in food are a totally different matter – with food there is no trade-off between a risk and a cure. Indeed, some people would say that we already accept quite enough risks from the agro-chemicals created by the same companies that are producing GE food.

Moreover, most drugs are taken in tiny quantities for a relatively short time. We consume food in far greater quantities, daily, over a lifetime. So the risk of cumulative effects is far greater. In addition, food is indiscriminate. Some drugs are never given to the very young or the very old, or to those made vulnerable by operations, disease, or pregnancy. GE food is eaten by almost everyone. Doesn't this mean that food needs to be far safer – not less safe – than drugs.

Is ethical testing possible?

The only scientifically valid approach is to feed these foods to human volunteers and see how they respond. Such testing is required by the FDA before new foods or additives produced by other methods can be marketed. Why should genetically altered food be the exception?

Professor John Fagan

* Argentina banned glyphosate-tolerant oilseed rape lest it create herbicide resistant weeds. It may be Britain's first GE crop.

The case against testing

It is one thing to say that if GE foods were drugs they'd be tested on animals and humans. It is quite another to say that they *should* be tested that way. The justification for testing drugs on animals and volunteer humans rests on the fact that drugs relieve pain and sickness. Currently GE foods benefit only the giant companies which make them, Far from fulfilling its promises, it seems set to *increase* the use of agrochemicals, and *increase* poverty and hunger in the Third World.

In America $95 million was poured into creating one GE tomato – which failed. Worldwide, thousands of millions are being spent to create other GE crops. If even a fraction of that money had been spent on developing normal crops, and on researching low input and organic farming, far more good could have been done.

Some people, such as the distinguished microbiologist Professor Richard Lacey, say there is no justification for using GE to create foodstuffs at all. Rightly, he points to an inevitable Catch 22. It is this. Since GE foods could be harmful they cannot, ethically, be sold without full safety tests on humans and animals comparable to those used to test drugs. However, ethical tests cannot be done for there is no justification for exposing people to health risks needlessly. And, since GE food isn't needed such exposure would be needless. His analysis has characteristic common sense.

I don't believe it would be ethical to test genetically engineered food on people. There is no justification for exposing people to that risk. The food should be banned.

Richard Lacey, Emeritus Professor, Leeds University

∗ Oilseed rape pollen can travel 2.5 kilometres. The official separation distance between GE rape and non-GE crops is 400 metres.

Logically, Professor Lacey is right and there is a growing body
of opinion that a world ban on GE food is needed. Until then
we remain experimental animals.

The method of science is the method of bold conjectures
and ingenious and severe attempts to refute them.

                                                    Karl Popper

4

Labelling: The Law with a Hole in the Middle

Three Myths

GE food will keep down prices.
Only three GE foodstuffs are in use.
The labels tell us about most ingredients that are
engineered.

Consumer . . . groups argue that . . . regulations should
protect the public not only against known safety risks,
but also against risks that cannot be anticipated by science. They view safety as only one component of a far
broader range of concerns about the impact of biotechnology on individuals, society, and the environment . . .
one aspect of a much wider range of social values.

Professor Marion Nestle, Department Nutrition and
Food Studies, New York University[1]

The Labelling Farce

The extraordinary thing is that full labelling of genetically
engineered (GE) foods hasn't been automatic, comprehensive
and universal. You'd think that if any radically new products
of techno-wizardry suddenly entered a nation's food chain any

responsible government would *want* comprehensive labelling. For logically, there are only two possibilities. Either the food is safe – in which case there is nothing to lose by labelling. Or there may be a risk that it could be unsafe. In which case a responsible government would use labelling to give people the choice of not taking that risk, and to ensure that any ill effects could rapidly be traced to their cause. It would also set up systems for recording adverse reactions and tracing products linked to them. No country has done this automatically and the British government has only begun to inch in that direction after considerable pressure from shoppers and NGOs.

Having authorised the sale of GE foods, are governments afraid of repercussions? Or have powerful agro-tech companies persuaded them to hide GE ingredients to make it harder for us to prove liability when something goes wrong? Or is it simply that preserving an unfettered market for biotech products has mattered far more to most governments than consumer rights, safety, or respect for people's ethical and religious principles?

Follow my leader

Amazingly, America accepted GE food almost without noticing. From the start the FDA, America's regulatory body, decided GE foods would be treated like any others. There is no compulsory pre-market approval, testing, or even labelling to give consumers choice. This is perhaps no surprise, given the interesting intimacy which seems to exist between key gene companies and the FDA. It is even less surprising in a land where such corporations have contributed generously to both political parties at every level.

Unfortunately, in areas like technology, where the pressure is on to seem 'progressive', America often sets the benchmark. Worldwide, governments have been trying *not* to label, or to restrict labelling to a point where it is virtually useless. What's more, laws seem to be timed so that any new GE food has a clear, unlabelled launch period in which to get established before labelling kicks in. GE food was sold here for four years before Europe got around to a law on labelling – and it only did so then under pressure. As early as 1995 a major survey showed that 93 per cent of British consumers wanted clear labelling. They were not alone. Yet the EU did nothing.

A Good Question

'Is it true that thirteen Monsanto staff now work for the Food and Drug Administration in the US?'

'No. You have got it all wrong,' Dr Bill Blowes, technical director for Monsanto Australia said, 'Those thirteen people came from the FDA to work for Monsanto.'

Bob Burton, Environment News Service,
Australia, 13 March 1999

A secret EU agenda

Perhaps believing the economic carrots the biotechnology companies cleverly dangled before governments and legislators, the EU has a secret agenda to foster biotechnology – which was shared by the British government. So instead of giving us full labelling the EU gave us propaganda. Over 552 million Ecu (roughly £380 million) of our money was spent by Europe, in four years, on promoting the 'social acceptance' of biotechnology.

This EU fostering of biotechnology goes far beyond a desire to ensure that good use is made of all technologies for the benefit of society. The agenda of the EU's Biotechnology Work

---

✳ By a vote of 407 to 2 the EU parliament condemned the EU Commission for approving a crop most member states had opposed.

Programme includes 'addressing hurdles which hamper successful utilization of relevant technologies, such as competing technological alternatives [organic farming perhaps?], and the resistance of potential users [you and me] to change'.

Clearly, the EU believes nothing must stand in the way of genetic engineering. No other technology is to have equal support, all 'resistance' must be overcome. The officials who wrote those words are ostensibly there to protect us and embody our democratic decisions, yet their statement smacks chillingly of dictatorship. Since the EU had – and continues to have – such an agenda, what kind of labelling could we expect?

> The regulators didn't want to get caught up in wrangles about trade and inhibiting a burgeoning new industry. They had to leave themselves room not to label. I think the legislators are now in a hole and they should stop digging. But you can't expect logic to come from the likes of the European Commission.
>
> Professor Barry Law, R & D consultant to the food industry

Too little too late

One of the most absurd, and confusing, laws ever created by the European Union must surely be EC Regulation 1139 – the regulation that sets the GE labelling standards of every country in the EU, including Britain. This dubious little number, passed in 1998, covers no more of the essentials than a stripper's G-string. Blind to our fundamental right to know what we eat, it ignored more than it included, excluded long-standing products, such as tomato paste, and made no provision for future ones. Most bizarre of all, under US influence it created a food apartheid which is still mystifying half Europe. For it means that one part of a soya bean or maize kernel has the

---

∗ Even tiny sugar substitute tablets may contain maize and soya starches.

privilege of being labelled and all the rest of it is excluded. The basis of this curious division is that only 'protein and DNA' (explained soon) from genetically engineered maize and soya need carry the words 'genetically modified'. This splitting of hairs means that, for example, soya textured vegetable protein (TVP) has to be labelled, but soya oil from the same beans needn't be labelled. Yet in making such a division officials give themselves away. The only plausible reason for such divided labelling is a belief that one is more dangerous than the other. Evidently, while telling us that everything is safe, both the EU and the British government know very well that GE food may carry risks.

Tomato Paste as a Trojan Horse

You wouldn't expect tomato paste to pose as a Trojan horse, would you? But it has. In the dim and distant days of 1994, when few of us knew much about GE and the Internet was young, GE tomato paste was born. Trumpeted as the latest thing throughout the media, this inno-cent-looking product was even labelled as genetically engineered. It needed to be. It was the industry's test product. If we bought that, we'd probably buy the rest of their Pandora's box, they thought.

The fact that it sold opened the door to all the other GE products. Even after all the consumer protests, the illusion continues that the sales of tomato paste prove we want GE. While debating GE both a politician and an agro-giant spokesman have said to me, 'Look at tomato paste, it's selling. That proves the public want GE food!'

Since the tin was bigger and cost less its sales were predictable. All they really show is that GE food creates a new injustice. If new or unpopular GE foods are cheap, the less well-off will buy them.

So What Are Protein and DNA?

If you find it hard to identify soya and maize 'protein and DNA' you're in good company. I doubt if one person in hundred can define them accurately.

For there is no brief, clear and scientifically exact description. Roughly it translates as 'soya and maize solids': soya and maize flour, soya-based TVP and so on. As you'll find in the lists below, they're in a huge range of manufactured foods.

Understanding GE Food

There's a lot of confusion about which foods have been genetically engineered. At a business breakfast my host pointed proudly to a display of eggs, tomatoes and mushrooms, assuring us that they were all organic – not GE. They were delicious. Yet none of those foods have GE versions in Britain – yet. He had, however, overlooked the ketchup, Danish pastries, croissants, bread and yoghurt – none of which were organic and all of which might well have contained GE ingredients.

So what food might be genetically engineered?

As I write (in early 1999) no GE crops are grown in Britain for sale as food – only as seeds – and the only foods from GE crops allowed to be imported into Britain are:

• GE soya beans and soya bean by-products

∗ The EU approved a GE maize variety which 13 out of 15 member states had voted against – a variety the British Medical Association also opposes.

- GE maize and maize by-products
- GE tomato paste/purée

By a remarkable 'coincidence' soya and maize are probably found in more manufactured food and drink than any other crops. Oilseed rape, another staple of food manufacturing, may be next past the post in Britain. The GE industry thinks big. They were the biggest sellers – and the most invisible. A clever move. Another huge market for GE maize and soya is animal feed. So GE also reaches your table indirectly through meat, poultry, eggs and dairy products.

Why GE foods are everywhere

You wouldn't think that three GE foodstuffs – tomato paste, maize and soya – could make much of a contribution to our diet. But these GE ingredients end up in at least eight out of ten manufactured foods – unless the brands are GM-free or organic. This is no accident. America has tried to ensure that GE versions of soya and maize are lumped together with non-GE ones at harvesting. So, unless a manufacturer finds special GE-free sources, most consignments will have GE varieties mixed in. The proportion of GE varies with the source, but it can already be high and, if the acreage of GE crops increases, it's likely to keep rising.

Soya and maize alone provide the food and drink industry with:

- much used flours
- useful thickeners
- vital stabilisers
- useful sweeteners
- two of the most-used oils
- the basis of various food colours

On top of that, manufactured food contains more than a dozen GE enzymes and other food additives.

No one knows the true extent of GM [GE] in food, because so little is labelled and monitored. It could be used in up to 90% of the processed foods in our supermarkets.

Dr Sue Meyer, Director of GeneWatch (UK)

How the Labelling Rules Work

The labelling rules apply to any maize or soya. But only a few varieties have been approved for sale in Britain. So, for the moment, fresh GE corn on the cob isn't sold here, nor do I know of any GE polenta – but things change fast in this industry, so read the labels. Spain will soon be growing thirteen different varieties of GE maize, so maize will be traded within the EU. Once that happens it may not be long before we see a wider range of GE corn products.

How GE protein or DNA must be labelled

When food contains soya or maize protein or DNA, from GE crops, it must be shown on the label in one of three ways. Using soya as an example, the ways it can be shown are:

- 'soya (genetically modified) flour'
- 'soya flour (produced from genetically modified soya)'
- 'soya* flour' ... then 'genetically modified' or 'produced from genetically modified ...' at the bottom of the ingredients list.

Ingredients which should say if they have GE sources

May contain protein & DNA	They may be in
cornflour	In mass market foods expect to find
modified cornflour	these in any foods in which flour
maize flour	would be used: bread, cakes, pastry,
soya flour	coatings, batters, and for thickening
	sauces, soups, desserts and custard.

soya protein soya protein isolate TVP	These are much used in vegetarian food but may also bulk out any meat products, such as ready-made meals.
polenta	This is unlikely to be GE yet.
soya milk	Any milk substitute could have this in. Soya baby formulas may contain GE soya but some companies are now avoiding it. Check with the company (see Baby Formulas below).
soya sauce	Don't assume that if it's from China it's not GE. China is well into GE.
tofu	This is in a mass of meat-free and dairy-free products that would otherwise contain meat and dairy products: burgers, sausages, ice creams, puddings, even custard.

A Point to Remember

The fact that something is on one of these lists of potentially GE food does *not* mean it *always* comes from a GE source. In some cases it just means it *could* come from one.

The following list may surprise you. But soya and maize have a range of by-products which don't need to be labelled. A number of other approved foodstuffs, such as enzymes and riboflavin, made by GE yeasts, bacteria and even fungi, don't need to be labelled either.

* The UK's Vegetarian Society bans the use of its 'V' logo on any GE foods except cheese made with GE rennet: chymosin.

However that doesn't mean you will never find any of the following on labels. By law none of them need say they have even danced with a GE gene. However, more and more supermarkets and manufacturers are labelling the main by-products of soya and maize – lecithin, and soya and maize oil – to show if they are GE.

These foods need not admit to any GE origins but may have them

Some 13 permitted – GE enzymes	unlikely to be named on labels but widely used in the food industry to make many manufactured foods: e.g. protinase is used in cheese sauces and snack foods, lipoxygenase in bread, and alfa-amylase in brewing.
aspartame (if made in USA)	– an artificial sweetener in many soft drinks and some foods.
chymosin	– the GE enzyme used to replace rennet in much cheese-making.
dextrose and glucose	– sweeteners used in confectionery and desserts
maltodextrin (often comes from maize)	– curries, soups, and many ready-made meals, breakfast foods, ice cream, food coatings, canned and bottled drinks, hot chocolate and other mixes for hot milky drinks, bread, buns and pastries.
high fructose corn syrup (HFCS) (from maize)	– very widely used sweetener in soft drinks, colas, and other canned drinks.
lecithin (E322)	– so widely used in manufactured

(from soya)	food that it's very hard to avoid. Most chocolate and chocolate coatings contain it and it's often in yoghurt, desserts, sauces, mousses, cakes, biscuits, pastries, foods with sauce or gravy, nut spreads.
maize/corn oil	– many home cooking oils, breads, biscuits, cakes, pastry, chips and many fried foods, snacks, some hydrogenated fats and margarine, salad dressings, mayonnaise, soups, and often in 'anything saying vegetable oil'.
meat, poultry, game, dairy products and eggs	– these don't come from GE sources but most animal feeds contain GE maize and soya.
milk from BST-injected cows	– American foods using dairy products.
modified starch	– a thickener used in pies, sauces, soups.
monosodium glutamate (E621)	– a flavour enhancer in many foods.
riboflavin (Vitamin B2, also on labels as E 101, 101)	– a vitamin and food colouring, used to 'improve' food and often in slimming foods, breakfast cereals, baby foods and soft drinks.
soya oil	– very widely used in cakes, biscuits, snacks and as large-scale catering fat; may be in some hydrogenated fats and margarine, could be in any 'vegetable oil'.

∗ The GE foodstuff which worries consumers least is GE rennet.

tomato purée or paste	– sold for home cooking, used commercially for pizzas, sauces, soups, chilli con carne, and could be in any products using 'tomato purée' or 'tomato paste'.
xanthan gum (often from maize) (E415)	– jelly-type confectionery, yoghurt, desserts, gravies, sauces, meat dishes with gravies, pet foods (that lovely meaty jelly some pet foods have).
yeast and yeast extract	– a GE brewing yeast exists and other yeasts are being worked on; as new ones are unlikely to hit the headlines, regard any yeast product as potentially GE.

E Numbers to watch out for

Food additives with the following E numbers may come from sources which have been genetically modified, or use GE oils. For example, some industrial food colours use soya oil as a base.

E101 E101a E150 E153 E160 E161 E306 E307 E308 E309
E322 E415 E471 E472a E473 E475 E476b E477 E479a E479b
E570 E572 E573 E620 E621 E622 E623 E624

Customer power

Additive labelling is under discussion but, as yet, none of the foods above *have* to be labelled although shops and manufacturers will do so if enough customers ask for it. We have all seen how many supermarkets, which only months ago were backing GE, have gone totally GE free for their own brand goods. Overwhelmed by customers' letters, they did a smart about-face.

Companies which genuinely do this need support and appreciation from everyone who wants non-GE food to remain in the shops. For re-sourcing is a remarkably painstaking process. Bill Wadsworth, Technical Director of Iceland Supermarkets, told me he was offered what claimed to be GE-free chicken Kiev. On the Kiev were breadcrumbs; in the breadcrumbs was pepper; blended with the pepper was GE soya lecithin. Iceland said it had to go. Such attention to detail takes time and care which were never necessary before GE was introduced, and which may be preventing food prices falling during a farm slump.

Unexpected GE

There are some surprises among the foods which could contain GE ingredients. Most arise because oil from GE soya or maize may have been used. They include:

- **salted nuts** (which may have been cooked in oil)
- **ready-to-cook flavoured rice** (which could use oil and MSG)
- **dried fruit** (which may be moistened with oil)
- **salad dressing** (which could contain oil and thickeners)
- **dips of all kinds** (oils and thickeners again)
- **frozen stir fry vegetables** (possibly oils and sweeteners)
- **honey** could have been contaminated by pollen from GE crops

---

Coming soon to a table near you?

With only three GE crops entering Britain in five years, it's easy to suppose that it will be a long while before we see a wider range. But 'what America does today we do tomorrow' is a saying which has proved true of GE. In America the range of GE foods is growing steadily. In addition to having GE cotton, maize and soya, some Americans are eating GE versions of:

papaya	rape oil
potatoes	summer squash
radicchio	tomatoes

Food crops being developed or having field trials include:

carrots	asparagus
celery	sugar beet
cabbages	malting barley
sprouts	

These could be coming here soon. Under EU law each new food will be considered on a 'case by case basis'. The EU still hasn't labelled tomato paste five years on, and took almost two years to pass its G-string law on soya and maize. So new GE foods may well sell unlabelled and unsung for years – unless the public insists on immediate labelling.

GE and drink

The really big users of GE ingredients are the makers of non-alcoholic drinks. Most of them, from squashes and so-called 'fruit drinks' to colas and other canned drinks, are chock full of sweeteners and food colours which could have been specially engineered or are likely to have come from GE soya or maize. Confusingly, the canned and bottled versions may have different ingredients. One may use sugar, another a maize by-product. So you may need to check every time.

It's hard to tell what part genetic engineering plays in alco-holic drinks. There are no GE vines or hops yet, but fermenting any alcohol could involve the addition of GE yeast. At least one GE yeast is already used in brewing and more are coming. How widely that GE yeast is used is impossible to say. As alcoholic drinks don't have to list their ingredients you won't be able to tell which drinks have used yeast in their making. The GE brewing enzyme alfa-amylase need not be labelled either. Beer and some spirits may also contain caramel colouring (E150) which could come from burnt GE material, though I doubt if that should worry anyone. It will, however, be a sad day when GE barley invades the whisky industry. Yet even that is planned.

Baby and Toddler Foods

Despite babies being the most vulnerable group of all neither the EU nor the British government has done anything to stop GE foods being fed to babies. The guidelines on the content of baby foods could have banned GM ingredients – but they didn't, and the GE labelling laws are the same as for adults.

There is no evidence that your baby will have been harmed if it has been eating or drinking GE foods. But, as GE foods have never had safety trials on human beings, it may be wise to avoid giving babies GE foods if you can. Unfortunately, there are more ways that GE food can reach your baby than you might think.

1 Most cattle are fed on GE crops and the engineered genes in the crops may get through to the milk or milk formula. Governments should have researched this before allowing GE crops into animal feed. They didn't – but research on mice suggests it may be possible
2 Formulas will probabaly contain ingredients which could come from GE maize or soya. See adult food for the safety issues.
3 If BST is allowed in future, formulas will contain BST itself, higher levels of a growth factor and higher-than-usual levels

of antibiotic residues. The residues may kill good bacteria in a baby's stomach, which isn't healthy. There's no evidence of how the BST and growth factor affect babies.

4 Policies vary on baby food. Companies, such as Heinz UK, began avoiding GE ingredients, for adult and baby foods, long before the outcry over GE food. But, as I write, Heinz still uses GE lecithin, and some animal products may come from animals fed on GE crops. Not perfect, but they're working on it. There are also excellent ranges of organic baby food – such as Baby Organix.

5 The greatest risk may be from soya formula made for lactose-intolerant babies. Soya formula will probably be from GE soya unless it's organic or says it is GMO-free. Unable to tolerate cow's milk, these babies will drink large amounts of soya milk at a formative time in their lives. Nobody can say that GE soya is unsafe for babies. But I know of no research to show it is safe either, and there are three potential risks to be aware of:

a   GE soya may have been sprayed with poisonous weed-killer later in the season than normal crops and carry a heavier chemical load than other soya.

b   There is a possibility that GE soya may contain more plant oestrogens. These can affect the human body much like normal female hormones – which could be as harmful to girls as to boys.

c   Any GE crop may, in the long term, turn out to cause allergies. Babies should not be exposed to allergens.

The GE brain builder?

On top of the standard GE ingredients, babies may be getting LCPs (long-chain fatty acids). These special fats may help build a baby's brain and eyesight. As breast milk has more LCPs than cow's milk, some companies are adding LCPs to baby formula. Some companies source LCPs from natural

✻ Coffee creamers and whiteners may contain GE soya.

foods, others use LCPs created through genetic engineering. The label won't tell you which is which. So you need to ask the manufacturer.

What to buy

Companies vary enormously and alter their policies fast when the public protests. So, the situation could change overnight. The food a child has in its early life is the bedrock of its lifelong health. So, if I had a baby, I'd buy organic. Then I'd be sure there were no GE ingredients in either formula or food. Failing that I'd write to the manufacturer with the following list of questions:

1 In which of your soya formulas do you use genetically modi-fied soya?
2 Are the cows whose milk is used for formulas given geneti-cally engineered feed at any time?
3 Please say which of your baby formulas contain each of the following:

- genetically engineered LCPs
- genetically engineered riboflavin (Vitamin B2)
- vegetable oil from genetically engineered plants
- lecithin from genetically engineered plants
- maltodextrin from genetically engineered sources
- glucose from genetically engineered sources
- other ingredients derived from any GE sources, even indirectly

With the infant formulas and infant foods we're seeing now, we've no idea what the impact on babies and young children is going to be . . . Subjecting newborns to this mass human experiment is wicked. It's a callous disre-spect for their humanity. And the government's failure to stop this is an abuse of trust.

Elisabeth Sterken, Director, Infant Feeding Coalition, Canada

Travellers beware

Avoiding GE foods and milk while travelling is hard;
avoiding them in Canada and North America is hardest
of all. As I write, there is no compulsory labelling of
GE ingredients in the States. American milk-based baby
formula, sold in America and Canada, may contain milk
from cows injected with the GE hormone BST (called
BGH there) and largely fed on GE crops. If you buy soya
formula it's a racing certainty that it contains GE soya –
unless you buy organic. When a baby moves on to infant
foods it will begin eating the 75 per cent GE diet that is
normal there – and if you make baby food from fresh
ingredients check them out. A constantly expanding list
of fresh foods are also genetically engineered in the US.
So many American products are imported into Canada
that the same may be true there. When travelling, organic
is safest.

Avoiding Genetically Engineered Food

The astonishing thing about GE foods is how rapidly a few
crops have sneaked into every nook and cranny of our diet.
Tomato paste was only introduced in 1995, and maize and
soya only a couple of years ago. However, their rapid spread
is probably part of corporate strategy. The more foodstuffs
contain GE ingredients the harder they are to avoid or ban.

They almost certainly hoped that, having eaten GE food
unawares – and found we didn't drop dead – we'd accept it,

∗ In 1998 the British government spent £52 million fostering
   food biotechnology research but only £1.7 on researching
   organic farming.

ignoring the possibility of long-term effects, and other issues. However, if you want to avoid GE foods it's still possible – just.

Foods which are GE-free – or may be

In Britain and the rest of Europe these foods should either be GE-free or are less likely to contain GE ingredients:

- any food *certified* organic, but see box on the next page for meat, dairy, etc.
- fresh fruit and vegetables – GE versions are still some way off
- frozen fruit and vegetables unless they are part of a ready-made dish
- tinned unsweetened fruit, but some have GE additives
- plain tinned vegetables – but a few have GE additives
- fresh fish and shellfish, but GE salmon and talipia may be coming
- frozen plain fish and shellfish not in ready-made meals (and not salmon or talipia)
- tinned fish and shellfish unless it is in soya, corn/maize or 'vegetable oil'
- tea, coffee and herb teas in their basic forms, but check mixes
- sugar (British Sugar will refuse to use GE beet)
- pasta, but cheap brands may add soya or maize flour
- nuts – if plain unsalted
- olive oil, and other named oils, but not maize, soya or 'vegetable oils'
- pure, unsweetened fruit juices, *not* fruit drinks
- many quality products made by small specialist producers
- Iceland's range marked 'made with no GMOs'

✶ Organic food is now delivered to the door by many companies.

An Organic Solution

Contrary to some incorrect rumours, all certified organic food is GE-free. So, one sure way to avoid GE foodstuff is to buy organic. Any food certified organic by the Soil Association, or any of the other British or European certifying bodies, has to meet strict standards. Those standards are as tough in relation to genetic engineering as they are to chemicals. These European standards apply to imported food too. It's illegal to sell imported food as organic unless it has been approved by an EU certifying body.

Organic crops are never grown from GE seeds. And where certified milk, meat and poultry are concerned, no animal which contributes to organic food may eat any of the GE crops or animal feeds.

In addition, ready-made organic food and drink *must not* use any GE ingredients, or anything remotely linked to GE. The regulations do not indulge in the hair-splitting practised by the other labelling law – they ban the lot.

But beware. The law on organic animal products isn't as strict as the law on crops or other foodstuffs. So some people claim to be selling organic animal products when they aren't. When buying milk, eggs, meat or poultry, only a certification label from one of the recognised bodies will ensure it is GE free. Look for these names:

- Soil Association
- Organic Farmers & Growers
- Scottish Organic Producers Association
- UKROFS6
- Biodynamic Agricultural Association
- Organic Food Federation

- own-brand goods from supermarkets which say they are *totally* GM-free
- own-brand goods from food-makers which say they are *totally* GM-free.

Shortcuts to Spotting Hidden GE Food

If any of these get a *yes* the food is likely to contain GE ingredients – unless it's organic, or a brand that is guaranteed GE-free.

- Has it been fried?
- Is it a snack food?
- Is it sweetened?
- Is any part of it thickened (i.e. not runny)?
- Does it use chocolate?
- Could it contain flour?
- May it contain tomato purée?
- Might it be artificially coloured?
- Is it vegetarian?
- Is it made by a big company?

Once you know these warning signals you don't need to keep chuntering through the list. You just know at a glance where the biggest risks lie and when it's vital to check the ingredients list.

Should we trust the supermarkets?

You may notice that I haven't named any supermarkets except Iceland. That's because Iceland took a stand against GE foods unprompted, launching its range, which uses no GMOs what-

---

✱ Britain has no organic honey: sprayed fields are never more than a bee flight away. GE trial crops can be equally close.

ever, at a time when other supermarkets were still putting out glossy pro-GE propaganda. Iceland's commitment is clearly real. But can we be as confident about companies which for a long time were pro-GE? Which put out 'information' leaflets decidedly biased in favour of GE? Should we take their conversion on trust? Or should we keep asking questions to make sure they haven't backtracked?

Some Monsanto research which reached my desk may shed light on this. Having interviewed senior people at Marks and Spencer, Waitrose, Tesco, CWS, Asda and Safeway (probably in late summer 1998), the report commented:

> Monsanto has made some progress among retailers. The retailers we spoke to are quite well briefed, in some cases citing Monsanto briefing statistics word for word . . . They are largely comfortable with the use of biotechnology in foods. In contrast to a year ago . . . they no longer seem focused on safety concerns [interesting] . . . they believe in the technology and think the long-term benefits outweigh the risks [notice that reference to risks].

Nonetheless, one retailer did have a gripe, apparently saying:

> 'We're relatively angry at the way things have been introduced and foisted upon us without proper preconditioning of the consumer to their arrival.'

Notice those words – *'proper preconditioning of the consumer'*. Surely one conditions leather, not people. Clearly, at least one senior person in at least one supermarket does not believe we should make a free choice based on accurate information but thinks we should be 'preconditioned' by propaganda until we buy what they want us to buy.

✱ The Australian government has spent $500,000 on boosting the image of biotechnology – targeting science teachers.

Checking out your supermarket

All those attitudes were expressed not long ago. I know St Paul was instantly converted on the road to Damascus, but can we really believe that whole management teams in most of the major supermarkets have had such instant conversions? If you stopped believing in the tooth fairy some time ago you may want to keep quizzing shops rather carefully to make sure 'GM-free' (GE-free) really is GM-free – and remains so.

We all have our own feelings about whether we want our shopping basket to be totally GM-free, or as close to that as we can reasonably get, or whether we simply don't care. If you do care, it may be wise to ask questions and take nothing at face value. Here are some points you may want answered about ingredients that don't need to be labelled:

Have all of the following come *totally* from normal, non-GE crops?

- lecithin
- modified starches
- sweeteners such as glucose, dextrose and maltose
- high fructose corn syrup (HFCS)
- corn, maize and unnamed 'vegetable oils'
- tomato purée
- riboflavin
- yeasts
- xanthan gum
- enzymes, colours and other additives used in manufacturing

You might also want to ask if the animals which contributed butter, milk, cream, yoghurt, cheese, eggs, or meat were given GE animal feed. After all, if we are what we eat, so are they. If you're a perfectionist you might even ask about the E numbers given earlier. In which case they'll probably pay you to shop elsewhere.

How Free is 'GE Free'

While narrowly restricting the substances which must be labelled, the law fails to say how much of those substances need be present for labelling to be mandatory. Industry may interpret this as it pleases. It has been suggested that if less than 2 per cent is GE the maize or soya should be deemed 'GE-free'. By what logic? For most of us 'free' means 'free' – as in zero GE. If a company makes a free offer we don't expect to pay a little bit. Why should we expect a little bit of GE protein in a 'GE-free' product? Even suppliers are confused.

> How can you tell if you're in compliance with the law if they haven't set a minimum level of genetically modified ingredients allowed, and haven't approved a testing method?
>
> US agriculture official wanting to export to Europe

This failure to define free is a striking example of how the laws on GE repeatedly lag behind the real-life situation. Only now, several years after permitting the sale of GE foods, is the EU trying to define 'GE free' and establish test standards. If safety is the sole issue they might, wrongly, argue that negligible levels of GE substances don't count. However, it is not the sole issue. Even if GE foods were 200 per cent safe there remain social, religious and ethical values which may be violated by some GE foods. As there is no predicting what genetic combinations might be created, laws need to anticipate such problems and ensure that 'free' means precisely what it says. However, they say that's impossible.

The Failure of Law

EU regulators seem to have forgotten their responsibilities to the people they are meant to serve. They allowed totally new and unproven foodstuffs to be introduced into our diet without our consent. At present we are only in the foothills of this new technology. If it continues, vegetables may contain fish or animal genes, meat may contain human genes. Such gene transfers have already been done. Those who favour this argue that the inserted genes aren't originals but only copies. Or that having a few animal or human genes among the thousands already in the plant or animal is no reason to refuse to eat it. They fail to see that values are not about numbers but about feelings and beliefs.

The debate on labelling needs to move right away from arguments about safety. Scientists can argue and counter-argue the safety issue till the sea freezes over. However, safety is only part of a far larger issue of human rights. The threat which GE food has introduced is not simply that of unexpected health hazards. It is a threat to the very core of individual liberty: to our right to care for our own bodies, and to express our values and beliefs through the food we eat. Moreover, it is a threat which will become ever greater if transgenic foods are created which challenge deeply held values and beliefs.

We have already seen how soya and maize were invisibly incorporated into almost every manufactured food without most of us even being aware of it. If legislation does not insist upon it can we expect any greater openness over foods we are more likely to reject? Some would like to see GE food banned entirely. To return to the GE-free status quo we so cosily took for granted would indeed remove the dilemma of labelling. Meanwhile, surely the bottom line in a democracy is to have labelling so comprehensive that we are given all the facts we need to make our own decisions and choose which aspects of GE techno-food we accept or reject.

Clearly officials fear that the more GE food we can find the more we will reject. And that if GE food fails so will biotechnology. Whether or not the future of biotechnology rests on its application in food is debatable. Science is like a river, and when its creativity can no longer flow down one channel it tends to find another route, which is often far more interesting. If the creative energies of biotech scientists no longer had to be channelled into achieving fast profits through food, they might well develop uses of infinitely greater benefit to humanity – and perhaps with even greater economic potential.

However, even if they could not, surely technology is there to serve humankind, not vice versa? And if human rights run counter to any agenda to foster genetic engineering, or any other technology, is there any good reason why human rights should not come first?

The Law That is Needed

Ninety per cent of people want fair dinkum labels.
Bob Phelps, Director, Australian GeneEthics Network

The EU labelling law rests on a scientific definition which is meaningless to most people outside a laboratory. Surely what is needed is a law which acknowledges people's right to make choices based on values – whether or not bureaucrats share them. A law which also reflects the way we think and talk about GE.

For most of us, genetically engineered food means food which is linked with GE in any way. So a law which restores freedom of choice needs to be very clear with no ambiguous or technical phrases, no weasel words, no fudging of boundaries. It must cover every kind of food and drink. And it must label not only organisms which are themselves GE but also any that have links with genetic engineering.

The list of such categories is long but its application could

A Cautionary Tale

At the height of the public outcry against GE foods, I heard that the American-owned Mars confectionery company was telling people: 'None of our products contain any genetically modified material.'

Most people would take that to mean that nothing in the product was ever part of a genetically modified plant. But in EU law those particular words simply mean that the products contain no protein or DNA from genetically engineered soya or maize. They may still contain sweeteners, thickeners, oils and other by-products from the very same GE maize and soya.

Knowing how the EU law opened the door to confusion and weasel words, and noticing how closely Mars kept to the words in the law, I smelt a rat. Chocolate and soya lecithin are like bread and butter. You seldom have one without the other. Yet lecithin, being a by-product, isn't classed as 'genetically modified' by EU law. Companies with genuinely GE-free products were doing rather well. Was Mars using the letter of the law to jump on the bandwagon – while still using lecithin and a host of other by-products of GE beans and maize?

Three days, several phone calls and some determined questioning later, Mars' chief press officer eventually told me they *did* use lecithin from GE soya. And no, they weren't specially sourcing for non-GE ingredients.

This story shows how easily the law may confuse or deceive. The statement by Mars was legally correct yet potentially misleading. If a company like Mars, which sits on the government's Food Advisory Committee, can apply this law with such curious precision, who else may be doing so?

be very simple. *What is needed is a front label* (looking on the back of products wastes time) showing that a food has links with genetic engineering. For example, the letters LGE: Linked to Genetic Engineering could be used if any ingredient fell into any of the categories listed below.

On the back, any ingredient which was itself genetically engineered could have GE beside it. Those with less direct links could have LGE. Additives need only have an all inclusive 'GE additives' or 'GE manufacturing aids'. That would be far neater and more comprehensive than the current labelling and would speed up shopping. The categories classed as GE or linked to GE would include all those below ('creature' includes fish, birds and animals) – which shows how widely GE can affect our food:

- any part of any GE plants, or microorganisms
- by-products of GE plants, or microorganisms
- any part of any GE creature, or its descendants
- by-products of any GE creature, or its descendants
- any part of any creature which has eaten GE feeds
- by-products from any creature which has eaten GE feeds
- dairy produce and eggs from any creature which has fed on GE foods
- by-products of such eggs and dairy produce
- any part of creatures which have been given GE hormones, GE medication, or similar products
- by-products of such creatures
- dairy produce and eggs from creatures which have been given GE hormones or medication
- by-products of the above
- all by-products of by-products of any of the above

That's quite a list. Especially when you consider that the current law doesn't even cover one line of it. It may seem

✷ Novartis says 78% of its maize is used in animal feed.

ridiculously detailed, needlessly cautious. But this isn't a question of safety. It is about restoring freedom of choice. Diet is always a personal thing. We each draw our own lines as to what we will and will not eat. And if GE food is not still further to erode our freedom, it is surely we, not officials, who must draw the lines on GE, we who must choose how we categorise, accept or reject its products and all that is connected with them. To do that we must know where they are.

As the law did none of these, Britain's compulsory labelling of GE foodstuffs is barely worth the name. That the EU, famous for restrictive, detailed laws on trifles, should opt for a law so scanty is perhaps a testimony to the power of America and its giant corporations. A power that appears to reach round the globe, for governments elsewhere seem equally reluctant to label.

The Gene Giant Network?

In Australia and New Zealand, scientists, doctors and NGOs have been calling for full labelling. There, as in Europe, regulators have leant towards minimal labelling, if any. Curiously, the GE foodstuffs Australian officials seem loath to label are the very ones Europe chose not to label too. Do the Australian authorities like to play follow-my-leader with Europe? Or could the gene giants have been whispering the same suggestions around the globe? After all, the more inadequate the labelling the harder it will be to lay any ill effects that may occur at the door of gene-foods. And the harder proving liability will be.

✳ A woman in the UK billed Monsanto for £6,418.82 for the cost and effort of avoiding GE soya.

A double failure

We have, however, experienced a double failure to uphold our individual freedom of choice. The EU law only set low standards. The British government had the power to press the EU to give us comprehensive labelling. It chose not to: biotechnology took precedence over people.

Then, panicked by rising consumer concern, as a face-saver, the British government took advantage of something the EU law had left uncovered. True to its G string approach, the EU law hadn't compulsorily covered meals in restaurants, canteens or any other eatery. Overnight the British government said that every catering establishment must be able to tell its customers which of its foods were genetically modified (i.e. contained soya DNA or protein) – if they asked. The government then boasted of its achievement.

> The government is determined that consumers should be able to choose whether or not to eat genetically modified foods. This includes foods sold in restaurants, cafés and take-aways and not just supermarkets. The UK is the first member state of Europe to take steps to ensure that consumers eating out have the same right to choose . . . as those buying in shops.
>
> Jeff Rooker, Food Safety Minister, 18 March 1999

Fine words, but a farce. Some 125,000 businesses, from multi-million-pound restaurant chains to tiny cafés, found themselves facing £5,000 fines if they couldn't tell customers whether their food contained genetically engineered soya and maize protein and DNA. The average government minister couldn't tell if his own breakfast cereal contained soya DNA. Expecting such scientific niceties, from every eatery was clearly

* In Australia in 1997 one person in five signed a petition calling for a ban on GE foods.

ridiculous, especially as an enormous number buy in ready-made foods whose ingredients they couldn't identify without research. And customers still wouldn't be protected because the law did not require full labelling.

> By telling shoppers that only four forms of food are affected, the government is misleading shoppers into thinking other forms of food must be GM-free. Tony Blair says we must 'proceed with very great care and caution not to get the facts mixed up' . . . the first step must be for the government to publish the true facts about the full extent of the use of GM foods.
>
> Dr Sue Meyer, Director of GeneWatch, 15 February 1999

Why Don't They Want Us to Know?

> Some industry leaders have already concluded that labelling will do more good than harm, whether or not the demands for it are scientifically justifiable . . . if they are producing beneficial, safe, and ethical products, labelling should encourage the public to purchase them. Industry attention to the quality and utility of its products should create a more favourable marketing environment, now and in the future.
>
> Professor Marion Nestle[4]

A curious reticence

One of the great mysteries about GE foodstuffs is the way in which those who create them break all the normal rules of business. If you created one of the wonders of the modern world, as GE crops are claimed to be, wouldn't you want to trumpet it? Wouldn't you be using all your influence to make sure every jot and tittle of the food you believed in so passionately was labelled for all to see – and buy? But have you ever heard a GE company asking for better labelling? Asking for real consumer choice – instead of trying to fool us that they'd given it to us? If their products are all they claim, why not advertise them? What have they to hide?

It pays to advertise

Of course, Monsanto might say it did advertise. It certainly did. What it notably failed to do in its British advertisements was to *advertise the GE crops it was selling to us*, still less tell us how to find and eat the food that contained them – should we want to. A series of six large advertisements failed to name a single Monsanto foodstuff being sold to Britain or even a product which contained material from Monsanto's crops.

Nor did the pictures help. Monsanto scored an advertising coup by advertising other people's products: a tomato, a strawberry, a potato, a baby, and an unidentified green field. No skin off Monsanto's nose if implied links between genetic engineering and tomatoes, strawberries, potatoes, green fields and babies reduce their sales. It wasn't selling babies or tomatoes.

'Monsanto believes you should be fully aware of the facts before making a purchase,' one Monsanto ad proclaimed, adding promises of 'real benefits of biotechnology for both consumers and the environment', and of GM crops grown in a 'more environmentally sustainable way' – promises which brought the company before the Advertising Standards Authority. As I write, the ASA has yet to make its final decision on the advertisements, and may revise its views after discussion with Monsanto but, by a happy chance, a draft of the ASA's reaction reached the *Observer*.

---

* The law does not define who will be liable if any GE food proves to be harmful.

It [the ASA draft report] says the US giant expressed its own opinions 'as accepted fact' and published 'wrong' and 'misleading' scientific claims . . . The authority also dismissed Monsanto's assertion that GM crops were grown 'in a more environmentally sustainable way' than ordinary crops as unproven.

John Aldridge, *Observer*, 28 February 1999

In Britain and France Monsanto spent £1 million on advertising the wonders of GE foods in general. Yet according to a leaked Monsanto report which appeared on my desk: 'Those who read the Monsanto advertising campaign were more predisposed than other ABs [professional people] to be hostile to the GM issue.'[5]

What a disappointment to spend £1 million on advertising and find that people saw through it. Yet Monsanto must be comforted to know that you can always fool some of the people some of the time. The report also says that 'among the political élite [top MPs and civil servants] there was clear evidence of progress. Fully half the MPs, for example, see benefits as outweighing risks . . . these members of the élite saw the advertising and clearly understood the messages.' Clearly a modern version of 'those that live by the sword shall die by the sword' is 'those that live by propaganda shall believe propaganda'. And who better to persuade than the man at the top? Tony Blair's statements on GE foods are so enthusiastic a gene company could have written them.

Information politics

If GE foods really do offer the claimed benefits why haven't companies positively pressed for full labelling? This failure is doubly odd in view of the fact that they say GE gives us 'more

---

* The market for the products of biotechnology is estimated to reach US$278 billion in the year 2000.

consumer choice'. If so, why this bashfulness about GE foods even in America, the country that invented publicity overkill?

If they really do believe in their products, and think them safe, surely it's time for all the creators of GE crops to persuade manufacturers to blazon the GE foods across every pack that contains them. Imagine splashed across cereal packets from the Pacific to the Atlantic:

MAIZEGRITS
MADE WITH NEW SUPER HERBICIDE-TOLERANT
MAIZE FROM GENETICALLY ENGINEERED PLANTS!
WITH FREE EXTRA HERBICIDE
The maize that has boldly grown the way no maize has
grown before!

Who could possibly resist such an offer. A bowl of cereal with free herbicide-resistant genes, plus – if you're lucky – that extra herbicide! Agro-giants claim that herbicide resistance reduces the overall use of such chemicals. They may, or may not be right. But what they don't say is that such crops let farmers spray later in the season – closer to harvesting – sometimes risking a greater herbicide load in our food. So they shouldn't have to worry about advertising standards authorities saying they promised herbicide that never reached the plate.

When people have a product which is genuinely good they want everyone to know that they made it. So, at the very least, the gene giants' reticence is curious. We cannot be blamed if we draw the obvious conclusion.

5

The Myth of Choice

Three Myths

GE reduces the cost of food.
GE food increases consumer choice.
Normal crops and GE crops must be mixed at harvest

Choice has become a buzz word for the propaganda machine. Agro-giants and politicians have united in saying that GE food *increases* choice. Anyone who believes this has no grasp of science, economics, or even shopping. Any look at the facts shows there has been a dramatic, but hidden, erosion of choice. An unseen removal of freedoms we didn't even know we'd had until they were taken from us.

Had this been by chance it would have been disturbing enough. It has not been by chance. Those in power have taken advantage of the fact that we were off guard, taking millennia-long freedoms for granted. We feel surrounded by so many options, and are so used to believing that manufacturers *add* to them, that it may be almost inconceivable that the reverse should happen. That big business, Eurocrats and our own government should have joined forces to take real choice away. Yet that is what has happened and is happening. That makes GE food not just a matter of preference, or safety, but of human, and democratic, rights.

What Choice Do You Really Have?

Those who deny freedom to others, deserve it not for themselves.

Abraham Lincoln

We all lost the choice not to have GE food in our lives the moment it was imported. The only remaining choice is whether we eat it or not and even that choice is, to some extent, an illusion. For choice between GE and normal food is only real if:

- GE foods never contaminate normal foodstuffs
- we always have a choice of eating GE or normal foods
- normal products are no more expensive than GE equivalents
- there is always a normal version available everywhere
- we can see at a glance which foods contain GE elements and which do not

On none of these counts do GE foods allow us real choice at present. We all know how, without us even being aware of it, GE soya and maize replaced normal ones in almost every manufactured food. We weren't told. It wasn't labelled. And we weren't given a chance to protest. Food shopping has been changed from a pleasure into a label-reading marathon. Favourite products which now contain GE ingredients give us the choice between pleasure and safety. An interesting concept of increased choice.

There may be greater erosion of choice to come. To sell more of their chemicals the gene giants are systematically converting to GE all the major crops for which there is no good substitute. If nothing prevents it we may soon see GE invading all the staples: rice, potatoes, sugar, wheat, and so on. The more farmers they can convert to growing GE versions, the harder it will be for food companies to find enough of the non-GE crops. And companies are marketing to farmers very aggressively.

> The OECD organised conferences in which the voices of caution were simply swept aside so that the industry agenda could be rubber stamped.
>
> Dr Alex Hankey, Natural Law Party

Essential rights

Agro-giants and politicians would have us believe that extra choice consists of simply having some new element in our food which we have never had before. There is one fundamental choice which they are failing to discuss: the choice to have no GE foods, or crops, at all in our country.

The right to choose what food we eat, or avoid, is a basic human right. Food and water are the two things without which we cannot live (interestingly Monsanto is moving into water too). If we can't control what we eat we cannot control our health. For that reason alone opposition to GE food is not the storm in a teacup some politicians like to suggest.

As time goes on, some of us may have serious reactions to certain GE crops. Some people can have life-threatening reactions to oils which have only been in contact with the substance to which they are allergic. So someone developing an allergy to a GE food could have a reaction to any food which uses its oil. Soya oil, for example, is in a huge proportion of foods. Yet the extreme restriction of choice which that might bring to susceptible individuals doesn't seem to have been considered.

> Genetically engineered foods are just out of the petri dish and their impacts ... will not be known for years. An

∗ The next GE foodstuff sold in the EU may be oilseed rape: much used in margerines, vegetable oils, and cosmetics.

adverse reactions register should be set up as a precautionary measure, so any patterns of illness from gene
foods will be recognized quickly.

Bob Phelps, Director, Australian GenEthics Network

Not every GMO will be damaging. However, there is a
real risk that any given GMO will be hazardous. Therefore
it is essential to establish clear cut guidelines for assessing
health and environmental effects.

John Fagan, Professor of Molecular Biology

Hermits 10: Ordinary Mortals Nil

Only hermits, hidden away in caves, totally control
what they eat. The rest of us eat with friends, eat in restaurants, schools, canteens, or are given meals on
wheels.

Government claims of increased choice vanish the
moment anyone is a guest. As guests, how can we turn
down GE food? How can a mother who feels strongly
about GE food prevent her children eating it at friends'
houses – or on the way home from school? And what
consolation is it to have GE foods labelled in restaurants
if choosing a good meal becomes an obstacle race, not a
pleasure? In none of these situations does real choice
exist.

Equally neglected are those of us who feel strongly about such
issues as cruelty to animals, respect for life, avoidance of
cannibalism, and other such matters which our legislators
deem unimportant. Many might want to shun milk from
BST-injected cows and meat from engineered animals even
if they were proved to be safe. It is only possible to avoid
GE food on any of these grounds if we can easily identify

products which have even a trace of GE origins. If we can't there is no option but to avoid milk and meat. Another loss of choice.

A matter of the spirit

Genetic modification – irreversibly alters the original framework of God's creation when there is nothing wrong with it in the first place. If we do not act now genetic pollution will spread, changing the life on this planet permanently.

Dr Mazammal Hussain, Islamic Concern

At present no crops on sale contain genes from animals or shellfish. But frog genes and fish genes have both been put in trial crops, and human genes have been experimentally put into farm animals. And doubtless, if animal engineering takes off, cow or pig genes may be put into lambs, so violating both vegetarian and religious taboos.

The use of animals to create pharmaceuticals may also create new religious dilemmas. For there will be no precedent for substances such as vital blood factors for haemophiliacs being made in animals which may be taboo.

Such medical aspects don't seem to have been considered and, on food, the authorities talk of the percentage of a food which is GE-free. They fail to understand that a belief is a belief and not a matter of numbers. Yet in any civilisation the moral and religious taboos of an individual or group should be respected. Everyone should have total freedom to avoid what is abhorrent to them.

Those who permitted GE foods to be introduced also seem unaware that food is powerfully symbolic. So retaining its natural form has a meaning which goes far deeper than issues of safety. For many food is the cornerstone of family rituals, an expression of love, the focus of celebration. The foods we choose to eat, or not to eat, mark our origins, our affiliations, and our relationships. For some engineering a plant or animal strikes at the heart of life.

> I personally have no wish to eat anything produced by genetic modification, nor do I knowingly offer this sort of produce to my family or guests.
>
> HRH the Prince of Wales, *Daily Telegraph*[1]

In an urban environment non-engineered food may be an important link with the non-mechanical world, a gift from nature. For some, the recognition of that gift is an important part of their inner life – a part which the rituals and injunctions of faith only symbolise. The bread of life, the communion wafers, the offerings at the temple, the unleavened bread of Passover, and the fasting of Ramadan bridge the divide between human and divine, reminding believers of gifts they have been given and of a debt they owe.

One might ask, what is altered when the wheat for the communion wafer contains scorpion or petunia genes? Does it matter that the integrity and identity of that organism are no longer intact? Is the communion wafer equally sacred if it is made with wheat not as creation designed it? Are the matzos less worthy of Passover? Is the bread we break with our loved ones any less of a shared gift?

But these are questions to which we must all find our own answers – whatever our faith, or lack of it. Scientists would argue that crops lost their natural integrity long ago. This is not, however, an issue of technical niceties but of human feelings. Feelings which are every bit as important as balance sheets and which labelling alone may not satisfy. Religious and moral concerns inevitably raise the issue of contamination.

Three Levels of Contamination?

Non-GE foods are only GE free if they can avoid contamination at these different stages:

- in the fields
- at harvest and during delivery
- during the processing of raw materials
- during manufacturing

Contamination in the fields

Freedom of choice starts in the fields. We have no choice at all if normal or organic crops cross-breed with GE ones. For next year's seeds will carry engineered genes. Government ministries talk of 'safe margins' and 'pollen banks' around trial sites and fields – measured in yards. But caught on the updraughts and eddies of the wind, pollen can travel up to 120 miles they've found and bees can travel several miles. What use are safety margins then?

Moreover, American research on maize, published in the science journal *Nature*, has shown that pollen from GE plants has twenty times the normal pollination power. Nobody knows why, but here, as so often, GE plants have behaved in a way that nobody predicted or can understand. But, since converting us to GE crops and food is definitely their aim, is it pure chance that GE companies picked on maize, *par excellence* a plant that dangles pollen tassels in the wind, as one of their first crops?

And, if choice vanishes when GE crops are grown in countries which lack the space to put a hundred miles between two crops, should GE crops be grown at all? Or does growing any such crops, even in trial sites, violate rights of choice?

✳ The European Society of Chartered Surveyors wants a GM land registry so buyers can choose to avoid GM sites.

Contamination at harvest?

They [the biotech companies] insist on thwarting consumer choice, bulldozing elected governments, and forcing their wretched products on the world's population.
They need to be brought within democratic control,
urgently.

Norman Baker, Liberal Democrat MP

One of the great myths has been that normal and GE foods
can't be kept apart. They said it about milk (sold in America)
from cows injected with the hormone BST. And they said it
when GE crops were first approved by Europe. But America
had no trouble finding normal soya to sell to us before GE
imports were approved. Then, when Europe accepted GE soya,
suddenly, before the ink was dry, keeping normal soya apart
became 'impossible'. And our governments let them get away
with it.

The question is: why did our governments let them get away
with it? Why did freedom of choice for voters count for nothing? The argument that GE and non-GE food are substantially
equivalent simply doesn't wash. Identical twins are substantially equivalent. Yet they are different people. Nobody would
dream of suggesting that someone who is married to one
identical twin must also sleep with the other. And, no matter
how equivalent GE foods are to normal foods – and there are
serious question marks over that – they are no more the same
than twins. Why should we be forced into bed with one
because we've long enjoyed the other? A child could see it's
nonsense.

Government statements about 'consumer choice' will
have a hollow ring whilst the Government does nothing
to prevent unsegregated GM foods entering the UK.

Friends of the Earth, 18 March 1999

The claims about segregation have continued. Early in 1999, at an American State Department meeting, Dan Amstutz, President of the North American Export Grain Association, said, yet again, that segregation of non-GE soya was 'impossible'. Yet only weeks earlier America's Pioneer Hi-Bred boasted of introducing twenty new varieties of soya, including ones with special 'oil profiles' for special markets. If twenty strains can be separated, why not two: GE and non-GE? They can – if it's profitable. With consumers shouting for normal soya beans, US Soy, in Illinois, is suddenly doing the 'impossible' – processing segregated non-GE soya beans in a massive new plant.

A whole area of southern Brazil has also decided to be GE-free. And if whole areas stay GE-free the risk of cross-pollination, or accidental mingling in transit, is removed. All of which shows what consumer demand can do. Yet so strong are the vested interests in converting us to GE that such regions may face sabotage.

Sabotage Afoot

When the supermarket chain Iceland pioneered own-brand food made without GE ingredients, it found soya suppliers in an area of Brazil where no GE soya was grown, and which no GE soya lorries had any reason to pass through. Fortunately the company organised strict security in case anyone didn't like their GE boycott.

One night a lorry was stopped in the area with a load of GE soya. Bill Wadsworth, one of Iceland's directors, told me they could never *prove* it was an attempt at sabotage. But what else was a lorry-load of GE soya beans doing there?

---

* The non-segregation of GE maize lost America around \$200 million in sales to Europe in 1998.

Contamination in processing?

Even if GE and normal crops aren't lumped together at source, there's still a risk that they'll become mingled during processing. For how do you stop flour flying? The answer is: you can't. Avoiding contamination during processing either means using a separate plant or the whole plant has to be rigorously cleaned between sessions of processing GE foods and normal ones. How many food factories are equipped to do that, do you think? And what extra costs in equipment, labour and lost processing time must it add? These costs will either be spread across all foods, or be added to the price of normal foods, not GE ones.

Unavoidable pollution

If crops are segregated, and manufacturing plants cleaned scrupulously, is food as free of abnormal and mutilated genes as before GE was introduced? Not always. Even if you carefully buy food which genuinely isn't made with any GE ingredients, or anything that comes from GE foodstuffs, you'll be lucky if the food is 100 per cent GE-free. There are, of course, exceptions, and organic food is struggling to remain so. But it isn't easy. Genetic material is as invisible as the dust and pollen causing hay fever. And once it's out there it's out there. Even the most careful of us are eating it and breathing it. Strikingly, when Iceland launched its range of non-GE foods, it immediately announced it could not call them GM-free.

> We would like these products to be totally GM free. We don't make these foods with anything that has been genetically engineered. They are as GM free as is humanly possible and we go to enormous lengths to make sure

✳ Britain's Trading Standards officers are meant to police GE food labelling – but are too underfunded to do so.

that they are. But that's the best we can do. Genetically modified organisms are in the air. When they're in the air we can't totally keep them out. That's why our labels say 'not *made* with any genetically modified organism'.

Malcolm Walker, chairman of Iceland Supermarkets

Governments accepted GE foods without ever looking at the issue of gene pollution. Advised by committees often dominated by those who represent industry – or are beholden to it – governments have pandered to the biotech industry and ignored their voters' needs. A new form of pollution has come into our lives. The only option available to us is to minimise it.

The extraordinary thing is that we have to talk in these terms at all. That we are forced to think about degrees of pollution, not principles. The central question isn't how many genes can sit on a sausage. It is whether, in a world which has already seen so much contamination, a new pollution should be allowed at all. It is whether we need these foodstuffs and whether the claimed benefits exist and are worth the risks. Since the World Trade Organisation seeks to make it illegal to exclude GE foods, we may also want to ask whether a country should have the right to turn its back on GE crops if its people wish it. This is the kind of issue on which there could be a referendum. Yet governments do not seem prepared even to discuss this option.

A Child's Rights

The Children's Charter of Britain's NHS says that you can expect your child to be offered a choice of children's menus which are healthy and which suit all dietary and cultural needs.

So if you don't want your child to have GE food you have a right to ask the hospital to provide other options.

Paying for choice

The firm behind Häagen-Dazs ice-cream and the Green Giant food brand [Pillsbury] has warned British consumers of huge price rises if they continue to snub genetically modified produce ... and consumer tastes split between pro- and anti-GM purchases.

Mail on Sunday, 14 March 1999

Those comments from Paul Walsh, Chief Executive of Pillsbury, are clearly designed to frighten consumers into accepting GE foods to keep prices down. Yet independent proof that GE food reduces prices is notably lacking.

Far from making food cheaper – as we've been promised – GE often puts up the cost of shopping. America probably sells more GM food than any other country, with the possible exception of China. American food prices have not come down as GM food has expanded. They have stayed fairly level in a falling market. However, if more and more farmers are persuaded to convert to GE crops, normal ones will gain a rarity value with a higher price, which could rise and rise as supplies dwindle. If that happens real choice will go.

One of the great injustices of the introduction of GE food is surely that, if non-GE food becomes scarce, the less well-off won't be able to afford it. So GE will create a food apartheid. Single-parent families, the elderly, the sick and disabled, and the unemployed will become the human guinea-pigs on which GE safety is tested long-term. There would be an outcry if laboratories used the least well off to test drugs. Isn't it even worse that they will, in effect, be paying to test this unproven technology?

Some supermarkets already put a mark-up on organics out of all proportion to the price paid to the farmer. At the same

* The limited shelf-life of foods has helped keep food prices down. 'Stay-fresh' GE food could end that.

time, if an organic crop is polluted by pollen from GE crops the whole crop can no longer be classed as organic. Every time this happens it's disastrous for the farmer. It also means there is less organic food to meet a growing demand so the price of organic food will go up. It's basic supply and demand. So we will either pay with our purses or with our principles. Since we don't need GE foods, and never asked for them, is that right? It certainly doesn't represent increased choice.

Unwanted Choice

The higher price paid for special GE foods may also be in flavour. One of the early American 'wonders' of GM was a tomato designed to be firm, perfect and unblemished for up to six weeks. The answer to a supermarket's prayer? They thought so.

They priced it, as something new and special, at double the usual tomato price. Initially it sold. What nobody had checked was the *taste* after all those weeks. Within less than two years this 'wonder of the world' had been withdrawn. I'm told the public simply ceased to buy it.

If Things Go Wrong Who Pays?

Who pays if things go wrong is just one of the many unanswered questions surrounding GE.

The gene giants would, of course, deny that GE food carries any risks at all. However, there was a surgeon in the eighteenth century who scoffed when a fellow medic suggested hygiene was important when operating. Unable to imagine infection

---

✳ Some insurance companies are reluctant to insure against GE accidents, seeing the risk as too great.

could be caused by invisible organisms, he wiped his scalpel on his boot before performing a Caesarian. His patient died: the court case is part of medical history.

GE is so new, and the techniques so unpredictable that neither we nor the companies that make GE food know much more about the effects of GE than that doctor did about germs. Yet, while telling us that GE foods are safe, internal government and company documents talk about a balance of risks and benefits. Well they might: we take the risks and they get the benefits.

Proving Liability

I've heard people say that if GE foods do make them ill they'll sue Monsanto and retire on the proceeds. They could be dreaming of fool's gold. It's almost fifty years since Sir Richard Doll first linked smoking with ill health. With smoking the issue's clear-cut – either you smoke or you don't. Over 5000 studies link smoking with ill health, and in Britain alone 6 million people have died of smoking-related diseases since the war. Despite all that, I have yet to hear of anyone who has received a penny in compensation – and many have died waiting. When smokers win, tobacco giants simply drag cases slowly through the appeal process. Can we expect better of biotechnology companies?

> With smoking, even with good information, and thousands of good studies, people still found it unbelievably difficult or impossible to hold manufacturers to account for harm caused by their products. With unsegregated genetically engineered food it's hard even to know what GE ingredients you've eaten. So the chances of getting any compensation if things go wrong would be very slim indeed.
>
> Clive Bates, Director, Action on Smoking and Health

The issue of liability is one possible reason why the industry has pressed for GE and normal supplies to be combined. The more that GE foods are mixed with normal produce, the harder it will be to pin the blame on GE crops if – or should I say when – things go wrong. If proof were needed that companies know that some GE foods may not be safe, it can be found in their desire to hide them in this way.

The Power of the Shopper

Despite all the lack of honest information, the propaganda, the inadequacies of the law, GE foods have been a gift. They have shown the enormous power of the purse and the pocket. When enough people asked for it, supermarkets – despite their secret belief in GE food – changed their policies and switched to non-GE ingredients in many products. They also showed remarkable collaboration. Iceland helped other companies source GE-free supplies. Sainsbury's formed a consortium of European supermarkets to jointly source GE-free soya and maize. These have been immensely important moves, for they showed farmers how well normal crops could sell – a vital encouragement to keep growing them. They demonstrated the power of the market, which was the last thing the gene giants expected. True, the supermarket turnaround only gave us back a slice of our pre-GE freedom, but a slice of a loaf is decidedly better than no bread.

It is a victory which belongs to everyone who questioned the supermarkets, wrote to manufacturers and politicians, phoned the media, or in any way, even for an instant, stood up for the right to know and to choose. Those who oppose such freedoms have tried to smear protests against GE as hysterical and ill informed. The smear is groundless. There has undoubtedly been an increase in risk. This is referred to

---

✳ Austria is almost GE-free, few shops stock any GE food.

privately by both GE companies and officials. It is a risk which, whatever its size, you and your family have had to take, and are taking, without having been given a choice. Yet the benefits from that risk go to big business.

That injustice has naturally raised the temperature of the debate. Yet, however intemperate the language, or colourful the images, the bottom line is that there has been an erosion of freedom and human rights which is unacceptable. This can only be made good by food labelling as comprehensive as that I have outlined, or by a total abolition of genetic engineering from every aspect of the food industry or, at the very least, from crops. It is also essential that all other applications of biotechnology are openly acknowledged, publicly discussed, and fully labelled. Without that consumer choice will be history.

Free to Choose

No matter how eloquent the corporate rhetoric I contend that:

- an uninformed choice is not a free choice
- an unavoidable choice is not a free choice
- an unaffordable choice is not a free choice
- an unacceptable choice is not a free choice

Patricia Young, US National Co-ordinator,

World Food Day, 1991

Patricia Young was speaking about women's choice. It is no less true of human choice. Freedom has no gender.

∗ GE products will soon be everywhere. Oilseed rape is being modified to produce lauric acid for use in soap.

6

Farm & Country

Three Myths

GE crops reduce the use of chemicals.
GE poses no danger to organic farming or wildlife.
GE crops always produce higher yields and greater profits.

Whose freedom is it when small, independent farmers, food processors, retailers, the world over, are undermined by the power of a very few giant corporations?

The Marchioness of Worcester, Associate Director,
The Society for Ecology and Culture

At the heart of the many claims made for GE crops has been a three-pronged justification concerning their contribution to farming – and through that to consumers and to the Third World. The selling pitch to farmers has been the implication that high technology means high yields and low outputs on chemicals and labour. That has allowed GE companies not only to persuade farmers to accept their seeds but to accept the fact that GE seeds cost more – sometimes far more. It has also allowed some companies to slap a technology tax on top. One company is said to have made $51 million in a year from the technology tax alone. Money that, having come out of the farmer's pockets, is added to the price of food.

In contrast, the public, after careful market research, were approached through the heart. These new wonder crops would be healthier, tastier and, we were told, were essential to feed the exploding world population. As icing on the cake, they said that GE would be good for the environment: That it would mean less use of harmful chemicals, and more wildlife. A brilliant piece of marketing. However, GE crops have been around for long enough for us to see what is really happening. The picture is almost the opposite of what we have been told.

Have We Been Here Before?

Far from bringing us crops which are more nourishing at least 8 out of 10 crops are engineered either to survive some all-purpose weedkiller or to contain a substance which kills caterpillars. And already, there are signs that weeds and insects are adapting and fighting back.

The very companies that now engineer crops previously engineered the so-called 'green revolution', with its dramatic increase in the use of farm chemicals. Significantly, that increase failed to deliver the healthy, pest-free crops farmers wanted. In the last forty years crop losses from diseases and insects have doubled in America – at a time when pesticide use rose eight-fold.

The idea that GE crops would reduce the use of agricultural chemicals and be kinder to the environment was therefore an alluring prospect. However, logically, it was always slightly improbable. Why should chemical companies suddenly come up with products which *reduce* the use of chemicals? And why should we believe they want to protect nature when they are tampering with its very essence?

∗ Since 1992 there have been over 500 trials of GE crops in test sites in Britain – often with poor safety controls.

The Decline in Birds

The past thirty years have been a period of intensive farming with heavy chemical use. Despite all the environmental claims GE crops are simply a new club in the golf bag of intensive farm practices which have already struck such blows to wildlife. The British Trust for Ornithology reported the following decline in farmland birds from 1971 to 1995:

- turtle doves: 79 per cent decline
- linnet: 49 per cent decline
- reed bunting: 61 per cent decline
- bullfinch: 75 per cent decline
- corn bunting: 80 per cent decline

When creatures as visible as birds die off to such a tragic extent, we can be sure that other, less visible creatures are dying in far greater numbers. The authors of the report recommend a '*switch to organic farming*' and '*a reversion to other less intensive farming techniques*'.

That is not what GE offers. When ladybirds dine on aphids which have eaten certain GE crops their lifespan is halved. Birds, being next up the food chain, may be equally vulnerable.

Far from being concerned for nature the impact of GE crops on the environment doesn't appear to have been thoroughly researched before the crops were grown in America. Had it been, the companies would surely have known that pollen from some engineered crops could kill butterflies and would not have planted them in the Monarch's path. Moreover, since the claim to environmental benefits was so central to the sales pitch, it is significant that even the most moderate and restrained environmental organisations are warning of the need for caution. In 1998 English Nature, the government's own environmental adviser, called for a three-year moratorium, saying it was vital for the impact of GE on wildlife to be researched before GE crops were introduced into Britain. The Royal Society for the Protection of Birds supported this.

> 'The ability to clear fields of all weeds using powerful herbicides which can be sprayed onto GE herbicide-resistant crops will result in farmlands devoid of wildlife and spell disaster for millions of already declining birds and plants.'
>
> Graham Wynne, Chief Executive of the RSPB

> We have a small, densely populated island where the flora and fauna are very closely linked to agriculture so we have to be very careful about how our arable system might affect wildlife such as wild flowers, birds and bees.
>
> Professor Ingrid Williams, Institute of
> Arable Crops Research, Rothamsted

The concern of English Nature and the RSPB is felt by many other organisations worldwide, which believe that GE crops will increase the destruction of wildlife already caused by intensive farming. This concern is amply justified by recent evidence of increased spraying of GE crops.

Pest-resistant Crops

The idea of crops with built-in pest control, so doing away with the need to spray was an appealing one – but somewhat flawed. Crops are often attacked by more than one kind of pest, so insecticides are still needed to kill those not affected by the built-in insect killer. Nonetheless, several of the big companies engineered into plants like cotton and maize a soil bacterium, known as Bt (*Bacillus thuringiensis*) which carries a toxin which is only activated in the very alkaline gut of caterpillars. This bacterium, has been used by organic farmers for 40 years as a very effective insecticide spray. Experts warned from the start that engineering Bt into plants was very different and that it would create a whole series of problems – and it does.

Warning and findings

Cross-pollination and gene-transfer

Bt crops will cross-pollinate with weed relatives and with non-GE crops, carrying their characteristics into the natural world, so contaminating normal food. Oilseed rape will be a particular problem as it has several relatives to breed with. But the transfer of engineered genes doesn't totally depend on pollination. Engineered genes can move out of their host plant and into any crop or wild plant. Such pollination or gene transfer could make wild plants poisonous to wild animals which depend on them.

Plant-resistant super-pests

In nature most traffic is two-way. So the response to pest-resistant plants is plant-resistant pests. In any group of insects there are usually some which can munch deadly leaves unharmed. As the rest are killed off they have only each other to mate with – the ideal conditions for breeding super-pests which can destroy Bt crops with impunity. Such potential for resistance to Bt crops was found ten years ago in two pests – a grain beetle, *Piodia interpunctel* and larvae of the diamond back moth. With short insect life cycles, and all the best food for themselves, resistant super-pest numbers can build up very

---

* Bees are the main pollinators of oilseed rape – a GE crop already in trials in Britain and the rest of the EU.

fast indeed. A question of survival of the fittest. In experiment with Bt pests developed resistance 1000 times the normal and, resistance was still high 15 generations later.

It may also help the creation of resistance that, for reasons nobody understands, the Bt toxin doesn't seem to be evenly distributed throughout the plant.

Farmers were told to surround Bt crops with wild areas to act as reservoirs of non-resistant creatures. But nobody really knew how wide those refuges should be. So, in only a handful of years, Bt resistance has begun.

A far higher proportion of insects are naturally resistant than experts used to think. According to the University of Arizona, 1 in 350 tobacco bud worms can munch Bt crops and come up smiling. A high proportion, given the rate at which insects breed. And the Californian cotton pest, rather charmingly called the pink bollworm, was resistant by this year. What's more, resistant pests may also develop resistance to other toxins and be harder to kill. So, before long, these 'no need to spray' crops may need more insecticide sprays than other crops.

Migrant pests

Insect pests may not be as stupid as we think. If one crop is deadly some of them wander off in search of another – becoming pests of some crop they've never eaten before. Those which experiment by eating non-Bt crops, of a different kind, will live to see another day – and to breed. By natural selection the pests which used to plague one crop just shift targets. It's probably too soon to say if this is happening. But it's on the cards.

Soil damage

Scientists at New York University found that engineered Bt behaves differently from its natural cousins and can damage

* Bees given sugar solutions containing substance found in pest resistant oil-seed rape confused different flowers.

soil organisms. As the plants decay the natural insecticide attaches itself to particles of soil and keeps on killing for up to nine months. Moreover the techniques of GE alter the Bt-toxin making if harmful to a for wider range of insects, and other organisms including those needed for soil fertility. As quantities of plant material get incorporated into the soil this could do serious damage.

Monarch butterflies threatened

Pollen from GE crops flies onto non-GE crops and wild plants. This means that both we and wildlife eat it. When caterpillars of the beautiful Monarch butterflies were fed milkweed dusted with pollen from Bt maize, half of them died. It could also be deadly for 159 European butterflies including the Red Admiral and Large Skipper.

Beneficial insects killed

As big eaters of greenfly, ladybirds are among the gardener's greatest friends, and their health is a measure of environmental balance. When ladybirds ate aphids which had dined on GE pest-resistant potatoes, it halved their lifespan and reduced their fertility. The Swiss Federal Research stations for Agroecology found the same mortality with lacewings, known as 'aphid lions' for their aphid eating. This means that such crops may also harm other friendly insects and aphid eating birds, such as blue tits and warblers.

> If you are going to kill 'bad' insects, there is always a risk you kill 'good' ones too. It was always going to be fairly indiscriminate. We urgently need a five-year GM freeze to allow for detailed research into the risks of such crops.
>
> Adrian Bebb, Friends of the Earth

✳ GE crops doubly harm butterflies: Bt pollen kills them, broad-spectrum herbicides kill plants needed for survival.

Bt in Organic Farming

You may be wondering why the problems of pest resistance and damage to beneficial insects don't occur when organic farmers use Bt as a spray. One difference lies in the fact that, in organic farming, sprays are only used occasionally. Also, when sprayed, Bt only lands on the surface of the plants and degrades in sunlight. Whereas Bt built into a plant is there all the time. It's the constant presence which creates resistant pests, not intermittent use. So Bt crops mean organic farmers may find there are fewer beneficial insects and now fear they may be plagued by pests which have become resistant to Bt through its misuse in GE plants.

A dubious success

It looks as if the honeymoon period of insect-resistance may be very short. Resistance is developing so fast that some agricultural experts say that – within four years – ten at the outside – the situation will be worse than before the introduction of Bt crops. During that time, pests may also have migrated to other crops, and large numbers of beneficial insects may have been killed. So pest problems will be increasing on every front. This will be especially tough for subsistence farmers who may suffer all these ills because of neighbouring Bt crops.

All of that will have farmers crying out for newer, stronger insecticides.

Isn't it interesting how Bt crops, while promising to reduce chemical use, are creating perfect conditions for increasing the use of chemicals? This may well have been the agro-chemical companies' chess game: sacrifice a pawn to gain a bishop. After all, why would chemical companies devise crops which genuinely reduce chemical use in the long term?

Insecticide Needed with Bt Crops

On top of doing all that harm to the environment Bt crops may not even save farmers from spraying. As Bt only protects against one kind of pest isn't unAmerican farmers have found they may need to use chemical sprays to kill other pests. So the benefits of Bt in organic farming have been squandered without it even ending the use of insecticides on GE crops.

> ... when using tools such as Bt cotton, pyrethroids [insecticides] and other traditional control aids can still play a vital role in stopping pests and boosting yields. Plant bugs, fall armyworms, boll weevils, and stink bugs were an early to late season problem in Bt cotton in 1996 that was not treated on a regular basis ...
> ... over-spraying with a pyrethroid on a seven to ten day schedule ... can be very beneficial starting at first bloom.
>
> Charles Hagedorn, Crop and Environmental
> News (USA), July 1997

So supposedly insect-resistant GE cotton may need chemical sprays several times in a season, and as often as at seven- to ten-day intervals. It makes you glad GE isn't used to ensure world peace doesn't it.

It would take a very big-hearted chemical company to be genuinely sorry that damage may be done to the soil (more

✳ Over 500 species of insects and mites already resist one or more insecticides.

fertiliser sales) and one of the most valuable tools of organic farmers is rendered less effective. But all this hardly makes insect-resistant crops the .environmentally friendly products the industry claimed them to be.

> A spirit of violence of the most ruthless kind has invaded man's agricultural activities . . . The spirit of violence and impatience ruled the earlier phases of the industrial revolution and is still endemic in modern industry.
>
> E. F. Schumacher[3]

GE Trees

Trees are one of the fastest growing areas of GE. They also have a far wider range of modifications than crops. For example, some trees are being modified for faster growth – for paper or biomass. Some western trees are modified to produce substances, such as rubber, which would otherwise come from the Third World – so perhaps threatening Third World jobs and economies.

Others are being experimented with as sources of medicinal products and substances used in industry. Indeed, comparing the range of modifications on trees with those on crops shows the extent to which crop modifications have been chosen mainly to benefit the agro-giants, not to benefit either farmers or consumers.

Herbicide Worldwide

Despite all the claims in 1998 about GE creating healthier food, 71 per cent of the world's GE crops are engineered so to survive being sprayed with some branded weedkiller.

The idea is that, instead of farmers spraying with several different weedkillers, they'll just use one – which can be used at any time in the growing season and will kill every non-engineered plant it touches. So far, such crops have mainly been engineered to survive weedkillers based on two chemicals – glyphosate and a glufosinate. The lion's share of this market belongs to crops engineered to withstand Roundup, Monsanto's glyphosate-based herbicide. This is the world's biggest-selling weedkiller – but was one nearing the end of its patent. So creating crops to withstand it, and ensuring farmers use it with the crops, has given Roundup a new lease of life. For farmers it means signing a contract promising only to use Roundup and not to save seeds on pain of grave consequences.

Pinkerton's detective agency was hired to nose out contract breakers and they have been publicly 'named and shamed'. American farmers have been encouraged to use a freephone line to report rule-breakers and, over 450 US and several hundred Canadian farmers have been sued. Bundled with that reign of terror was the promise that weedkiller- and insect-resistant crops mean, in theory, less time on pest control and less money on weed- and insect-killers.

Creating GE crops resistant to their herbicides has enabled companies to sell two products, rather than one. However, experts warned companies against it. It's interesting to compare the warnings with what's now happening on farms.

Warnings and findings

Weedkiller resistant weeds
Experts warned that this Weedkiller resistance can rapidly be created in weeds if only one weedkiller is used. So, before long, an even stronger weedkiller will be needed. This happens

---

✳ GE crops are boosting the sales of glufosinate weedkiller so much that its sales rose by $200 million in one company.

remarkably easily. In Australia rye grass which was only sprayed with Roundup ten times in fifteen years became resistant to it.[5]

Botanists also warned of weedkiller-resistant super-weeds being created. Through cross-pollination between these GE crops and weed relatives or through genetic material moving from crop plant to weed. This was said to have happened when GE crops were only at the trial stage. In field trials 72 per cent of potatoes grown close to GE potatoes took on the resistance gene. And 35 per cent of those *1,100 metres* away had also been contaminated.

Crops, also self-seed in surrounding countryside and these 'volunteers' can themselves become weeds. All this will create a need for even stronger weedkillers to kill them.

With GE crops Monsanto at first, recommended only one application of Roundup. Then two. Unconfirmed reports say some farmers already need to use Roundup three to four times.

> Growers have been happy with the weed control but not happy with the varieties . . . [however] there are several species of weed which, if the timing is wrong, can't be controlled at all. Glyphosate is not a one-shot solution.
>
> Dr Ford Baldwin, weed scientist, University of Arkansas[4]

Weedkiller drift

There were warnings that drifting spray from an all-purpose weedkiller would be especially damaging to the surrounding countryside, and to neighbouring non-GE crops. In the Third World this might kill enormous numbers of wild foods on which the poor often depend.

This is already happening. In some areas of the States, complaints from neighbouring farmers have reached record levels.[6]

✱ Herbicide resistance builds up easily. Worldwide at least 270 weed species already resist some herbicides.

Some farmers and scientists say Monsanto's reformulated Roundup includes chemicals which seem to create a finer spray, which drifts further. But may be chemical companies hope that if farmers get sick of drift damage they'll go over to GE crops themselves.

More weedkiller in food
As the crops won't be killed by the weedkiller farmers can spray later in the season, close to cropping. The more leafy the plant the more weedkiller it may absorb. So late spraying may mean more of the weedkiller gets into food, though this will vary with the crop.

Cattle Feed: Double Jeopardy

Only organic animals, and animals from a few selected farms, eat a weedkiller-free diet. However, in the past, their feed has contained varied chemicals. In contrast engineered crops used in cattle feed, such as soya, maize and cotton, to be sprayed with a few power herbicides means cattle will eat unprecedented levels of certain chemicals. In addition some GE cotton is producing a toxin in its seed. The effects of toxins in cattle feed is not known.

What nobody knows is whether a higher dose of one particular chemical cocktail will be more harmful or less, to the creatures themselves and to those who eat their meat, eggs or dairy products. As so often, this is something which should have been conclusively researched *before* GE crops were launched, and it wasn't. Nor do we know the effects of animals eating more than one kind of engineered crop. For animal feed may also contain crops engineered to contain Bt to resist insects. That in turn affects the meat, poultry and animal products in our diet in ways not yet known.

Monsanto has asked for the permitted maximum level of its weedkiller Roundup in food to be substantially increased from 0.1 mg per kilogram of crop to 20 mg per kilogram.

Fewer beneficial insects (yet again)

Could I have the same rights for my bees as MPs have in their members' dining room – to feed off non-GE food? . . . to most people 'pure honey' and 'contains food from GE sources' are exact opposites.

John Phipps, Editor, *Beekeeper's Quarterly*

The International Organisation for Biological Control showed that Roundup killed vital beneficial insects such as ladybirds, lacewings, a predatory mite and a predatory beetle.[7] There are also rumours of bees being affected. Other herbicides used with GE crops may be equally harmful.

With GE crops some farmers are spraying later – which can mean spraying at a time when beneficial insects are at a more vulnerable stage in their life cycle, and will be killed more easily. Here again their death, because of GE crops, disrupts the natural pest control balance on which organic farmers and gardeners depend.

Water pollution

It was hoped that GE crops would reduce harm to water life through chemical pollution. But herbicide resistant crops may increase water pollution.

In March 1999 Water UK called for a moratorium on GE crops, as the chemicals used with them might pollute rivers, lakes and reservoirs, saying: 'We have genuine concerns about the widespread use of crops which rely on just two chemicals . . . We need time to find the answers. We need several years.'

Here again nobody knows the size of the danger. It very much depends on the formulation of any chemical used. For example, glyphosate, the main ingredient in Monsanto's Roundup, seems to be especially harmful to fish and water life and has been mentioned in a number of chemical accidents. Also weedkillers are blends of many chemicals, some perhaps more poisonous than the main one. So the harm done by regular doses of these, singly and in combination, has to be considered, yet there seems little data available.

I say 'regular doses' because, if large numbers of farmers convert to using GE crops, immense areas of countryside will be sprayed with just one or two chemicals. As not everyone will spray at the same time, waterways may be repeatedly dosed with a particular chemical cocktail – and that steady input could be harmful in ways that an occasional dose might not be. Nobody has researched the effects of frequent doses of such chemicals on water, and water life, when another dose arrives before the previous one has dispersed. For example, as fish seem to be the most sensitive of all creatures to glyphosate a constant trickle of glyphosate into rivers might perhaps wipe out fish and other water life – and with them, river fishing.

Soil Damage

There were warnings that broad-spectrum herbicides could poison many beneficial soil organisms, such as the fungi which help plants take goodness from the soil. This can make the soil less fertile for all plants and may especially harm trees as many of them depend on a mutually beneficial relationship with soil fungi.

There is extensive research to show that soil fungi and nitrogen-fixing bacteria are harmed by such weedkillers and that they also reduce the growth, and shorten the lives of earthworms.

A Cycle of Destruction

You might think that the discovery of the world's oldest fossil couldn't possibly have anything to do with genetic engineering. But it does.

Discovered early in 1999, the oldest fossil was an alga. One of a family of neglected little plants, ranging from seaweeds to the green coating on garden paths, algae are the bedrock of the food chain. Growing on, or just under, the soil's surface, they provide food for a mass of tiny creatures that are vital for soil fertility. These creatures, which feed on algae, are also food for the next layer of life, such as birds. Apply that pattern to evolution, and you can see that, without algae, we probably wouldn't be here – and we may still need them.

All-purpose weedkillers are created to kill all plants. So they are likely to devastate algae and may also affect the tiny fungi and other micro-organisms in the soil. We still know remarkably little about the subtle inter-action between the immense range of organisms which keep soil fertile. What we do know is that the soil has its own unseen life, and that to disrupt its balance risks a long-term reduction in soil fertility. One American body concerned with pesticide harm says research shows that Roundup slows the development of earthworms, reduces nitrogen fixation in the soil, and inhibits beneficial fungi.[8]

Land Pollution

The Royal Institute of Chartered Surveyors has called for a register of all land which has grown GE crops at any time. It has warned that prospective purchasers would want to know about this, and that land which had grown GE crops would probably fetch a lower price. So any tenant growing GE crops might have to compensate the owner for that drop in value.

If you are thinking of buying a house, or land, it's a point well worth raising with the estate agent.

What we should sensibly do in any new situation is to weigh the risks against the benefits ... It is extremely difficult to tinker with the genome in a way that actually *improves* anything but a very narrow range of its performance.

Professor Colin Blakemore, University of Oxford

The Promise of High Yields

Although the gene companies have talked as if high yields go hand in hand with GE – that isn't quite the case. The Catch 22 for genetic engineers is that something as fundamental as productivity is unlikely to be controlled by one gene. Yet the more genes are inserted the more the plant is disrupted and the more unpredictable the results are. So they have mainly gone for insect resistance and weedkiller tolerance hoping that high yields, would result.

✱ In 1997 the UK was penalised by the WTO for growing too much oilseed rape. The coming GE rape claims higher yields it may be the first GE crop Britain grows commercially.

When asked for evidence that GE seeds improve yields agro-giants have been known to point to the millions of acres American farmers have planted. 'Why would farmers plant GE crops if they aren't successful?' they say. One reason could be because GE seeds are so powerfully advertised and so warmly recommended by seed merchants – on which farmers may rely for information. Seed merchants are some times on very intimate terms with GE companies. Indeed, some of them *are* GE companies, at least in parentage.

The great cotton bud fall

One of the most extraordinary aspects of the GE story is that farmers were still planting GE crops even after some astonishing GE crop failures in other areas. One of the jewels in Monsanto's GE crown was meant to be cotton. Some cotton was engineered to survive Roundup, some with Bt, to be pest-resistant. Across America over a million acres were planted with GE cotton in 1996. Everyone looked set to make a killing. Some of them did, but not quite in the way they intended. To their dismay Texan farmers found their 'pest-resistant' cotton positively overrun with pests.

In 1997 farmers in the South had other troubles with Roundup Ready cotton. The cottony heads (boll) were deformed and dropped off the plants. By autumn nearly 30,000 acres of Mississippi alone were affected, and its said that some growers faced losses of between $500,000 and $1,000,000. The same year the University of Georgia tested Monsanto's Paymaster 1220 cotton, noticed the roots were deformed and warned against using it.

Yet the following year, farmers not a million miles away in Georgia, Florida and North Carolina planted GE cotton. There are reports of Monsanto facing claims for millions of dollars from cotton farmers in these states, as well as Texas, Oklahoma, Mississippi and Louisiana. Some of the lawsuits are said to accuse Monsanto of 'fraud and misrepresentation'. But these failures are a striking example of the unpredictability of GE crops – an unpredictability that can affect safety as well as yields.

A Sorry Farmer

Andrew Thompson was one of this victims of the GE cotton disaster. He was so excited by what GE cotton promised that in 1998 he devoted a large chunk of his 1,600 acres to it. Nearly a quarter of his cotton crop withered in the field, costing him $250,000. His lawsuit alleges that the companies rushed the seed to market without adequate testing. Then, when complaints started, those responsible hid the size of the problem from growers and agriculture officials. So he was wrongly advised and it wasn't just Andrew Thompson's pocket that was hit.

When you have strangers . . . see this sorry crop they say, 'That's a sorry farmer.' It's straining emotionally.

Augusta Chronicle, USA, 25 January 1999

Whatever the mechanism turns out to be cotton boll development is not obviously related to herbicide resistance and would not have been predicted as an outcome of adding a resistance gene. The boll problems [therefore] contradict claims that gene splicing is a precise technology which allows scientists to reliably predict risks based on knowledge about the added genes.

Union of Concerned Scientists, USA[9]

* Transgenic crops rose from zero sales in 1995 to US1.35 million in 1998.

In India, Monsanto's GE cotton, apparently, fared little better. According to Dr Vandana Shiva, Monsanto announced good results for its field trials. But when members of Dr Shiva's science research institute talked to the farmers themselves, it was a very different story. Dr Shiva told me that many farmers experienced a dramatic drop in yields, one farmer's dropping to a small fraction of what it had been.

Some reports of Bt cotton say it failed to deter insects, and that the cost of seeds and chemicals was up while the yields were down. As the whole point of Bt cotton is its built-in insecticide, what were those extra chemicals for? Of course, there may be places in which GE cotton succeeds but it's interesting that, in 1998, Monsanto withdrew the GE cotton 'value guarantee' it had offered to Australian cotton growers.

Soya yields

Soya has had troubles too. Nothing as striking as the cotton bolls falling off, but quite enough to cast doubt on the much-boasted 'high yields' of GE crops. In this highly competitive industry, dog predictably eats dog. Early in 1998, the agro-chemical company Cyanamid said it had evidence that yields and profits were lower with Monsanto's GE soya than with good normal varieties – and that farmers growing GE soya were losing up to $43 an acre.

Comparing yields for GE Roundup Ready (RR) soya and normal soya the University of Arkansas found that in 30 out of 37 cases normal seeds had higher yields. The difference was sometimes considerable and often the GE crops failed to even reach the average yield for the area.[10]

Of course, one set of figures – however striking – doesn't prove that higher yields are impossible. There may well be some corner of a foreign field that is for ever a Roundup Ready

---

* There is evidence that spontaneous transfer of genes from GE trial crops to other species has already occurred.

success story. However, the Arkansas figures do cover six different varieties of RR crops. So it can't just be that one variety is poor. All six varieties seemed equally unable to excel. After all the hype about high yields being worth the extra cost of seeds – up to twice the price of normal seed, plus a technology fee – farmers must feel as if they've bought tickets to see a singer billed as the next Frank Sinatra, only to find the man can't sing.

Less corn on the cob

In Virginia Bt corn fared no better. In 1997 the biotechnology specialist of the Virginia Cooperative Extension, reporting on the first generation of GE Bt corn, wrote:

> Yields were very similar to the non-Bt [non-GE] varieties. However, significant [lower] yield differences were seen in some of the newer Bt varieties. Growers should not sacrifice yields just to use Bt lines. There will also be a technology fee of $15 to $18 a bag.
>
> Charles Hagedorn, Crop and Soil Environment News,
> USA, March 1997[11]

Tellingly Charles Hagedorn added that 'corn could be produced fairly successfully throughout the Southeast without too much concern for insects', provided it was planted early and maybe had some 'at-planting insecticide.' So much for Bt crops being insecticide free.

Rape rules OK?

However, such honesty isn't always evident. In Canada, seeds have to obtain 108 points in trials to be accepted into the seed lists. When two GE oilseed rape varieties came up for approval the committee simply upgraded them in because of the 'desirability of the herbicide tolerant trait'. That was in 1995, but in 1998 the director of the Ontario Canola (Rape) Growers Association said that his yields had fallen by almost a quarter.

> Engineering in one trait can disrupt other aspects of a plant. Already this has led to lower yields. How long will it be before this technology triggers changes which harm our health? This 'suck it and see' approach is unscientific and utterly unacceptable when we are dealing with global food security.
>
> Mark Griffiths, Land Management Adviser to the RICS

Flawed data and illegal trials

In the face of protests governments and gene giants claim that strict controls are imposed on GE trials. But the proof of the pudding . . . In 1998 a trial field of sugar beet in Holland was accidentally harvested and processed into sugar and animal feed. In Britain this year Monsanto was fined a mere £17,000 for failing to keep the required pollen boundary around a trial field of GE rape – a financial pinprick compared to the £600,000 claim Monsanto made against two ordinary women who pulled up a GE crop – a crop which could have ruined an organic farmer had the pollen drifted onto his land.

In reality the data companies submit when asking for crop approval may be no more meticulous than some field trials, and poor data get past many regulators. In January 1999 the government advisory body ACRE called a major agro-giant 'incompetent' and accused it of submitting sloppy, 'wholly unacceptable' research, far below the required standard.[12] The row occurred when it asked permission to import a herbicide resistant GE crop for human and animal food and ACRE discovered the company hadn't even correctly defined the gene which had been inserted. ACRE spoke of 'lack of rigour in the

---

* An official report by the John Innes Centre said that pollution from GE crops could not be contained.

first analysis', 'poor interpretation of data' and 'a standard well below that expected . . . to place products on the market'.[13]

Blows to Organic Farming

We are faced with one of the most important and urgent choices of our time: whether we want genetically engineered food or organic food. If we do not act, all our food – even organic crops – will be contaminated with genetic pollution. We must ban genetically engineered crops and promote what British people want in ever increasing numbers – organic food.

Lord Peter Melchett, Greenpeace, and Patrick Holden,
Soil Association

It's ironic that GE is almost tailor-made to drive consumers to buy organic food, even if they weren't doing so before. Yet, at the same time, GE crops are almost tailor made to destroy it. Indeed, almost every step on the GE road has been perfectly calculated to undermine organic farming: the risk of contaminated seeds, crops which cross-pollinate more easily, genes which may create virulent crop diseases, harm to beneficial insects, and an increase in Bt-resistant pests making an important organic insecticide less effective.

The Soil Association, which sets the standards for organic farming in Britain, supports the call for a moratorium on GE crops but goes even further. Richard Young, himself a farmer and policy adviser to the Soil Association, told me that the organisation would like British farming to be a no-go area for GE crops – a move ideally suited to an island and one which could immensely benefit British foodstuffs in world markets. He says:

∗ Monsanto's 1996 revenues equalled Britain's contributions to the EU in 1997.

GE crops aren't compatible with sustainable agriculture of any kind. In Britain even conventional farmers have been moving towards more care for the environment, more sustainability. GE just puts the clock back. It's a technology dependent on increased chemical inputs damaging to the environment and consuming non-renewable resources.

Richard Young, Soil Association

The proof of the soil . . .

One of the most important claims made for GE has been that it is needed to save the world. However even if some GE crop yields were, genuinely, as impressive as the gene giants claim, that need not be the only way to feed the growing world population. New research, reported in the science journal *Nature*, confirms the claims of experienced organic farmers that well-managed organic farming can be as productive as intensive farming.

A 'conventional' site used a 'high-intensity system' with pesticides, and mineral nitrogen fertilisers, as on 'typical farms'. The first organic plot used a manure-based system, feeding cattle grasses and legumes grown as part of a crop rotation system, then using the cattle manure on the land. The other organic option used no cattle but dug in nitrogen-rich plants as 'green manure'.

Nature reported, 'Amazingly, ten year average maize yields differed by less than 1% among the three cropping systems . . . and were nearly equally profitable', and 'measures of soil fertility increased markedly in the manure system'. However 'the conventional system had more environmental impacts ×60% more nitrate was leached into groundwater . . . than in the manure or legume systems'.[14] The same article said soil can take fifty years to recover full fertility after damage by chemical farming, suggesting that, given time, the yields from organic methods would have *exceeded* those from chemical farming.

GE Boosts Pollen Transfer

Organic farmers have always said their crops were in danger of being pollinated by GE ones – even from trial sites – especially with a wind-pollinated crops like maize. They are right. In autumn 1998, *Nature* published evidence from Professor Joy Bergeleson showing that GE plants fertilise other plants 20 times more easily than normal plants. The researchers said their findings had serious implications as 'this altered gene has been introduced into dozens of altered crops'.

In 1999 the National Pollen Research Unit found that maize pollen lives for twenty-four hours and in some winds can travel up to 120 miles. And even the Ministry of Agriculture's own figures say bees can fly 3–9 miles. Put all those facts together and there's an enormous risk of organic farms being ruined by even one field trial. For any crop contaminated with GE cannot be sold as organic.

Yet the Ministry of Agriculture insists on accepting the agro-chemical industry's claims that 200 metres is the appropriate space to allow between engineered crops and organic growers. Dr Jean Emberlin of the Pollen Research Unit estimates that at 200 metres 1 in every 93 kernels on an organic cob would be contaminated with GE genes.

That risk isn't limited to organic crops. Ordinary non-GE maize will also be cross-pollinated by GE crops. So GE genes will be in our diet even when we buy non-GE food. That's why the EU is now trying to define non-GE food as food containing only a limited amount of engineered genes. If this happens GE-free food will be a thing of the past.

* In Britain there are 90 organic farms within a bee flight (6 miles) of one of the GE trial sites.

The thinking behind GE?

It is possible that the growing interest in organic food was one factor which persuaded the biotech industry to push GE crops so hard and so fast, rushing them into the fields without long-term trials, Maybe they needed to lock farmers and consumers into acceptance of GE before the tide turned too far against the agro-chemical industry.

Over the last twenty-five years the industrialised world has been waking up to the damage which has been done to the environment. Concern has been growing about the human risks of aggressive, chemically based farming. Organic and low-input farming has mushroomed, and herbal remedies have been outselling some of the drugs made by the gene companies' pharmaceutical arms.

GE was the natural tool with which to control markets. The really clever move was launching their GE offensive with products which looked, at first sight, as if they really could reduce chemical use. They forgot that quite a few people knew the story of Little Red Riding Hood.

> Genetic engineering represents a whole new biological attack on nature – the latest in a line of environmental devastation caused by 50 years of intensive agriculture.
>
> Lord Peter Melchett, Greenpeace, and Patrick Holden,
> Soil Association

Feeding the World?

> There are still hungry people in Ethiopia, but they are hungry because they have no money, no longer because there is no food to buy. We strongly resent the abuse of our poverty to sway the interests of the European public.
>
> Tewolde Egziabher, Ethiopian delegate at the Biosafety Talks[15]

You might suppose that, having claimed to be able to feed a hungry world, the companies would be specially engineering crops to meet Third World needs. Far from it. Most Third World crops are being given the same old duo – either genes to resist weedkillers, or deter specific pests. As the use of such crops should create huge markets for their agro-chemicals, agro-giants are trying desperately to get them into the Third World and to persuade the rest of the world that GE crops are needed there.

They are neither needed nor wanted and could do immeasurable harm to local crops and wild foods. Their use would also increase the cost of farming and aggravate the poverty which is at the root of Third World hunger. Their use would be a continuation and aggravation of the tragic situation in which many of the countries' children have, tragically starved while their country grew cash crops for export, often animal fodder for cattle in richer countries.

In February 1999 over 120 out of the 170 countries at the Biosafety Protocol talks at Cartagena argued against GE crops being forced upon them. Those countries were overwhelmingly from the Third World. Ranged against them was a powerful biotech lobby group from America – which Britain supported. Predictably the arguments of the poorer countries were overridden.

It is not surprising that agro-giants should target the Third World. Huge populations mean huge markets. The Third World is also a reservoir of organic farming – the last thing chemical companies want to see. So the gene giants are trying to lure Third World farmers into discarding their traditional methods in favour of more 'modern', more 'progressive' alternatives. This could set the scene for a tragedy. The high chemical inputs needed by the hybrid seeds which have been adopted may be beyond the means of small farmers in poor countries.

Engineered seeds, farmer contracts, plus perhaps Terminator technology, which makes seeds sterile to prevent seed saving (see Patents), could lead to an environmental disaster. In many supposedly 'less developed' countries, crops are fostered and pests and diseases limited by companion planting – often with what we might call weeds. The destruction of such fruitful partnerships by broad-spectrum weedkillers would undermine long-term food security in those areas. For countries and alliances come and go but 'weeds' go on for ever.

A rich tradition

In the West we rarely see Third World agriculture unless famine strikes and images of parched fields are splashed across the media. So it's easy to forget that what agro-chemical giants portray as primitive agriculture is in fact immensely diverse and successfully feeds millions.

According to the United Nations, major aid charities, and leaders of the countries themselves, undernourishment in the Third World isn't due to lack of food but to lack of money to buy it. While Britain can boast less than a dozen varieties of wheat in active use, India can boast over 17,000 varieties of rice, each perfectly suited to its area of cultivation. There were over 50,000 before the 'green revolution' wiped out huge numbers of crops and crop varieties.

An FAO report on plant diversity listed the adoption of 'modern' seeds, in place of local ones, as the main reason for varieties being lost in 80 out of 154 countries. Some Western seeds may well bring benefits. But abandoning the immense range of non-GE seeds, and local varieties, in exchange for a few varieties of uniform GE crops, as gene giants recommend, could mean catastrophic crop failure. For, the more uniform the crop the greater the risk of devastation by a single disease.

Using GE crops which destroy beneficial insects and risk a build-up of resistant pests would also create a need for insecticides which are beyond the pocket of many small farmers. It will mean abandoning diversity in the hope of higher yields which may, on present showing, be illusory. In little more than a year 400 Indian farmers committed suicide, unable to face the debts which chemical farming caused them.

> Monsanto technologies will push Bangladeshi peasants into debt as they have to spend more money on herbicides, seeds, royalties and technology fees. This rising indebtedness of farmers is the reason why only 2 per cent of farmers survive in the US and thousands of farmers have committed suicide in India.
>
> Dr Vandana Shiva, Director of the Foundation for Science,
> Technology & Ecology

In countries where many people work small plots, providing just enough for the family, with the surplus going to market, even minor crop losses from weedkiller drift from larger farms could bring hunger to a family, or a village. Drifting spray can also devastate wild vegetation. In the Third World this has a special importance. Many tropical countries are rich in wild foods and the poor depend on these foods for much of their diet. In West Bengal 124 'weeds' are eaten, in Tanzania 80 per cent of the vegetables eaten by the less well off come from uncultivated plants. In rural Mexico over 400 species of wild plants and animals are used – and over 200 eaten. If all-purpose weedkillers destroy such plants, thousands could starve. And if wild plants are destroyed, or contaminated with GE genes it will also destroy reservoirs of natural resources which they and the world may need in centuries to come. The risk of this is all the greater because many western crops originated in the Third World and weed relatives abound.

> The biotech companies promote GM foods as a way of saving the world . . . All that, to me, is the most disgraceful and cynical marketing. The majority of crops are

* Tests at the University of California showed glyphosate can drift 400 metres.

herbicide-resistant. We forget that these biotech companies are simply manufacturing companies with a new
product they're trying to flog.

Malcolm Walker, Chairman, Iceland supermarkets

GE Crops and the Third World

The great promise has been that GE crops are vital to feed
the world's growing population. Yet, looking at the following
catalogue of disadvantages suggests the opposite is likely to be
the case – bearing in mind that the Third World will need to
feed itself and cannot depend on Western exports.

- All-purpose weedkillers destroy wild foods which are an
  important part of the diet in many parts of the Third World.
- Such weedkillers also destroy reservoirs of wild plants
  essential to the interactive ecology of beneficial insects,
  birds, and other elements of the natural world.
- The destruction of beneficial insects makes farming harder
  and perhaps more dependent on toxic chemicals.
- Huge acreages growing the same GE varieties are extremely
  vulnerable to disease (as in the Irish potato famine).
- The best results are likely to be obtained with very varied
  seeds adapted to thrive in very diverse soils, climates, and
  altitudes throughout the world.
- Seeds bred locally can be interbred to adapt to weather
  changes caused by the world's changing climate whereas
  GE seeds are patented and must not be interbred.
- Total dependency on imported seeds leaves countries vulnerable. At times of international friction survival may
  require self-sufficiency in seeds.
- If GE technology renders the seeds produced by a crop sterile

✳ A soil-web of over 100 billion microbes, surrounds a plant's
  roots: many of them are vital for it to thrive.

farmers suddenly cut off from imported seeds, by disaster or war, will have nothing to plant. Yet, by then, they may have lost their native varieties.

- Local farmers who have interbred seeds over centuries may be best at creating the varieties they need for their diet and local conditions.
- GE seeds are mainly designed for cash crops, yet switching from smallholding to cash cropping may be less sustainable and feed fewer people.
- GE seeds are designed to require high chemical inputs which few in the Third World can afford. The cost of using even hybrid crops is already forcing small, self-sufficient farmers and their families off the land and into unemployment – and hunger and even suicide.
- GE crops may react very badly to stress – such as the extreme weather conditions which could be coming as world weather changes. A sudden decline in yield is catastrophic for small farmers.
- GE fosters the use of chemicals – the more used the greater the risk to fish and wildlife used as food.
- If Terminator technology makes GE crops sterile it will force farmers to buy fresh seeds each year and bring debt and ruin to many.
- Research shows that chemical farming seriously reduces soil fertility and reduces yields, requiring high chemical inputs which small farmers may not be able to maintain.
- GE methods which reduce soil micro-organisms might extend that damage still further, increasing soil erosion.
- The insect-resistant GE varieties will encourage super-pests to evolve which will spread to non-GE farms as well.
- Herbicide-resistant plants may cross-breed with local varieties and local edible weeds, creating unknown toxins or allergens
- Such crosses may create invasive super-weeds which oust valuable local wild plants altering the ecology for ever.

The Farming World.

There are many other disadvantages which could be listed but the bottom line is that food security – in any country – cannot be achieved without control over the sources of food, and without sufficient diversity to avoid widespread crop losses from any one disease, or from freak weather. In place of that GE offers farmers worldwide uniformity and dependency.

If Third World farmers, or farmers over here, buy into GE crops it may be a noose around their necks. As I show later, patents recently taken out by gene giants reveal that the agenda for GE crops is very far from being beneficial to consumers, farmers or the environment. It threatens the food security of the whole world and will put the farming industry in bondage to the agro-giants. Already this is beginning to happen. Lax regulations fail to control the gene giants, yet the advent of GE crops and clever mergers have enabled them to put farmers under contract and gain ever greater control of farming.

The tougher the rules for small farmers, the easier it will be for gene giants to put people out of business if they blow the whistle on accidents or problems. If things start going wrong, farmers may stay quiet rather than risk lawsuits against major companies. As one American farmer put it, after signing a contract to grow Monsanto's GE potatoes: 'It gives corporate America one more noose around my neck.'[16] The noose is part of tomorrow's corporate strategy.

Farmers will be given just enough to keep them interested in growing the crops, but no more. And GM

---

* In Brazil a court ruled that Monsanto must assess the environmental impact before planting GE 'Roundup Ready' crops.

companies and food processors will say very clearly how
they want the growers to grow the crops.

Friedrich Vogel, Head, BASF Crop Protection Division[17].

The European Position

All this is extremely bad news for the rest of us. Our freedom
to buy food which is not GE, to have organic food or food
with low chemical inputs depends on the successful survival
of small farmers. They in turn depend on a farming climate
which makes small farming viable.

Until very recently the British government has been all in
favour of GE and remarkably insensitive to the needs of small
farmers. Though token sums have been given to organic farming they are a drop in the ocean in comparison to the huge
grants given to the already rich biotech sector. The government
has shown little real interest in small farms, organic farming, or
even healthy eating. Though faced with rocketing NHS costs, it
has apparently failed to make the connection between food
and health.

However, the enormous public opposition to GE, combined
with the Trojan work of dozens of independent pressure
groups, has persuaded the government that it is in its interests
to tone down, or at least conceal, its yearning to consummate
its love affair with biotechnology by sanctioning the growing
of GE crops in Britain. In March 1999 the government
appeared to accept the need for a moratorium to assess the
impact of GE crops. The advisory body ACRE has – at last –
recognised that the European farming environment is different
from its counterpart in North America, and that 'there is
increasing evidence of a link between the decline in wildlife
and the intensification of agriculture'. However, whether the
change of heart is real remains to be seen. The government's
actions are contradictory. Officially it eventually backed a
moratorium. Yet within days, it was said to have given certain

GE crops a special fast-track route to approval. One minister has been busy restructuring ACRE to make it less industry-dominated – which sounds positive. Yet another minister has continued to assure everyone that field trials of GE crops covered no more land than a few football pitches. In reality there are well over 300 trial sites – none of them small. So a substantial acreage of Britain is already growing GE crops with all the inherent risks of genetic pollution, and cross-pollination. Is he trying to fool us or does he simply not know the facts?

Equally contradictory behaviour is shown by the EU. So it's hard to tell where to stand. However, it would be extraordinary – given the strength of their previous pro-GE stand – if there had been a real change of heart. So the future of our food almost certainly depends on whether those who oppose GE food have the doggedness to keep making their feelings abundantly clear even if only by where their money goes – and leave politicians in no doubt where votes will go if those feelings aren't considered.

7

BST: Madder than Mad Cows?

Three Myths

Just injecting cows with GE hormones can't hurt.
Milk from cows injected with BST is just like other milk.
Britain would never permit anything cruel to animals.

The genetic engineering of animals violates their biological integrity and frequently results in a huge burden of
suffering. It is a prime example of science acting as God
– but a God of exploitation and devoid of compassion.

Joyce D'Silva, Director, Compassion in World Farming

When thinking about genetic engineering in relation to animals,
it's important not to start out from a false viewpoint. We do not,
of course, live in a world in which wild cattle and mountain goats
browse virgin pastures. So the application of genetic engineering to animals must be seen in the context of our current use of
animals. However, that's an advantage, not a disadvantage.

This is such a controversial topic that before embarking on
two chapters on animals I feel I should 'declare my interests',
as MPs say. I'm not a vegetarian, belong to no religion, have
never campaigned for animal rights, and am excited by science.
Starting out with few preconceptions. I brought to this topic

curiosity rather than criticism. Yet the more I have satisfied that curiosity, the more appalled I have become. Some of the work repeatedly raises the questions, 'How can this possibly be wise, justified or ethical?' and 'Why do it?' In this area of genetic engineering, GE, as in some medical applications, science seems to be entering an ethical minefield which human beings still capable of the atrocities in Yugoslavia are ill equipped to negotiate wisely or humanely; a minefield which calls into question not only the rights of animals but how to define a human being. It is a measure of the length to which other GE work on animals goes that the least bizarre of all these applications is injecting animals with an engineered substance which radically alters their metabolism.

BST: The Coming Threat

The genetically engineered hormone BST is a prime example of how engineered substances to make animals more productive can cause them suffering and put human health at risk. There's no shortage of milk in the Western world. Yet in America BST is injected cows to boost their milk yields. The profits go to vast agro-chemical companies. The price is paid by the cows – and by consumers.

Canada has recently banned BST, for causing harm to cows, and the distinguished British medical journal *The Lancet* called it 'one of the most controversial drugs of the decade'. For the price of increased milk can be terrible suffering for the cows, and the milk may well increase the risk of cancer. Despite that our farmers may soon be using BST. And, if the milk is pooled with other milk, as it is in America, we may find it hard to avoid.

Having a milk surplus, Europe put a temporary ban on BST until the year 2000. America is now pressing to have BST accepted. Despite a wealth of evidence against BST inside information suggests Europe may lift the ban. And, it looks as if

So What Is BST?

BST (bovine somatotrophin) is a GE version of nature's milk-making hormone. It's made by combining 'BST genes' with the common gut bacterium *E. coli* and triggering them to become a mini factory. Sold under names like Posilac and Nutrilac, it's injected into cows fortnightly and has been a multibillion-dollar earner for Monsanto and others.

Scientifically speaking, the GE version is rBST or rbST (recombinant bovine somatotrophin), and informally BST. But Americans call it bovine growth hormone (BGH), rBGH or rbGH and drop the 'h', calling it somato-tropin. As Bernard Shaw said, Britain and America are two countries divided by a common language. So I shall call it BST.

the British government may not oppose that. So very soon, thanks to genetic engineering, we may be expected to drink milk which comes from cows which have suffered needlessly, and which may cause cancer – and more.

However, the BST story isn't simply one of harm to animals, risks to health, or even misuse of GE. It's an extraordinary example of how poorly GE products may be regulated. Their regulation has been variously described as 'sloppy', 'corrupt', 'inadequate' and 'biased'. It also shows GE's potential to amplify the worst aspects of factory farming and extend the exploitation of animals in ways that may not even pay off – still less be good and compassionate animal husbandry.

* According to the FDA's figures, Monsanto has inflated the number of American cows injected with BST by more than 40% per cent.

More cow madness?

Bovine spongiform encephalopathy (BSE), the 'mad cow disease', and BST don't just sound alike – they have a lot in
common:

- each can cause cattle terrible suffering
- officials have claimed that BST also poses no risk to humans
- independent experts disagree and say human health may
  be gravely harmed

The difference is that BST is injected into cows deliberately –
in the knowledge that it will cause suffering to many, and
ignoring evidence that the milk may increase human cancer.

BST: The Risks for Cows

Monsanto isn't famous for admitting the disadvantages of its
products. So when it warns of snags we'd better believe it.
When its version of BST was launched in America, the FDA
approved it (on the basis of much criticised tests – but more
of that later). But even the permissive FDA was sufficiently
concerned to insist that Monsanto include a warning label.

Poor cow

The warnings said that cows might suffer twenty-one side
effects – some of them very painful – including:

- pre-mastitis or mastitis (painfully infected udders)
- disorders of the womb
- cystic ovaries
- indigestion, bloat and diarrhoea
- foot problems
- sores where they were injected

Giving cows an extra, man-made dose of nature's milk hormone clearly isn't the small matter it may sound. With milk increases ranging from zero to as much as 50 per cent, I've heard of udders sometimes bloated almost to the ground. Mastitis in a woman's breast can be agonising. The suffering of cows with mastitis in such udders is unimaginable. On top of that the fortnightly injections are often given in the root of the tail – where excrement may infect the wound, creating painful sores.

The knacker's yard

BST channels all a cow's physical resources into milk production and away from its own health, leaving it terribly depleted. It needs an extremely rich diet and expert husbandry. Even then its own hormones may be so out of balance that it's slow to heal and falls sick more easily. Some cows become infertile or give birth to dead or deformed calves. With good husbandry a cow can normally live twelve years. But Jose MacDonald, former pedigree dairy breeder and agricultural adviser, says the extra milk production on BST takes so much out of cows that few even begin to reach that age. Even on a rich diet some may be little more than skin and bone, suffer burst blood vessels and be barely able to stand. There are accounts of cows having be slaughtered as young as four or five.

> The cows become very emaciated . . . and many go down . . . many had multiple births . . . and many of these calves died . . . as many as 50 cows in some of the herds had to be sold . . . when they reached the market some were unable to get off the truck, they had to be dragged off.
>
> John Kinsman, a Wisconsin farmer on
> BBC Radio 4's Farming Today[2]

* The swellings on injection sites can be up to 4 inches across and last for 6 weeks.

No ideal world

I've been told that BST can spare cows extra calvings, and maintain steady but not excessive milk yields. Under ideal conditions, maybe, but when the Canadian Veterinary Medical Association opposed the licensing of BST, it quoted farm figures showing a dramatic difference between the rate of illness in cows on BST and other cows. The problems included:

• 18% more infertility than normal
• 25% more mastitis than normal (some studies say 45%)
• 50% more lameness than normal
• a reduced life span

The price of 'progress'

Giving cows BST means extra feed, higher vets bills, more antibiotics, infertility, loss of calves, and a shorter lifespan. So you'd think it would be hard for farmers to break even, let alone make a profit. According to John Verrall, Director of the Food and Farm Society, BST is far from being the huge success it is claimed to be: 'most US commentators say the product is becoming a major commercial disappointment.'[4]

America's Department of Agriculture reports that many farmers who tried BST are giving it up. If so, small wonder that manufacturers are redoubling their efforts to press BST on the rest of the world.

The British charity Compassion in World Farming says that using BST in Europe would violate the Protocol on Improved Protection and Respect for the Welfare of Animals. Although the EU signed up to this protocol at the Amsterdam summit in 1997 it's very doubtful whether that will stop it approving BST. Where genetic engineering is concerned protocols don't seem to carry much weight. What may carry more weight is the issue of human health. And here America's FDA has been roundly criticised – both by public interest groups in Europe and America and by Canada's health department.

A Farmer's Story

Chuck Knight, a family dairy farmer in Watchula, Florida, thought he was the only farmer having problems with cows on BST (rBGH). Then he saw another farmer on CBS News describing the same troubles. He rang him and learned that even farm managers with herds of 500–1,300 cows were having problems. Yet he alleges that Monsanto vets kept telling him he was the only one, and failed to file a report of his cows' sickness with the FDA – as it should have done.

My vet claims the mastitis was a result of the rBGH, and for six weeks our herd had 1–2 new cases of mastitis every day. Every time I got a cow off a new one came on. Laminitis occurred in the older cows – this is where the hoof actually peels off. We lost 10 cows that we had to slaughter – they were crippled so bad we couldn't market them. We got $250 a piece – cost cost me $1,200 to replace them – didn't pencil out too well . . .

Our cows' udders were so sore that they kicked and fussed and swung all over when massaged or milked. They hurt so bad that some of them would not let down their milk properly. They'd milk a bit and then quit and then let down a bit more. It was just a nightmare . . .

I talked to Monsanto . . . Monsanto tried to make me feel incompetent, so I kept quiet and figured I should try to solve this thing on my own.

∗ A Monsanto report of adverse reactions to BST, sent to the FDA in 1994, included numerous cows dying spontaneously.

BST: The Risks for Human Beings

With the active complicity of the FDA, the entire nation
is currently being subjected to an experiment involving
the large-scale adulteration of an age-old dietary staple
by [an] . . . unlabeled biotechnological product. Disturbingly, this experiment benefits only a very small segment
of the agrichemical industry while providing no matching
benefit to consumers. Even more disturbingly, it poses
major potential public health risks for the entire US population.

Professor Samuel S. Epstein, University of Illinois, USA

Professor Epstein, who is an adviser to the US Congress on
cancer and the environment, is one of many critics who say
that milk boosted by BST may increase the risk of breast, colon
and prostate cancer. The risks to human health don't stop
there. It may also spread antibiotic resistance, and revive the
risks of Mad Cow Disease – in humans. So it may seem extraordinary that only a milk surplus has let Britain and the rest
of Europe keep it out for the past five years, and that the
manufacturers and their White House supporters are pushing
to have it accepted. However, the stakes are high. The Consumers Union (USA) thinks BST could earn Monsanto alone
$500 million a year in the States, and $1 billion internationally
– and this isn't the only company making it. Those are trade
figures any government would welcome and a report by
Canada's health service suggests the world can expect a hard
sell.

In November 1993 the FDA approved rBST . . . There are
reports on file that Monsanto pursued aggressive marketing tactics, compensated farmers whose veterinary bills
escalated due to increased side-effects associated with the
use of BST, and covered up negative trial results. All four

US manufacturers refused to disclose the lists of their research grants to US universities.

Health Protection Board, Health Canada, Canada's health department

More of that later. For Health Canada has revealed how BST is a good example of the inadequacy of screening procedures for GE foodstuffs government bodies may as approve GE products on the wrong evidence and how dubious some of that process may be.

Assessing the risks

It is most important to remember that BST is not a therapeutic drug to which the public has limited exposure.

John Verrall medical pharmacologist and Director,

Food and Farm Society

One of the best measures of BST's human health risks is the fact that Americans, who accept GE crops so readily, have tried to get it banned. In 1998 several American consumer groups filed a joint legal petition to have BST taken off the market, saying there was growing evidence that the original testing of BST was 'fundamentally flawed'.

As usual with GE foods, the tests, which had convinced America's FDA that BST was safe, were done by the companies which stood to profit from BST and were astonishingly brief. Drug trials normally take several years and involve large numbers of animal trials – followed by trials with volunteer humans. In contrast, because BST was being used to produce a food, there were no long-term tests to see whether the milk or meat from animals injected with it would be safe for humans. Monsanto merely did a ninety-day trial with thirty rats to see if the milk would be safe, then presented it to the FDA saying that the rats showed no toxicologically significant changes.

Doctors from Health Canada, the government health department, disagree. They looked at Monsanto's data and found the very opposite. The most obvious human health risk from BST is that some of it gets into the milk. The brief rat research showed that BST is absorbed in the gut. A disturbing number of rats had developed immune reactions. Cysts had also formed in the thyroid and prostate glands of some male rats. Changes which, according to America's Consumer Policy Institute, suggest a risk of cancer and should have prompted Monsanto to do a full assessment for immune reactions and carcinogenic effects. Seemingly, no such assessment was done.

> I don't understand the glib way people talk about hormonal products. When you get out of sync you don't know what's going to happen.
>
> John Verrall medical pharmacologist,
> Director Food and Farm Society

A dangerous growth factor?

> A search by the *Independent* of the FDA's literature on BST does not show any investigation of IGF-1 levels in milk produced by injected cattle.
>
> Charles Arthur, *Independent* 22 March 1999[8]

The reason why milk from BST cows may increase the risk of cancer is that BST makes cows produce more of a hormone called IGF-1 – standing for Insulin-like Growth Factor-1 – which gets into the milk. This hormone is abundant in human breast milk soon after birth, and may help a baby's early development, perhaps helping its stomach to grow and adapt to food. But the amount of IGF-1 in breast milk tails off later on. The fact that nature tunes down this hormone as a baby grows suggests we don't need much of it. To back that up, some cancers are associated with high levels of IGF-1 in human blood. So:

- Does extra IGF-1 in dairy products lead to extra IGF-1 in the bloodstream?
- How much IGF-1 in the bloodstream is too much?
- What are the dangers of having too much IGF-1 from this source?

How much is too much?

> Levels of IGF-1 are significantly elevated in milk from rBST treated cows and will continue to rise with increased use of BST. It is the IGF-1, not the BST per se, that is the main cause of concern regarding possible adverse effects on human health . . .
>
> Consumers International submission to Health Canada[9]

IGF-1 isn't destroyed by milk processing. So one of the disputed points is whether IGF-1 from milk can get into our bloodstream. The FDA passed BST supposing IGF-1 was destroyed in the gut – as Monsanto claimed. But, two years *before* the FDA approved BST, the British milk expert Dr Ben Mepham had said that the casein in milk would be likely to protect IGF-1 from destruction. Surprisingly, Monsanto's evidence of the safety of BST milk was based on giving IGF-1 to rats on its own – without milk.

The amount of IGF-1 in milk probably yo-yos during the injection cycle, but Monsanto told the EU it 'went up substantially (about five times)'. Whatever the level, there's now evidence that besides being active in the gut itself – with potentially dangerous results – three-quarters of the IGF-1 in BST dairy products gets through into the bloodstream. The question is: does that matter?

Governments in Britain and America say no. Many scientists say yes. Canadian doctors reported that IGF-1 can be 'absorbed

* IGF-1 is a potent mitogen: it makes cells divide. Cancer is unwanted cell division.

intact [into the bloodstream] from the gut'. They felt the greatest risk might be to newborns, but there may be grave risks to adults too. When we understand this hormone better, it may prove innocent. But on today's evidence I, for one, wouldn't want extra for breakfast, lunch or dinner. Still less would I want to give such milk to my children.

In the case of a drug used in a therapeutic capacity, a margin of safety (at least 3 × the dose) is needed for approval – yet, here we have a drug used over longer periods of time for a non-therapeutic purpose, which produces serious side-effects at . . . normal dosage levels. Why this is tolerated, allowing no margin of safety, is a mystery, and how it complies with the veterinary equivalent of the Hippocratic oath is a question which needs an answer.

John Verrall, medical pharmacologist, Director, Food and Farm Society[14]

Dying for a drink of milk?
As milk is a staple food of infancy and childhood children may be most at risk. So what does extra IGF-1 do to children? Nobody knows. The generation of children born in America since 1994 are, yet again, guinea-pigs in a vast uncontrolled experiment.

Exposure during infancy and childhood raises some additional concerns, because these age groups drink the largest amount of milk on a body weight basis, and because growth and development are most rapid during childhood. Higher exposure to IGF-1 in childhood could set life-long processes in motion that determine later risks.[10]

Consumer Policy Institute, USA

One of the risks may be of childrens developing osteosarcoma, a tumour of the bones which tends to strike during periods of rapid growth. At a conference of America's National Institute of Health (NIH) it was suggested that IGF might play a role in this cancer and that 'reducing circulating levels of [this] growth[11] hormone . . . may have therapeutic potential'.[12]

A year before the FDA approved the use of BST, Dr Ben Mepham, of Nottingham University's Department of Physiology and Environmental Sciences, published in Britain's *Journal of the Royal Society of Medicine* a detailed analysis of the risks involved. In it he pointed out that EEC Directive 81/852 defines acceptable safety margins for such substances as 'to be a dose devoid of effect in man . . . of a safety margin of 1/100'. Using Monsanto's figures on how much milk an infant would drink and the level of IGF-1 in milk, he added that 'according to this criterion an infant would be exposed to a dose of IGF-1 which was 12.5 times the recommended minimum'. It is hard to see how exposing babies and children to this risk can possibly be justified.

A cancer promoter?
Cow IGF-1 is chemically identical to human IGF-1. In both humans and cows it's involved in cell growth and it can operate throughout the body. Just what newborns need. But inappropriate cell division is called cancer.

> Not surprisingly, most of the cancers that IGF-1 is associated with occur in tissues where [it] plays an important growth role, including the mammary, cardiovascular, respiratory, and nervous systems, the skeleton, and the intestinal tract.
>
> Michael Hansen, Consumer Policy Institute, USA[13]

Breast and prostate cancer booster
Evidence of links between IGF-1 and cancer is increasing. In January 1998 *Science* published research showing that raised IGF-1 could increase the risk of male prostate cancer by up to

four times. In May 1998 *The Lancet* published a major American study involving over a thousand women. It showed a close relationship between women's level of IGF-1 and their risk of getting breast cancer. Pre-menopausal women under fifty-one with the highest levels of IGF-1 were seven times more at risk of getting breast cancer. Other work suggests that even slight rises in IGF-1 levels may increase such risks.

However, these studies weren't looking at people with raised levels from BST milk. Nobody knows whether the raised levels of IGF-1 cause cancer or are caused by it. However, that may be irrelevant. For what is clear is that, if someone has cancer, extra IGF-1 could make it worse.

A report by America's Consumer Policy Institute says, 'IGF-1 appears to play a strong role in breast cancer. Breast cancer cells react strongly (i.e. grow and divide) in the presence of low levels of IGF-1.'   The report also says that reducing IGF-1 levels, by using drugs, such as tamoxifen, can inhibit the growth of breast cancers. It concludes: 'data suggest that IGFs are likely to be involved in breast cancer at the level of tumour growth and perhaps at the level of initial development and later metastases [creation of secondary cancers]'.[16]

So the more IGF-1 there is in the blood the faster breast cancer grows and the less there is the less it grows. As BST boosts IGF-1 in the blood the conclusions are obvious. And what is true of one cancer could be true of others. At a time when breast cancer is increasing alarmingly, can there be any excuse for introducing a food which may promote it?

A dangerous gut reaction

Although it can operate anywhere in the body IGF-1 also seems to have a special affinity with the gut and beyond. The cells lining the colon are so sensitive to it that even small amounts can boost their growth rate. As IGF-1 is produced by

---

* The National Farmers' Unions of both Britain and America oppose the use of BST.

colon cancers, so one of the risks from BST milk is that extra IGF-1 may convert common polyps into cancer.

> If you have higher levels of IGF-1 in BST-treated milk, it could increase cell proliferation in the small bowel, and there's always a possibility they could form abnormally into a tumour of some kind.
>
> David Challacombe, Somerset Children's Research Unit[17]

Increasing antibiotic risks

Though cancer is the gravest health risk it's by no means the only one. British research shows increased mastitis means there is more pus in the milk. The germs are killed during pasteurisation, but it's not a pleasant thought. More seriously infection means more antibiotics and antibiotic residues, Monsanto's own package insert admits: 'Use of Posilac is associated with increased frequency of medication in cows for mastitis and other health problems.' Understated words, but infection of the udder, and injection site sores, can mean repeated treatments with antibiotics and cows on BST may be slow to recover.

A Vermont study[19] found BST increased mastitis sevenfold and America's Consumer Policy Institute says cows on BST need antibiotics for more than twice as long as other cows. Others reports found that BST cows recover so slowly that they may be on antibiotics six times as long.[21] Combine the worst of those figures and BST may sometimes increase the use of antibiotics by more than forty times – a huge increase. What antibiotics residues end up in the milk no one can say. Farmers are usually meant to discard milk from cows on antibiotics for a set period of time. But who can tell if they bend the rules? Accurate tests for low-level residues in milk simply don't exist.

Antibiotic resistance

> Antibiotic use in dairy cows can lead to resistance that
> . . . could then be present in meat or milk, which could
> produce human exposure to infection that was resistant
> to antibiotics.
>
> Michael Hansen, Consumer Policy Institute, USA[24]

High use of antibiotics doesn't just cause antibiotic residues; it also makes it more likely that bacteria on the farm will develop resistance to antibiotics. And, as you'd expect, antibiotic-resistant bacteria are far more common in BST cows. From cows they spread to people. The British Medical Association opposes the use of antibiotic markers in crops because many human infections no longer respond to antibiotics because the bacteria have become antibiotic resistant. With BST, as with crops, GE is putting human health at risk. For even 'safe levels' of antibiotic residues in milk can speed up the development of antibiotic resistance by 600 to 2,700 per cent in *Staphylococcus aureus* – a very common bacteria which causes severe infections.

> Greater use of antibiotics in dairy cattle . . . may contrib-
> ute to the growth of antibiotic resistance in bacteria [in
> animals]. . . . Resistance can then be transferred to
> disease-causing bacteria that infect humans, with the
> end result that a given antibiotic may not be effective in
> treating disease.
>
> Michael Hansen, Consumer Policy Institute, USA[26]

The increase in antibiotic-resistant bacteria is one of the most serious problems facing medicine today. In Britain, both vets and doctors have been warned to use antibiotics less. Yet here

✳ A strain of *Staphylococcus aureus* in America now resists all antibiotics.

we have a product which, is of no benefit whatever to the public, and which, by increasing mastitis and sores, demands greater use of antibiotics in farming. On this fact alone the wisdom of using BST must be extremely doubtful.

An encore for mad cow disease?

You might think those were enough risks for any food. But that is not all. To keep churning out extra milk – and survive – cows need a very rich diet. So BST creates a demand for high-protein cattle-feed. An obvious source is animal remains especially in the Third World where protein is short. And, despite the fact that most Western countries have banned the feeding of animal remains to their own cattle, there is nothing to stop them exporting to the Third World potentially contaminated animal feed they can't legally sell at home. And some say Britain did so, even during the BSE crisis.

America's Consumers Union is concerned that, by creating a demand for such cattle feed, BST will increase the danger of BSE. Despite the problems in Britain – and European and American bans on feeding animal remains to cattle – many countries still allow them to be used. What's more, research suggests that IGF-1 may work hand-in-glove with the infective agent in BSE. So there's a possibility that using BST could make cows more vulnerable to Mad Cow Disease. If BST use grows worldwide, we could soon be importing BSE in cans.

Law and Disorder

When anyone raises issues of GE safety the companies ask what evidence there is of harm in America. That may convince politicians. But it's hokum. It's no good looking to America for evidence. Cancer was increasing in most industrialised

---

✴ BST is used in South Africa, and some developing countries.

countries before BST was introduced. If IGF-1 was stepping up that increase it would be impossible to prove it. What's more, five years may be a short time in the evolution of cancer.

According to the report by Health Canada, the ninety-day safety trial with rats, on which America's FDA approved the use of BST, was both inadequate and misinterpreted. The data suggests that further safety trials should check whether BST could cause cancer. Therefore, the approval of BST in America has been surrounded by suggestions of scandal. As has its near-approval in Canada.

There have been extraordinary allegations of revolving doors between regulators and manufacturers. At least one key man involved in the approval of BST had worked for Monsanto and had publicly argued against an American law which prevents cancer-producing substances being included in food. In addition, the 'Gaps' report by Canada's health service implies that the close relationship between Monsanto and some members of the approvals body in Canada may have meant that their judgements on BST weren't totally impartial. Such closeness could exist in other countries too.

No major industrialised country, except America, has approved the use of BST. The Canadian government turned it down in December 1998. That only increases America's desire for Europe to take it, it's saying a further ban would infringe free-trade rules.

It Europe tries to extend the ban on using BST beyond the end of 1999, the WTO may show its muscle. There are caveats in the WTO rules which could allow such a product to be banned but the WTO may not face strong opposition. For, astoundingly, despite all the evidence of animal suffering and ten years of ever-growing evidence of the connection with cancer and other health risks, some British and EU bodies have backed BST's introduction. Could there be 'revolving doors' here too? Or is this just an example of official incompetence?

The central fact about BST is that it is of *no benefit to consumers* and may put all of us at risk. Yet, if it is used here, it may not even be labelled as coming from BST-injected cows. In America, BST milk is combined with other milk, and not labelled. Monsanto even threatened to sue those who tried to show that their milk was BST-free by labelling it as *not* from BST sources. Europe's love affair with technology and willingness to be swayed by trans-nationals could well mean that BST milk is unlabelled, and mixed in with other milk, here too.

When the [US] Government granted the Monsanto company permission to sell rBGH, recombinant growth hormone, which increases cows' milk production, some states and several dairies tried to label their products as free from the hormone. Monsanto threatened to take them to court.

Marian Burros, *New York Times*, 20 July 1998

Do we need it? Should we accept it?

Consumer pressure could be crucial in preventing BST being approved in Europe. For, unless there are vigorous protests, BST milk, and dairy products, may be in our shops from the start of 2000. That doesn't just affect those who use a lot of dairy products. Milk finds its way into many ready-made foods – from ice-cream to sauces, confectionery and desserts. So, as with GE soya, everyone will be eating it.

As a GE hormone, merely injected into cows, BST may seem one of the less radical examples of genetic engineering. Yet clearly it may seriously undermine animal welfare, our health, and our right to choose what we eat. Despite all that, some officials in the British and European governments are still arguing that it is safe.

They say, 'Prove it's unsafe'. What we've got to say to the manufacturers is, 'Prove it's safe'.

John Verrall medical pharmacologist, Director,

Food and Farm Society

8
Animals: Human Triumphs that Shame

Three Myths

Very few animals die in GE experiments.
Scientists would never put human genes into animals.
There are strict limits on how animals can be engineered.

There is a risk to the integrity of the organisms themselves
. . . an enormous risk to the animals themselves. Even
to engineer a mouse can involve suffering in new and
unpredictable ways.

Professor Colin Blakemore, Department of Physiology, Oxford

One of the most disturbing aspects of genetic engineering (GE)
is its attitude to animals – its lack of respect for the nature, integrity and identity of living things. There seems to be no sense that
animals are more than bodies – no awareness that species have
their own integrity – nor that individual animals feel, have iden-
tities, instincts, and rights. Both plants and animals are simply
treated as grist to the biotech mill: mere genetic store cupboards
which can yield, or receive, genes researchers find useful.

Unfeeling children may pulls wings from flies. Looking at
the range of animal biotechnology it sometimes seems as if
the same unfeeling spirit of curiosity is being harnessed for
corporate gain. As an extension of factory farming there is

research on factory 'pharming': engineering animals to become live factories. Calf genes are being inserted into chickens. Human genes have been put into pigs, sheep and cows. There are no longer any boundaries. If cat or dog genes promised benefits, they too could end up on our tables.

All this, and related work in medicine, raises questions about how research should be regulated. How far it is reasonable for science to go?

For in treating living creatures as mere objects, biotechnology calls into question not only the rights of animals but the rights of human beings. Our characteristics, too, are held in the remarkable, self-perpetuating, bundles of genetic material which humankind is now reorganising in animals. At a biological level, we and the animals are one. The more their identity is violated the greater the danger of this technology failing to respect ours. Indeed, as aspects of patenting show, that is already happening. So perhaps the questions we should be asking, at every step along the biotech yellow brick road, are: where is this eventually leading? Do we want to go there?

And what part all of us should play in decisions which could alter the nature of the human race and the animal kingdom?

Engineered animals: the fashionable science

When organisms are treated as if they are machines, an ethical shift takes place – life is seen as having instrumental rather than an intrinsic value. The manipulation of animals for industrial ends has already had major ethical, ecological and health implications. The . . . machine view of animals removes barriers to ethical concern for how animals are treated to maximize production.

Dr Vandana Shiva, Foundation for Science,
Technology and Knowledge

* Britain created more than 60,000 transgenic animals in 1996 alone. Most of them were for use in research.

Engineering animals themselves is by far the most fashionable aspect of biotechnology. It is not viewed with distaste – indeed, clever marketing has given it the greatest media attention, and the warmest accolades, of any aspect of GE. Yet strip away the pictures of cuddly lambs, the child-designed jumper in Dolly wool, and the reassuring face of Dolly, and there is a very different scene. A science in which animals endure distress, pain, death and deformity for ends which often seem ill-conceived, and inappropriate. Far from being the jewel in the crown of GE, it is probably the most dubious, and one of the most dangerous aspects of this science. Engineering an animal usually means micro-injecting unnatural genes, from man or some other animal, into an egg cell in a laboratory. To produce one such transgenic animal, this may be done to hundreds of eggs, for a few to 'take'.

An egg cell isn't a blob of jelly – it's the essence of life. A miraculously complex, harmonious community of genes and microscopic, functioning 'organs', about which we still know so little that to try to improve on it has all the wisdom of you or I rewriting a Beethoven symphony.

The new genes invade the harmonious, well-ordered relationships between the genes of a living, feeling creature, and disrupt the life which that egg would have been. The results are unpredictable, and often horrific. We only see the successes. But how do you define success?

> The movement of a single gene . . . results in uncontrolled random splicing of the foreign gene into the host DNA. This invariably disrupts to a greater or lesser degree natural genetic order and biochemical activity. The splicing of a piece of the Spice Girls' music into the middle of a Mozart symphony (or vice versa) would hardly be called harmonious.
>
> Dr Michael Antonio, molecular geneticist, King's College London

✳ A transgenic mouse was born with a single eye in the middle of its forehead.

Whether the creature is a mouse, a sheep or a monkey, science has violated an animal's essential self and taken away from it what I can only call its 'beingness' – that which it was intended to be, had man not interfered. This is not the place to explore animal and human consciousness, and what it rests on. It is enough simply to consider the fact that, even if only at a physical level, humankind can now deprive an animal of its 'self'. This is not a little thing but an immense and grave one – yet the issue is barely discussed.

Of course, ever since artificial insemination, mankind has been manipulating blood-lines. So it would be easy to portray GE as a natural extension of that. In some ways it is. But the 'achievements' of transgenics and cloning would not be trumpeted as they are, if they were simply more of the same. By crossing species, inserting human genes into animals, and creating young lambs by cloning old cells, GE has broken the 'gene barrier' as surely as aviators once broke the sound barrier. The question is: does any anyone have a right to do that? If so, what right, and in what circumstances? And, if not, why is it being done?

What Are Animals Engineered For?

There must be many answers to why animals are engineered. Some of the reasons are praiseworthy – even if the means are debatable. Yet, some work may be tainted with two other answers: to make money, and because the challenge is there. Because it has been considered impossible. I am not suggesting that these are the only motives, simply that they may unconsciously be driving forces. Many mountaineers risk their own lives climbing 'impossible' mountains for the sheer joy of the challenge. Those with such a mind-set may well enter science.

Lacking adequate government funding, as they do, research bodies depend, as never before, on industry. What companies want for their money is saleable products and good publicity.

When Dolly, the Roslin Institute's cloned sheep, made head-lines, it is said to have added £25 million to the market value of its partner company. How many scientists, supported by grants from industry, and with that sort of money in the balance, could say, 'I could do this to an animal, and it might produce a money-spinning product, but I don't think it would be right'?

> If you look at the laboratory animals they're creating it's just horrific what they're producing. The list is endless.
> Joyce D'Silva, Director, Compassion in World Farming

The use of animals

Whatever the motives, genetic engineering is used on animals right across the board, from insects to apes. The reasons include:

- producing uniform animals for use in experiments
- creating animals prone to particular diseases, on which to test treatments
- giving creatures different food qualities, e.g. leaner meat
- creating creatures which grow faster and bigger
- creating animals which produce medicinal substances
- making farm creatures more resistant to diseases
- providing organs for transplants to humans
- providing specific cells or organs for medical use

The Price of Cloning

Who can forget the likeable face of Dolly the sheep? She wasn't the first mammal to be cloned; she was just the first cloned by that particular method. Yet she's probably the most photo-graphed sheep in the history of the world, and will go down

A Very Dangerous Game

A prime example of how engineering animals can be dangerous to humans is some work done on mice. In the late 1980s a major centre for disease research injected the fertilised eggs of mice with the AIDS virus. The mice were born with the virus in every cell of their bodies. Scientifically a big success: it was the first time a human virus had been genetically engineered into an animal. Yet Dr Robert Gallo, the original discoverer of the AIDS virus, pointed out, in the journal *Science*, that the AIDS mice had created a totally new danger. The AIDS virus was able to combine with normal mouse viruses to make 'super-AIDS'. And super-AIDS was able to infect new kinds of cells. Most dangerous of all, whereas normal AIDS could only be passed on by body fluids, super-AIDS might be spread by 'novel routes' – such as the air.

All this is, of course, on top of the risk of such mice simply escaping and breeding with other mice, which would be eaten by cats, which would . . . Need I go on? You'd think nobody would do anything as irresponsible as creating mice with AIDS. That they did so – without seemingly considering either the risk of the mice escaping, or the well-known ability of viruses to alter in new environments – is just one example of irresponsibility in the GE community.

in the annals of science. She was presented to us as a small miracle of human ingenuity – a miracle it seemed churlish to question.

When we hear of some feat of extraordinary scientific

∗ Dolly was rapidly followed by Polly – a cloned sheep with human genes ingenuity, requiring knowledge and skill which we personally lack, it is easy to let admiration blind us to the fact that 'clever' and 'wise' are not the same thing. Yet, if we accept such miracles at face value, we are handing over responsibility for the future of the natural world over to science, inviting a nanny state in which the nanny who knows what's good for us is someone in a white coat, transferring genes in a test-tube.

What the animals endure

The current state of knowledge in the neurosciences amply demonstrates that animals are provided with cognitive abilities which, without reaching the degree of development of human beings, are sufficient for us to acknowledge that animals feel not only physical but also psychic suffering.

Dr R. Dantzer, INSERM, France[2]

When the media trumpet accounts of successful cloning journalists have rarely been told about the animals which enabled the clones to be born. You may, reasonably, think that a 'ready to grow' embryo is simply popped up in a sheep's womb to develop to term. Far from it. Cloning involves surgical procedures and many dead animals. With sheep and pigs, especially, the procedures are far harsher than you might expect. For example, the usual system for sheep is this.

1 The donor ewes have hormone injections, and their eggs are surgically removed.
2 The 'fertilised' eggs are placed, surgically, into the temporary hosts.
3 Those animals may be killed to remove the multiplied eggs.
4 The eggs are surgically inserted into the final mothers.
5 Many of those mother animals do not carry to term.
6 Often the resulting 'babies' need surgery to deliver them.

Unmentionable distress

Out of any batch of young born from one cloning experiment, those which aren't stillborn may only live briefly or be abnormal. The two cloned sheep Megan and Morag of another media grabbing experiment, were just the ones that hit the headlines. There were other, unsung lambs. Several of Megan and Morag's live siblings had deformed internal organs. Some were far larger than normal. This isn't unusual: its called 'large offspring syndrome'. There are accounts of cloned animals up to five times normal birth weight. Can you imagine the suffering of the mother animal?

> Greater than normal weights can cause distress at parturition to both the offspring and the dam, and often require delivery by Caesarian section. Immediately after birth many lambs and calves have breathing difficulties, are lethargic and often will not suckle. As a consequence, perinatal mortality is high, even with the help of a veterinarian.
>
> Dr Lorraine Young, the Roslin Institute Annual Report 1997/8.

The waste of life

The number of animals used in all this is extraordinary. Cloning Dolly was no exception:

- cells were taken from the udder of a Finn Dorset ewe and cultured
- 277 sheep's eggs had their genetic material removed and a cell inserted
- these eggs were temporarily put into other animals to mature a little

* At the University of Bath they produced a headless frog embryo.

- 6 days later, at the multi-cell (blastocyst) stage, they were removed
- 29 were found to have multiplied normally
- 13 ewes had those eggs implanted into them
- only 1 had a live lamb: Dolly

Had anyone lined up for the cameras the pathetic remains of all the 'failed' and deformed foetuses and stillborn animals, and their surrogate mothers, Dolly's image might have been different. Yet this 'wastage' is typical. In 1998, when a scientist in Hawaii cloned mice, this is what it took to do it:

- in a laboratory, over 1,125 egg cells were 'fertilised' with cells from an adult animal and allowed to multiply into a tiny bundle of cells (blastocysts); over 320 failed to multiply
- 800 blastocysts were implanted into 54 foster mothers
- 17 live foetuses were born
- 6 died on delivery, 1 died within a week
- out of the original 1,125 only 10 lived on

With both Dolly and the mice, the success rate is less than 1 in 100. Yet, on hearing of the work with mice, Professor Lee Silver, author of *Cloning and Beyond*, said, 'There's not a single reason why it wouldn't work with humans.' Of course, it can be argued that it's still early days: by the time anyone gets around to cloning humans numerous aborted foetuses and dead babies wouldn't be necessary to produce one live one. But, that is by no means certain.

When a human being has to resort to implantation to become pregnant, the medical ordeals can be tough enough. But the human being, to some extent, understands what is happening and can complain of pain or distress. Animals subjected to surgery do not. They cannot understand post-

---

∗ Dolly, the cloned sheep was announced in *Nature* on 27 February 1997.

anaesthetic confusion, or ask for post-operative painkillers. Nor do they choose to be involved.

In scientific terms, Dolly's greatest achievement was showing that even mature adult cells can, under the influence of an egg cell, differentiate to create a whole creature. That was an exciting discovery which went clean against conventional wisdom. It seemed as if the biological clock could be wound back. But it may not be that simple. There are now signs that Dolly is aging faster than normal sheep. The question is: was there no other way to make this discovery?

Cloning transgenic animals

Cloning, though not strictly genetic engineering, has been included because a prime reason for much work on cloning is that the perfected techniques will be used to create large numbers of genetically engineered animals. Scientists are trying to engineer animals in the hope of creating better farm animals and also to make animals into 'living factories' which produce medical products. However, the process is so tricky, so hit-and-miss, that umpteen attempts may result in only one animal that both thrives and carries the new genes. Not much good for breeding. Indeed, the best indicator of the failure rate in creating transgenic animals is that cloning, with all its failures, is the surest way to create more.

Cloning can also be used to multiply the number of animals engineered to develop some particular disease or disability, or tailored for use in experiments. One of the most distasteful recent examples of this is that in America, a batch of monkeys were to be cloned for use in experiments. For monkeys are expensive to buy, and identical animals were seen as an advantage. An expected 'achievement' the scientists concerned have announced with pride.

Transgenic Animals

Creating transgenic animals, which contain genes from a totally different species, is now a major part of biotechnology. The main thrust of this work is three pronged: creating tailor-made animals for research, engineering them to produce medical substances, or 'improving' creatures for eating. More unusual applications include an Australian attempt to produce 'self-dipping' sheep, which will produce a substance that kills flies and sheep parasites. While, insect work includes an attempt to engineer the bug that carries the deadly Chagas disease, in South America, so that the infectious parasite will die in its gut, and to modify mosquitoes so they can't spread malaria. Unfortunately, though that may sound appealing some biologists say GE could make mosquitoes more dangerous, not less.

Eating Uncle Harry

The first attempts to exploit transgenic technology in livestock were directed at the manipulation of conventional agricultural traits such as growth and feed efficiency . . . Although transgenic pigs carrying *human* [my italics] growth hormone genes did exhibit a slightly enhanced growth rate and substantially reduced carcass fat composition, these animals suffered from widespread deleterious effects including susceptibility to stress, lameness, and reduced fertility.

Roslin Institute Report 1997/8

Super-beasts

The matter-of-fact tone of that statement is, perhaps, as surprising as the fact that *human* genes are being put into animals one day destined for our tables. In farm animals: they are aiming for super-beasts, creatures which are bigger, leaner, grow faster, resist disease or have some other desired quality. Fortunately, to date, this hasn't exactly been a success. Even so, there is talk of such cloned transgenic animals being the future of the livestock industry. There have been attempts to produce grazing pigs, pigs which produce appealing milk, and muscular chickens containing calf genes. More successfully, they have created turkeys which produce more eggs, and sheep containing mouse genes have been created to grow more wool.

All very clever, but not necessarily sensible. Even if the nature of the animals wasn't being violated and they could persuade us to eat copies of human genes in our meat – and would you? – there's an obvious snag. If they manage to create whole herds of healthy, cloned, transgenic beasts, all with the same transgenic asset, they will have created a time bomb. If the animals all have the same strengths they will all have the same weaknesses. Instead of some of the flock or herd dying from the next animal illness, they all will.

The day of transgenic herds is, however, some way off. Genetic engineering in animals is no more an exact science than in plants. The genes can't be inserted in any precise position, and they interact with the host genes in totally unpredictable ways. Some of the resulting animals fail to show the transgenic characteristics; others die or are weak or grossly deformed. To obtain even a few 'usable' animals, many embryos and stillborn and crippled animals are discarded.

I think they started out optimistic that they'd get faster-growing super-animals, then they found that they were often terribly deformed and suffered greatly. Surprise, surprise.

Joyce D'Silva Director, Compassion in World Farming

Human Genes: Super-Pigs

Among transgenic farm animals the most conspicuous failures were the Beltsville pigs engineered with human growth hormone to produce super-pigs – or so it was hoped. There was, of course, the usual 'wastage', but some lived. The poor creatures were impotent, partially blind, arthritic and had ulcers. Even so, the researchers at USDA were so proud to have created any living animals that they showed them to the press. They were not impressed. A film shows one animal floundering on its knees, clearly sick, and too crippled to even stand.

Fishing for trouble

Fish are one of the 'success' stories. As yet no GE fish are on sale, but work is officially being done in several dozen laboratories around the world, on species such as flounders, talipia and salmon. The main aim is to create GE mega-fish which grow larger faster – one salmon reached thirteen times its usual size in a year. They've also tried putting flounder genes in salmon to help them tolerate cold better – so as to extend the range of fish farming, and tried to create salmon which will breed in the ocean, instead of in rivers.

Despite being seen as a success, there are several risks with fish engineering. Although cages have been devised which seem escape proof there is no certainty that everyone will use them. Even captive fish bring hazards, but the dangers are increased by some research being in secret.

∗ Escapes from fish farms are so common that in parts of Norway escaped fish outnumber wild ones five to one.

- GE fish could displace other varieties – reducing the gene pool of its species and making it vulnerable to extinction.
- Some GE fish have had deformed jaws and other physical problems. Such fish could spread weaknesses to others of their kind if they escape.
- Changes in size and breeding patterns could affect all the other creatures which feed on that fish, from the fish-eat-fish hierarchy, of rivers and oceans to mammals, such as bears, which feed on salmon during spawning. So upsetting a balanced ecology which has evolved over millennia.
- The naturally invasive inserted genes, which will float into the oceans in any particle of the fish, may transfer themselves to other sea organisms, and genetically modify them – with incalculable results. It's a *very* improbable scenario, but just suppose the genes which made salmon thirteen times bigger did the same to a white shark. A more likely scenario is a series of small unseen changes disrupting the complex, interactive world of sea life – a hidden world already suffering gravely from human and chemical pollution.

In addition, if engineered salmon, for example, escape and breed with normal salmon engineered genes could spread throughout the world's salmon stocks. Non-GE salmon would cease to exist. Shoppers who didn't want GE salmon would cease to buy – and the salmon industry would be devastated. Yet once genetically altered salmon escape, there is no going back. They cannot be recalled.

✴ The GE SCID-hu mouse has a human immune system, using cells from an aborted foetus, and is used to test drugs.

Lab rats with a difference

> It's part of a whole historical institution of animal experi-
> mentation in medicine. Central to the thinking is that
> animals are models for humans. Today this is a bit old
> fashioned-but they still think that way.
>
> Dr Jacky Turner, Compassion in World Farming

Engineered animals are also due to be increasingly used in
medical tests – animals deliberately created to be prone to
diseases like cancer, such as the well-known 'oncomouse' patented by Du Pont. This use of animals is not only morally
but scientifically dubious. Even if the transgenic animal shows
signs of the required condition – and many don't – animals
remain animals. The value of using animals is now hotly
debated. Since nothing but a human reacts like a human, the
real advantages of having a mouse a little bit less mouse-like
may be minimal.

Indeed, it may be counterproductive. There is a risk that
because the mice are 'a little bit human' researchers may put
too much weight on experimental results – downplaying vital
differences between the two species. Research on BST using
ordinary rats to test the drug's safety was considered enough
evidence of the milk's fitness for humans. So it may well be
even easier for research on transgenic animals to allow unsafe
products to be approved. What's more, here, as to often GE
seems out of date. At the very time when researchers are busily
creating what they believe will be better test animals, other
branches of technology are coming up with increasingly sensitive and inventive ways of testing without using animals at
all. If needless animal suffering is to be avoided, it is important
that biotechnology does not siphon off money better spent
developing non-animal testing.

✱ Many mice engineered to have human medical problems
  fail to have them. Others die soon after birth.

What concerns the society is that the issues raised are not being addressed yet. We are calling for an independent body to review all potential research before it is done. To look very carefully at the impact of the techniques on animals before the animals have suffered – not afterwards.

Dr Julia Wrathall, Senior Science Officer, RSPCA

Animal pharm factories

One of the most extraordinary and almost science fiction, uses of GE is the way animals are being turned into living factories. 'Pharming' is the jokey name for it. By inserting human genes into the egg cells of animals scientists can, with a little bit of luck, create 'bio-reactors', creatures which produce human proteins – blood-clotting factors, and other substances used in modern medicine – in their body fluids. Any body fluid will do: milk, blood, even urine and semen.

This promises to yield marketable products which the pharmaceutical industry is waiting to snap up. So it's set to be a big growth area for GE in animals. Tellingly, the Roslin Institute, commenting on the huge demand for a serum used in treating burns, doesn't mention the number of burns cases needing such treatment – merely that 600 tonnes are needed a year.

In this booming field pigs have been genetically modified to produce milk containing a human blood-clotting factor missing in haemophiliacs. It's claimed that harvesting this from animals is safer than doing so from human blood. Not everyone agrees – animals too carry diseases. Anything you can do with a pig you can do with a sheep, it seems. So, the creators of Dolly produced Polly, a sheep with human genes said to produce the same blood-clotting factor that pigs can already produce – a duplication which suggests that the sole aim may not be pushing back frontiers purely for the benefit of humankind.

✳ Companies say that using animals as 'furry little [pharmaceutical] factories in fields' can save them millions.

A Real Benefit

Some animal pharming is already in trials. In Britain cystic fibrosis is being treated, in trials, with the protein alpha-1-antitrypsin from milk from GE sheep, and other trials are going on in America. The contribution such treatments could make to the lives of those who suffer from such conditions is not in doubt. The question which must constantly be asked, however, is whether the same product, could be produced without turning animals into factories. If it could, it is hard to see how using animals can be humane or ethical

The coming thing

Meanwhile, a more original scientist in Canada has engineered pigs to produce human protein in their semen. It seems boars start producing semen at 110 days old, ejaculate half a litre at a time, and will mount anything remotely resembling a sow. Perhaps amusing, but another duplication. The protein could already be produced by transgenic cows and ewes. However the researchers claim there is more protein in semen than in milk. If so, how long before it's also in our food?

Farm animal research has always been business-driven, but 'pharming' transgenic animals has taken the rewards from animal use into a whole new dimension. With the right product, and the right patent, huge money can be made. The US market for therapeutic proteins alone is expected to reach $18.5 billion in 2000. When there is huge money to be made the temptation to push the violation of animals to ever greater extremes is inevitable. At present, animals used in pharming seem to be excellently cared for. But for how long? It's a man-made extension of the way some pregnant mares have their urine collected for use in the contraceptive pill – a practice made easier by keeping them constantly tethered and immobile. So why should we expect better treatment for 'pharm' animals?

Why Do It?

There's an assumption that this is the way to go. The enormous resources involved and the rigidity of the structure mean people are channelled into a certain mind-set, that using animals is the way of doing things.

Dr Jacky Turner, Compassion in World Farming

The question which nobody in power seems to be asking is: Why produce human proteins this way? They used to come from human blood, until diseases such as AIDS made that too risky. But is animal engineering the best alternative? Surely not because:

- animals too carry infections: sheep, for example, can suffer from lentivirus, similar to HIV
- the changes engineered into animals may well harm the animals themselves
- all GE can be unstable (sheep engineered to produce more wool only did so for the first year and didn't pass the trait on to their lambs)
- human proteins can be made without using animals
- the benefits may not always outweigh the harm to animals

Research is going ahead without proper concern for the welfare of the animal. We need to monitor the long-term effects and there is absolutely no mechanism for systematic long-term monitoring once animals are away from the laboratory.

Dr Julia Wrathall, Senior Science Officer, RSPCA

A lack of discrimination

The irony is that animal experimentation is charging ahead at precisely the time that less glamorous work, which might replace it, is being done on micro-organisms. Genetically engineered bacteria, yeast and similar organisms have already been created to produce a wide range of substances – for the food industry and for medicine.

They may also be capable of producing human proteins, and other useful substances, far more easily than an engineered animal. And they should be able to make large quantities faster than animals could. If you've enjoyed any 'vegetarian cheese' you have benefited from this. The chymosin, which starts the cheese-making process, is made by a yeast genetically engineered to contain genes from a calf. In a similar way, cells can be cultured and engineered to be mini-factories. Already, several blood-clotting factors needed by haemophiliacs are produced commercially from cell cultures. With enough investment many other medical products might also be produced in laboratories, not fields.

Of course there may be limits to what can be produced in this way. And there are risks with any GE products from micro-organisms – risks which both the tragedy of GE tryptophan and the difficulties with GE insulin (covered in Medical Matters) illustrate. The proteins may also be hard to purify and may need to be modified. But these risks aren't necessarily any greater than those from using animal products. As the enormous obstacles to creating transgenic animals can be overcome, why should it be impossible to overcome the obstacles to creating safe, well-tailored proteins from lesser organisms? If the risks from engineered micro-organisms are weighed against violating the nature of animals, surely using micro-organisms is the lesser of two evils?

Does it make sense to do it any other way? If AIDS is a bar

∗ A transgenic 'pharm' goat has been valued at $1 million.

to using human blood, it should be an equal bar to animal blood. Haemophiliacs were infected with AIDS because the virus was unknown and couldn't be identified at the time. Exactly the same could apply to an unknown virus in the blood of an animal, and the disease could be just as harmful. However, the risk may be even greater, not just for the haemophiliac but for everyone else. Animal blood containing an animal virus might transfer to the human population a new disease every bit as devastating as AIDS. Of course, animals destined to give protein are carefully selected and kept in immaculate conditions. Even so, nothing is perfect.

> Practically speaking, it is impossible to ensure that production animals retain the same disease free status from day to day. Certain viruses are endemic in particular livestock species in all parts of the world, and sub-clinical infections would go unnoticed.
>
> A. Coleman, American Journal of Clinical Nutrition.

Engineering 'breast milk'

Creatures part-human part-bull are the stuff of mythology. Biotechnology threatens not only our compassion but even our myths. Herman, the gene-spliced humanoid bull, already exists – a prime example of how gravely misapplied this technology can be. He's a bull with human genes engineered to sire cows with a difference. The idea was that the milk from these cows with human genes should contain two human enzymes – so making it better for babies. Even if this worked would it be a great achievement? Not really. The perfect milk for babies already exists. The difference between breast milk and cow's milk isn't just two proteins; it's a complex balance of many proteins tailored by nature to a baby's needs. Research shows that only a tiny percentage of women would prefer not to breast-feed. The rest have practical problems, lack encouragement and support, or have medical conditions which are poorly treated. Solving these problems by engineering a bull to create cows with human milk is like losing your front-door key and hiring a Sherman tank to get you in, instead of going to a locksmith. It may be rather fun to use a tank – but is it wise?

An insane bias

What kind of society is it that will expend animal lives, and a small fortune, to engineer a bull in order to get marginally modified baby milk to enrich multinationals; yet neglects to help mothers to breast-feed it they want to? Surely it shows a gross disrespect for science itself. Science has shown that a child's long-term health and intelligence benefit from the tailor-made nourishment of breast milk. Why should that vital knowledge be misused to marginally tweak the milk of a totally different species? A tweak which will do very little for babies but enable some multinational to cash in on a trivial change by being able to say their formula is closer to mother's milk?

That work is not alone. A Roslin Institute report talks of altering the content of cow's milk to make it suitable for premature babies. Why violate the nature of cows without first seeking a more obvious, though far less glamorous and complicated, solution – for instance, enabling the mother of a premature baby to give it her own milk or providing safe milk from donor mothers?

Unfortunately, all this is typical. Biotechnology is viewed by business, government and economists as the engine of tomorrow's economy. As such it has become an icon, able to do no wrong. Meanwhile, other branches of science, and non-technological solutions, have to some extent become ugly sisters, and common sense doesn't even get a hearing.

* On average breast-fed children score 10 IQ points higher than those which were bottle fed.

Questions to Be Asked

In considering any experiment involving animals, even of the mildest, least invasive kind, there are surely basic questions which should first be asked. For example:

- Why do this?
- Is it really worth doing?
- Is involving animals the best way to do it?
- Can animals be involved in ways that respect them?
- Can animals be involved in ways that leave them unharmed?
- How great is the risk of harm – if harm is possible?
- Is the harm of a kind which can ethically be justified?
- Given any potential harm, is it *really* worth doing?
- Is the work really essential?
- Is there absolutely no other way of doing it?
- Can it *really* be justified?

The circularity is deliberate. It is one thing to think something is worth doing in principle; another to feel it is worth doing when the price paid by animals is considered.

The Money Machine

When one reads that a sheep or a pig has been given human genes to enable it to produce some human protein, there is no mention of whether that protein could have been created without involving animals. There is no attempt to justify such extreme interference with a creature's existence. Nor does there seem to be any recognition that such interference should be only a very last resort, in the most extreme circumstances.

Should we be surprised? There is money and prestige in

manipulating cows and little or none in the solutions I've suggested. A company that funds the research to make cow-milk suit premature babies is in a win-win situation. It will have a product to sell worldwide – plus a publicity coup. With a little luck, the company will be praised in the press for saving babies' lives, complete with picture of smiling executive and contented cow. So the company gets: a product, an employee morale-booster, an executive vanity aid, and free publicity on top. All good for the share price and the bonuses of those involved. Game, set and match to industry. Animals nil.

The glamour factor

Such spurious glamour is what industry is using to lure govern-ments into making grants, relaxing rules, and pandering to their whim of iron. There is no such photo opportunity in a 'vat' producing medical products from cell cultures.

A Question of Values

If human genes are going into animals, what about animal genes going into humans? You haven't heard of that? Well, that's understandable. So far animal genes aren't being put into humans – it's about the only thing they aren't trying. But what if scientists believed they'd isolated the genes which enable an eagle to see for miles? Or the one that lets lizards regrow their tails? What if parents in years to come are offered a choice of giving birth to 'ordinary nature-poor' babies or 'gene-enhanced' babies?

Molecular biologist Professor Lee Silver of Princeton Univer-sity has speculated that at some time in the future there could be two kinds of human beings: the gene-rich and the gene-

---

✽ Large segments of human DNA are now used in 'pharm' animals. This risks creating new human-animal viruses.

poor – the gene-rich, of course, being those whose parents can pay to have them gene-enriched. Suppose you were told that if your baby-to-be was enhanced with lizard genes it could regrow its limbs if they were injured? Or that with eagle genes it would have incredible eyesight all its life? What would you do? Would you mind a child, or grandchild, which was, biologically, part lizard and part bird, provided it looked normal? And how far would you go? How many genes would it take? How many 'benefits' would there have to be before you felt enough was enough?

I raise these issues because at present biotech is busy changing animals, not people. However, unless there is something to prevent it, science does what science can do. It may not be so very long before equally bizarre options are offered to parents-to-be. For the moment there are no plans for animal genes being used to create a superhuman-race. But it is not unthinkable in the light of what is already being done. Already plans are afoot to put animal organs into humans – which is no less strange.

Natural boundaries?

As you were reading some of this chapter, did it strike you as odd that you were reading about copies of human genetic material being put into animals – not just for medical reasons but to improve their eating quality? Was there, even for an instant, a drawing back from the idea? Perhaps not. One of the most extraordinary aspects of this whole issue is how rapidly the idea of such a breach of natural boundaries has been accepted. In order for science to go too far, gaining our acceptance will be half the battle.

As yet most genetic insertions have been tiny. But it won't stop there. Two years ago Japanese researchers inserted fifty times more human DNA into a mouse cell than anyone had thought possible. Where need it end? If we, the public, will accept a couple of human genes in an animal, why not fifty, a hundred, a thousand . . . As time goes on, researchers are likely to become more daring, transferring larger and larger strips of DNA from one species to another. The sole criteria for this technology seem to be:

- Can it be done?
- Will it pay off?

With such criteria, what could possibly be the limiting factor? Preserving the identity of the animal? That has already been violated. Morality? Ethics? A sense of decent boundaries? Those seem to have vanished long ago. The disquieting fact is that there *is* no limiting factor once this work has begun – unless we, uninvited co-partners in this enterprise, require it. I say co-partners because some of this work is encouraged, even funded, by the government, and we are always, in theory, the beneficiaries.

That, of course, raises interesting questions. Do we want transgenic meat, fish and poultry. If so where should the lines be drawn? Should carcasses of GE animal 'prototypes' already be allowed into food? Should such meat or fish be sold for food even if the creature contains human genes? How many human genes would a substance need to have before eating it would be cannibalism? Does it make a difference the they are *copies* of human genes? Is cannibalism a question of degree or kind? Or is it like pregnancy: you either are, or you aren't? These are just some of the many moral issues about which there has been far too little discussion and on which we, the public, haven't been consulted.

GE crops entered the shops long before public protests began. Is this an issue on which we need to think ahead and make our feeling known before our Sunday lunch has a little bit of Uncle Harry?

✳ They have tried to create featherless chickens – which need no plucking.

The ultimate beast

Setting aside the issue of eating an animal containing human genes, there's a more important question: How far should scientists be allowed to go in combining human and animal genes for any purpose? Once this has begun – as it has – there is no logical end point. Some people have already proposed creating an underclass – part man, part animal – of GE semi-human animal slaves.

There are laws against human slavery but how human need a creature be to have that protection? This question is barely being discussed. Meanwhile biotechnology is rushing ahead, mingling genes as it pleases.

Research pressures

If a department does animal work at all there is a huge incentive to use GE – even if it may not be the best way to solve a particular problem. This technology is changing at a far greater speed than the laws which should be controlling it and ensuring that animals are protected. In Britain, the 1986 Animals (Scientific Procedures) Act is meant to protect animals from being needlessly used in experiments. It requires scientists to check that the work can't be done any other way – and confirm in writing that they have done so. In reality, some branches of biotechnology are so specialised that scientists may have no way of knowing how else such work could be done. And with money and prestige in prospect, how many researchers will leave no stone unturned?

> The RSPCA believes that there is an urgent need for all regulatory inadequacies in the various fields of

* The sheep Tracy produced large amounts of valuable alpha-antitrypsin in her milk – but unexpectedly her offspring didn't.

biotechnology to be identified and appropriately rectified, in order to ensure that the application of these technologies to animals is effectively controlled with due regard to animal welfare.

Dr Maggie Jennings, Head of the Animal Research
Department, RSPCA

I am not, for an instant, suggesting that those who use animals in genetic engineering are cruel or callous. I am sure they all believe that they are moving science forward in ways that benefit society. But nobody has twenty-twenty vision – especially about their own work. The issue which has not been addressed is what if society disagrees? What if the general feeling is thanks but no thanks'? It is easy to say that science should not be censored. In reality science always is censored – by money. What can't be funded isn't done. Unfortunately, animal work is flavour of the month and brings in grants from government or industry. Whether using an animal in this way is appropriate or justified may not even be seriously considered. Yet, when the very nature of a living creature is about to be violated, what could be more important?

It's always can we do this, not should we do this, and who can we get to commercialize this. They never stop to think, is this what we should be doing? Is this right? What will the consequences be for the animals? And have we the right to muck about with other living creatures?

Joyce D'Silva Director, Compassion in World Farming

Negative engineering

Whatever your feelings about the animal work undertaken so far the objectives have, at least, been positive. However, judging by work on plants which I cover later, there is also a long-term possibility of genetic engineering being used negatively. Genes could be inserted which act like on/off switches,

A Very Dangerous Bias

Genetic engineering has an extraordinarily free hand, not only because laws are failing to keep up with it, but also because it's seen as a frontier science, a technological sacred cow. There's considerable prestige, and perhaps money, in doing it. If research grants aren't beating a path to the door of a research body, or department, the solution is to get a name for genetic engineering, especially of animals. Consider contrasting cases. Dolly the sheep put the Roslin Institute very much on the biotech map. At a different institute, Dr Arpad Pusztai's work suggested that biotech food might be unsafe – within weeks a distinguished career had ended.

Dr Pusztai is not alone. Professor Elaine Ingham, of Oregon State University, used to be well funded by America's Environmental Protection Agency (EPA). Then she discovered that a GE micro-organism, *Klebsiella planticola*, engineered to ferment farm waste, which would then be put on farms, damaged soil life. Since then, the EPA has not been interested, she says.

This bias of towards research which shows genetic engineering in a positive light is one of the most disquieting aspects of the biotech scene. The standard criteria for obtaining a research grant, from government or industry is that the outcome will be of use to industry-research which reveals flaws and hazards isn't regarded as useful. Yet, when radical changes are being made to the nature of life itself, how can it possibly be wise to underfund and stifle those who reveal dangers?

turning on and off different characteristics of the animal. This switching would be triggered by a shot of proprietary chemical.

So, for example, one breed of pig might be made capable of

producing lean or fatty meat depending on which genes were switched on or off by an injection. Or animals might be engineered so they only ovulate if given proprietary food X. Or even so that they die if not given a particular drug. That is just speculation, so far as animals are concerned. But patents on equally destructive manipulations already exist for plants and its a short step from injecting engineered BST into animals to injecting animals with substances they've been engineered to respond to.

Our part in all this

In Holland the rule on animal engineering is 'No unless'. All animal engineering has to go before an expert, and wide-ranging, approvals committee and is only allowed if it can be totally justified. If we have any compassion and respect for animals isn't such a policy essential? However, those on such a committee have a thorny task.

Ben Mepham, director of the recently formed Food Ethics Council, has raised the important question: at what point does GE violate *the fundamental nature* of an animal – or any other living thing? Is it when we alter its hormones and much of its body chemistry by injecting a substance like BST? Or must violation involve the animal's genes being altered? If so by how much? When corporate scientists first defended GE vegetables on television they made much of the fact that GE crops looked exactly like normal crops. Yet they don't behave like normal crops in many ways – normal crops don't decimate Monarch butterflies. Appearances can be deceptive.

Does a creature need to look different before we feel its essential nature has been violated? Or do we alter that by changing the way its body works, or by turning it into a cloned, mass produced, chemical factory? Moreover, under what cir-

---

* The first successful transgenic mammal was a mouse, born in 1981.

cumstances is it permissible to commit such a violation? Is it justified if it saves life but not if it simply makes money? Or are animals simply there for us to exploit in any way we wish? We will each have different answers, different points at which we personally draw the line on engineering animals.

I ask these questions because however much animals are engineered to further the interests of agricultural and pharmaceutical companies, we are the end consumer. In the last resort, only we can draw the lines between what is and is not acceptable to us. I also ask them because we too are animals – in time radical changes to human beings may also be on the cards. In pondering how to define the essence of an animal we pave the way to decisions over where we draw the line with human beings as well.

What is happening to animals today reflects how all those involved expect us to behave. They wouldn't be engineering animals for meat, medicinal products or anything else if they didn't believe we'd buy the products.

Plant biotechnology took most of us by surprise. One moment it was a possibility found only in the pages of science journals. Then, before we knew what was happening, it was in almost every product. With animals we have a chance to draw the lines before things go too far. This is a far more complex issue than whether we have a right to choose what we eat. In most cases, animal engineering is unlikely to be the only solution to a problem. But, to produce treatments for some medical conditions, it may be. There are difficult choices to be made, both personally and as a society.

* A Japanese GE mouse contains an entire human chromosome.

9

Medical Matters

Myths

They can now engineer perfect drugs from micro-organisms.
There's no danger anyone will clone a human being – it's illegal.
Soon human organ donors won't be needed, they will get organs
from animals.

The fundamental ethical consideration that should
underlie both routine medical treatment and medical
research is respect for the individual patient as a human
being.

Dr Rory Collins, Professor Sir Richard Doll and
Professor Richard Peto[1]

Medicine is both the most positive story in the genetic saga
and one of the most difficult ethically. On the one hand doctors
are successfully using a large range of genetically engineered
(GE) drugs and medical products. On the other, the ability to
clone human beings has created the disquieting prospect of
cloning human embryos for research, and growing headless
cloned bodies to provide transplant organs. While the
possibility of treating genetic disorders before birth has also
raised the dark spectre of eugenics, and the mythic 'perfect
baby'. With this has come the possibility of a future in which

there is growing state and technical control over every aspect of having children.

Between those two extremes there are for example exciting advances in tissue culture and some over-publicised genetic treatments which medical geneticists say are nothing like as advanced as some media reports have suggested. This makes it an extremely controversial area in urgent need of thought, discrimination and public participation. For the dilemmas centre on issues of ethics and human values which concern every one of us.

Medicine is also an area in which some extraordinary experiments are going on. One company has put human genes into kiwi fruit to produce human proteins. Another is trying to create vaccines in bananas.

More ingeniously, Dutch researchers are engineering petunias so that honey from their nectar will contain a vaccine. Responsibly, the flowers and the bees are being kept safely within a glasshouse. However, kiwis and bananas are large plants. If planted in the open some of the engineered genes will inevitably 'move house', finding new hosts and recombining with other organisms. Such feral vaccine genes would be dangerous. So although vaccines-bearing fruit promise easy, needle free, vaccinations strict containment is vital.

Their ability to generate yet more viruses that attack a wide range of species should not be underestimated.

Dr Mae-Wan Ho, Genetic Engineering: Dream or Nightmare

Drugs from taboo animals

The creation of animals which produce pharmaceutical products raises totally new medical and ethical issues. Someone whose religion makes the eating of pork or beef, for example, taboo may have the same taboo on medication which has been produced by a pig or a cow. So the religious and ethical implications need to be discussed *before* such products are routinely used. If full labelling detailing the animal source isn't a condition of licensing it may be far harder to introduce it later – and deeply held beliefs may be violated by certain medical treatments. But unless the public initiates the discussion the licensing authorities are unlikely to even consider it.

GE Skin Creams

Plant oils, such as rape and soya, are used in many skin creams and may be included not only in cosmetics but also in creams used medically. The unpredictability of GE crops means there is always a risk that any GE plant oil may prove to be allergenic. This possibility should now be considered if there is a reaction to any cream.

Genetically Engineered Drugs and Treatments

Among all the applications of GE this stands out as the most appropriate and least controversial, and one of the least-known areas is tissue engineering. Tissue engineers are working on ways to engineer most human tissue, from bones and cartilage to the delicate structures of the nervous system. Skin graft replacements have been grown and used for the past ten years, but now it's possible to do quite remarkable things, such as promoting bone regrowth in the jaw, or creating veins to be used in grafts. The hope is that such tissues, grown from a patient's own cells, will greatly reduce the risk of complications and rejections and all the overheads, in human and financial terms, which accompany them.

∗ A GE drug designed to cure dwarfism has sales of $500 M – mainly to build the physique of those of average height.

Far better known and far larger in scale is the production of GE drugs, new vaccines and other medical treatments. Yet few people realise how many medical products are now produced by yeasts, bacteria and fungi which have been genetically engineered to create a 'pharmaceutical soup'. Such engineered products may now treat anything from cancer to strokes. There are also hopes that GE will allow the creation of totally new kinds of 'designer drugs' to treat conditions which have previously been untreatable. However, as with GE crops, there are doubts about the safety of some processes used to make them. And a question hanging over some GE medical products is whether the techniques used to make them will avoid needless exploitation of animals.

A child's needs

Somatic therapy, mainly done on babies after they are born, is an exciting area which may give a normal life to children who are gravely ill. For example, it's nine years since a little girl was born with the rare disorder, severe combined immune deficiency (SCID). For lack of one enzyme she was so vulnerable to germs that she would have spent her life in a plastic bubble. But doctors were able to introduce into her blood a gene which enables her to make that enzyme. Today she can go to school with other children. Some attribute this to the gene therapy, others to a drug she was on.

Gene therapies are being tried for various cancers, haemophilia, Duchenne muscular dystrophy, and many other disorders. The idea is to give people healthy DNA which will override malfunctioning or absent DNA. Such DNA can be delivered in surprising ways. At Britain's Windeyer Institute they have been developing a very concentrated gene aerosol

---

∗ Unfortunately patients sometimes develop immune reactions to engineered viral vectors used to deliver GE treatments.

which those with cystic fibrosis can breathe in – rather like using an asthma inhaler. However, somatic therapy is very much in an experimental stage, very rarely available, and may not be risk free. Those in this field are constantly turning away would-be patients who believe this work is in a far more advanced stage than it is.

The insulin story

Although GE medical products seem to be a success story, they aren't all trouble free. Insulin is a good example of a medication which has been around for years and which has also been produced by genetic engineering. Worldwide, about fifty million people have diabetes (*Diabetes mellitus*).

Diabetics don't produce enough of the hormone insulin and have trouble controlling their blood sugar levels. For over fifty years diabetics injected themselves with insulin from cattle or pigs. Not identical to human insulin, but it did the job. Then, in the 1980s, genetic engineers produced insulin from bacteria, which they claimed was identical to human insulin.

Marketed as 'human insulin', it seemed a step forward and, despite a higher price, most doctors switched to prescribing it. Then reports of problems began to come in. Some diabetics were no longer getting clear physical symptoms of blood sugar imbalance, such as sweating, weakness and hunger, and were in danger of unexpectedly going into a coma. Some also experienced personality changes.

A report commissioned for the British Diabetic Association (BDA) reveals that when patients reported these symptoms most doctors just explained them away, often saying it was just a matter of adjusting to the new insulin.

A diabetic doctor

Dr Matthew Kiln is both a diabetic and a specialist in diabetes. He says about three diabetics out of ten do better on animal insulin than on the supposedly perfect GE insulin. He contests the idea that problems only occur when people switch over. He himself switched to human insulin. Nine months later serious personality changes began. 'I just wasn't the reliable person I used to be. I'd get mood swings. I didn't realise I was changing but by wife would have left me if I'd stayed on it. Quite a lot of people have got divorced afterwards and blame it on the insulin, and it's understandable.'

Back on animal insulin, he became himself again. Experimentally, he tried 'human insulin' again. After a 'honeymoon' period he again changed into the person his wife nearly left. Yet his consultant tried to persuade him that he was imagining things. It took his wife's insistence to convince the consultant that the changes were real.

Jenny Hirst, who now runs the helpline for the Insulin Dependent Diabetics Trust, which advises those with such problems, had a similar experience with her diabetic daughter. But on top of the mood swings there was a massive weight gain, and disastrous exam results. Within three days of returning to animal insulin her weight began to drop, and her memory and academic ability returned.

Jenny Hirst feels many doctors have put undue trust in the perfection of biotech products and that this has led them to deny the reality of changes in their patients.

What makes me angry is it destroys people's lives. People have lost their jobs, lost their driving licences, had accidents. And the behavioural changes destroy relationships. People who've never been aggressive in their lives can become really aggressive and even violent.

Jenny Hirst, Insulin Dependent Diabetes Trust

The implications for GE drugs

At least seven out of ten people seem fine on GE insulin but any medication can cause unexpected side effects. Normally patients are believed when they say they have side effects. The overwhelming picture from the BDA report is that, on GE insulin, they were not. It looks as if the fact that the insulin was genetically engineered, and claimed to be identical to human insulin, led doctors to discount genuine side effects. This exemplifies a recurring problem. All too often, those in key positions to blow the whistle when GE shows signs of going astray are too starry-eyed about this new technology to accept the evidence.

Insulin may not be the only GE treatment to cause problems There are reports that when some people with Gaucher's disease were switched to a GE version of the treatment, they experienced a reaction they didn't have with the older version. Here as with insulin, not everyone was affected. Clearly, GE drugs may contain unknown substances, to which some people react badly. So shouldn't there be a scheme to alert doctors to this risk? Yet there seems to be a dangerous reluctance to admit that this blue-eyed baby of the techo-era isn't perfect.

Clearly what's happening is that these products which are supposed to be totally pure aren't and have unknown contaminants which may, or may not, be part of the genetic engineering process.

Dr Michael Antoniou, medical geneticist, Kings College, London

In licensing engineered products the authorities seem to have done nothing to ensure that doctors knew that GE was not infallible. Nor did they stipulate that the older versions must

✳ Before the GE growth hormone, children with pituitary dwarfism were injected with growth hormones from corpses. Some developed CJD.

not be withdrawn. This shows serious lack of forethought. For any company with a new medicine is likely to price it more highly than the older one. Then, by the normal laws of business, the less paying proposition will be phased out. Already non-GE insulin is on the way out. Yet, despite the evidence of serious reactions to GE insulin, and the higher cost to the NHS of GE insulin, such is the charisma of GE that the authorities appear to think it can do no wrong and ignore the issue.

Medical choices axed

The fact that drugs are set to be a booming area of genetic engineering makes this replacement of normal drugs with engineered ones a serious threat to health care. To retain choice, for doctors and patients alike, GE drugs should only have been approved on condition that normal ones aren't discontinued.

There is a large group of patients, on long-term medication, whose whole quality of life depends on a carefully adjusted drug-dose regime. Any change in formulation can send such patients back to square one – bringing pain, illness or side-effects. Since individuals differ in their response to drugs, there will always be some who react to the engineered version of a drug.

Because genetic engineering interferes with the complex and *very little understood* mechanisms of nature, that will apply even if the manufacturer believes the product to be an identical twin to that in the human body. With genetic engineering there is only one rule: expect the unexpected. Manufacturers may *say* two molecules, two drugs or two plants are identical, but they cannot possibly *know* they are identical because the

---

∗ GE drugs offer rich pickings: the world pharmaceutical market is worth US$297 billion.

science which would underpin that knowledge doesn't yet exist.

If you aren't on long-term medication you may feel this doesn't affect you. But GE isn't just being used to make drugs for the chronically sick. It's being used to create products for every aspect of medicine including brief medication and accidents and emergencies. So your life could depend on your personal reaction to a GE product. If effective, long-established drugs are already being withdrawn in favour of GE counterparts, your future health could be in jeopardy and the cost of health care needlessly increased. Yet there is a serious risk of this happening across the board.

Nutraceutical and Functional Foods

Genetically engineered 'health foods' are tipped as tomorrow's boom area. Like the food supplement tryptophan implicated in so many deaths and illnesses, these 'functional foods' are likely to come from great 'vats' of engineered micro-organisms producing vitamins, amino acids and so on.

These will create, or be added to, a food product and sold at a premium price as a dietary supplement Perfect for drug companies tired of the long and expensive vetting procedure needed for medicines, and wanting a faster return on research.

However, the fact that the industry seems to think there will be a big demand for dietary supplements suggests they may know what we don't know. Engineered genes are unstable and evolving. Could it be that the companies know that GE crops are likely to become less nourishing with time?

∗ The nutraceuticals market is predicted to be $30 M a year.

Genetic Screening

> The science of genetics has been transformed into a major
> new industry, with public and private investment con-
> tinuing to skyrocket ... Much of this research focuses
> on genetic diagnostics: tests designed to identify genes
> thought to be associated with various medical conditions.
> More than 50 genetic tests have been developed in the
> past 5 years.
>
> The Council for Responsible Genetics (USA)[2]

'It runs in the family,' we say. The idea that certain looks and
characteristics are passed down from generation to generation
is universal. So you might expect that genetic research would
be revealing a mass of inherited conditions. Not so. The human
genome still holds many secrets but, so far, specific genes
linked to particular medical conditions are proving hard to
find. Genetic engineering may have enabled science to create
'more than fifty' genetic tests but no one has found that many
conditions which depend on a single gene. Single gene disorders and conditions seem to be rare. Nonetheless, genes
allegedly 'for' homosexuality, Alzheimer's disease, cystic
fibrosis and Huntington's disease have made world headlines.
So how far can such labelling be taken?

Most inherited conditions seem to be connected to a number
of genes. Yet already some researchers claim that knowing
your genes means knowing how you, or your children, will
die. Is this true? What about emotion, and the man who had
cancer and laughed himself better? Are 'predictive' genes any
more than clues to a human being's destiny? And what costs
and benefits do such tests carry?

* Bone marrow cells give rise to our blood cells. There have
  been attempts to insert functioning genes into bone marrow
  to replace faulty genes.

No more gene dictators

Many people have the idea that genes are destiny and that genes are some sort of master-puppeteers that are jerking our strings, sexual and otherwise . . . that's a very incorrect view of how genes act.

Dean Hamer, ABC-TV *Four Corners* programme, 1994

Dean Hamer was the man who discovered what was dubbed 'the gene for homosexuality' yet it's clear from those words that he did not see genes as dictators. The more that human genes are understood the clearer it becomes that, like all other genes, they form a dynamic and fluid community, work together in groups, move around, and respond to the 'world' around them. Since they are so reactive, our genetic inheritance doesn't give us a blueprint but a range of possibilities. And some aspects of our genetic potential may never be activated. That's just as true of genes predisposing you to illness, as of genes giving a child on a desert island the potential to play great golf.

The biologist Garland Allen pointed out that we shouldn't talk about a gene *for* some factor but about *a gene which has a norm of reaction*. Something normally has to happen before your genes react by bringing out a particular characteristic. As genes collaborate, the gene usually has to get others to join in. The question is: what activates genetic possibilities? We've all met people whose 'obesity gene' is switched on when their partner leaves them. But whether it collaborates with the 'death by chocolate' gene or the 'curry is heaven' gene may depend on both ancestry and experience. That is a frivolous and totally fictitious example. Yet it's far closer to the way genes really work than the false belief that if your parents are fat you must have an obesity gene and will get fat too.

✻ Genetically engineered beta-interferons are used in the treatment of multiple sclerosis.

Genes and expectations

According to aerodynamics bumble-bees can't fly. Luckily they don't know they can't.

Anon – from a poster my daughter loved

Psychology tells us that beliefs and expectations hugely influence our performance. If you think you're a fool you'll do poorly, no matter how high your IQ. But if you think you're brainy you can outperform your equals. Being what we think we are applies just as much to illness as to brains. Research shows that our mental state affects how efficiently our body fights disease.

Genes can tell us only part of the story about why some people get sick and others do not. Even if we are able to know exactly what genes a person has (and we are a long way from doing that) we would still be unable to predict their future health needs.

The Council for Responsible Genetics (USA)[3]

The more sensitive genetic tests become the more genetic testing will pinpoint the genes which carry a potential – no more than that – for a particular disease. Unfortunately, this may, in itself, be a killer. The danger is that, as genetic screening becomes more common, people will think the results are far more predictive than they are. So someone may imagine they are destined to have a particular illness. As there is a powerful feedback mechanism between emotions and the immune system, controlling the body's ability to fight off illness or heal, that could be life threatening. It's therefore important that the limitations of genetic screening are understood.

* There is a risk that gene replacement therapies could cause disease and generate virulent viruses.

Buck-passing genes

Regarding genes, and genetic screening, as predictive also provides an excuse for buck-passing. Already, the lion's share of research on cancer, and many other conditions, is devoted to developing treatments from which pharmaceutical companies can profit. Far smaller sums go into research on the relationship between diseases and the pollution of air, water and land by toxic chemicals – often manufactured by those same companies. Genes which predispose to cancer or certain other conditions may well make people vulnerable to certain pollutants. Blaming genes alone for illnesses focuses attention away from a situation which could be changed onto one which can't. The central question is: how does chemical pollution interact with genetic predispositions? A question drug companies aren't queuing up to answer.

There is already a danger that, searching for scapegoats, genes and genetic tests may be misused to explain behaviour or to stigmatise. In one American city there was a proposal to look for a criminality gene in black youths. By such reasoning Welsh miners might have been held to carry genes for lung disease. That may seem absurd, but crazier things have been proposed.

Having, lacking and faulty

Surprisingly, an expert in genetic medicine could not think of a single condition that was due to the presence of a normal gene. For, although all the talk is about genes for X or Y it's the *lack* of a functioning gene which may be most medically predictive. And it's this that many genetic tests are looking for. If a key gene is missing or damaged the body may be unable to do something it needs to do, or may perform in a way that causes problems.

Although genes aren't *dictators*, some medical conditions will almost always occur if a particular gene is missing or faulty.

That's the case in a range of medical conditions, including muscular dystrophy, thalassaemia, sickle-cell anaemia, haemophilia, Huntington's disease and cystic fibrosis.

Some of those diseases can take years to show. The symptoms of Huntington's disease, for example, usually start between the ages of thirty and fifty. Until then, potential sufferers can live normal, healthy lives. Some people in families with a genetic condition may want to know if they too lack the gene, so they can make the most of what years they have. Others may prefer not to know. The value of genetic screening depends on whether they are allowed that choice.

Bill Clinton used to wax lyrical about the day when a baby would come complete with a print-out of its genetic future saying, 'All kinds of decisions about your child will be made on the basis of that information'.

His dream is still a long way off, and if it ever came true it could well be a nightmare. Parents and schools might treat a child very differently if they knew its life would be blighted by some future disease.

Genetic Screening and Eugenics

In 1995 China introduced compulsory screening for those about to marry. The screening includes tests both for sexually transmitted diseases, such as AIDS, and for hereditary diseases – including some 'hereditary' diseases which are only possibilities, not certainties.

Those with so-called hereditary diseases may only marry if they agree to measures to prevent children, such as long-term contraception and sterilisation. So genetic screening is already being used to limit personal freedom and 'improve' at least one race.

Screening for breast cancer

Genetic tests for breast cancer show both multiple genes and patenting at work. Breast cancer has links with mutations in at least four genes, two important and two minor. In 1994 the American company Myriad Genetics discovered that mutations in a gene called BRCA1 were linked with breast and ovarian cancer. The same year a British team discovered that mutations in BRCA2 were also linked to breast cancer. The American company patented its test and charges over £1,000 for it. The British researchers had to patent theirs, or others might have done so, but allowed another company a licence on their patent on condition that it was free to the British NHS, and sub-licensed to hospitals and 'non-profit organisations'. Two very different attitudes.

> 'If it's not patented, you won't get some group to spend money to develop it, and you won't get a high-quality, inexpensive test.'
>
> Mark Skolnick of Myriad

> 'We do not believe pieces of the human genome are inventions; we feel it is a form of colonization to patent them . . . I don't think it is appropriate for [such genes] to be owned by a commercial company because . . . there is inevitably a demand for profit,'
>
> Mike Stratton, who gave BRCA2 to the NHS.[5]

Current research suggests that having faults on those genes only increases the risk of breast cancer in those who have a family history of breast cancer. Equally, if these genes are normal someone with a family history of breast cancer may be at no greater risk of contracting it than anyone else. For

✷ Part of the US Orthodox Jewish community is encouraging young Jews to test for Tay–Sachs disease before marriage.

such a woman from such a family to have a test and discover her genes were fine could be life changing. Unfortunately, when such tests are as highly priced as Myriad's policy has made its test the less well off will rarely get them.

Mind over matter

In 1994 *Time* magazine featured a woman surrounded by photographs of relatives who'd died of breast cancer, with the caption 'Malignancy is simply part of her pedigree'. How does it feel to be such a woman? To feel predestined to develop a dread disease? Being destined to get breast cancer is not the same as being destined to die from it. Yet how could this woman's immune system be fighting fit after posing for such a photograph?

A growing threat to freedom?

The information produced by these tests is increasingly being used out of context in ways that are contrary to the interests of the patient. This practice, called genetic discrimination, affects a growing number of people.[6]

P. Brown & K. Kleiner, *New Scientist*, 1994

The British government has recently set up an advisory committee on genetic screening. The challenge lies in developing valuable and moderately priced genetic tests. And in setting up ethical codes for the use of genetic tests which take account of personal rights, and of the impact of such tests, rather than being driven by administrative convenience or profits.

Drug companies develop these tests, or buy the patents on them, and market them very effectively. Mail-order screening tests are already sold for some conditions, and in America genetic tests are already a routine part of diagnosis. Elsewhere their day is rapidly dawning. In America it hasn't been hard to persuade insurance companies and employers to do so, and Britain has begun to follow suit.

In most countries nobody can force you to take a genetic screening test – but even here refusing could count against you. So, in reality:

- people may be forced to take screening tests they don't want
- so they are forced to learn if they have genes for a fatal disease
- carrying the weight of that knowledge may take the joy from their lives
- the knowledge may prevent them marrying and/or having children
- they may be excluded from long-term training (e.g. medical school)
- employers may assume they'll be dead soon and choose not to promote them
- health and life insurance may be impossible to get
- lacking life insurance they may be refused mortgages

The stress of all this might make an inevitable disease show sooner, or cause a predisposition to turn into a disease when it might not have done so. Death by genetic screening, you might say. And with a condition such as Huntington's disease every brother, sister and child has about a 50 per cent likelihood of having the disease too. So, if one person in a family has a test it can blight a circle of lives – especially if there is no counselling or support.

Doors slam on insurance and jobs

Already, in Britain, genetic screening for a range of ailments can be a condition of life assurance policies of over £100,000.

✴ Scientists have warned that GE crops with antibiotic resistant genes in them make it harder to treat fatal diseases such as meningitis, typhoid, and AIDS related illnesses.

It is probably only a question of time before such screening applies to insurance more widely. The risk is not just that an individual's right not to know their future will be infringed but that they may end up uninsured, or paying a far higher premium. For some companies may apply the results ignorantly or retrospectively. In America, people have been refused insurance cover for having a 'cancer gene' – even though it indicated only a potential, not a certainty. Americans insured for medical care have also had their insurance invalidated by a genetic test taken later, the companies claiming that they had a 'pre-existing condition' which would have rendered them uninsurable. That is not allowed in Britain – yet – but if you are taking out insurance, and fail to declare the results of a genetic screening test in your application your insurance will be invalid. All this inevitably means that some people will refuse life-saving screening tests lest they lose the chance of insurance cover.[7] The Advisory Committee on Genetic Testing monitors, and aims to prevent the misuse of such tests but they cannot alter human nature.

Genetic tests could also close other doors. Someone's chances of selection for higher education, jobs and promotion could be reduced to a matter of odds. Instead of simply assessing someone's ability, the odds on their 'useful life' might also be calculated. 'Why spend hard-earned taxpayers' money on educating people who may never pay it back?' governments may argue. 'Why train those who may not last the race?' or 'Why promote anyone who'll be dead before she reaches the top?' companies may say.

According to America's Office of Technology Assessment (OTA), some top companies already use genetic tests to screen out 'bad risks'. Unless such use is prevented by law, such testing, and such attitudes, could be adopted with frightening ease. For 'born less healthy than' is just a new version of the old idea that certain classes and races are born 'mentally less than'. This doesn't just harm those with genetic disorders. For it makes it easier for companies to see employees not as human beings bringing multiple intangible assets to an enterprise, but as cogs in a machine – cogs whose value is judged by how soon they may wear out. This penalises everyone, and changes the nature of employment. Yet such a policy doesn't even pay off in material terms. It would have written off the brilliant scientist Stephen Hawking, and business would have lost innovations from hundreds who burned brightly, if briefly.

Suspicion or test?

In a staff workshop on caring for chronic illness, Kim, an American social worker, spoke about her mother having Huntington's disease. Her employers knew that if her mother had it she had a 50 per cent chance of getting it too.[8] A week later she was fired – despite outstanding performance assessments only a month before. If mere suspicion can cause dismissal laws against discrimination on genetic grounds are clearly vital whenever such tests are used.

Ironically, had she taken a genetic test they might have discovered that she was among the other 50 per cent – the ones who haven't inherited the gene.

Perfect Babies: Shadows of Eugenics

Scientists are like space explorers: they have an irresistible urge 'to boldly go where no man has gone before'. That's fine when it's space. But when it's boldly changing the nature of your child or grandchild, boldness may not be quite what

---

✶ By 1931 thirty US states allowed eugenic sterilisation and tens of thousands had been forcibly sterilised.

you're looking for. However, the whole history of science is one of pushing back frontiers.

The sky's the limit

The huge step which some scientists want to take is to engineer a baby by altering the genes in the sperm and/or egg which create it. The crucial difference between this and all other genetic therapies used on human beings is that this 'germline therapy' not only changes the nature of the resulting baby but changes for good or ill its descendants.

In the early 1980s an important American report, 'Splicing Life', drew a sharp distinction between this 'germline therapy' and 'somatic therapy', also called 'gene therapy', which alters other cells. Germline therapy was deemed unacceptable. That is now the position throughout most of the world: even therapeutic work on egg cells is seen as too close to eugenics to be allowed.

However, there is pressure to lift the ban on modifying children-to-be. Already, scientists in America are talking of using such therapy to create people who are totally resistant to almost any disease – and of dramatically affecting intelligence. They seem to think that such therapy is coming, Few of their claims are likely to be fulfilled: genes are too complex for that. Yet the climate for such attempts is being created.

In treatments for infertility, babies which have been conceived in laboratories, are genetically screened as embryos before being implanted in the womb. This already gives parents a chance to decide what disabilities, if any, they will accept. As knowledge of human genes grows, that process may change. Saying 'no thank you' to a girl, or an embryo with a disability, may progress to refusing on wider and wider grounds. Parental eugenics has already begun. For some people germline therapy is the natural next step.

The risk of error

Not everyone sees it that way. In other areas of GE there have been extraordinary errors. What if they occur here too? Though some scientists confidently talk about 'tweaking' human genes, others say mistakes are unavoidable, the result inevitable.

> If widely applied [it] will progressively corrupt the blue-print of our species with genetic errors. These will irreversibly burden future generations with genetic diseases, causing millions to suffer. Such manufacturing defects cannot be recalled.
>
> Professor John Fagan, Wall Street Journal, 2 May 1997[9]

As a molecular biologist, John Fagan knows what he is talking about. Applying GE to a mammal's reproductive cells means altering every cell in the resulting body – including the reproductive cells of the next generation. An 'inevitable slip of the genetic scalpel', as he puts it, could result in genetic changes which would initially be undetectable yet lead to unknown disorders down the line and blight the lives of generations.

Unfortunately, success in somatic therapy is a two-edged sword: the more it succeeds, the more people will see it as demonstrating how well GE can work – so why not allow germline therapy too? If it fails it will create pressure to use germline therapy instead. But to what end?

A dark history

There was a British TV series enticingly called *Perfect Babies*. But what is a perfect baby? Who is to define it? If people can choose to have 'perfect' babies, what price is acceptable for this 'advance'? And how will society deal with the immense

✳ Sweden practised eugenic sterilisation from 1922–1976.

moral and social challenges the altering of babies brings? These are questions which the human race may be ill equipped to answer wisely.

Altering babies also brings other serious dangers. Logically, if some babies are perfect and totally desirable, other babies must be, by comparison, imperfect – and undesirable. The history of what happens to those seen as undesirable is shameful – and recent. In the 1930s Germany had some of the world's most knowledgeable geneticists. Some of them fostered Hitler's dream of an 'ideal' Aryan race and encouraged him to improve Germany's gene pool by killing 'undesirables' such as gypsies, homosexuals, cripples, the mentally ill and, of course, Jews. The infamous Josef Mengele, who tortured twin children in Auschwitz to study their responses, was a geneticist seeking answers on heredity.

It is worth remembering that there have also been more secret genetic 'purifications'. Countries widely regarded as civilised, such as America and Sweden, have sterilised people against their will as 'unfit' to have children. Officialdom had decided which babies were fit to be born and which were not. Aboriginal children were forcibly taken from their parents and placed with white families, on the assumption that it was better for them (or at least for society). Whatever reasons were given for this cruelty, it suggests an underlying belief that all Aboriginal parents were bad and all white parents good. The key difference was their genes.

Babies with bathwater

Even on scientific grounds re-engineering a human being is a problematic area. The impression is sometimes given that all that needs to be done is to whip out one gene and slot in another to produce a Mozart instead of a drop-out. In reality far too little is known about genes to do any such thing, and what *is* known suggests that very often a gene which carries a disadvantage also confers an advantage. Swings and roundabouts apply in genetics just as they do in life. That is unlikely to stop attempts to create 'perfect' babies being on the agenda before long. Initially germline therapy will only be used to treat illness, but such limitations are unlikely to last.

Some physical illnesses go hand in hand with mental disabilities. It will seem the natural thing to treat both – to restore a child to 'normal' and give it a chance of a 'normal life'? It is, however, a very small step from removing a disability to trying to introduce an ability. Of course, since genes are part of a gene community, and most qualities are attributable to several genes, or even to many, there is no guarantee whatever that tampering with human genes can confer any benefits However, people will almost certainly try. It is hard to say which will be more tragic – success or failure. One will spur people on to ever greater eugenics. The other will result in dead and disabled babies damaged by human meddling.

> I suggest projects should be vetted by ethical committees comprised of eminent people in various disciplines. Such ethical committees should be universal.
>
> Professor Sir Joseph Rotblat, Nobel Prize winning physicist

Enginering human beings may seem outlandish. But genetic engineering assumes that nature is a defective machine which can be improved by man-made genetic changes. If it proceeds to change every other area of life why should human beings be left out? It is the logical next step in the increasing masculinisation of childbirth which has led to women having less and less control over the process and to a soaring rate of Caesarians.

As this mind-set increasingly encourages people to see nature as defective, we can expect more and more babies to be conceived in laboratory dishes, and either carefully selected or

---

* 300 American parents have sued doctors for 'wrongful births' – allowing a disabled child to be born.

genetically modified. At present the main limiting factor is that modifying animals has yet to be perfected and an enormous amount of 'wastage' occurs. Such wastage might be unacceptable if human embryos were the discards. But they're working on it.

All this isn't just a matter of science but of human values – and the value of a human being. Once 'modified' babies become possible there is a risk that to have a child which is visibly 'imperfect' could become socially unacceptable. With medical costs rising there could be strong economic pressures to regard parents who simply want the child nature creates, with all its abilities and disabilities, as socially irresponsible. Such attitudes don't just disadvantage the disabled and their families; they alter what a society values in every human being – from the most to the least able – rating someone's least important and most superficial aspects above their inner qualities.

State-controlled babies

It is not too far-fetched to think that, in time, parents might lose the right not only to have the child nature gives them but even to decide how it will be changed. Criteria could subtly shift from what parents want to what is economically desirable or saves taxpayers the burdens of long-term healthcare.

A baby's very identity having been decided in a laboratory, why should nature be allowed to do the rest? Mechanical wombs don't yet exist but a false stomach does, so wombs may not be far off. No less a publication than *Scientific American* described four years ago how a baby could be gestated in a fluid-filled artificial womb. A professor of medical ethics at the University of Virginia even had the gall to suggest that it would be an improvement on nature:

The womb is a dark and dangerous place, a hazardous environment. We should want our potential children to be where they can be watched and protected as much as possible.

Professor Joseph Fletcher[10]

If genetically engineered babies and artificial wombs became available, what price the right of parents to do it the 'old-fashioned' way? For a woman to lose working hours by 'primitively' using her own womb? Such a dramatic change of attitude may seem unlikely. But why should it be? It's not so long since big business convinced women that baby formula was better than breast milk – and made many women feel that breast-feeding 'like an animal' was disgusting. Some women, against all logic and medical evidence, still remain convinced that what is unnatural is best – and in the Third World babies are still dying because of it. If we can be fooled once, how can we be sure we won't be fooled again? Think of the money to be made by all the technology involved and by producing special nutrients to be dripped into artificial wombs – and the marketing budgets companies would deploy to convince us it was best for babies. If one medical professor can back such an idea, how many doctors might not join him?

Suppose too that preconceptual correction of genetic 'faults' becomes the norm. Will those who become pregnant accidentally be compelled to have abortions? Or will their children, born with disabilities into a world of 'perfect' children, be viewed as freaks? Could we see a gradual return to the view that those with disabilities are less than human? Alternatively, will the manipulation of human genes to avoid hereditary illnesses become too great a drain on the public purse? Will it become a rich person's privilege to have children without certain disabilities? Could Professor Lee Silver's warnings

---

✳ A Harris poll in 1992 showed 43 per cent of Americans would approve of gene therapy to improve a baby's physical characteristics.

become reality: a society divided into the modified 'gene rich' and the 'gene poor'?

Animal Organs for Humans

> Twelve voices were shouting in anger, and they were all alike. No question, now, what had happened to the faces of the pigs. The creatures outside looked from pig to man, and from man to pig, and from pig to man again: but already it was impossible to say which was which.
>
> George Orwell, *Animal Farm*

The world shortfall of organs for transplants is about 100,000 organs – and the market for them worth about $6 billion. So animal organs (xenotransplants) may seem a way to meet that demand. At present such transplants are banned. But there could be huge money in them, so companies like Novartis hope such bans will soon be revoked. Meanwhile, animals are being engineered with human genes in the hope of reducing rejection. Pigs have been chosen as being closest to humans, but even so there are a lot of differences between pigs and humans. Even monkeys immediately rejected pigs' hearts. However, during an operation, human blood has already been passed through a pig's kidney, outside the patient's body.

What they call 'the graft survival time' was 'improved', in monkeys, when the hearts came from pigs modified with certain human genes. But they were still rejected. To stop that rejection, anyone who receives a pig organ may need to take drugs which suppress their immune responses. Nobody knows how long such drugs would be needed, and, while on them, the user would be open to infection.

There is only limited information to suggest how well a foreign organ might function in a human subject, yet clearly this question is of the greatest clinical importance.

Dr Jeffrey Platt, xenotransplant researcher, Duke University USA[11]

The virus wild card

Even so, external infection wouldn't be the biggest risk. The most serious danger is of the organ transferring an unidentified animal disease to its human host. In 1997 it was found that an unknown pig retrovirus could infect human cells in vitro. By engineering a pig to be closer to humans, and transferring the organ across, animal and human viruses are brought into intimate contact: an ideal situation for enabling them to go one step further and combine into new, serious and possibly fatal human diseases, which any pig-heart carrier could transmit to the rest of the human race perhaps causing an epidemic as serious as AIDS.

> Most new pandemics arise through inadvertent transmission of viruses from another species ... to humans ... Scientists do not have the luxury of a crystal ball for predicting the outcomes of these experiments. What we do have is AIDS as a reference point.
>
> J.S. Allen, Science[13]

So great is the risk of such infection that when a group of American researchers called for a moratorium on xenotransplants, their grounds were that, even if a particular patient benefited from an animal organ, the risk to the rest of the population was too great for the decision to be left to an individual and a medical team. They recommended that such transplants should have to be approved by a regulatory body which would include ordinary citizens as well as experts.

* Amgen's GE drug Erythropoietin is successfully used by hundreds of thousands of kidney dialysis patients.

Doubtful benefits

Even setting such infections aside the risks may outweigh the potential benefits. For there is no certainty that the heart of a creature that lives on all fours will function well in a vertical human. Nor can it be expected to last very long – pigs live some fifteen years. Similarly, a pig's liver may not be able to process the substances encountered by a human liver. Richard Nicholson, editor of the *Bulletin of Medical Ethics*, estimated that, even if the xenotransplant works perfectly, it will only increase life expectancy by 0.02 per cent.

There is also the curious fact that some people who have heart transplants seem to undergo changes of personality. There is growing physiological and psychological evidence to show that memory doesn't simply 'live' in our heads: our body carries memories of our life's experiences.[14] It's too early to say whether the organs which might be transplanted – such as the heart, lungs, liver and kidneys – are exempt from memories. If they aren't, a human body would contain not just a pig organ but an element of pig consciousness. A curious thought.

There are other issues to be considered. The psychological impact of accepting any transplanted organ is huge. To accept it from an animal would be extraordinary. How would you see yourself if you knew your very life depended on a pig's heart? Would you feel that you were, in part, no longer fully human?

Baboon man

The bodies of two patients who, in 1992, under Dr Thomas Starzi, received baboon livers were directly affected by the implanted organs.[16] Though one only lived for twenty-six and the other for seventy days 'baboonisation' took place. Baboon white blood cells, cholesterol, albumin and other factors appeared in every tissue of the body. Knowing that one's blood was becoming more like that of an animal would not only be disturbing psychologically; it could disrupt the intricate inter-actions of the body itself. The companies waiting impatiently in the wings for the moratorium on xenotransplants to be lifted and human transplants to go ahead don't seem to under-stand that human beings aren't cars. The human body is an interactive system in which you cannot unbalance one part without unbalancing the whole.

Yet why would they not push ahead? Having once been free, transplant organs have become a multimillion-pound world-wide business – and money is the name of the game. However, the final irony is that. If the use of substances such as BST continues to boost the use of antibiotics in farming, and antibiotics continue to be used as casually as they are currently used, transplants may become too dangerous to undertake at all. For there will be no cure for post-operative infection.

˙ Cloning People

Of great concern is the way human biological material is being taken into private ownership . . . Thinking ahead, we need to consider the prospect of human clones and human-animal hybrids being taken into private multi-national ownership. Changed life-forms can now be owned by multinational corporations. This . . . threatens human independence and freedom, human health and survival.

Manfred Davidman, 'Creating, Patenting and Marketing New Forms of Life', 1996[17]

'Which Elvis would you clone? Young Elvis?' Of course not, I'd clone big fat Elvis.'

Club Buggery, ABC-TV, 16 August 1997

According to some scientists it's already possible to clone human beings. When patents on the techniques used to create

Dolly the sheep were applied for, the application originally covered humans too. That is no longer so. Shortly after Dolly was cloned, President Clinton, a man well versed in drawing fine lines, banned the use of government money for research on human cloning. This does not mean that research is not continuing.

Having cloned Dolly, the Roslin Institute set up Roslin Bio-Med to exploit its cloning expertise commercially. Having bought all Bio-Med's shares, an American company now plans to use human cloning to develop treatments for conditions ranging from diabetes to Parkinson's disease. Unfortunately, the step from that work to a cloned human being may only be a matter of implantation. Currently the question is not whether a human being will be cloned, but when. In a sense, it has already happened. Scientists in Korea claim to have cloned a human being and taken the embryo to the stage at which it would normally be implanted before destroying it. That work could be taken further in any country with lax laws and able scientists. And there are plenty of them.

> Mainstream commentators, including 'bioethicists', are already peddling the idea of cloning dying children.
>
> The Council for Responsible Genetics[18]

Yet the idea of cloning human beings is almost universally regarded with alarm. Around the world human cloning has been the subject of bans and debates. The most alarming feature is that people are drawing fine distinctions about when cloning may and may not be acceptable – ignoring the fact that a human being is more than a lump of meat. Scientists have, for example, said that there should be no ethical objections to cloning human embryos for use in research. Provided they are not implanted, embryos could be used for a whole host of experiments and research projects. It wouldn't – in scientific eyes – be a human being that was being used in this way. This was, amazingly, the position taken by a paper published jointly in 1998 by Britain's Human Genetics Advisory Commission (HGAC) and the Human Fertilisation Embryology Authority (HFEA).[19]

As the idea of using animals as organ donors seems set to fail because of the enormous risks from infection, clones have been suggested as a solution. Apparently it needn't even involve the growing of whole donors. In 1997, when British scientists created a headless frog embryo, it was heralded as the first step towards headless human clones which could provide organs for transplants.

If a headless body, why not a bodyless head? Come in, science fiction, all is forgiven. But is it? When such things are done by science they are done on behalf of us all. They are regulated by people appointed by those we have voted for, and done in the name of medical progress, Progress from which we may benefit – however indirectly. What are we prepared to have done in our names? Where does research end and abuse of science begin? What is life? And what is a human being? If genetic engineering progresses at its current pace it will not be very long before any one of us may be involved in personal decisions about where to draw the lines – about how to respect the essence of life without depriving the sick of healing. We will each have different answers. The important thing is that we do not accept the idea that possessing a particular gene stamps our future, or the future of any human being. That we remain aware of the value of the stuff of life which genetic engineering now treats merely as raw materials. Most important of all, we should not leave all these issues to others, otherwise:

... we shall slip quietly and insensibly into an era of human genetic engineering dictated purely by corporate interests exploiting the sick and the gullible for profit, while simultaneously giving rein to the worst excesses of human prejudices.

Dr Mae-Wan Ho

10

Patents: Patently Wrong

Three Myths

You own your body.
A living thing can't be patented.
If genes couldn't be patented it would hamper research.

They're not only taking living blood. They've been
opening graves and taking from the dead. Going into
museums and sampling mummies. But they don't seem to
think how it's violating people – and all they hold sacred.

Dr Pauline Lane, social anthropologist, University of East London

Genetic engineering has not only reshaped nature. Behind our
backs its applications have affected key aspects of patent law
in ways that touch every one of us. Patents, granting exclusive
rights to commercial exploitation for 17–20 years, have been,
and are, the fuel in the engine of genetic engineering (GE).
Without them the industry would be very different. As it has
expanded, patents have both fostered it and become the main
limiting factor. Since profit is the main aim what can't be
patented won't, on the whole, be done. By default, patent
officers worldwide have become the guardians of public safety
and ethics, a role which may be neither welcome nor appropriate in a controversial field, with immense ramifications for the

human race. Faced with such an unlooked-for role they might have adopted the precautionary principle. They did not.

Biotechnology companies, which unthinkingly change the nature of living things, now call themselves 'the life industry' and pretend to foster life. Their 'fostering' has made life itself a commodity and created a multimillion dollar market for unusual, and exploitable, genes to use in GE.

Their industry has used patents to annex traditional knowledge from indigenous people, to take away our rights to our own bodies, and to gain monopolies on living things. Used them in ways which rob the poor of natural resources to enrich the already rich. And used them in ways which threaten the food supply of every one of us – rich or poor – the world over.

Today, biotechnology and patents have a circular relationship. Biotechnology puts patents on biological raw materials – blood, hair, plants and so on – uses them in genetic engineering, then puts another patent on the finished product. Through its use of patents, and all that stems from them, genetic engineering is reshaping attitudes to life itself, to the natural world, and to what it is to be human.

It is doing this without regard for what is sacred to individuals or communities, without regard for the integrity of nature, often without ethics, and frequently without the consent of the individuals or societies whose genetic inheritance is taken to enrich corporations.

In today's knowledge-based economy, intellectual property assets have surpassed physical assets, such as land, machinery, or labour, as the basis of corporate value. Life industry companies are securing and protecting information and technology via monopoly patents, and that quest is, in many cases, driving a restructuring of the industry.

Rural Advancement Foundation International (RAFI)[1]

Patent Injustice

Patents have a chequered history and dishonourable origins – stemming as they do from kings granting buccaneering explorers rights to discovered land. But that was 500 years ago. In this century patents came to be seen as a tool to protect the weak against the strong. They have been an easy and affordable way for individual inventors to safeguard their inventions against unjust exploitation by big business.

In most countries, the law set strict limits to what could be patented or become intellectual property. It was usually impossible to patent common knowledge, any form of life, or a discovery. However, since the advent of biotechnology, patent decisions in America have gradually removed those fundamental boundaries. Once the patenting of whole living things was possible in America, the pressure was on to harmonise patent laws worldwide to make it easier for bio-giants to take out identical patents in any country they wished.

The EU Directive introduced in 1998 made it possible to patent whole plants and human body tissue. Moreover, when the European Parliament inserted a clause that those whose body samples were patented must first give informed consent, the Commission deleted it, and the EU Parliament caved in. In Europe new biotech-friendly patent laws come into force in 2000, unless an appeal against them succeeds.

The adoption of such laws has been fiercely opposed by the Third World which sees Western patent laws as enabling bio-prospectors to patent their traditional medicine, their specialised crops and even their human genes.

---

* The 13th Amendment of the US Constitution forbids the granting of any property rights in a human being. That has not stopped US companies parenting human genes.

No individual, institution or corporation should be able to claim ownership over species or varieties of living organisms. Nor should they be able to hold patents on organs, cells, genes or proteins, whether naturally occurring, genetically altered or otherwise modified.

The Council for Responsible Genetics

Unfortunately, refusal to adopt such laws is only partial protection. Bio-prospectors can still take genetic material from the Third World and patent it elsewhere. So today, patent laws in the West have come full circle. Once more patents reward piracy, discovery and colonialism – the only difference is that now the discoveries are not land but genes. Patent law now enables big business to patent plant varieties carefully bred over centuries by Third World communities. It allows centuries-old medical knowledge to be patented by outsiders and upholds the rights of big business against those of individuals and communities.

Guess What?

What have all these got in common?

- a mouse which gets cancer easily
- cells from an umbilical cord
- basmati rice
- John Moore
- a Solomon Islander
- the neem tree

Answer: They have all been patented without consent.

Countries which are reluctant to adopt such laws may come under pressure from the World Trade Organisation (WTO) – an organisation which seems hell-bent on arming Goliath against David. This is being done despite the fact that such laws may violate not just the traditions of some countries but their deepest values. For the new patent laws of the industrialised world allow no place for respect for life, for the natural world, or even for that which is held sacred.

The bounty hunters

Biotechnology, and increasingly permissive patent laws, have fostered a new, ever more exploitative approach to the living world. Genetic material is now a richly marketable commodity. Today's bounty hunters are not buccaneering pirates sailing the high seas but smooth-talking, smart-suited gene scouts who scour the world for plant, animal or human genes to sell for high prices to giant corporations. Bio-prospectors is the polite term for them, bio-pirates is what they often are. Yet the steps which have made life a commodity have seemed almost insignificant.

It had always seemed reasonable to exempt living things from patents. They were, after all, 'products of nature' as was every part of them. Humankind didn't invent plants, animals or cells. So how could anyone claim a monopoly on them by taking out a patent? But in 1980 that bedrock of patent law was shattered when an American court allowed the patenting of a genetically modified bacterium. It had been created to clear up the pollution of oil spills. Ironically, the legal pollution this decision caused has spread to every major landmass in the world. The next landmark decision was the patenting of the oncomouse – a mouse genetically engineered to be prone to cancer. For the first time a living animal was considered an 'invention'.

Today, if you undergo any medical procedure, they'd better not discover anything unusual. If they do, your blood could find its way into somebody's pocket and your genes into a gene bank – patented for others to profit from. In few countries will you even have any chance of redress – or a share in those profits. You may think you own your own body but you may not own all of it.

Patenting Humanity

A most alarming aspect of patenting life is the patenting of human genes, cell lines and tissues . . . these 'products of nature' are patentable once they have been isolated to produce a form not found outside the laboratory.

The Council for Responsible Genetics

The 'isolation' referred to here need not be very complex. It seems increasingly easy to patent human genes merely by the act of possessing them. That has, after all, isolated them from their owner. The case of John Moore was crucial.

Without His Consent

I am known as Patent #4,438,032. Some of you may be familiar with pieces of me in your laboratories . . .

I am concerned because the dehumanisation of having one's cells conveyed to places and for purposes that one does not know can be very, very painful. Why should I or any individual or group of individuals have their unique genetic materials borrowed, stolen, or bought for some fraction of their value for some project of others? . . . How can anyone set a price on what may be priceless or sacred to someone else? I am concerned because even in this country where the rights of the individual are supposed to be protected from the grasp of institutions, and certainly from the greed of private corporations and researchers, they are not . . . I have had a very sad experience.

John Moore, speaking before a committee of the US
National Academy of Sciences, 1996

An unjust precedent

In 1976 John Moore, an American, was being treated for a rare form of leukaemia which caused his spleen to swell to many times its usual size. His consultant, having noticed that John's blood contained unusual proteins, which might be used in other areas of medicine, took a blood sample and patented them – without John's knowledge or consent. In collaboration with the University of California the doctor then created a cell line which was sold to a Swiss pharmaceutical company for almost $9.5 million.

When John Moore eventually discovered what had happened he sued the doctor for a share of the money. After years of expensive wrangling the court agreed that the doctor should have told John what he was doing. Yet it ruled that John Moore did not own the cells from his body – and had no right to any of the money. In making that extraordinary ruling the court said that to allow him ownership of his cells would 'hinder research by restricting access to necessary materials'.

At a stroke the human body had legally been deemed a raw material, like coal, iron or oil. A raw material which could be taken at will to fuel the engines of the world's fastest-growing industry – biotechnology. That is not an American aberration. In much of the world the same applies, or will soon apply. In fact very soon we may all have to take out patents on ourselves just to hang onto our own bloodline – and be sure our genes aren't engineered into a pig.

> Our goal is now to have sequenced, mapped and filed for intellectual property all the novel and most commercially relevant genes by the second half of the year 2000.
>
> Incyte Pharmaceuticals[2]

✳ In 1991 the European Patent office granted its first patent on a human gene.

Who owns your body?

Under the two European patent laws, which apply in Britain and throughout Europe, a doctor could take a sample of your blood, to test for some suspected disorder, then put a patent on it without even asking for your consent. Here, as in America, obtaining informed consent is advised but not legally required.

Patent laws don't just allow others to patent your genes. They can also deny you access to your own cells. For example, the cells from umbilical cords, discarded after a birth, used to be freely available to treat bone marrow diseases. Then an American company took out a patent on them. The patent is being contested. But, if it's upheld, it will create an extraordinary injustice. Suppose umbilical cord cells are needed to treat a child's bone marrow disease. Its mother is about to have another baby, so she suggests that, after the birth, the baby's umbilical cord could provide the cells. What could be more natural? Yet, if the patent is upheld, she would have to pay the company in order to use cells which came from her own body. What is true of those human cells is becoming true of many others. And with every patent the cost of health care rises.

> Patents on life enclose the creativity inherent in living systems that multiply in self-organized freedom. They enclose the interior spaces of the bodies of women, plants, and animals. They also enclose . . . intellectual creativity by transforming publicly generated knowledge into private property.
>
> Dr Vandana Shiva, Director, the Research Foundation for Science,
> Technology and Ecology[3]

Cashing in on disability

The raw materials of genetic engineering – including human cells – are now traded as eagerly as stocks and shares. Companies large and small – gene giants, middlemen and prospectors – are all out to patent whatever they can get that is different. In the great patents race unusual cells can be very valuable. Yet it is not their original owners who make the killing. Anyone with an unusual genetic inheritance could find that, in the process of giving a blood sample or tissue for some personal health reason, or even while having an operation, the rights to their own genes have been taken from them.

Australian researchers found, in the DNA of a handicapped child, an unusual trait, which could be cloned for use in gene therapy for several disorders. The child's DNA was patented by an Australian drug company which now stands to make millions from it. Neither the child nor its parents are likely to get anything.

> There should be a ban on patenting human genes because they are 'discovered' not 'invented'.
>
> Bob Phelps, Director, Australian GenEthics Network

Body parts from babies

Since patents were first allowed on living things, companies have kept pushing back the frontiers. Yet there has been little discussion on what techniques, or life-forms, could morally be patented. When Stuart Newman and Jeremy Rifkin applied for a patent on a creature half man, half monkey, they did so only to draw attention to the extremes to which biotechnology and patenting are going.

> Rifkin and Newman point to work by Johns Hopkins researcher John Gearhart involving cells from aborted human embryos. Gearhart has applied for patents on the cells, which he hopes will further research on embryo development and may even be induced to grow into body parts.
>
> Rick Weiss, *Washington Post*, 11 May 1998

Not long afterwards, Bruce Lehman, Commissioner of the US Patent and Trademark Office, announced that he would deny patents to 'monsters' and other 'immoral inventions'. The Newman–Rifkin patent has been refused. But the question it rightly posed was: how many genes, how many cells, how much biological material, must go into another animal to make it a monster? That remains unanswered.

There has been no serious debate on how far GE should be allowed to go, and who should control it. In Britain such matters are reviewed by official committees. However, questions which challenge how a human being is defined surely go beyond the remit of any government committee. They raise ethical and religious issues about which many people feel strongly – issues which patent officers were never intended to regulate. Yet, worldwide they often regulate them by default, while the public are never consulted. Without anyone noticing government officials and committees have become the arbiters on life itself and on how a human being is defined. Is that what we want?

The vampire project

Perhaps the most astonishing aspect of all this is that making human genes a commodity has invited gene theft – a modern version of body-snatching which is now happening all over the Third World. In Victorian times the body trade shipped whole slaves from country to country. Today's body-snatchers do it a cheaper way – but they steal a human being's rights over his or her own body just as certainly.

* The worldwide market for cell lines and tissue cultures is over US\$500 M a year. It is expected to be over US\$910 M by 2002.

The human hit list

The Human Genome Project (HUGO) was launched in 1990, as a public undertaking by America and Britain, to decipher the whole genetic code of humankind. Since then HUGO has been gazumped by private enterprises, which are trying to race them to it. Linked to HUGO's respectable research is the Human Genome Diversity Project (HGDP) – otherwise known as 'the Vampire Project'. Its aim is to collect hair, skin and blood samples from 700 native peoples worldwide, and to catalogue their genetic codes. A project which combines genetic anthropology with prime opportunities to discover unusual genes which could be useful in genetic engineering.

> Over the last 200 years, non-Aboriginal people have taken our land, language, culture, health – even our children. Now they want to take the genetic material, which makes us Aboriginal people, as well.
>
> John Liddle, Director, Central Australian Aboriginal Congress[4]

No longer do white men open the mouths of slaves to check their teeth. Instead they open the mouths of indigenous peoples to get cheek scrapings. At this moment there are soft-spoken college graduates doing just that to log the tissue types and genes of other living human beings in what is called a catalogue of 'Isolates of Historic Interest'.

I downloaded from the Internet a sixteen-page 'hit list' of peoples from every corner of the globe whose genes are targeted for collection. It reads like anthropology from the 1930s, each group diminished to a neat number – those not yet dead. This is a tiny section of it:

Community	Country/Region	Population
Coorgis	Karnataka	300,000
Gawda	Goa	95,000
Namboodri	Kerala	100,000
Nairs	Kerala	200,000

Lyengar	Tamil Nadu	100,000
Vellalas	Tamil Nadu	300,000
Kalans	Tamil Nadu	100,000
Kammas	Andhra Pradesh	500,000
Reddis Chamars	Uttar Pradesh	300,000
Rastogis	Uttar Pradesh	100,000
Brahman Kayasthas	West Bengal	10,000
Thakurs	Bihar	500,000
Ahmediyas	Kashmir	100,000
Sarguja Brahmans	Madhya Pradesh	50,000
Aggarwais	Madhya Pradesh	100,000
Kalitas	Assam	200,000
Rajbansis	Assam	50,000
Syrian Christians	Kerala	100,000
Anglo-Indians	West Bengal	100,000
Cochin Jews	Kerala (Cochin)	800
Parsees (Zorostrians)	Gujrat	100,000
Moplas (Muslims)	Laccadives	100,000
Dawoodi Bohras	Rajasthan	10,000
Meos	Haryana/Rajasthan	1,000,000
Ladakhis	Kashmir	12,000
Tibetan Refugees	Himalchal Pradesh	10,000

Collecting their genes is not simply to enable the characteristics of these people to be catalogued. Such sampling is now done at the behest of both industry and governments. What the gene hunters are often looking for, in this new gold rush, are genes which can be exploited. The race is on to patent as many unique human genes as possible – for use in research, transgenic work with animals and other branches of biotechnology.

In this worldwide, multimillion-pound trade the case of the people of Tristan da Cunha is typical. Canadian bio-prospectors noticed their asthma rate was unusual. Their blood samples went to an American gene company which allegedly sold some of the rights to a German pharmaceutical giant for $70 million.[5]

Chillingly, the gene buyers may include those working on weapons of biological warfare. Biotechnology's growing skill with genes is paving the way for weapons which could be targeted at particular ethnic groups. So collecting the genes of indigenous people may provide the genetic insights needed for such targeting. Those involved in collecting the samples for the HGDP project are often private companies and there seems to be no restraint on how they obtain the genes or whom they sell them to.

> They . . . offered us diabetes tests while they took samples of our blood. We agreed. We had no idea that a few months later, our blood would be in the US being tested [and perhaps] exploited in ways of which we do not approve.
>
> Leonor Zalabata Torres, an Arhuaco leader from Colombia

In theory people whose genes are taken by the HGDP should give informed consent, but it isn't legally necessary. Even if their consent is sought, how can someone living deep in a forest, sharing food and possessions within a small community, even conceive of the avarice which would make rich men in smart clothes take her very blood, and her children's blood, to profit from it? The selfishness of a patent is inconceivable: the genetic manipulation which will exploit it beyond all imagining. Informed consent is therefore meaningless. This has not prevented the genes of such people being taken. Nor has if meant that requests for their return have been respected, as the following exchange shows.

Ambassador Rex Horoi
February 1, 1994

Mr. Ron Brown
Secretary of Commerce
United States Department of Commerce
Washington, D.C.

Dear Sir,

**Re: World and U.S. Patent Claim by the Government of the United States of America on Human Cell Line of Solomon Island Citizen
Publication Number: WO-9215325-A
Priority Application Number: US-662368**

In my capacity as the official representative of the Sovereign Government of Solomon Islands, I write to bring to your immediate and urgent attention the above matter.

Non-governmental organisations Swissaid and Rural Advancement Foundation International have brought it to our attention that the Government of the United States of America (Department of Commerce) has claimed both U.S. and World patents on material derived from the cell lines of at least two Solomon Island citizens. Details of the claims are attached.

On behalf of the Government of Solomon Islands, I request you to withdraw the patent claims, for the following reasons:

1. My Government believes, on moral grounds, that human genetic material should not be patentable.
2. As a matter of national sovereignty, we assert that the Government of the United States of America has no right to claim patent protection over material

derived from the cell line of a citizen of the Solomon Islands.

3. We believe that the people whose blood was sampled could not have given prior informed consent for the patenting and possible commercialization of material derived from their cell lines.

For these reasons, we respectfully ask you to withdraw your patent applications.

I would also like to point out and state unequivocally that arrangement for the repatriation of the material on deposit at the American Type Cultures Collection in Maryland must be made immediately as well.

It would be in the interest of my Government to expect an early response from you.

Mr. Secretary, your co-operation and assistance in this matter will be valued.

Yours faithfully,

Rex Horoi

Ambassador/Permanent Representative

But Ron Brown's reply was as follows:

His Excellency Rex Horoi
Permanent Representative of the
Solomon Islands Mission to the United Nations
820 Second Avenue
New York, New York 10017
Dear Mr. Ambassador:

Thank you for your letter concerning patent applications on a human cell line derived from Solomon Islanders. The applications, assigned to the United States Government, were filed both here and abroad.

Under our laws, as well as those of many other countries, subject matter relating to human cells is patentable and there is no provision for considerations relating to the source of the cells that may be the subject of a patent application. Should you have questions regarding the circumstances that led to the invention claimed in the patent applications to which you refer, you may want to contact Dr. Harold Varmus, Director of the National Institutes of Health, 9000 Rockville Pike, Building 1, Room 126, Bethesda, Maryland 20892.

Sincerely,

Ronald H. Brown

The [HGDP] project has very little interest in helping indigenous people to survive . . . For Solomon Islanders . . . the traditions and customs that protect the sanctity of human materials – be it blood, cloth, saliva, or mucus – are very strong. It pays no respect to our dignity, culture or identity, and at the same time it will eventually turn our people away from medical help.

Ruth Liloqula, Solomon Islander

Selling indigenous people

Officially the HGDP's aim is to preserve the genetic codes of every ethnic group in the world before shrinking tribes die out. The US government has claimed to have 'immortalised' human cell lines taken from those in such places as New Guinea, Panama and the Solomon Islands. I'm sure there are people involved in all of this who genuinely believe they are doing good and would be horrified to hear their work criticised. But which of us would consider ourselves, or our nation, to have been 'immortalised' by having our cells taken and refrigerated? Especially when the aim is often not only 'immortalisation' but exploitation.

There is a bitter irony in such genes being commercialised.

For the 'dying out' of indigenous people is usually due to the destruction of their way of life by encroaching industrialisation, destruction by the same industrialised world which plans to make money from their body samples. It is as if, before sending Jews to their destruction, the Nazis, as well as stacking their glasses and shoes for future use, also took samples of their hair, blood and skin to preserve their genes for later use.

Moreover, there is a risk that native people will be seen as redundant – once their genes have been collected. Already, a major reason why industry and governments even consider preserving rainforests is that the trees may yield valuable medicines. The genes of some native people may also lead to medical treatments. But, once their genes are secured, what price the people themselves? I am not suggesting that they will be slaughtered like the Jews, merely that 'Operation Vampire' is removing a major incentive to preventing their demise as human beings and communities.

> If there is concern for our demise, then help us survive on our own terms.
>
> The Chief Leon Shenandoah of the Onondaga Council of Chiefs

---

Eugenics Rides Again

The types of genes being collected for research approved by the HGDP suggests that they are not just being catalogued but that people are also looking for genes which could create a super-race – of animals or humans. Listed are:

- oxygen absorption genes from Tibet which improve 'reproductive fitness'
- genes from Mongolian cold-tolerant pastoral nomads
- resistance-to-cancer genes from the Plains Apache

A Bitter-Sweet Harvest

The giant companies driving forward genetic engineering have claimed that it will feed the Third World. What they do with Third World resources tells a different story. In Gabon there's a plant with extraordinary berries. They contain a sweetener 2,000 times more effective than sugar, weight for weight. Seeing locals eating it, a researcher took some, tested it, and an American university took out a patent on it.

This might have meant a fruitful berry trade. It didn't. To add insult to patenting injury, the berries were analysed, and a genetically engineered substitute created. GE substitutes for vanilla and coconut have also been created. In Madagascar 70,000 farmers depend on vanilla and GE coconut threatens the livelihoods of 21 million people in the Philippines and many more in Southern India. GE substitutes for other spices may follow, impoverishing farmers and damaging the exports of tropical countries. Yet poverty, not lack of food, is the root of Third World hunger.

Patenting Traditional Medicines

Genetic engineering has also created a huge demand for patentable plant genes. Here again bio-pirates have turned to the Third World. One of the great unsung resources of the non-industrialised world has always been knowledge of wild things. Of edible wild foods, medicinal plants, animals and

∗ A multinational pharmaceutical giant paid a prospector US$4 million for rights to a treatment used by local healers. The healers got nothing.

fungi, of leaves which will heal a cut, or soothe a burn. We in the industrialised world may be tempted to view the Third World through the tunnel vision of media images 'of' disaster and starvation, or the curious tasters afforded by brief holidays in luxury hotels. There is, however, another Third World, which few of us begin to understand: communities holding enormous local wisdom about the properties of everything around them.

This shared knowledge is their unwritten library, their treasure-house. It is not simply something they possess, as you or I might possess a book. It is not an acquisition, a property; it is the essence of their identity – part of what they are. As intrinsic to their culture as the language they speak and the clothes they wear. Only by applying that knowledge of the natural world down the generations have such communities survived. Survival not of the fittest, but of the wisest. Today bio-patenting is enabling big business to annex exploit their knowledge of medicinal plants and wild foods – without even giving anything in return.

Today's carpetbaggers

The term 'patent medicines' has always had a dubious ring to it. Yet the carpetbaggers of the Wild West seem positively virtuous compared to some bio-prospectors. National plant collections and indigenous people are being systematically raided for knowledge of medicinal plants which can profitably be patented for large corporations to use in biotech medicines and other pharmaceuticals. Patents which ignore the fact that indigenous plants have been used medicinally for centuries. As with human genes, the work is often undercover. A nice young botanist arrives at a remote village saying s/he is

---

∗ 57 per cent of the most frequently prescribed drugs in America originated in plants.

studying nature, then watches to see what the local people use as remedies.

Before long s/he'll be thanking the village and flying home with baggage full of patentable plants. Often a plant is patented for its traditional uses – the companies don't even have to be creative to get a patent. Consider these:

- **Turmeric**, for centuries used in India for healing wounds, was patented by Mississippi University for healing wounds.
- **Barbasco**, long used in the Amazon to paralyse fish, was patented by the UK's Foundation for Ethnobiology for, among other things, 'regulating muscular activity'.
- **The neem tree**, India's medicinal tree, has had substances from it patented by western companies for medicinal uses.

The catalogue of such thefts is long; the stories shabby. One rich university repeatedly pleaded poverty when asked to supply a translation of the contract local people had been asked to sign. Another proposed to fly in plant prospectors and soldiers to forcibly obtain medicinal knowledge from a remote tribe in South America. With extraordinary insensitivity even a sacred tree of South America has been patented.

A precious inheritance

When the remedies of the Third World are annexed and patented much more than the plants themselves are being stolen. With them goes inherited wisdom, which is priceless. People in non-industrialised countries have, for centuries, created their own remedies from natural sources. In countries like India these vital medicines have been used by rich and poor alike, but upon which the poor depend most heavily, the common property of everyone. Such remedies never were, or could become, private property. So, when the bounty hunters of the biotech industry use patent laws to steal them, they do more than annex what isn't theirs. They undermine a community.

Aboriginal smokebush patented

In 1997 the Australian smokebush (genus *Conospermum*) was patented by Americans. Aboriginal people had used the plant medicinally for centuries, and the Western Australian Herbarium had helped the US National Cancer Institute to find such medicinal plants.

After an outcry, a licence to develop anti-HIV drugs from the smokebush was acquired for the Australian company AMRAD. But would a less powerful country have been able to recover even those rights?[7]

Patenting Farming

> The patenting of food biotechnology is not about feeding the world or strengthening food production. It is entirely about monopoly ownership of the food chain. It is driven by an assumption that corporations have the right to patent life itself. It is the colonization of existence in the name of corporate greed.
>
> Alan Simpson, MP

The world over farmers have traditionally harvested grains, sold some of the crop, and kept a portion to sow the following year. Hybrid varieties have, of course, disrupted this to some extent. But they have no monopoly and seed-saving remains central to farming in many countries.

It's easy for those of us who live in towns to forget how vital the acts of sowing, reaping and seed-saving are to many worldwide. To most of us in the industrialised world, seeds are optional extras bought to fill our gardens or window boxes; with flowers. For millions around the world they are very much more than that: not only essential for survival but part of their inheritance. The seeds they sow belong to a long line of seeds, as valuable, and as symbolic of their ancestral line, as any stately home.

Year after year, their fathers and mothers, and grandfathers and grandmothers have carefully selected seeds from the best plants to sow the following season, stored them carefully, discussed and exchanged them with neighbours, mixing and interbreeding to obtain unique varieties perfectly suited to their plain, valley or hillside. A process not just of ensuring a supply of food to eat year after year but a community ritual, a sharing of collective and individual wisdom in which everyone can take pride.

Today key varieties from every major traditional crop are in danger of being patented. Even those in remote places aren't exempt. The quinoa of South America is just one example.

The World's Richest Grain

For centuries the native people of Chile, Bolivia, Peru and Ecuador have eaten quinoa (*Chenopodium quinoa*) as a central part of their diet. It is one of the most protein-rich grains in the world and, over time, they have carefully bred numerous varieties to suit the different microclimates of the Andes. Now two American scientists have been given the patent rights not just to part of a Bolivian variety but to all hybrids derived from it.

Bolivia's Association of Quinoa Producers protested in vain until the Canadian organisation RAFI took the case to the UN General Assembly and the International People's Tribunal on Human Rights and the Environment in New York, and the patent was relinquished.

∗ In one small area of Peru they grow 27 varieties of maize – all farm saved and inter-bred.

Sometimes the people win. Sometimes truth has a good day . . . Quinoa is the meat of the Andes and it was almost stolen from us.

Jaime Bravo, a Bolivian farmers' representative[6]

The unseen web

In the industrialised world patented biotech seeds combined with the strictest ever legal constraints on farmers are suddenly changing the face of farming. The clear intention is to change the face of farming worldwide. Wherever GE crops are allowed to be grown, the companies dangle the carrot of promised benefits.

In today's bad market farmers are desperate for anything they imagine might give them an edge. Having got their attention – possibly by using highly selective figures of crop yields – some companies persuade farmers to walk into the trap of restrictive contracts which limit their freedom and their ability to respond to people's needs. Increasingly, giant multinationals are taking control of what is grown, who grows it, how it is grown, the price it is sold at, and who can buy it.

From patent to contract

So far Monsanto seems to be the major company using patented GE seeds to sew farmers up in restrictive contracts. But who knows how long it will be before others follow suit. It's doing a remarkably thorough job and may well 'inspire' others. The contracts made possible by its patents prevent farmers from saving seeds, lock them into using a particular chemical, and give the company the right to inspect the farm for three years afterwards. One doesn't need to be a devotee of crime dramas to see that this is not only an extraordinary invasion of privacy but a dangerous precedent. Today's companies are not necessarily tomorrow's. Some unscrupulous future

---

✳ In Glasgow two people have already died of a *Staphylococcus aureus* resistant to all antibiotics.

company which copied such terms could ruin any farmer who ceased to buy GE seeds, by trumping up evidence of breach of contract during the three-year inspection period. The contract would give it a cast-iron excuse for going onto the farm – where it could plant 'evidence' of seed-saving. A perilous situation for farmers.

Rounding Up Opportunities

The lapsing of a single patent has been driving the creation of many GE crops and of new restrictions on farmers. Monsanto's Roundup is the world's biggest-selling all-purpose weedkiller. But its patent is coming to an end. Not one to sit crying over spilt milk, Monsanto had the bright idea from its point of view of engineering plants to survive spraying with a new version of Roundup, so guaranteeing a future market for the new version of its prime money-spinner. In theory, Monsanto's Roundup is the only all-purpose weedkiller these GE crops will survive. Other companies have also created patented GE crops which tolerate their patent weedkillers. All this seems to be less about improved seeds than about improved profits and greater control over farming.

Grower may not: sell or supply any seed purchased under this agreement to any other person or entity ... [the shalt nots go on and on, ending with an undertaking not to] save any of the seed produced from the purchased seed.

Monsanto Roundup Ready Gene Agreement, 1996

[The] Grower grants Monsanto, or its authorized agents, the right to inspect and test all of Grower's fields planted with soybeans and to monitor Grower's soybean fields for the following three years for compliance with the Agreement.

Monsanto Roundup Ready Soybeans Gene Agreement, 1996[9]

As if that weren't enough, contracts may also put the farmer's entire farm, home and livelihood at risk should there be any violation. According to RAFI, the agreement says that 'nothing contained in the agreement shall limit the amount of damages that Monsanto might recover for any violation of the agreement'. To give you an idea of the amounts involved, damages in one Monsanto agreement include: 'liquidated damages of up to 100 times the then applicable fee for the Roundup Ready gene, times the number of units of transferred seed, plus reasonable attorney's fees and expenses'.[10]

Patent crop controls

Under the guise of protecting the environment, industrial farming technologies seek to legitimize and reinforce chemically-based . . . agriculture with significant gains for the global agricultural input suppliers. Bioserfdom is not just a threat to farmers and peasants; it is a trend that jeopardizes global food security.

Rural Advancement Foundation International (RAFI)[11]

All this could increasingly affect what you and your family eat and the genetic pollution you live with. The day may be coming when farmers will be tightly controlled by the giant corporations that they will be unable to respond to the needs of the public.

Patents can also be used in other ways which limit farmers' freedom and make it harder for them to grow the non-GE crop varieties the public may want. A company can patent key non-GE varieties and use the patent to *prevent* those varieties being used – while offering GE varieties instead. The power of companies to do this is obvious when you look at these 1998 figures:

- 45 per cent of the world's grain seeds are controlled by one company: Cargill, now part of the Monsanto group
- 47 per cent of the world soya bean seed market is controlled by four companies
- 75 per cent of the global seed market is controlled by just five companies
- 87 per cent of the global cotton seed market is controlled by Monsanto
- 88 per cent of the world's GE crops are controlled by Monsanto

Apparently, Monsanto, a company never slow to see legal opportunities, took out a patent on *all* genetically engineered cotton (cotton seed is an important cattle feed) and on soya (*Glycine max*). The patent application for soya was blocked in the USA but has been granted in many parts of the world. It also holds amazingly wide patents on engineering rape, cabbage, cauliflower, broccoli, and the whole of the brassica family, using one of the most popular GE techniques. Sweeping patents on particular crops could also be used to prevent new, perhaps better, GE varieties being created by other companies – or give the patent-holder control over aspects of those GE crops.

The sting in the tail

The granting of such patents means that major patent-holders may have extraordinary control over which normal and GE seeds are sold. That control could be a greater threat to our health and the environment than patents being split between many companies. Suppose Monsanto were to have a patent

∗ Christian Aid estimates that patents from bio-piracy cheat the Third World out of US$4.5 Bn a year.

which embraced all GE soya beans – which it almost has. This wouldn't mean that nobody else could create GE soya beans; just that anyone who wanted to do so would need a licence from Monsanto. More than one characteristic can be engineered into a plant. So the obvious licence for Monsanto to grant would be one which said the engineered beans *had* to include genes to make them survive its weedkiller Roundup. Any such clauses could have serious consequences for all of us.

- If every version of a crop must resist a particular chemical every version will carry a particular, engineered gene or gene sequence. But any gene sequence may turn out to be harmful in undetected, slow-acting ways. And the more versions of a crop that contain that gene sequence, the greater our exposure to that risk.
- The more widely a chemical is used the more of it we eat – and the harder it is for our bodies to cope with it. 'The poison is the dose.'
- However harmful agro-chemicals have been in the past, farmers have tended to use a fairly wide range. So, wildlife and soil organisms weren't hammered by the same chemical everywhere, all the time. That at least gave some chance of recovery between onslaughts. Or what was killed on one farm might survive on another, which used different chemicals. Whereas the more that patents and GE foster the use of any one chemical, and the more farmers grow GE crops, the greater the risk that it will wipe out some key element in the fertility chain which is sensitive to it. Once again, the more frequent the dose, the greater the risk. Yet millions of acres around the world are now devoted to crops engineered for just one weedkiller – though not always Roundup.

∗ 80 per cent of GE patents are held by 13 companies. None are held by the Third World.

- If the patent is for a genetic manipulation which may endanger beneficial insects, the more widely that technique is used the more beneficial insects will be killed.

Do Patents Help or Hinder Research?

Those who take out patents on life argue that research costs millions. That if they can't make profits out of patented life-forms, research will grind to a halt, depriving humankind of all the benefits they expect from GE.

Many people would be delighted if research on GE ground to a halt for a while, if only to have time to take stock of the directions in which it is going. So that is not a compelling argument. However, although patents have aided and abetted the biotech boom, a more restrained use of patenting would not stop research. Research existed long before the current greed for patents took hold. Moreover, although patents can foster research, they can also retard it. There is no guarantee that a company which has the patent on a particular plant, gene or cell is the one best able to use it in the service of humanity nor that it will develop it swiftly. Yet, once patented, its potential may be locked away from other researchers.

Even when patented genes have been analysed commercial interests may cause the findings to be kept secret – even when they are needed to save lives. In America last year public health officials were struggling to find a treatment for a deadly strain of *Staphylococcus aureus* – one of the commonest serious hospital infections. The new strain of the bacterium was resistant to all antibiotics, and officials needed to know more about its genetic structure to devise a treatment. The company which had patented the bacterium refused to share its knowledge – and treatment was set back in a way that could have cost lives. The head of the government research institute commented:

Without this information, we don't have the insights we need. It's like keeping the map of the city of Washington secret.

John La Montagne, National Institute of Allergy and Infectious Diseases

The Road Ahead

Clearly, with patents, as with laws on labelling, or the regulation of experiments using animals, genetic engineering has set precedents, and created challenges, for which nobody has been prepared. At the same time, governments believing in the commercial potential of GE have often fostered bio-patenting, rather than restrained it – ignoring both justice for individuals and the long-term effects.

Some complex techniques took immense skill to develop and deserve to be patented. So there is nothing inherently wrong with bio-tech patents. Nonetheless, the lack of restraint on the patenting of human genes and life-forms enabled, and is enabling, companies to violate basic human rights and gain monopoly control over plant, animal and human genes. Genes which are part of the natural world, not their creations. This is unjust and extremely dangerous.

There is an urgent need for patents laws to be rethought and reformed, both to restrain bio-tech excesses and to safeguard resources justly. Nobody can predict where science is going next, what problems it will have to solve, and what resources it may need in order to solve them. Every time any part of the natural world comes under the sole control of any one company it either removes that resource from the scientific pool or puts a price tag on it. So the very patent laws which have fostered science in the short-term could be a long-term ball and chain.

At the same time the less industrialised world is being doubly disadvantaged. Bio-piracy is stealing traditional knowledge and annexing the genes of people and plants. Yet few Third World companies or countries have the resources to enter the gene race. Even fighting lawsuits to prevent a few indigenous plants from being patented, as India has done, uses money which could find better uses than filling lawyers' pockets.

While Third World countries refuse to adopt laws which allow patents on life they can at least prevent such patents applying within their borders. However, far from supporting this stand, most governments of the industrialised world seem to want them to adopt the very laws which would damage them. If Western governments and the WTO manage to bring this about it will be disastrous for the Third World. Its farmers and plant breeders will be unable to use patented traditional crop varieties. Its doctors, scientists and pharmaceutical companies may be prevented from using local resources in medical treatments.

Such injustice will, very reasonably, be a source of resentment and will either disadvantage them unfairly or lead to covert patent-breaking, international friction and lawsuits. This promotion of unjust patent laws is, ostensibly, being done on our behalf, in the name of exports and jobs. Is that what we want?

If compassion and a sense of justice is beyond our governments perhaps the way forward is for them to realise that it is far harder to export to poor countries than to prosperous ones: that every time they damage other economies they reduce the prospects for their own. That patent colonialism is not only wrong but also extremely short-sighted.

11

Terminator Technology: The Seeds of Strife

Three Myths

Terminator technology will never be used.
Terminator will stop GE crops harming the environment.
Terminator crops cannot cross-pollinate with normal crops.

The new patents pose a huge challenge to community and national food security. The new technologies will be dominated by no more than half a dozen transnational agro-industrial firms (or Gene Giants) that already control virtually 100% of the transgenic seed market. Their ability to insert and externally manipulate vital DNA sequences within crops (and, possibly, insects and livestock) threatens national sovereignty over agriculture and biological resources.

Rural Advancement Foundation International (RAFI)[1]

Behind those measured words is a far darker story – a story which should be central to the whole debate about genetic engineering in agriculture. The reference to 'threats to national sovereignty' is an understatement. Logged on patent office computers the world over are innocent-looking sets of numbers which could license giant agricultural companies to threaten our health, our freedom and even our survival.

Some three dozen patents for GE crops, recently applied for by major international companies, are not what they appear at first sight. Disquietingly, those patents show the transnational agro-chemical companies in their true colours and reveal the extraordinary battle for global power which is taking shape.

The use of biotechnology is indeed set to remove control of agriculture from sovereign nations. But the main thrust of what these companies intend to achieve may be something far more dangerous. With the consent of governments worldwide, vast transnational corporations are acquiring what are, potentially, some of the most insidious weapons of war ever devised.

These weapons need no bombs or canisters to deliver them, no soldiers to carry them, no explosive devices. They can be sold across a counter, laid out, in plain sight, for all to see, without anyone being aware of their potential to control millions without a shot being fired or a window shattered. With these weapons a handful of men could, from the discrete security of office suites, blackmail governments and starve millions to death. Yet the first of these weapons was created with the support of America's Department of Agriculture – and, before long, they may be coming to a field, or a table, near you.

The war-mentality underlying military-industrial agri-culture is evident from the names given to herbicides which destroy the economic basis of survival for the poorest farmers in the rural areas of the Third World.

Dr Vandana Shiva, Director, The Research Foundation for Science,
Technology and Ecology

Making War, Not Food

The weapons are killer seeds. The so-called Terminator seeds can destroy their own fertility and shatter the seed-to-plant-to-

∗ 75 per cent of the world's market in vegetable seeds is already controlled by just 5 companies.

seed cycle of fertility which has sustained life throughout evolution. And there is worse to come. The destructive potentials of other seeds for which patents on pending are more suited to science fiction than to science fact.

It is tempting to dismiss the potential uses of such seeds as a 'what if' scenario which, mercifully, will never happen. Yet to do that would be to throw away the chance to prevent their use. For all wars – even economic ones – are like relationships. The conflagration may appear swift and unexpected but, in reality, wars always have three stages.

As with an affair of the heart, the match is put to the fuse by a sudden flash of awareness of the possibilities which could unfold if . . . Next, as in the prelude to an affair, it's a time to size up possibilities, test methods of persuasion, and discover weaknesses and points of resistance.

> Biotechnology promises the greatest revolution in human history. By the end of this decade, it will have outdistanced atomic power and computers in its effect on our everyday lives . . . Nothing will be the same again. It's literally going to change the face of the planet.
>
> Michael Crichton, Introduction to *Jurassic Park*.

Today's short game

Ironically, we can most easily recognise these stages when it is not a matter of life and death. When it is love that is made not war few of us find it hard, secretly, to appreciate either that first moment of recognition or the power games that follow. Yet, if history is any guide, when real danger looms we play the ostrich. Announcing 'Peace in our time' we deny the fact that the war has already begun. We are already in stage two of the biotech war – the waters are being tested – and the price of ignoring it will be high.

The biotech war

I am concerned about the possible harmful effects that may result from genetic engineering. I worry about the possibility of a weapon of mass destruction coming from it . . . Can biologists assure us that no research can lead to such a weapon and that no scientist will work on such a weapon? I do not believe it.

Professor Sir Joseph Rotblat,
Nobel Prize winning atomic physicist

War is usually thought of in terms of territorial conquest. That view may, in its literal sense, be outdated. Power is always the final objective and that can be acquired without territories. Global communication has changed the boundaries of power. Just as information wings its way around the Internet, no longer limited to tangible books and paper, so power no longer needs a location. Power and the trappings of power – wealth, influence, domination, control – can be achieved at a distance; the weapons of persuasion can be invisible. Such a war may be waged in any country in the world without us even being aware of it – until too late.

The two resources gene giants possess in unique abundance are, of course, biotechnology and chemical technology. For governments these have already produced the world's most deadly weapons. Oddly, there is no sign that governments have even considered the possibility that gene giants might also produce weapons. Yet the writing is on the wall.

The biotech kings

The last few years have seen an intense escalation in bids for supremacy by some of the biotech companies. Like medieval kings and princes, they have increased their power by strategic marriages (takeovers) and alliances, bolstered their finances by enforced levies from the people (technology fees from farmers) and demanded feudal rights (to inspect farms to ensure no seed is saved).

Already we begin to see the medieval scene of governments playing lapdog to gene giant kings and of these biotech kings posing as protectors of their nations. It may not stop there. There is a grave danger that, in time, key companies will control such a large slice of the world's food supply that they will be able to use it to have governments dance to their tune on any topic they please. The latest biotechnology has given them the perfect tools to do that in the economic war which has already begun. A war in which gene giants are battling to see which of them can gain the greatest power over us.

> In 10 years' time genetic engineering will be seen, not as a solution but as part of the problem.
>
> Dr Geoffrey Clements, physicist and leader of
> the Natural Law Party

Unless something is done swiftly, the world may soon face not only the greatest-ever threat to its food supply but perhaps an even greater threat to democracy and individual liberty. In the past year patents have been taken out, or applied for, world-wide which will permit companies to cripple the world's main crops – rice, maize, soya, whatever people can least live without – making them totally dependent on proprietary chemicals if they are to germinate, survive and bear crops. Once a sufficient acreage of such a crop is grown, a gene giant will be in a position to threaten to starve millions – simply by withholding the vital chemicals.

Some of the companies have said they will never use these patents commercially. Should we believe them? Not if history is our guide – and not if we look at assurances given with Terminator.

✳ Delta and Pine Land, co-inventor of Terminator, and owned by Monsanto is the world's largest cotton seed company.

The Terminator

> When we began to work on the atom we had some idea
> of its potential but we did not imagine that it had the
> potential for mass destruction . . . It has happened once
> and I believe it will happen again. Every citizen should
> be concerned to avert such a catastrophe.
>
> Professor Sir Joseph Rotblat, Nobel Prize winning atomic physicist

Terminator technology and its even deadlier descendants
give the lie to claims that GE crops will benefit the world.

It's said that the history of Europe was changed by the
invention of the longbow – a piece of technology which
immediately gave unprecedented power to the side whose
archers possessed it. The atom bomb did the same. Now, in
the same century, we have another such piece of technology
– the Terminator. Yet, in this instance, it is not simply the
Terminator itself which is so dangerous: it is the concept. A
concept which other companies have taken even further.

The aim of the seed war is control of the world's food supply.
The chief obstacle: the age-old farming tradition of saving part
of the crop to sow next year. In the Third World it's the only
way poor farmers can survive, and even in America about one
farmer in four saves seed. But every seed saved means less
profit and less control for the seed companies. Hence America's
brainchild, which Rural Advancement Foundation International (RAFI) aptly called the Terminator.

The first real Frankenstein

As a seed which kills, the Terminator is perhaps the first
product of biotechnology to truly deserve the Frankenstein

✱ Half the soya planted in tropical countries is from saved
seed.

epithet so much used elsewhere. Yet compared to some of its successors, its killing powers are positively understated.

On 3rd March 1998, the American Department of Agriculture (USDA) and the Mississippi-based Delta and Pine Land Company announced their ownership of US Patent No. 5,723,765 for 'Control of Plant Gene Expression' – a shocking technological trick which programmes a plant to make its own off spring sterile. Known as Terminator these seeds look like normal seeds, grow like normal seeds, and the plants even set seed which looks normal – but it is as infertile as a rubber duck. Any farmer rebellious enough to save seeds from the crop to sow next year will reap bare ground.

Terminator Worldwide

The gene manipulation which creates Terminator seeds has no limit; it can be used on *all plants and seeds of all species*. It can be applied to fruit, flowers, vegetables, crops ... from the first spring cabbage to the last over-wintering vegetables nothing need be Terminator-free. All the world's crops and vegetables can increasingly have their fertility taken from them.

The patent is said to have been applied for in more than eighty-five countries. It will especially affect self-pollinating crops such as wheat, rice, cotton, soya beans, sorghum and oats – some of the world's most vital crops.

This is an immoral technique that robs farming communities of their age-old right to save seed and their role as plant breeders. Farmers and governments everywhere should declare use of the technology as contrary to

✱ Of India's 100 million farms, 80 million depend on saved seeds.

public order and security. This is the neutron bomb of agriculture.

Camila Montecinose, Centro de Educación y Tecnología, Chile

My main interest is to protect American technology. Our mission is to protect US agriculture.

Melvin J. Oliver, prime inventor of Terminator technology

Predictably, Monsanto, already hot on farmer contracts, snapped up this destructive use of technology. Within months Monsanto had acquired the rights to it. However, Monsanto carefully played it down, and even made out it had no plans to use it. In September 1998 Australia was being told that there were no plans for the Terminator.

The Terminator is just a concept. We have no plans for Terminator technology at this time.

Murray Willcocks, Monsanto's NZ business manager[2]

An interesting denial: at the time Monsanto was spending millions on developing a second-generation Terminator. Not something a company does because it's bored with filing its nails. In February 1999 AstraZeneca's research director said the company would 'not develop any system that would stop farmers growing second generation seed'. Less than a week later a division of the company received a patent on such seeds. We can expect to hear equally firm denials – made with equal sincerity – from all those researching destructive uses of GE.

This patent is profoundly immoral. It will fundamentally change both the biology and economics of agriculture to the detriment of the poor. It must be stopped.

Farhad Mazhar, South Asian Network for
Food Ecology and Culture

Talking round America's farmers

By January 1999 a very different story was being peddled by the American Seed Trade Association (ASTA). The association wants to seduce American farmers into accepting a technology which removes their rights. So, by a feat of double-think, it is being marketed as a benefit. In a piece of writing so slippery you could break your neck on it, it is claimed that American farmers have been paying for advanced seed technologies and that 'some of these technologies have leaked into other countries without payments by farmers receiving the advantages of these traits, creating an uneven playing field'.[3] Then it says that Terminator has been created to:

> 'ensure a more level playing field for North American farmers when competing in commodity markets worldwide'
> 'stimulate breeding and marketing efforts in countries which have not benefited from advances currently available in the developed world'
> 'prevent transgene movement'

Not one claim bears examination. Nonetheless, it's a very clever piece of writing. What farmer wouldn't want a level playing field? And how many would realise that the unevenness is already in their favour, compared to many of their counterparts elsewhere in the world? At first hearing, 'seed leaking' sounds like money running out of American pockets. But have you ever heard of seed leaking – from country to country, across oceans? In reality, marketing, using every device in the book, is taking place in countries not part of the 'developed' world.

✴ Officially the Terminator is called a Technology Protection System (TPS). Significant. For Terminator is about patent protection – not farming.

In trying to sell Terminator to US farmers ASTA compares Terminator seeds to hybrid seeds – a false comparison since most hybrids still produce fertile seeds, but fail to breed true. Not the same thing at all.

The propaganda then assures farmers that 'there is no correlation between TPS [Terminator] and lack of genetic diversity'. Obviously incorrect. Far from stimulating breeding, sterile seeds remove the incentive for companies to breed new varieties to ensure sales.

The ASTA document ends: 'it is in everybody's interest that more choices be available to all the world's farmers and TPS is the means of achieving this goal.' In reality Terminator reduces choice.

In recent months Monsanto has come under fire for pushing so-called 'Terminator' seeds in India and Africa.

Jeffrey St Clair, *In These Times*, USA, 7 March 1999

Moreover, as Third World protests at the Biosafety Protocol conference early in 1999 showed, those countries and their farmers – are bitterly opposed to GE. American seed companies are frantic to get such GE seeds into those countries. If they succeed it will benefit neither the farmers there nor those in America. Only the gene giants.

They are also trying to find ways to encourage farmers around the world . . . especially in the huge market represented by farmers in South America, Mexico and Asia, to switch to genetically engineered, proprietary seed instead of relying on the eons-old practice of saving their own, locally produced, and conventionally bred, seed. If they can . . . offer their 'improved' seed cheaply enough to convince even poorer, Second and Third World farmers to switch, they will have captured much of the global market.

Gedi Guidetti, the Ark Institute[4]

Terminator II

While denying that it intended to do anything with Terminator technology, Monsanto spent a fortune developing a newer, more profitable version. Terminator II seeds, once again, look normal and grow normally but their seeds are sterile – this time however, fertility can be restored, by the antibiotic tetracycline. Those seeds can then grow and they in turn produce seeds which are sterile unless the chemical is applied.

Dying for modern agriculture

Already the use of hybrid seeds needing expensive chemicals has brought unbearable losses and debt to many Indian farmers. Terminator seeds will do far worse.

In the central Indian state of Andhra Pradesh, an extraordinary drama is unfolding: [in 1998] 500 farmers killed themselves ... 700 farmers killed themselves [in 1997]. Nothing like this has happened before in India. The farmer's preferred way of dying is swallowing insecticides and dying in the fields which failed them. The ... reason, victims' relatives said, was the volatile combination of debt and farm chemicals that no longer worked to kill the pests.

Bill Lambrecht, *Post Dispatch*, Washington, 27 December 1998

This chain of chemical dependency stretches on for ever, generating profits which are not only guaranteed but likely to

✶ Tetracycline is used in medicine, dentistry and by vets. Its use in 'terminator' will foster resistance to it, putting such uses in jeopardy.

escalate. For such seeds can be used as leverage on farmers to buy other products. For example, the company might incorporate the fertility restorer into a soil treatment, so pushing up the cost of farming – and food. But no treatment, no crop.

Dangerous leverage

The use of Terminator technology could create grave dangers for farmers and consumers.

- Terminator plants may cross-pollinate with non-GE crops nearby, making their seeds infertile. This will reduce supplies of non-GE food and create conflict and pressure to switch to GE crops.
- Cross-pollination will happen most where space is limited, and farmers poor. For any farmer to have partial crop failure is hard. For subsistence farmers it can mean hunger – even starvation – for a whole family or village.
- If any GE crops *do* have the advantages the companies claim, the Terminator will either exclude less well-off farmers who need to save seeds or lock them in a cycle of debt.

The sterility trait will take millions of farmers out of plant breeding, leaving no one to care for their specific agricultural needs.

RAFL, *Terminating Food Security*

- It may be hard for some Third World farmers to believe that anyone would do anything as unnatural as *destroying* the fertility of seeds in the name of progress. So some may disbelieve the warnings and plant sterile saved seed. The crop losses could be devastating. Once again children may starve.
- Wild relatives of Third World cultivated plants, which are a vital part of the diet of the poor, will be made sterile and

lost through cross-pollination with Terminator. This will be another cause of hunger.

- The loss of those wild plants would mean the destruction of a vital reservoir of plant diversity and will also damage the whole ecosystem of creatures that depend on them.
- The control system used in the Terminator, or the chemicals put on the seeds to make them germinate, may prove toxic to seed-eating birds. – perhaps causing them to die out.
- Seed-saving has acted as a price control and a stimulus to new varieties. If seed merchants charged too much or failed to offer improved varieties, the farmers saved their seed. So a balance was maintained. The more varieties go over to Terminator technology, the more price control companies will have and the less need to create new varieties.
- Terminator takes from nature the right to cross-pollinate and improve on what exists. At a time of rapid climate change all natural adaptations should be welcome. To prevent this is both arrogant and imprudent.
- Terminator takes from farmers the right to interbreed varieties to suit them, their location and local weather. This deprives both them and the world.

We work with farmers who may buy a commercial variety but its breeder wouldn't recognize it five years later. Women select the best seeds every year. And, over time, the rice moulds itself to the farm's own ecosystem ... Terminator ... could put an end to all of this and increase crop uniformity and vulnerability. It poses a threat to seed sharing and exchange that is primarily led by women farmers.

Neth Dano, South-East Asian Regional Institute for Community
Education

✳ Worldwide some 1,400,000,000 resource-poor farmers depend on saved seeds.

Squandering antibiotics

The use of Terminator varieties whose fertility depends on antibiotics will squander a valuable medical resource and increase antibiotic resistance.

- Using an antibiotic in the huge quantities needed to treat seeds may foster the development of antibiotic-resistant bacteria wherever the seed is handled or used.
- Antibiotics kill bacteria. Yet soil fertility and plant growth depend on the good offices of bacteria. Putting antibiotics into the soil may kill vital soil bacteria – making the soil less fertile.
- Not all the bacteria in the soil will be killed; some will become antibiotic-resistant. So the land itself will become a vast reservoir of antibiotic-resistant bacteria with which other bacteria can 'cross-breed'.

The potential reservoir of antibiotic resistance is no small matter. In 1998, in America, 18 million acres were planted with
GE soya – and doubtless more will be planted in future years. So, if soya beans alone were 'equipped' with Terminator II, America would have created an 18-million-acre reservoir of resistance to antibiotics. And that reservoir would grow with that every new sowing of such crops. If Terminator II seeds are sold worldwide we can expect such reservoirs to be created in every country in the world.

All this may most hurt the least well-off. In the Third World there can be a narrow margin between self-sufficiency and hunger. Disease is already a problem, and few can afford the latest antibiotics, to which bacteria are not yet resistant, if they

✳ RAFI wants people worldwide to write to their governments asking for pending patents on Terminator and traitor seeds to be rejected.

become ill. The very people who Monsanto has claimed will benefit from GE will be most harmed.

Among other farmers the damage will not be limited to the multiple harms I have listed. These seeds would take from farmers worldwide the very heart of their business – the right to choose what to grow and how to grow it. The Terminator, would take control of the food supply out of the hands of farmers into the hands of big business. Farmers would no longer be able to help out a neighbour during hard times. They would be bioserfs yoked to a buying cycle dictated by seed suppliers. The more farmers lose their freedom to breed seeds according to their needs the more the freedom of consumers is also eroded.

> . . . food security . . . will be surrendered to the monopoly control of a few corporations that will determine the genetic qualities that will be grown; under what costs and conditions; and how (or if) positive or negative traits will be triggered by external agents. The creation of such a level of dependency related to such a basic human need is unprecedented . . . If the Terminator technology is widely utilized, it will give the multinational seed and agro-chemical industry an unprecedented and extremely dangerous capacity to control the world's food supply.
>
> Rural Advancement Foundation International (RAFI).[6]

Some say farmers will always be able to buy normal seeds from the public sector. But will they? It was USDA that developed the Terminator, and once it is widely used why wouldn't government crop research institutes also adopt it 'to protect the taxpayer's investment'?

✳ Zeneca says the 'Verminator' gene is an 'uncoupling protein' from the brown fat of a rat: *Ratus ratus*.

The Lack of Buffer Zones

With Terminator, as with all else in GE, the law lags far behind the technology. In many countries there is no set buffer zone that must exist between normal crops and GE crops – including any engineered to include the Terminator. Nor need a farmer even tell his neighbour that he is growing GE crops. And, where they do exist, buffer zones and notification periods are usually totally inadequate.

No system of compensation has been worked out for seed-savers whose crops are cross-pollinated by the Terminator and who thus lose part of the following year's crop, nor for organic farmers whose crop can no longer be classed as organic.

Plant Junkies

The notorious Terminator patent is just the tip of the iceberg. Every major seed and agrochemical enterprise is developing its own version of suicide seeds . . . insidious techniques for sterilizing plants and seeds – even animals. Novartis, AstraZeneca and Monsanto [have] sterile seeds in the pipeline, while others like Pioneer Hi-Bred, Rhone-Poulenc and Du Pont have technologies that could easily be turned into Terminators.

Pat Mooney, Executive Director, RAFI[7]

Once one company had destructive seeds everyone had to have some. In the past year more and more patent applications have been filed for techniques which genetically mutilate seeds.

What is happening is a battle for world economic control. There are three basic resources without which economies grind to a halt: food, water and oil. Oil used to be the favourite. Now that biotechnology is showing its power to control, and water may run short, companies are moving out of oil and into food and water. In the battle for the world food supply, the British firm AstraZeneca has gazumped Monsanto with patents on plants which can't even survive without a chemical fix, including a particularly nasty brainchild – dubbed 'the Verminator'.

In the Verminator AstraZeneca has enlisted 'fat rat' genes in patents which take plant-disabling to new depths. RAFI calls these seeds 'Traitor' seeds because, besides removing fertility, this technology converts normal healthy plants into chemical junkies. If a farmer fails to spray, an in-built assassin will kill the plant. So fertility and growth depend on repeatedly applying one of the company's chemicals. No ifs, no buts, no 'I can't afford the chemicals till next week'. The result will be a *far greater use of chemicals* and farmers shackled to AstraZeneca.

False innocence

Yet, carefully marketed, Traitor seeds could avoid a lot of the criticism aimed at Terminator. Nobody can say they are sterile. They aren't. They're chemical-dependent. Nobody can say cross-pollination with their offspring will make wild plants die out. It won't – not if enough patent chemical is sprayed on them. Nobody can say that cross-pollination will ruin a neighbour's crop next year – unless it's organic. The company will be only too *glad* to sell the neighbour chemicals to restore lost health. No longer need greedy patent-holders prevent farmers saving seed. Farmers can save seeds to their hearts' content. The seeds are useless without the chemicals – but nobody is stopping them being saved.

✱ If we grow Traitor seeds America need only withhold vital chemicals catalysts in the next banana/beef war – and cripple crops.

Yet life has been mutilated, the rights of farmers removed, and an unlimited thirst created for chemicals which may very well harm the environment – and us. So Traitor seeds do even more harm than Terminator and concentrate more power in the hands of a gene giant. By making plant health depend on chemicals they can be used to put the world's food supply and in even greater jeopardy.

Will Traitor seeds sell?

By the time you read this, these Traitor techniques may have been patented in seventy-seven countries – for application to 'all plants', starting with:

apples	maize	sorghum
barley	mangoes	strawberries
cabbages	melons	sugar beet
canola (rape)	onions	sunflowers
carrots	peaches	tobacco
cotton	pears	tomatoes
lettuce	rice	wheat

Dying for a fix

You think farmers won't be mad enough to buy such seeds? They will: these seeds won't be sold as *dis*advantaged seeds, but as *ad*vantaged seeds – farmers need never know that Verminator technology even exists. They can be told that soaking the seeds, before planting, in chemical X is vital to bring out whatever other '*benefit*' has been built in.

It's too soon to say how often farmers will have to spray, what chemicals will be used and how great the toxic load on the environment and in food will be. The ideal regime, for a

---

* 'Cloning' may mass produce Terminator/Traitor seeds creating uniform, disease-vulnerable, sterile crops.

chemical company, would be one in which spraying was so frequent and so costly that it put small farmers out of business. The more small farmers go out of business the cheaper the price of land, and the easier it is for the giants or their allies to snap it up.

Still greater mutilation of life

Plant junkies aren't limited to AstraZeneca. Novartis has trumped AstraZeneca's three destructive patents with a dozen – all potentially more damaging than AstraZeneca's.

While executives from Novartis publicly peddled the idea that GE would offer better, healthier food – with less chemical input – behind the scenes the company was working on ways to make plants cripples without chemical sprays. Novartis has plans to take strong, tasty, nutritious, disease and pest-resistant plants and suppress all those assets. A process it blandly calls 'inactivation of endogenous regulation', as if long words could make such misuse of science respectable. A dozen patents applied for in more than eighty countries would enable it to *turn off any plant's natural*:

- ability to flower
- fertility
- attractive flavour
- pest resistance
- disease resistance
- nutritional value

The solution: a bottle, straight from Novartis. As the company puts it:

> . . . genes which are natively regulated can be regulated exclusively by the application to the plant of a chemical regulator . . . a chemically regulatable non-coding sequence can be associated with a gene controlling flower or fruit ripening, a gene affecting tolerance or resistance to herbicides or to many types of pests, for example, fungi

∗ The world agro-chemical market is valued at US$30.9 Bn.

viruses, bacteria, insects, nematodes, or arachnids; a gene controlling production of secondary metabolites; male and female sterility; dwarfness; flavour; nutritional qualities and the like.

Allegedly, Novartis plans to weaken the defences of most staple crops. Agricultural biotechnology – which posed as the saviour of the world and a revolutionary tool to improve crops – is now seen in its true colours: as a destroyer of life. It is to be ruthlessly used to increase chemical use, and dependence on chemical companies.

Insect Invaders?

Among the list of topics covered in a March 1999 conference in North Carolina was 'genetically engineered insects'. They would of course, be engineered to make them less productive. Having seen how if could backfire when GE tried to make crops *more* productive are we about to see an insect version of *Jurassic Park* in which we are all eaten alive in our beds by huge colonies of over-fertile ants looking for *lebensraum*? But it seems this is no joke.

Up to now, living organisms have evolved very slowly, and new forms have had plenty of time to settle in. Now whole proteins will be transposed overnight into wholly new associations, with consequences no one can foretell, either for the host organism, or their neighbours ... going ahead in this direction may be not only unwise, but dangerous. Potentially it could breed new animal and plant diseases, new sources of cancer, novel epidemics.

Professor George Wald, Harvard University, Nobel
Prize Laureate in Medicine, 1967

Grim Technology

It is only too obvious to concerned scientists . . . that we are about to repeat the mistakes of the insecticide era even before it is behind us.

Dr Hans Herren, Director-General, International Centre of Insect
Physiology and Ecology, Nairobi

The final twist to the deadly use of technology involves insects. Grim is the apt name Texas University gave to its biotech pest control. Grim by name and grim by nature.

At the University of Texas they have engineered a fruit-fly gene so that it will kill the creature that contains it – to order. In theory, any signal could trigger the killer gene – even a change of temperature or the scent of roses.

The idea is to breed Grim insects, then release them to mate with relatives. Once the gene has been spread sufficiently, huge numbers can be killed by the trigger signal. The idea may be appealing, but Grim insects could be one of the most dangerous GE applications yet.

- Pests carrying killer genes can transmit the genes throughout the insect family on that continent. Any pest is part of a chain of life; if too many are killed a link in that chain is broken and birds and other creatures which lived off it, or in association with it, die too.
- Genetic engineering is inherently unstable. There have been many examples of changes which worked during trials failing in practice. If that happens, and Grim killer cells fail, the number of pests will have been increased, not decreased.
- Most seriously of all, this killer gene seems to work in any living thing – including man! – since engineered genes, are

* Millions of poorly protected agricultural workers in developing countries risk poisoning by agrochemicals.

born travellers able to move from host to host. So the great danger is that the Grim gene sequence could carry its fatal trait to any other creature – bees, wild and farm animals, and even man. The contact wouldn't have to be direct: there's evidence that engineered genes can be picked up by the soil and can be transferred to insects, birds and animals and carried in water supplies.[8] Such things are random and it would be unlikely to occur at once – but the possibility would increase with every insect that carried the gene.

Hitch-hiking Genes

People often forget that GE genes aren't only transferred through pollen: They are quite happy to hitch a lift on pollen or anything else, but they need no such transport, and can carry the plant or animal genes with them independently. Sterile and fatal Terminator, Traitor and Grim genes are no exception.

We all live in an invisible 'fog' of bacteria and viruses which float in the air, live in soil and water, and in and on plants, animals and us. They are so numerous and so varied that we live in their world, not they in ours. There are no boundaries to where any genetically engineered genes may end up – nor to the effect they will have.

Agro-chemical Power Games

While using GE to gain more control over plants, companies have also been merging and expanding. More and more power has been concentrated in fewer and fewer hands. Today a

---

✳ In 1998 global mergers and acquisitions were valued at $2.4 *trillion*.

handful of companies hold unprecedented control over the products upon which we depend for life: food and medicines.

Playing monopoly 1998–9

- Monsanto spent over $8 Bn buying seed and genetics companies
- German Hoechst and French Rhone-Poulenc merged to form Aventis – which claims to be the world's largest company in this field
- Du Pont acquired the massive seed company Pioneer Hi-Bred
- British Zeneca merged with Swedish Astra, with assets of over $70 billion. Assets greater than the gross national product of almost a hundred developing nations

Each expansion stimulates the expansion of others. Takeover trumps takeover, each merger giving the company control of a bigger slice of the world's crops, chemicals and pharmaceuticals.

No company seems too large or too small to be acquired. Worldwide, as buy-out succeeds buy-out, small – and medium-sized seed companies are becoming rarer. As they are gobbled up, opportunities for farmers or market gardeners to buy non-GE seeds are steadily reduced. Already gene giants have more than enough power to persuade governments that national seed collections ought not to be available to less 'advanced' seed companies. Unless GE crops continue to be strongly opposed we could soon see a time when normal seeds – and therefore normal food – will be virtually unobtainable.

Freedom Under Threat

Earlier I compared the contests between the agro-chemical giants to struggles between competing medieval kings and princes. There is, however, an essential difference. To gain extraordinary power today all that is needed is the ability to make a sufficiently powerful threat. The Cold War was fought on the basis of the threat of nuclear devastation, the balance of power preventing action. If the crop war is not stopped there will be no balance of power: gene giants will have the weapons; farmers and consumers will be the targets on the road to power; and governments will be defenceless.

Terminator, Traitor and Grim technologies are very much more than tools with which to sell chemicals. Gene giants claim that they were created simply to protect patents. However, their *potential* is far more sinister. By giving companies control over the fertility of crops – and therefore over the supply of food wherever these crops are grown – they can be used to threaten mass starvation.

They offer a return to the siege tactics of history – except that this siege is by threat alone. What can more easily, or cheaply, destroy people than depriving them of food? Moreover, they can be used at every level: to control farmers, landowners, regional governors, governments – and even in battles for supremacy with other gene giants.

Core crops: the Achilles heel

The power offered by Terminator and Traitor goes way beyond the influence which we all know is wielded by vast corporations. Chemically dependent crops would set the scene for companies to gain an unprecedented degree of covert

✳ Seed crippling technologies may violate the UN Convention on Biological Diversity, signed by 170 countries.

political control in almost any country they choose. In some countries this could amount to dictatorship, for governments of all political complexions would be forced to dance to their tune.

In most countries there are one or two staple crops which are major exports, without which millions would starve. These are vital to the balance of trade, to the nation's economy, and to its ability to import other food. Whether that core crop is rice, wheat, soya, maize or sorghum the gene giants have already created GE varieties, or are working on them. Already they have taken out patents on key varieties of virtually all such vital crops worldwide. Not even little-known staples, like South American quinoa, have evaded the trawl of their all-embracing net.

To see how this could be exploited to gain ever-growing political control, let's use a fictitious company: Biga-corp and fictitious countries. Any similarity to any corporation or country alive or dead is totally coincidental. Moreover, I'm not suggesting that any existing company would do any of what follows. However, what could be more appealing to some unscrupulous future company than acquiring such destructive uses of technology?

Biga-corp wants power both at home and abroad. Its home country is Industra – a major Western industrial nation. Biga-corp markets aggressively in many countries at once, always pushing hardest with each country's major crop. It has three objectives:

- to gain a bigger percentage of world sales than its rivals
- to control key governments in any country it chooses
- to have enough international power to manipulate its own government

Tactic 1: the chemical fix

Let's suppose a Third World country called Dajan is one of its targets, with maize the staple crop. Using normal business methods, plus alliances with local food processors, powerful individuals and the usual range of respectable, and local, business practices, it acquires a bigger and bigger share of the seed market for maize – selling GE varieties. When farmers prove resistant to GE seeds, Biga-corp has ways of persuading them.

Seducing with 'generosity'

Fantasy: Biga-corp gives free seed to aid agencies operating in Dajan. It even gives free 'spray-on fertiliser' to every farmer. The agencies check: the crops have no infertility genes. The farmers can save seed. What the aid agencies don't know is that the seeds have been made disease-prone. The 'spray-on fertiliser' is really protection against other negative traits they carry. Biga-corp didn't build infertility in because it *wants* this maize to cross-pollinate with nearby non-GE maize. This will create crippled, poorly performing plants among the non-GE maize of seed-saving farmers next year.

The GE crops thrive. Nearby non-GE ones do poorly. GE crops look like winners. Within a few years some farmers who refused GE seeds are ruined. The rest are persuaded to sign up to multi-year contracts – how can they refuse a company that gave them free seeds and 'fertiliser'?

Reality: I know of no evidence that any company has used such a ploy or ever would. But companies change hands. Who knows what future parent companies might plan? Meanwhile, the scene is set: giant companies already offer seeds to charities in target areas. The plant-crippling technology isn't yet in use but, if it ever is, who would ever know if a company changed the labels on its sacks to make mutilated seeds look innocent? Crop failures can occur naturally.

Attractive terms and incentives

Fantasy: Biga-corp offers incentives: discount prices, free chemicals with seeds, buy now, pay later – using cross-pollinating chemical dependent seeds as above.

Once again non-GE seeds do badly.

Reality: Companies already offer incentives and discounts. Oddly, if a country subsidises farmers it's an offence against free trade, but if a vast corporation offers discounts, which amount to the same thing, it is not seen as an offence against trade by smaller companies.

The Black Revolution

GE crops have been heralded as the new 'green revolution'. For many the green revolution was a black event:

- the green revolution forced 1 in 4 Punjabi small-holders off the land; many were left destitute
- during the green revolution the number of house-holds affected by rural debt in South Korea rose from 76 per cent to 98 per cent.

The gene revolution promises to be blacker still for small farmers.

Becoming a moneylender

Fantasy: Through innocent third parties Biga-corp lends farmers money to buy 'the latest seeds' – Biga-corp's GE seeds.

It can't lose: those who use the chemicals succeed and sign on for more. Those who don't are indebted and can be made to sign on, or bankrupted and forced off the land. Small farmers are less use to Biga-corp than large ones.

✳ The Novartis Traitor patents says the chemical regulator could be combined with a fertiliser or pesticide.

Reality: Monsanto is 'striving to have at least one microcredit project operating in each of its world areas and working with third-party organizations'[9] to do this – and may not be the only company offering such largesse. It is possible that some such companies may like the wolf in 'Little Red Riding Hood' have very big eyes. And farmers who take the cake of microcredit, could risk being gobbled up. And Monsanto may not be the only company offering such largesse.

No more Mr Nice Guy

Fantasy: GE seeds, and the stocks of bacteria and viruses which Biga-corp uses to test them, open the door to strong-arm tactics which this purely fictitious company isn't too scrupulous to use. I'm not suggesting that any real company would even consider such tactics, but this scenario illustrates the power which biotechnology gives to seed companies – and its potential for misuse.

As Dajan's major maize seed supplier, Biga-corp has to look as if it sells normal seeds as well as engineered ones. But farmers who insist on normal seed get sacks doctored with a proportion of GE seeds of the same variety, disabled to be disease-prone. They see neighbours' GE seeds always doing better. For good measure Biga-corp secretly releases viruses and bacteria for plant diseases into areas of non-GE maize. Increasing disease and lower yields persuade farmers to try GE.

If thwarted in prime areas, Biga-corp is not above using more direct strong-arm tactics against farmers who continue to hold out against GE. The large number of mercenaries left by wars in Africa and elsewhere, and now employed by international 'security' firms, make this a simple, and discreet, matter. Accidents have always happened on farms.

Patenting starts as a fundamental argument about

✶ The WTO could ban the use of seed-crippling technology for putting the environment at risk.

whether we should have the right to patent life. But ultimately it is about a corporate desire to own death as well. All biotech crops in the not too distant future will have their own patent protection built into them. It will allow them to produce but not to reproduce. Effectively it will give corporations the power to sterilize nature. This is a shift from corporate entities to corporate deities. It gives them the power of life and death and turns us into indentured labourers and share croppers with fewer rights than peasants in the middle ages.

Alan Simpson, MP

When such tactics have gained Biga-corp a big enough stake it tightens its grip. In mid-season, with junkie crops due for the next chemical fix, Biga-corp suggests that farmers should sign long-term contracts to ensure it can plan ahead for the chemicals they need. The threat need not be explicit. Farmers understand the choice: sign up, or be without chemicals, lose the crop, and be ruined. They sign up. The terms allow Biga-corp huge control over what farmers grow, whom they sell to and what they charge – a branch of Biga-corp will buy the crop. At a stroke farmers have become serfs on their own land, unable to respond to the needs of those who don't want GE food.

If the major seed and agro-chemical multinationals have their way Terminator and Traitor technologies will come on the heels of the millennium to a farm near you . . . with potentially disastrous consequences.

Pat Mooney, Executive Director, RAFI

✳ An official report says that in 3–7 years disabling traits may be hard to trace or to police. Seeds could contain them without buyers knowing.

Tactic 2: the government fix

Fantasy: With enough farmers using dependent GE seeds, it's time for the next step on the road towards control. Dajan is a typical small Third World country with a fragile economy and no food to spare. Biga-corp controls the lion's share of the maize seed market. Without a mid-season chemical fix the crop will fail, exports be lost and some people starve.

In the long term Biga-corp wants real power in Dajan. In the short term it wants laws which make life tough for the few farmers who have stood out against it, or control of the country's seed collections. All Biga-corp need do is tell Dajan's government that there's a shortage of the vital chemical without which Dajan's crops will fail. But hint that, since 'friends' do 'friends' favours, if X or Y is done, Biga-corp could juggle its orders and supply the chemical concerned.

What government would risk the social and economic fall-out of saying no? Or let such a 'crisis' become public knowledge? A secret deal is struck. The government of Dajan can now be blackmailed at will. If it fails to grasp the strategy it may even feel indebted and be even more amenable to the next request. While the beauty of such moves from Biga-corp's viewpoint is that they:

- can be made in secret
- cost nothing
- can be made in many countries simultaneously
- can be made to look like a genuine problem well solved
- can produce legislative changes in its favour

With such tactics Biga-corp has no need to do anything overtly aggressive. Nothing-need appear on the surface which would alert the public, or shareholders to its lust for power. The use of chemically dependent crops has made countries dependent on it. Without the chemicals a large part of the nation will go hungry. Using this leverage is child's play.

Biga-corp acquires a seed bank here, a legal concession there, and an ever-growing share of the market. Each move gains it more power, more control – and makes the next one easier. This war not only costs nothing, it's profitable. But as Biga-corp gains power, everyone else loses it. In any country heavily dependent on a few crops, power over those crops is power over the food supply, the economy – and the government. Once Biga-corp has that it can make its preferences clear to the government on any issue – alliances, education, wars, healthcare (perhaps Biga-corp has pharmaceuticals) – there is no limit. Where its economic clout isn't quite enough, a combination of unspoken threats and strategic donations to political parties, or individuals, tips the scales.

Home gains from abroad

Power gains abroad bring power gains at home. Industra's embassy in Dajan (and elsewhere) reports Biga-corp's growing influence with foreign governments – influence which could be politically useful to Industra. So as Biga-corp increases its power in foreign countries, its own government increasingly smooths its path at home. Here too seed banks change hands, laws are passed which favour GE, blind eyes are turned to violations, new crops approved on the nod, consumer protests ignored.

This desire to favour Biga-corp is boosted by the fact that, following a series of mergers and buy-outs, Biga-corp has become Industra's major player internationally in the field of seeds, chemicals and pharmaceuticals. Biga-corp is seen not

---

✱ The British Medical Association has urged the strengthening of the Biological and Toxin Weapons Convention.

so much as a company greedy for power but as Industra's representative in a world fight for supremacy in this vital sector of business. 'What is good for Biga-corp is good for Industra' is the message Biga-corp feeds Industra's politicians.

A loss of rights

Little by little the people of Industra lose their right to eat non-GE food; farmers become bioserfs. Across the board the same tactics can be used at home, the same secret political power gained – though this time it is through the combined power of owning the biotechnology and of huge control over crops. Of course, from time to time GE foodstuffs go wrong, stressed plants produce unexpected toxins, there is an unaccountable rise in the number of deformed babies, allergies and cancer increase, people fall sick and die of new unexplained diseases.

Government toxicologists find other explanations. There is nothing wrong with biotechnology, they say.

The Reality

That was fiction. The reality of Traitor technology is that the only block to a biotech company's expansion is another biotech giant. In any country in which it does good business, an agrogi-ant can quietly clear the way to covert political power. If it uses its power to withhold the chemicals on which junkie crops depend, governments will make concessions, thinking they are protecting their country – when in reality they are doing the reverse. The beauty of it, from a gene giant's view-point, is that this is a war which costs nothing. It can threaten a bio-siege without even losing its reputation.

Undoubtedly GE companies will say they would never use their technology to harm people. Yet how can we trust such

---

✳ Vast transnational corporations now account for more than two-thirds of world trade.

companies to respect human life when they have shown such disrespect for life in other ways? When they have planned something as inherently destructive as crippling healthy plants. And when such destructiveness would enhance their profits while exposing farmers to the risk of crop devastation, and nations to the risk of famine? For with all plant-crippling there will always be a risk that the chemicals intended to switch positive traits back on will fail to work. So crops – and lives – will always be at risk.

Giant mergers reshape the world

Disturbingly, gene giants have gained these tools at a time when mergers and acquisitions have already given some of them enormous influence.

Sizing Up Giants and Super-Giants

Gene giants expanded vastly in 1998/9 and their figures for that year aren't out yet. But even in 1997 turnovers were substantial:

Novartis:	US$4,199,000,000
Monsanto:	US$3,126,000,000
AstraZeneca:	US$2,674,000,000

But the 1997 sales of some food manufacturing trans-nationals make gene companies look puny:

Nestlé, Switzerland:	US$45,380,000,000
Philip Morris, USA:	US$31,890,000,000
PepsiCo Inc., USA:	US$20,910,000,000
Mars, USA:	US$14,000,000,000

✱ Some NGOs believe that if seed-crippling techniques aren't banned they could rapidly dominate the world seed market.

Wherever Monsanto seeks to sow, the US government clears the ground. In Japan last month, Agriculture Secretary Glickman and Trade Representative Barshefsky each told their government hosts that labelling modified foods wouldn't suit Uncle Sam.

Bill Lambrecht, *Post Dispatch*, Washington, 27 December 1998

When faced with the almost certain prospect that the EU would ban the import of Monsanto's genetically engineered corn in 1998, the company unleashed an unprecedented lobbying effort, flying in a group of critics to the United States, where they . . . were given a tour of the White House, including a rare visit to the Oval Office . . . Even Bill Clinton and Al Gore . . . engaged in some last minute arm-twisting of Irish Prime Minister Bertie Ahern and French President Lionel Jospin. Both the French and the Irish caved in to pressure.

Jeffrey St Clair, *In These Times*, USA, 7 March 1999

Since the potential power of biotechnology began to be realised, all the major companies have been positioning themselves to dominate large sectors of their industry, and of the globe. Mergers and buy-outs have put most of the world's seed and agro-chemical markets in the grip of a handful of companies. Some plan to go further and move into food manufacturing and retailing, creating vertical seed-to-plate monopolies.

There is however, another possibility. The world's biggest food companies are large enough to snap up gene giants.

If Nestlé, for example, bought up a biotech giant, the world's largest food company could at a stroke gain control over much of the world's food supplies and have seed to plate control, thus acquiring the power over life and death. The immense

---

✱ 'Recipes' for developing biological weapons are now available on the internet.

power all this would give it worldwide, coupled with financial resources greater than those of many governments, would give it extraordinary political influence in Europe. Such a move would be countered by a similar merger in America.

Consumers would then go to the wall as governments on either side of the Atlantic supported 'their' region's company even more strongly than they do today. Already, there is an extraordinary assumption in the White House that what is good for Monsanto is good for America. Yet America is surely her people, not her industry.

> Monsanto has always been able to count on the aid of the US government to sedulously promote its products. With the ceaseless encouragement of the [US] Department of Agriculture, American farmers have planted more than 50 million acres of Monsanto's genetically engineered crops over the past four years. The Food and Drug Administration (FDA) have played along, acceding to the company's demand that genetically engineered crops not be labeled as such.
>
> Jeffrey St Clair, *In These Times*, USA, 7 March 1999

Patently sick

When we look at risk assessment it's clear that we're always systematically overestimating the extent of intellectual control – especially in biology. The extent to which we can control the consequences is far less than we think. If we recognize that we can't control the consequences we should ask: Why are we doing this? Why are we taking the risk? Is the aim just commercial profits?

Dr Bryan Wynne, speaking at London University 1999

The Reality of Traitor Ownership

The top five seed and biotech companies all have self-destructive seeds. They are:

Monsanto	(USA)
Novartis	(Switzerland)
AstraZeneca	(UK/Sweden)
Du Pont-Pioneer	(USA)
Aventis	(France/Germany)

Terminator patents have also been taken out by organisations such as the Scottish Crop Research Institute, the John Innes Centre, BASF and the University of Texas.

Future imperfect

Now that gene giants can build destructive genes into crops and insects, will it stop there? Maybe not. In a debate on genetic engineering, one of my opponents was from Novartis. He said that GE crops had to be safe as they'd never be so mad as to harm their own customers. I replied that, although *his* company would not do such a thing, in principle any drug company involved in GE had much to gain from foods which made people ill, provided the blame couldn't be laid at its door.

His outrage was out of all proportion to my carefully chosen words. Maybe he knew that Traitor technology, on which Novartis has extensive patents, could be used to undermine human health, and thought I was implying that the company would use it that way. In fact I wasn't.

✴ The top ten corporations control almost half the world seed market.

However, in immoral hands, biotechnology *could* engineer crops so that their nutritional value falls after spraying. As 'substantial equivalence' can be based on unsprayed crops nobody would know that key foods were lacking in vital nutrition. These nutritional deficits could be made good by nutraceuticals which – quite by chance – would be made by the same company.

Nor, need boosting the demand for pharmaceuticals stop there. Hormones and other body chemicals control our mood, our immune system, and a mass of other functions. Since both plants and animals can be engineered to produce medical products, tomorrow's GE companies could secretly engineer crops, farm animals, fish or poultry to secrete substances which would make us depressed, damp down the immune system, increase hyperactivity in children – or create any of a host of changes of mood and metabolism which would need to be treated by drugs sold by the very companies that had engineered such harm. What today's companies won't do, tomorrow's may.

Traitor weapons

The danger of Traitor weapons, is already being discussed internationally. They include not only the misuse of drug-dependent crops but also sprays or 'fertilisers' containing Grim genes coupled with viral or bacterial vectors which would carry the genes into a non-engineered crop.

Very little is yet known about the extent to which engineered DNA is incorporated, intact, into the cells of those who eat GE foods. However, there is evidence that it can be – and that the fetus may be especially vulnerable. If that is so, or if future gene manipulations could make it so, Grim technology could create weapons tailor-made for genocide. For it could engineer into appropriate crops a substance fatal to humans, or to a specific ethnic group, which would be incorporated into their cells, to lie dormant until triggered by some seemingly innocent catalyst. Those not exposed to the catalyst could eat such crops without risk. Of those at risk, the children might die first. What more certain way is there to destroy a race?

> So much science is done in secrecy. A basic tenet of
> science should be openness. Yet, at the present time, we
> have thousands of scientists working in laboratories and
> nobody knows what is going on.
>
> Professor Sir Joseph Rotblat, Nobel Prize-winning atomic physicist

This is not currently possible. But not long ago all Traitor
technology was impossible too. The question of whether such
modifications would be allowed is academic. Now that plants
and animals can be engineered almost anything can happen
and the chances of detection would be virtually nil. Relaxing
the laws on the patenting of life-forms set biotechnology on
a road which could lead almost anywhere. The only limit to
the extent to which it could be used unscrupulously, or with
a simple lack of compassion and humanity, is the morality of
the companies concerned – and companies change hands.

It is not surprising that a technology based on the violation
and manipulation of core elements of life has so little respect
for life that it is prepared to create Terminator and its descendants. What is surprising is how quickly it has reached this
point. This is a field in which the speed of change is alarming.
Yet the alarm bells seem to be unheard by those in power.

> The history of humanity is a history of war. Scientific
> advances quickly lead to developments in weapons
> technology . . . It would be a tragedy if, in ten years time,
> the world faces the reality of genetically engineered and
> possibly genetically targeted weapons.
>
> Dr Vivienne Nathanson, British Medical Association

* In January 1999 a company told the American Association
  for the Advancement of Science that it was on the brink of
  constructing the world's first artificial life form – but would
  not do so as it could be misused as a biological weapon.

12

Reaping the Whirlwind?

Three Myths

Anything new is always progress.
In the modern world there is no place for the sacred.
If something really matters you can always put a price on it.

I happen to believe that this kind of genetic modification
[of crops] takes mankind into realms that belong to God,
and to God alone. Apart from certain highly beneficial
and specific medical applications, do we have the right
to experiment with, and commercialize, the building
blocks of life? . . . We simply do not know the long-term
consequences for human health and the wider environment of releasing plants bred in this way.

HRH The Prince of Wales

In Greek mythology King Midas was granted his wish to turn
everything he touched into gold. He revelled in this ability until
he touched his food – and it too turned into gold. Suddenly
he had everything – except that which sustains life. The folly
of King Midas was to succumb to financial greed which lost
him something he had taken for granted yet was of even far
greater value than gold.

What Is Important?

That story should be engraved on the doors of every agro-chemical company engaged in genetic engineering. For in their eagerness for profits they are following in the footsteps of Midas. But it is *our* food which they reach out to touch – and blight.

Most have played Midas for many years. In their quest to grow rich and expand they have left a trail of devastation behind them. The earth bears witness to the pollution they have master minded. Since 1900 the world has lost more than three quarters of its varied wild plants and creatures. Each of us carries in our tissues several hundred chemicals which would not have been there a century ago. Breast milk is contaminated with PCBs. Men's sperm counts have halved. Fish are failing to reproduce. More children suffer from asthma and allergies than ever before – and more under thirtys have cancer. Seas are poisoned. Forests are dying from acid rain. The polar ice caps crumble.

Our age has been the age of destruction. Everything in the natural world, from the minute traceries of corals to the irreplaceable forests of the Amazon, has been viewed through Midas' eyes – as something to turn into money.

The price of destruction

To criticise that is not to condemn profits. However, since the driving force behind genetic engineering is, once again, economic perhaps we should consider whether the balance sheets should be drawn up purely in terms of money. Or if the price of grief, death and the destruction of so much of the natural world should not also appear in the expenditure

✻ Worldwide 2.5 million tons of pesticides are used each year, selling for US$20 billion, GE will increase their use.

column? Whether it does so or not, it remains an invisible overhead – a high price already paid by the human and natural world for the incautious and inappropriate use and abuse of chemicals in industry and in farming.

That price is the result of an extraordinary cycle to which GE gives a new twist. As pests damage has increased in the face of chemical pesticides the proffered 'solution' has been more chemical pesticides. As land has lost its natural fertility under the onslaught of chemical fertilisers and crop sprays, the 'solution' has been more chemical fertilisers. Now, as pesticide resistance, soil erosion, and losses of wild life mount, we are offered a 'solution' which strikes at the very core of the natural world, violating the integrity of life itself. A 'solution' which will give another twist to the spiral of pollution: bringing the use of yet stronger pesticides and the prospect of plants which depend on agro-chemicals for the most basic processes of life. We could expect nothing else. If you were a chemical company would you create crops which needed *less* chemical input? Or *more*? However we are not chemical companies and only a befuddled drunkard over-indulges and believes that a hair of the dog which bit him is the best cure.

As a society we have been drunk. For we have imbibed a heady brew of false beliefs. The priests dictating the terms of that worship are giant corporations.

Greed over need

Trade is no longer the provision of goods which people want but the provision of marketing opportunities for corporations. Decisions about what will be manufactured and sold are no longer dictated by need, but by opportunities offered for big business to make money. The goods come first, the persuasion to use follows. Such persuasion has become all-pervasive, and so deeply woven into our thinking that we have witnessed the extraordinary spectacle of politicians accusing critics of GE of assuming that what is new must be bad. While they themselves have adopted the equally illogical belief that what is new must be good. For, on scientific evidence, GE crops have little to recommend them.

As a result of all this GE crops have become a prime example of greed prevailing over need. People have been asking for safer, genuinely healthier food. Such crops fail to meet that need. They will not protect the environment, they put it at risk in ways we cannot even envisage. How can they possibly be safe when even the EU, staunch champion of GE, has crop disaster plans? They are too unpredictable ever to be healthier, their yields too uncertain, their uniformity too vulnerable to devastating disease, for them to feed the world.

Yet, because it offers huge financial opportunities to chemical companies, the application of an untried technology to our everyday lives was sanctioned without open discussion. If any development might be dangerous to human health, or to the environment, those who might be harmed should be fully represented in fair, open, decision-making and able to ban the process or product if necessary. For if our society learnt from history the 'progress' offered by any technology would surely be seen as a gift horse whose mouth should be inspected very closely indeed.

The Burden of Proof

Moreover, when a totally new process or product is introduced the burden of proof of its safety should rest with the those likely to profit from it.

The following statement of the precautionary principle, which should guide those involved, was drafted by scientists, government officials, lawyers, and activists from Britain, America, Germany, Canada and Sweden, at a meeting in Wingspread, Wisconsin, in January 1998. They could have been adopted by governments considering the uses of genetic engineering – but they have not been.

Wingspread statement on the precautionary principle

The release and use of toxic substances, the exploitation of resources, and physical alterations of the environment have had substantial unintended consequences affecting human health and the environment. Some of these concerns are high rates of learning deficiencies, asthma, cancer, birth defects and species extinctions, along with global climate change, stratospheric ozone depletion and world wide contamination with toxic substances and nuclear materials.

We believe existing environmental regulations and other decisions, particularly those based on risk assessment, have failed to protect adequately human health and the environment – the larger system of which humans are but a part.

We believe there is compelling evidence that damage to humans and the worldwide environment is of such magnitude and seriousness that new principles for conducting human activities are necessary.

While we realize that human activities may involve hazards, people must proceed more carefully than has been the case in recent history. Corporations, government entities, organizations, communities, scientists and other individuals must adopt a precautionary approach to all human endeavors.

Therefore, it is necessary to implement the Precautionary Principle: When an activity raises threats of harm to human health or the environment, precautionary measures should be taken even if some cause and effect relationships are not fully established scientifically. *In this context the proponent of an activity, rather than the public, should bear the burden of proof.* [my italics]

The process of applying the Precautionary Principle must be open, informed and democratic and must include potentially affected parties. It must also involve an examination of the full range of alternatives, including no action.[2]

First published in Rachel's Environment & Health Weekly
February 19, 1998

The sacrifice of life

In our dealings with giant industries we have rarely adopted the precautionary principle. Instead we have repeatedly sacrificed the natural world to the insatiable demands of industry. Today we are being asked to make an extraordinary sacrifice. To sacrifice the concept of life itself as something precious and not of our making.

Genes contain the blueprint for everything that we are, and for everything that makes up the living world. Yet we are being asked to accept that they can be privately owned. That the blueprint for life is just a commodity like any other. They want us to believe that no respect is due to the innate identity of living things, that a science in its infancy should be allowed to violate the innate identity of animals at will. That animals have no self which should be respected. They also expect us to believe that human beings who don't even understand all the genes of an organism can manipulate them without repercussions – that in living things the whole is not greater than the sum of the parts, that nothing is, or should be, sacred.

Those who plan to make money from manipulating genes not only want us to accept GE food. They want to create a radical change in how our society views the whole of the natural world – microbes, plants, animals, human beings. Locked into their outdated, mechanistic view of genes, they fail to appreciate the danger of tampering with a system as subtle and interactive as the gene pool of the natural world.

∗ The USDA hopes to know the 7,500 genes in a cousin of mustard, *Arabidopsis thaliana*, by 2004. A breakthrough.

Losing control

Genetic engineering has entered, or is due to enter, almost every industry. There may be some applications in which its use is justifiable and worth while – as it is in medicine – if only as the lesser evil. However, most are a long way off. So it has been necessary here to focus mainly on specific problems – food pollution, the danger of creating new diseases, the risks of work on animals, the dangers of GE crops. However, the greatest threat is to the ecosystem of the earth itself, on which all life depends.

It has been estimated that free-floating engineered genes may genetically alter as much as one per cent of the natural world a year. That may be an over-estimate or an under-estimate. Who can tell? There is no precedent for cutting and splicing genes as they do today. What is certain is that while we release genetically engineered organisms into our environment we have no control over the process of change which we trigger. Unseen changes might go on for years with no apparent impact – then suddenly alter some key element in the chain of life. What might happen nobody can predict. Science may be able to cut and splice genes but it is only just beginning to understand the basics of the web of life.

The officials who regulate GE seem to think the 'food chain' is merely seed to plate. They appear to know nothing of the life-sustaining 'food chain' of the natural world. Yet, without it, the seed will not grow. We know of only a tiny fraction of the micro-organisms which sustain life on earth and almost nothing of their subtle, yet vital interactions. Without thought for the future, GE is putting at risk the fertility of the soil itself, and the delicate, invisible, interactive web of life which has supported us on this planet for millennia.

It is the task of scientists to discover the laws of nature; of

✳ Worldwide some 50,000 species become extinct each year.

inventors to invent; of industrialists to set up and organise useful production; and of governments to govern. But none of these activities, no matter how specialised, can be wholesome unless carried on by people who take full responsibility for their actions, being imbued with a fully developed sense of the sacredness of all existence – a knowledge that they have not made the world and have not made themselves.

E. F. Schumacher[3]

Science has claimed to have the answers but any truly able scientist will admit that, in science, there is no certainty. The only thing a scientist can ever be totally sure of is that what is known today will be outdated and disproved tomorrow. In our ignorance about the systems which GE is to alter, all we can do is speculate. What if a GE microbe mutates to a form which sterilises or kills bees – upon which so many plants depend for pollination? What if the micro-organisms which decompose every kind of rubbish, from dead leaves to waste tips, start to release toxic gas while rotting? What if GE crops cause delicate, unseen micro-organisms to mutate and destroy soil fertility? There are scores of such questions to which science doesn't begin to have the answers.

We can seal up Chernobyls and missiles, stop making chemical pollutants and CFCs. But genetically modified organisms are alive and, once out of the laboratory, unstoppable. Whatever emergency plans the EU may make, once out of doors microbes are not containable. Already far too many have been released. Even as I write, food made without GE ingredients cannot claim 'contains no GE material' – for GE organisms are already in the air. We cannot halt the movement of pollen or ring-fence viruses. Nor can we contain microbial damage to the soil within some man-made firewall. Moreover, if damage is done it will be done for all time. There will be no antidote: life is self-perpetuating.

When you eat an apple you do not analyse the constituents of the apple. Yet God gave it health benefits, benefits which are the basis of many plants. They have tunnel vision, these scientists. They change one thing – they don't know anything about the hundreds of other things in the apple. They think you change one thing and the rest is intact. They are so *stupid*! When you disturb something it is not isolated. You disturb one thing and you disturb the interactions of *everything*.

Dr Majid Katme, spokesman for the Islamic Medical Association

Facing the Future

In this book, and in the media, a great deal has been said about the dangers of genetic engineering. However, it is not simply physical safety which is at stake. In relation to almost every application of GE human values, personal freedom and democracy are under threat, and with them the right to the most basic choices. Yet it is easy to get so caught up in the details of the arguments that we fail to see the broad picture.

Asking why?

We live in a world obsessed with numbers. But in many aspects of biotechnology thinking in terms of numbers is no more relevant than wondering how many angels can sit on a pin. We can all dispute how far pollen flies, debate crop yields, or how soon a deadly GE disease will emerge, until the sea freezes over. The fundamental question is: why use biotechnology when it isn't necessary? Why not reserve its use for ethical applications where no other technique will do? When its use is unethical or inappropriate, as in the case of crops and some animal work, why permit it? The world neither needs nor wants GE crops – so why have them? Most pharmaceuticals can be made without turning animals into living factories – so why do it? When living creatures are needlessly used as factories, our ethics violated and our lives endangered, the time for numbers is surely over.

Collaboration or subjugation

Of vital importance is the context within which we are making such decisions. For millions of years humanity has seen the natural world as its cradle and succour. Like all the other creatures of the earth, we survived and developed because every step of the way there has been food to eat and water to drink. We evolved not through conquering and subjugating the natural world, but because most of the time the natural world provided for us like the most tolerant and generous of mothers. As humankind became more sophisticated we learnt to understand her and to reap still greater benefits. There was, of course, a gradual shift to exploitation as we learnt to gouge out minerals and dam rivers. Yet, in the span of humanity on earth, it is only in relatively recent times that we have had the arrogance to shift from collaboration to subjugation. Even so, the basic building blocks of life, the inherent structure of plants, animals and humans, have until now been left intact, not just as entities but as symbols.

As most of us in industrialised, mechanised environments become distanced from nature, wild plants and creatures have remained, if only in memory or imagination, a link with something greater and more mysterious than ourselves. For the religious, a symbol of God's love; for many of those who have no god, a spiritual haven – a reminder that the whole is infinitely greater than the sum of the parts and of the connectedness of everything. What is now at stake therefore is not just safety or even survival. It is our whole perception of what it is to be alive.

A world in which the essence of life is a commodity and in which everything alive is seen as a defective machine which technology can improve – is a different world from one in which nature is cherished and respected. Nature will survive, despite our abuse, but the world will become a profoundly different place.

Do we want our children to grow up in a world bereft of humanity, their identity defined merely as the sequence of the human genome? Even if there were no physical dangers from GE, can we really accept the prospect of tomorrow's children living in a mechanistic world in which nothing is sacred and all reverence for life has been lost?

A sacred duty

Non-cooperation with injustice is a sacred duty.

Mahatma Gandhi

It would be easy to simply condemn the misuse of biotechnology, corporate greed, naïve and duplicitous government, theft from the poor, patents on human life, the prospect eugenics and crippled plants and animals pressed into service as 'factories'. Yet it would be wrong to lay the blame solely at the door of the biotech industry. When we look at the lengths to which GE has gone we aren't looking at some rare exception. We are seeing an outsized reflection of the whole of our society. The question is: will the life-destroying prospects which the misuse of biotechnology shows us be writing on the wall writ large enough for us to read?

Looking ahead

Let us hope that wiser council will prevail . . . That we learn to apply the principles of non-violence not only to relationships between people but also to those between people and living nature.

E. F. Schumacher[4]

Most of us live our lives like rowers: always seeing where we've been, never where we're going. Yet such are the long term possibilities of genetic engineering that they may encourage us to turn round and face what the future will be like if we don't change course.

This has been a century of multi-nationals, whose reach has often exceeded their ethical grasp.

However, the GE industry represents much of today's thinking. In seeking corporate power and profits by stealing the blood of tribal people, by depriving plants of their fertility, farmers of their ancient freedoms, and consumers of the fundamental right to eat natural food, biotechnology is showing us the natural outcome of a trend which has been taking place throughout much of industry. Human values have increasingly been replaced by accountancy values. If heads of industry do not value those they employ a human beings why should biotechnology apply human values to genetic engineering.

In farming we as a society if not as individuals, have silently accepted the loss of song birds, the destruction of hedgerows, the extinction of wildlife of every kind. Provided the food on our plates looked good, and was cheap, we turned a blind eye to its toxic load. We have ignored the steady pollution of land and water with farm and industrial chemicals – chemicals whose sale fattened many of today's gene giants. We have helped to make pollution pay. Should we be surprised when those same companies go one step further in their contempt for nature by reassembling the building blocks of life and crippling plants?

As a society we accepted our government's failure, to control or monitor chemical pollution. We have stood by while they passed laws which progressively limited the freedom of individuals – including the right to protest. We did not seek the slow building of corporate power – but neither did we stop it. With almost every shopping trip, we have, in one way or another, bought into it. Directly and indirectly, through shares, pension funds, banks and building societies, we have let our money support industry without asking too many questions. We have not discriminated between those companies which fostered human values and those which violated them. Provided the return on investment was right, we, like the gene giants, have been content.

As stockbrokers, investment analysts, fund managers, accountants, financial advisers, financial journalists, and all the other cogs in the investment machine, we have not, on the whole, discriminated between ethical and unethical investments. Nor have we ensured that our clients knew about the true nature of the firms they invested in. As health professionals we have too often tried to prevent death without respecting the indefinable qualities of life. We have often seen bacteria as our enemy, rarely as our friends. We have not opposed structures which forced us to treat the parts, not the whole. We never dreamed how short a step it might be to the production of a headless clone. As midwives and obstetricians we have often failed to stand up for the wisdom of nature; accepted or participated in interventions which were not essential; failed to honour the act of birth and the coming together of mother and child. We never dreamed that this would take us ever closer to genetically engineered babies in mechanically engineered wombs, still less to experimental embryos.

Very few of us can put hand on heart and say that we have in no way contributed to the devaluing, mechanical, dehumanised, greedy, irreverent world which the excesses of biotechnology symbolise and embody. Like most people I stand guilty as charged. So why should we be surprised if biotechnology seems set to go further still? What we are seeing in biotechnology is a natural expression of almost every aspect of our society.

A human triumph

Despite all that, the remarkable thing is that it seems almost as if people have been waiting for an opportunity to stand up for other values. Instead of submitting to the control of gene giants people have rallied. One of the great achievements of this century may be that ordinary people have halted giant industries in their tracks. In a way which would do credit to Gandhi, shoppers have opposed oppression simply by standing up for what was right. Their refusal to buy has made GE products uncommercial and convinced giant food manufacturers like Unilever – once a staunch supporter of GE – to change tack.

With every company that has changed its policy the countries and the farmers that refused to grow GE crops have gained ground and the others have lost. The shift in export patterns has been massive – and salutary. Governments, especially in America, had been persuaded that to support, any aspect of GE was to give their economy an edge. The reverse is proving to be the case. However, there is strong evidence that both politician and industry intend to sit out the storm without changing their aims.

Moreover, the danger is that we will tackle the symptoms without touching the disease. If we will change the course of biotechnology without looking at the society which spawned it, and made it what it is, the disease will merely return in another form. The immense opportunity that the excesses of genetic engineering offers is that it touches every area of our lives: our health, our values, our freedom of choice, our democratic rights, the value we put on the natural world, our priorities, our childrens' future, our understanding of other cultures, our sense of what is sacred.

Precisely because it threatens to go too far in so many areas, it gives us an opportunity to re-evaluate how we live – perhaps even to enter a new age. We have had the Stone Age, the Iron Age and the Age of Steam; and now we are being told that we are moving into the age of biotechnology. Yet remove six letters and you have a very different age – the age of biology.

> Action Aid believes that the way the biotechnology industry is applying GM technology could threaten the food security of developing countries and could well increase poverty and hunger.
>
> Action Aid 1999

A New Vision

The age of biology would need to have a subtle vision of the future. In a crowded industrialised world we cannot suddenly revert to being smallholders digging-in manure. We can, however, think and feel biologically. We can question the legality of patents on life because they fail to respect life itself. We can use science to understand more deeply the interconnectedness of all things. We can use technology to help us to live in harmony with the oneness, which is a biological reality whether we choose to notice it or not. We can combine our personal insights with those of science to better understand our place in that harmony. In doing so we can perhaps see the world and our place in it as it really is, not through the blinkered arrogance of industrialisation.

> The forests are more valuable to all of us than we have yet grasped; like love itself, they are so valuable we take them for granted.
>
> James Lovelock, Gaia[5]

Respecting the earth

Is it too much to hope that in the biological age we will cease to take life for granted, value the whole of the natural world, and realise how profoundly we depend on the earth itself? And that life is something we have been given – not something we create. For surely it is madness for us, who do not even understand ourselves, still less the miraculous interactions between everything on this planet, to suppose we can improve on the building blocks of a natural world which has evolved over millennia? To allow genetic engineering with infantile arrogance, to mess with the blueprints of life itself as casually as a toddler mixes finger paints.

While retaining whatever is good, ethical and responsible, do we not owe it to future generations to do all we can to limit the damage done by this and all other irresponsible industries?

Nature is resilient. We can harm her, we can kill her insects, cripple her plants, poison her rivers, make the soil sterile, do what we will, but we cannot destroy her – it is only we who may not survive.

> Gaia [the earth], in all her symbiogenetic glory, is inherently expansive, subtle, aesthetic, ancient, and exquisitely resilient ... We remain brazen, crass, and recent, even as we become more numerous ... We cannot put an end to nature; we can only pose a threat to ourselves. The notion that we can destroy all life, ... is ludicrous ... Most of them, the microbes, the whales, the insects, the seed plants ... will continue their cacophonies and harmonies long after we are gone.
>
> Lynn Margolis, *The Symbiotic Planet*[6]

The Music of Life

They say that science is deciphering the information code of life, and that now multinational companies intend to cultivate life in their laboratories, so that it does not run around wild and unharnessed, squandering colour and gaiety with the coming of spring. But life is music. It has its own notes, and its rhythm and cadence, and its melodies. And it is a powerful and playful magic force that moves our heart and our feet, and our very soul. And life, like music, was made to spill over and flow freely, a gift to poor and powerful alike. There are a thousand tunes in this world, for those who want to listen.

And each tune is a little piece of the soul of people and – just like life – cannot be cultivated in the laboratory of a multinational company. For this very reason, now that capital wants to appropriate the notes that compose the diverse songs of life, we need to join efforts, and stop it.

Indigenous People's Biodiversity Network

If you would like to do that please read on.

Actions that Make a Difference

> Never doubt that a small group of thoughtful, committed citizens can change the world. Indeed, it is the only thing that ever has.
>
> Margaret Mead

The power of the purse and the pen is extraordinary. Companies from all over Europe are joining together to form buying groups to source GE-free ingredients. Multinationals like Unilever are dropping GE ingredients. Austria is now almost a GE-free country. Holland and Italy have joined together to oppose the new European directive on patenting, which rubber-stamps bio-piracy. Whole states of Brazil have declared themselves GE-free zones. Worldwide, countries growing non-GE crops have booming exports, while those growing GE crops have seen sales slump.

It's a magnificent start but it would be easy to think that the battle had been won. It hasn't. It is only a first step towards creating a much larger debate about broader issues and getting politicians to listen to the public.

As taxpayers we have the right to be told the truth, not bamboozled with EU and government propaganda. We have the right to be consulted on whether we wish life to be treated as a commodity, and whether the World Trade Organisation – which acts on our behalf – should foster trade at any price, even if it violates the traditions of the Third World, harms the environment and may starve those who are already hungry.

Yet, even on food, some of those in power seem to think that consumer opposition will be a nine-day wonder – and may need to be proved wrong. The following came from a survey of the views of top politicians:

> '*Messy for a few years and then everybody will wonder what all the fuss was about.*'

> '*I think long term positive, you have got a bit of a storm in a teacup in the near future.*'

> '*I'm sure in five years' time, everybody will be happily eating genetically modified apples, plums, peaches and peas.*'

If you'd like to be eating GE apples, plums, peaches and peas in five years' time, I warmly recommend that you do nothing. If, on the other hand, you want to make these people wrong, read on. The money we spend and invest is the life-blood of the global economy, and our votes are the life-blood of politicians. We all have far more power than we realise. Politicians are counting on the public getting tired of opposing GE. They think that if they just keep ignoring us all opposition will fade away. In reality people who care about this can keep buying non-GE food for as long as it takes. While we keep buying shops will keep stocking. The purse is mightier than the sword. It isn't however, the only way to make your views felt.

Postcard and internet power

How often have you planned to write a letter, of praise or protest, and failed to do so? Haven't we all? Yet a few words on a postcard can be just as effective, e.g. 'I've switched to your brand/shop/chain because it's GM-free. Thank you.

Please keep it up', or 'You support genetic engineering, so I no longer buy your products/you no longer have my vote. Please let me know when your policy changes.'

On the Internet, at www.i-sis.dircon.co.uk, the Institute of Science and Society has put up two petitions to be signed, one by scientists, one by non-scientists, calling for a five-year world moratorium on the growing of foods, and a ban on patents on living organisms, cell lines and genes. You may want to add your name.

Twenty actions that make a difference

> All that is needed for evil to triumph is for good men [people] to do nothing.
>
> Edmund Burke

1 If you oppose the use of BST, write quickly to your MP, *and* your Euro MP, asking for it to be banned.

2 Talk to people about all this and encourage them to talk to others and take action too.

3 Ask manufacturers and shops to label shelves and the *front* of products to show GE-free items. It's simple, legal and makes GE-free shopping faster.

4 Support companies which take a stand on the issues – and praise them for doing so. Use the call lines of supermarkets.

5 Avoid buying any products from a company which uses GE crops in its foods – and maybe write and tell the company what you're doing.

6 Ask for and buy organic produce – it gives shops a clear signal that consumers want natural food – not GE.

7 Ask the government/your MP/MEP to give more encouragement to organic farming.

8 Ask the government/your MP/MEP to boost scientific research into organic farming.

9 Ask the government to make it easier for farmers to convert

to organic farming by allowing an intermediate category during changeover.

10 Ask shops to create GE-free zones – or become totally GE-free.

11 Ask restaurants, cafés, pubs and food chains to become GE-free.

12 Ask schools, colleges, work canteens, meals on wheels, hospitals, children's homes to become GE-free.

13 Support charities opposing the misuse of GE. Some are listed in Sources of Information and many have active local groups you can join. Money is also welcomed and every pound helps.

14 Write to your MP, to relevant ministers, and others in power on aspects of GE which concern you. Postcards are often better than letters.

15 If any aspect of GE violates, or may violate, your religion, point this out to politicians, and urge your religious leaders to take the issue up on the grounds of human rights and respect for freedom of religion.

16 If you belong to an organisation, ask a speaker to come and talk on GE issues – there is much more to this than just food, so there's a GE topic for every kind of organisation.

17 Discuss the ethics of aspects of GE within professional bodies with which you are associated, and in their magazines.

18 Don't hold shares in any company whose policies seem to you unethical. If you decide to sell shares, you might also write and tell the companies why.

19 Write to organisations which invest money for you – building societies, pension funds, trade unions, professional bodies, and so on, questioning their policies on investing in biotechnology – especially GE farming.

20 Put your money into companies which pursue policies you feel are ethical and world-sustaining.

Sources of Information

Addresses

Government
The Prime Minister
10 Downing Street, London, SW1A 2AA
To find your MP dial 0171 219 4272 and give your town or city and post code.
To find your MEP dial 0171 227 4300.

Minister of the Environment
Dept. of the Environment, Transport and the Regions (DETR), Sanctuary Buildings, Great Smith St. London SW1P 3BT
Web: http://www.environment.detr.gov.uk/acre/register.htm
The web site covers applications for GE crops.

Minister of Health
Dept. of Health, Richmond House, 79 Whitehall,
London SW1A 2NS
0171 210 4850
http://wwww.open.gov.uk/doh/dhhome.htm

Minister of Agriculture, Fisheries and Food (MAFF)
Whitehall Place West, London SW1A 2HH
Information line: 0645 33 55 77
http://www.maff.gov.uk

Regulatory and Advisory Bodies

Advisory Committee on Releases to the Environment
(ACRE)
Department of the Environment, Transport and the Regions,
Ashdown House, 123 Victoria Street, London SW1E 60E
Tel: 0171 890 5275/5277
Fax: 0171 890 5259
Web: see DETR
Advises on releases of GE organisms into the environment.

Advisory Committee on Novel Foods and Processes (ACNFP)
Nobel House, 17 Smith Square, London SW1P 3PY
Tel: 0171 276 8187
Fax: 0171 276 8333
Advises on the approval of GE foods.

Human Genetics Advisory Commission,
Albany House, 94–98 Petty France, London SW1H 9ST

Relevant UK-based organisations

For information from any of these organisations please send
a large self addressed envelope with a first class stamp.

Action Aid
Hamlyn House, Macdonald Road, London N19 5PG
Tel: 0171 561 7561
Web: http://www.actionaid.org
Publishes an excellent free booklet on GE and world hunger.

Action Against Allergy
P.O. Box 278, Twickenham TW1 4QQ
Tel: 0181 892 2711

Baby Milk Action
23 St Andrew's Street, Cambridge CB2 3AX
Tel: 01223 464 420

Web: http://www.gn.apc.org/babymilk
Has information on safe baby milk.

Campaign Against Human Genetic Engineering
P.O. Box 6313, London N16 0DY
E-m: cahge@globalnet.co.uk

Catholic Institute for International Relations
Unit 3 Canonbury Yard, 190a New North Road,
London N1 7BJ
Tel: 0171 354 0883
Fax: 0171 359 0017
E-m: ciir@ciir.org
Web: http://www.ciir.org

Christian Aid
P.O. Box, London SE1 7RT
Tel: 0171 620 4444
Web: http://www.christian-aid.org.uk

Compassion in World Farming Trust,
5a Charles Street, Petersfield, Hants GU32 3EH
Tel: 01730 264208
Fax: 01730 260791
E-m: info@ciwf.co.uk
Web: http://www.ciwf.co.uk
Sells excellent reports on animal issues, including BST.

Consumers Association
2 Marylebone Road, London NW1 4DF
Tel: 0171 830 6000
Web: http://www.which.net/campaigns/gmfood/
contents.html

The Corner House
P.O. Box 3137, Station Road, Sturminster Newton,
Dorset, DT10 1YJ
Tel: 01258 473795
Fax: 01258 473748

e-mail: cornerhouse@gn.apc.org
Web: http://www.icaap.org./cornerhouse
Sells excellent briefing papers.

Corporate Watch
Web: http://www.corpwatch.org
Briefing papers on company misdeeds.

Council for the Protection of Rural England (CPRE)
25 Buckingham Palace Road, London SW1W 0PP
Tel: 0171 976 6433
Fax: 0171 976 6373
E-m: cpre@gn.apc.org
Web: http://www.greenchannel.com/cpre/

Earth First! UK
c/o Cornerstone Resources Centre,
16 Sholebroke Avenue, Leeds LS7 3HB
E-m: actionupdates@gn.apc.org
Web: http://www.hrc.wmin.ac.uk/campaigns/ef/
earthfirst.html
Network of local radical activist groups with monthly newsletter.

The Ecosystem
Environment Digest, 13–17 Sturton Street,
Cambridge CB1 2SN
Tel: 01223 568017
Fax: 01223 354643
E-m: ecosystem@reast.demon.co.uk
Web: http://www.gn.apc.org/ecosystem/

English Nature
Northminster House, Peterborough PE1 1UA
Tel: 01733 455000
Fax: 01733 568834
E-m: enquiries@english-nature.org.uk
Web: http://www.english-nature.org.uk/

Food Commission
94 White Lion Street, London N1 9PF
Tel: 0171 837 2250
Web: http://www.foodcomm.org.uk
Expert food information.

Food Labelling Agenda (FLAG)
P.O. Box 25303, London NW5 1WY
Campaigns for better food labelling.

Freeze Campaign
94 White Lion Street, London N1 9PF
Tel: 0171 837 0642
E-m gealliance@dial.pipex.com
An alliance of companies and organisations calling for a five-year freeze on genetically engineered food. Companies and organisations are welcome to join it.

Friends of the Earth (FoE)
26–28 Underwood Street, London N1 2PN
Tel: 0171 490 1555 or 0113 242 8153
Web: http://www.foe.co.uk
Very active on GE with many local groups taking action. Greenpeace, Friends of the Earth (FoE) and Genetic Engineering Network (GEN) have a joint campaign against GE food on hotline: 0171 865 8222.

Gaia Foundation
18 Well Walk, London NW3 1LD
Tel: 0171 435 5000
Fax: 0171 431 0551
Covers the Third World, patents and bio-piracy.

Gen Ethics News
P.O. Box 6313, London N16 0DY
Tel: 0181 809 4513
Fax: 0181 809 4513
E-m: genethicsnews@compuserve.com

Web: http://www.ourworld.compuserve.com
Produces a bi-monthly newsletter.

Genetix Food Alert
c/o Green City, 23 Fleming Street, Glasgow
Tel: 0141 554 6099
Web: http://www.essential-trading.co.uk/genetix.htm
A coalition of wholefood groups which wants the government to have a three-year ban on importing, growing or using GE in food. Campaign coordinator on: 0141 554 7633.

GenetiX Snowball
One World Centre, 6 Mount Street, Manchester M2 5NS
Tel: 0161 834 0295
Web: http://www.gn.apc.org/pmhp/gs
Gene Watch UK
Web: http//www.genewatch.org
Briefings on GE, particularly around policy issues. Good links to other sites.

Green Party
A Waterlow Road, London N19 5NJ
Tel: 0171 272 4474
Web: http://www.greenparty.org.uk
Campaigns for GE-free school dinners. For leaflets send an SAE or Phone 01484 430 738 for pack on GE issues.

G.M. Free
Khi Publications,
Beacon House,
Skelmesdale, Woodley Park,
Lanco WN8 6UK
Tel/Fax: 01695 50504
E-m: gmfree@cableinet.co.uk.
Bi-monthly magazine on GE and its risks to food, farming and the environment.

Greenpeace
Canonbury Villas, Islington, London N1 2PN
Tel: 0171 865 8214
Web: http://www.greenpeace.org/slgeneng/
http://greenpeace.org/comms/cbiog/geneng.
Commissions reports as well as direct action on GE. Wide range of leaflets.

Hyperactive Children's Support Group
71 Whyke Lane, Chichester, Sussex PO 19 2LD

Insulin Dependent Diabetes Trust
P.O. Box 294, Northampton NN3 2BN
Tel:/Fax: 01604 721 325
Helps those who react badly to 'human' insulin.

Institute of Science and Society
Web: http:/www.i-sis.dircon.co.uk
Has two petitions for a five-year freeze of GE. One invites signatures from scientists, the other from the public.

International Society for Ecology and Culture
Apple Barn, Week, Dartington, Totnes, Devon TQ9 6JP
Web: http://www.isec.com.uk
International globalisation issues and GE.

Nationwide Food Survey
Beacon House, Willow Walk, Skelmersdale,
Lancashire WN8 6UP
Fax: 01695 503306
Publishes a booklet listing GE-free foods.

Natural Law Party
Mentmore Towers, Mentmore, Buckinghamshire LU7 0QH
Tel: 01296 662211
Fax: 01296 662486
Very active with many local groups

Wessex Natural Law Party
Web: http:dRwww.btinternet.com/slnlpwessex/Documents/
gmocarto.htm
*National web site with very useful facts on the performance of GE
crops and the environmental impacts of GE.*

HRH Prince Charles
Prince of Wales genetic engineering web site on GE food
Web: http://www.princeofwales.gov.uk/forum/

One World On line
http://www.oneworld.org/guides/biotech/GE events.htm
Good site for the latest news.
*An internet community of 434 organisations concerned with human
rights, and sustainable and/developing world with excellent links.*

Excellent Links
The Panos Institute,
9 White Lion Street, London N1 9PD
Tel: 0171 278 1111
Fax: 0171 278 0345
E-m: panos@panoslondon.org.uk
Web: http://www.one world.org/panos/
*A development charity with information on the impact of GE on 3rd
World farmers.*

Pesticides Trust
Eurolink Centre, 49 Effra Road, London SW2 1BZ
Tel: 0171 274 8895
Fax: 0171 274 9084
E-m: pesttrust@gn.apc.org
Web: www.gn.apc.org/pesticidestrust/
*Health and environment issues related to chemicals. Newsletter. Web
has links to similar organisations in UK and overseas.*

Physicians and Scientists for Responsible Application of
Science and Technology
Web: http://www.psagef.org/indexgen.htm
Excellent web site for clear explanations of science issues involved in
GE, and why GE food is a bad use of science.

Soil Association
40–56 Victoria Street, Bristol BS1 6BY
Tel: 0117 929 0661
Fax: 0117 925 2504
E-m: info@soilassociation.org
Web: http//www.soilassociation.org
Main certifier of organic food, promotes organic farming and opposes
GE. Has lists of organic box delivery schemes for a GE-free diet.

Sustain – the Alliance for Better Food and Farming
94 Red Lion Street, London N1 9PF
Tel: 0171 837 1128

Student Environment Network
c/o Grassroots, UMU, Oxford Road, Manchester M13 9PR
Tel: 0161 275 2942

Townswomen's Guilds
Chamber of Commerce House, 75 Harborne Road,
Edgbaston, Birmingham B15 3DA
Tel: 0121 456 3435
Web: http://www.townswomen.org.uk/

UK Food Group
P.O. Box 100, London SE1 7RT
Tel: 0171 523 2369
Fax: 0171 620 0719
Web: http://www.ukfg.org.uk
An NGO forum on global food, agriculture and development issues.
Members include Action Aid, the Gaia Foundation and Oxfam.
Linked to it is the UK Agricultural Biodiversity Coalition, which has
a very informative web site on:

http://dspace.dial.pipex.com/ukfg/ukabc.htm

World Development Movement (WDM)
25 Beehive Place, London SW9 7QR
Freephone: 0800 328 2153
Fax: 0171 738 6098
Web: http://www.wdm.org.uk/

Women's Environmental Network (WEN)
87 Worship Street, London EC2A 2BE
Tel: 0171 247 3327
Fax: 0171 247 4740
E-m: TestTube@gn.apc.org
Web: http//www.gn.apc.org/wen
Campaigns on GE, produces useful briefing sheets on setting up local campaigns and ideas for action.

Women's Nutritional Advisory Service
P.O. Box 268, Lewes, East Sussex BN7 2QN
Tel: 01273 487 3666
Send an sae for a survey of companies using GE soya.

Organisations Worldwide

Action for Solidarity, Equality, Environment and
   Development (ASEED) Europe
P.O. Box 92066, 1090 AB Amsterdam, Holland
Tel: 31 20 668 2236
Fax: 31 20 665 0166
E-m: aseedeur@antenna.nl
Web: http://www.antenna.nl/aseed/
Coordinates action groups worldwide on food and globalisation campaigns.

Alliance for Bio-Integrity
http://bio-integrity.org
A useful American web site for information and campaigns. Religious principles.

Australian Gene Ethics Network (AGEN)
340 Gore Street, Fitzroy 3065, Victoria, Australia
Tel: 03 9 416 2222
e-mail: acfgenet@peg.apc.org
Web: http://www.zero.com.au/agen/ or
http://www.peg.apc.org/ãcfge.net
Network raising awareness of GE issues.

Californians for Alternatives to Toxics
P.O. Box 1195 (990 I St), Arcata, CA 95518, USA
Tel: 00 1 707 822 8497
Fax: 00 1 707 822 7136
E-m: catz@reninet.com
Web: http://www.reninet.com/catz/

Campaign for Food Safety
860 Highway 61, Little Marais, Minnesota 55614, USA
Tel: 00 1 218 226 4164
Fax: 00 1 218 226 4157
e-mail: alliance@mr.net
Web: http://www.purefood.org/index.htm
Formerly the Pure Food Campaign, it backs sustainable food production and opposes GE. Global information source.

Centre for Science and the Environment
CSE Centre for Science and Environment,
41, Tughlakabad Institutional Area, New Delhi-110062, India
Tel: 91–11–6981110, 6981124, 6981125, 6983394, 6986399
Fax: 91–11–6985879
E-m: webadmin@cseindia.org
Web: http://www.oneworld.org/cse/html/cmp/cmp13.htm
Excellent information on biodiversity, patents and the Third World

Chemical Injury Information Network (CIIN)
P.O. Box 301, White Sulphur Springs, MT 59645, USA
Tel: 00 1 406 547 2255
Advocacy by the chemically injured for the chemically injured plus

education, research and empowerment. Has over 5,000 members in 35 countries Monthly newsletter Our Toxic Times *countries.*

Community Food Security Coalition,
P.O. Box 209, Venice, CA 90294, USA
Tel: 00 1 310 822 5410
Web: http://www.foodsecurity.org.

Consumer Right to Know Campaign for Mandatory
Labelling and Long-term Testing of All Genetically
Engineered Foods
500 Wilbrod Street, Ottawa, Ontario, Canada KIN 6N2
Tel: 613 565 8517
Fax: 613 565 1596
E-m: rwolfson@concentric.net
Web: http://www.natural-law.ca/genetic/geindex.html

Corporate Watch
P.O. Box 29344,
San Francisco,
CA 94129, USA
Tel: 00 1 415 561 6568
e-mail: corpwatch@igc.org
Web: http://www.corpwatch.org/trac/undp/index.html
Information on the rise and influence of giant corporations. Resource centre providing tools to investigate and analyse corporate activity.

Council for Responsible Genetics
5 Upland Road, Suite 3, Cambridge, MA 02140, USA
Tel: 00 1 617 868 0870
Fax: 00 1 617 491 5344
E-m: marty@gene-watch.org
Web: http://www.gene-watch.org and
http://www.essential.org/crg/
Focuses on the social and environmental aspects of GE; patenting, genetic discrimination, food.

Edmonds Institute
20319 9 2nd Avenue, Edmonds, Washington 98020, USA
Tel: 00 1 425 775 5383
Fax: 00 1 425 670 8410
E-m: beb@igc.org
Policy analysis and research, scholarly, advises policy makers.

Genetic Concern
7 Upper Camden Street, Dublin 2, Eire
Tel: 353 476 0360
Fax: 353 476 0361
E-m: geneticconcern@tinet.ie
Web: http://www.vibrantplanet.com/geneticconcern
Is fighting a court case against GE crops being grown in Ireland.

Genetic Engineering and Its Dangers
Philosophy Department, College of Humanities,
San Francisco State University, San Francisco, CA 94132, USA
Web: http://userwww.sfsu.edu/slrone/gedanger.htm
Collection of good essays on GE, selected by Dr Ron Epstein.

Genetic Resources Action Network (GRAIN)
Girona 25, Pral, E-08010 Barcelona, Spain
Tel: 34 3 301 1381
Fax: 34 3 301 1627
E-m: grain@bcn.servicom.es
Web: http://www.grain.org/ in English, French and Spanish
Promotes sustainable land use and biodiversity based on local control over genetic resources, especially in developing countries. Good on patents.

Indigenous People
http://www.indians.org/wel ker/genome.htm
Opposes the patenting of life forms.

Infant Feeding Coalition,
10 Trinity Square, Toronto, Canada M5G 1B1
Tel: (416) 595 9819

Mothers for Natural Law
Web: http://www.safe-food.org/welcome,htd
Web: http://www.Lisco.com/mothers for natural Law
Aims to make opposition to GE a talking point in every American household. Site has scientific background, news and events.

National Association for Sustainable Agriculture, Australia Ltd
P.O. Box 768, Stirling, South Australia 5152
Tel: 61 (08) 8 370 8455
Fax: 61 (08) 8 370 8381
E-m: nasaa@dove.mtx.net.au
Web: www.earthlink.com.au/nasaa/

Organic Consumer Association (OCA)
860 Highway 61, Little Marais, MN 55614, USA
Tel: 001 218 226 4792
Fax: 001 218 226 4157
E-m: oca@purefood.org
Web: http://www.organicconsumers.org.
Supports high organic standards. Provides resources on how to buy organic. Addresses food safety issues such as GE and rBGH.

Organic Farming Research Foundation,
P.O. Box 440, Santa Cruz, CA 95061, USA
Tel: 001 831 426 6606
Fax: 001 831 426–6670
E-m: research@afrf.org.

Pesticide Action Network North America (PANNA)
49 Powell St, Suite 500, San Francisco, CA 94102, USA
Tel: 00 1 415 981 1771
Fax: 00 1 415 981 1991
E-m: panna@panna.org
Web: http:dRwww.panna.org
Campaigns against pesticides worldwide. E-mails a free newsletter.

Physicians and Scientists for Responsible Application of
Science and Technology
E-m: webmaster@psrast.org
Web: http://www.psagF.org/indexgen.htm

Purefood Campaign (USA)
http://www.geocities.com/Athens/1527/
Useful site with excellent links to other sites.

Rachel Carson Council, Inc.
8940 Jones Mill Road, Chevy Chase, Maryland 20815, USA
Tel: 00 1 301 652 1877
E-m: rccouncil@aol.com
Web: http://members.aol.com/rccouncil/ourpage/
*An association for the integrity of the environment. It has information
on chemical pesticides and alternative methods of pest control.*

Research Foundation for Science, Technology and Natural
Resource Policy
A-60 Haus Khas, New Delhi 110016, India
Tel: 0091 11 696 8077
E-m: twn@uvn.ernet.in
Web: http://www.indiaserver.com/betas/vshiva
*A small foundation deeply committed to conserving biodiversity and
sustainable agriculture.*

Rural Advancement Foundation International (RAFI)
110 Osborne Street, Suite 202, Winnipeg,
Maritoba, Canada R3L IY5
Tel: 204 453 5259
Fax: 204 925 8034
E-m: rafi@rafi.org
Web:http://www.rafi.org
*Excellent web site for information on patents, bio-piracy and trans-
national corporations.*

Third World Network
228 Macalister Road, 10400 Penang, Malaysia
Tel: 60 4 226 6728

E-m: twn@igc.apc.org
Web: http://www.twnside.org.sg/souths/twnhsbio.htm
Good web site for the facts on most Third World issues.

Union of Concerned Scientists
Two Brattle Square, Cambridge, MA 02238, USA
Tel: 00 1 617 547 5552
Fax: 00 1 617 864 9405
E-m: ucs@ucsusa.org
Web: http://www.ucsusa.org/
An alliance of scientists and consumers concerned for a healthier world. Publishes e-mail magazine The Gene Exchange, *details of how to receive it on the web site.*

Books Which May Interest You

On food

How to Avoid GM Food, Joanna Blythman, Fourth Estate, 1999.
Lists, item by item, some major brands of ready-made foods which contain GE ingredients.

The Shopper's Guide to Organic Food, Lynda Brown, Fourth Estate 1998. Focuses mainly on food standards, organic certification, residues in non-organics and so on.

GM Free: A shopper's guide to genetically modified food. Sue Dibb and Dr Tim Lobstein, Virgin 1999. Has an alphabetical list of food types with guidance.

The Organic Directory 1999–2000, Clive Litchfield, Green Books 1999. Clear county-by-county listings of organic shops, mail-order companies, restaurants, box scheme deliveries, etc.

Where to Buy Organic Food, The Soil Association 1998. Direct from the Association (see p. 330) it gives similar guidance.

On genetic engineering & the environment

Altered Genes, Richard Hindmarsh, Geoffrey Lawrence and Janet Norton, Allen & Unwin (Australia), 1998. Interesting Australian perspective.

Against the Grain: The Genetic Transformation of Global Agriculture, Marc Lappe and Britt Bailey, Earthscan, 1999. The impact of GE on agriculture, its dangers and failures.

Improving Nature: The science and ethics of genetic engineering, Michael J. Reiss and Roger Straughan, Cambridge University Press, 1996. Good, clear science basics and thoughtful ethical discourse by a biologist and a philosopher.

The Biotech Century: The Coming Age of Commerce, Jeremy Rifkin, Victor Gollancz, 1998. Thought-provoking analysis of the social implications of biotechnology.

Biopiracy: The Plunder of Nature and Knowledge, Vandana Shiva, Green Books, 1998. A well-argued case against bio-patenting from an Indian perspective.

Genetic Engineering: Dream or Nightmare? – The Brave New World of Bad Science and Big Business, Mae-Wan Ho, Gateway Books, 1998. A pioneering exposé by a distinguished scientist. Excellent for the scientifically inclined.

On related topics

Books which, while not about genetic engineering, offer a cautionary and illuminating perspective on it.

Gaia: the practical science of planetary medicine, James Lovelock, Gaia Books, 1991. Despite its ponderous subtitle, an extremely readable, beautifully illustrated book on the interactions of all life on earth. No home should be without it.

The Symbiotic Planet, Lynn Margolis, Weidenfeld and Nicolson, 1999. The latest book by an inspired biologist. A good read which explains our origins in the very organisms which GE so underestimates.

Toxic Deception! How the Chemical Industry Manipulates, Science and the Law, and Endangers You and Me, Dan Fagin and Marianne Lavelle, Centre for Public Integrity, 1999

The Feminisation of Nature! our future at risk, Deborah Cadbury, Penguin 1998

Genetic Engineering, Food, and our Environment, Luke Anderson, Green Books 1999. A pocket-sized, fact-packed rundown.

Acronyms

ACF	*Australian Conservation Foundation: an opponent of biotech releases into the environment.*
ACGM	*Advisory Committee on Genetic Modification: advises mainly on non-food uses of genetic engineering.*
ACNFP	*Advisory Committee on Novel Foods and Processes, the body which approves GE foods for sale in Britain.*
ACP	*Advisory Committee on Pesticides.*
ACRE	*Advisory Committee on Releases to the Environment, which has a subgroup which examines issues of biodiversity.*
ADM	*Archer Daniels Midland, a large American food manufacturer.*
AMRAD	*Australian Medical and Research and Development Corporation, a pharmaceutical company.*
ANZFA	*Australian and New Zealand Food Authority: the body responsible for overseeing food labelling.*
ATCC	*American Type Culture Collection. An international store holding tens of thousands of samples of genetic material for the purposes of patent procedures.*
BASF	*An agro-chemical giant now working on GE crops*
BINAS	*Biosafety Information Network and Advisory Service: seems to be an offshoot of ICGEB.*
BST	see *Glossary*.
BVD	*Bureau of Veterinary Drugs (Canada).*
CAP	*Common Agricultural Policy (of the EU).*

CBD   *Convention on Biodiversity – a UN convention.*

CBDC   *Community Biodiversity Development and Conservation Programme, a research network of rural civic societies.*

CGC   *Canadian Grain Commission.*

CGIAR   *Consultative Group on International Agricultural Research.*

CGRFA   *Commission on Genetic Resources for Food and Agriculture: a division of the FAO.*

CoC   *Council of Canadians: a citizens' group.*

COT   *Committee on Toxicology (UK).*

CRG   *Council for Responsible Genetics: an association of American scientists opposed to patenting life-forms.*

CVMP   *European Committee on Veterinary Medical Products.*

DETR   *Department of Environment, Transport and Regions (UK), the department responsible for approval of crop trials.*

DISR   *Department of Industry, Science and Resources.*

DNA   *See Glossary.*

DSB   *Disputes Settlement Body – of the World Trade Organisation.*

EC   *European Community (another term for the EU).*

EFB   *European Federation of Biotechnology.*

EPA   *Environmental Protection Agency (USA).*

EU   *European Union (also called the EEC: European Economic Community).*

FAC   *Food Advisory Committee (UK): advises the government on general food issues.*

FAO   *Food and Agriculture Organisation of the United Nations. Issues independent reports on food and farming worldwide.*

FDA   *Food and Drugs Administration (USA).*

FOE   *Friends of the Earth, one of the most long-established environmental bodies.*

GATT   *General Agreement on Tariffs and Trade: a global trade agreement implemented by the WTO.*

GE   *Genetically Engineered or Genetic Engineering.*

GEO   *Genetically Engineered Organism – the same as a GMO but a more accurate term. Some organisms, such as food-stuffs, are themselves engineered (or modified); others are produced by organisms which have been engineered or modified. Engineered covers both situations better than GMO.*

GGC   *Guaymi General Congress: Panama's largest organisation for indigenous peoples.*

GMAC   *Genetic Manipulation Advisory Committee (Australia).*

GMN   *Giant multinational*

GMO   *Genetically Modified Organism: often used for anything produced by genetic engineering at any stage. It is, how-ever, the weasel term the industry prefers: 'modified' sounds much gentler than 'engineered'. See GEO above.*

GRAS   *Generally Regarded As Safe: an American classification.*

HSCA   *Heritage Seed Curators Australia.*

HSD   *Human Safety Division – of the Bureau of Veterinary Drugs (Canada).*

HUGO   *Human Genome Organisation: a network of international scientists who coordinate their research to identity the full sequence of human genes.*

IBC   *International Bioethics Committee: a subsection of the United Nations Education, Scientific and Cultural Organ-isation (UNESCO).*

               Institutional Biosafety Committees (Australia): voluntary committees based in institutions and companies.

ICAR   *Indian Council of Agricultural Research.*

ICGEB   *International Centre for Genetic Engineering and Biotech-nology: an international organisation set up to 'promote the safe use of biotechnology world-wide'.*

IDRC   *International Development Research Centre.*

IPR   *Intellectual Property Rights: traditionally this was the right to the exclusive ownership and exploitation of some-thing such as a book, a design, or a musical score – as opposed to a mechanical invention. Recent laws have extended it to include ways of carrying out certain scientific processes. These have been interpreted as embracing not just the process but the genes or cells on which they are used. So life itself is now patentable.*

JECFA	*Joint Expert Committee on Food Additives.*
MAFF	*Ministry of Agriculture, Fisheries and Food (UK).*
MNC	*Multinational Company.*
MRL	*Maximum Residue Levels: usually used for the amount of pesticide per kilogram of food.*
NASAA	*National Association for Sustainable Agriculture of Australia, a certifying authority for organic crops.*
NFU	*National Farmers' Union: a name used in the UK, the USA and elsewhere.*
NGO	*Non-Governmental Organisation: usually a pressure group.*
NHS	*National Health Service: the government-funded nationwide medical service of the UK.*
NIH	*National Institute of Health.*
NOAH	*National Office of Animal Health (UK).*
NRA	*National Registration Authority on Agricultural and Veterinary Chemicals (Australia).*
OHE	*Office of Health Economics (UK).*
OTA	*Office of Technological Assessment: a Congressional office in the USA.*
PAMP	*Post Approval Monitoring Programme.*
PEGS	*Pesticide Exposure Group of Sufferers (UK).*
POEA	*Polyoxyethyleneamine: a* **surfactant** *(see Glossary), used in many glyphosate weedkillers.*
PSD	*Pesticides Safety Directorate (UK), a regulatory government body.*
RAFI	*Rural Advancement Foundation International, a Canadian charity which monitors the impact of new technologies on rural societies.*
RICS	*Royal Institute of Chartered Surveyors.*
SAGB	*Senior Advisory Group on Biotechnology (Brussels-based).*
SCF	*Scientific Committee for Food – an EU body.*

SCIMAC	*Supply Chain Initiative on Modified Agricultural Crops: formed by the NFU and other concerned UK bodies.*
SEARICE	*South-East Asian Regional Institute for Community Education, a Manila-based body concerned with agriculture and biodiversity.*
TNC	*Transnational Corporation.*
TPS	*Technology Protection System, an official name for Terminator seeds.*
TRIP	*Trade Related Intellectual Property. An agreement under GATT which opened the door to transnationals patenting both life-forms and traditional knowledge and remedies.*
UKROFS	*United Kingdom Register of Organic Food Standards.*
UNCED	*United Nations Conference on Environment and Development (see Rio Earth Summit in Glossary)*
UNCSTD	*United Nations Commission on Science and Technology for Development.*
UNESCO	*United Nations Education, Scientific and Cultural Organisation.*
UPOV	*International Union for the Protection of New Varieties of Plants: an international agreement which enables plant-breeders to obtain property rights over plants they breed, within set criteria, but which is less sweeping than a patent.*
USDA	*US Department of Agriculture.*
VMAC	*Veterinary Medicines Advisory Committee (USA): a division of the FDA.*
VMD	*Veterinary Medicines Directorate (UK): the regulatory body for animal treatments. It comes under MAFF but is 'self-financing'. Funding may come from industries it is meant to regulate.*
VPC	*Veterinary Products Committee (UK): a committee advising the government on such products.*
WIPO	*World Intellectual Property Organisation.*
WTO	*World Trade Organisation, the international body controlling and promoting world trade.*

Glossary

Adaptive mutation
A new and controversial concept of adaptation, at DNA level, in response to a selective pressure or stress.

Agenda 21
A set of action programmes for sustainable future development agreed at the United Nations Earth Summit. An important but not binding consensus on the part of world governments.

Agro-giant
Multinational maker of farm chemicals and agriculture products.

Allele
A variant of a particular gene. The cells of most organisms normally have two versions (two alleles) of each gene – one from each parent. One chromosome has one parent's allele for a characteristic, its paired chromosome has the other parent's allele. Sometimes both alleles cause the same characteristic (e.g. both cause brown eyes). But if two alleles carry different characteristics (e.g. one carries brown eyes, one blue), the more powerful (dominant) allele wins, the less powerful (recessive) one loses.

Allergen/allergy
Definitions of allergy vary but, broadly, an allergen is whatever triggers an allergy (i.e. symptoms of sensitivity) in those vulnerable to it. It may take several contacts before symptoms ranging from mild rashes to fatal shock occur. If GE creates new allergens, the allergies may not show at once.

Amino acids
The building blocks of proteins and peptides – and so of life – made from different blends of basic atoms like carbon and nitrogen. All animals have twenty common amino acids plus

many others. Essential amino acids are those an organism needs but can't make for itself. One of these is tryptophan. Humans and animals depend on their diet to provide a range of essential amino acids. Just as twenty-six letters of the alphabet can make millions of different words, so amino acids can make millions of proteins. To do this they form peptide bonds to link up in a chain. The order in which they link creates the properties and biological role of each protein.

Antibody
A vital protein created by white blood cells as part of the immune system which recognises and disables invaders, such as a germs.

Bacillus
A type of rod-shaped bacterium.

Bacteria
Microscopic single-cell organisms ranging in shape from oval to corkscrew, which can live in the mouth, gut and wounds, and in soil, water or air. Some are beneficial to us, e.g. by helping a compost heap decay. Others causes diseases in plants, animals and humans and produce poisons to do so (endo-toxins, exotoxins). Antibiotics kill them, but bacteria are constantly evolving and many serious infections now resist all but one or two antibiotics. The use in GE of antibiotic-resistant bacteria or genes providing resistance to antibiotics is therefore a serious issue.

Bacteriophage (or phage)
A virus that infects bacteria.

BGH
See BST.

Biochemistry
The study of the chemistry of living things (e.g. proteins, etc.).

Biodevelopment
Normally means the use of biology by industry.

Biodiversity
All earth's life-forms: the species of creatures and plants and the ecosystems of which they are a part. Protecting biodiversity means protecting the full range of plants, creatures and other life-forms in the natural world. The aim is to maintain the balance of nature by retaining its full range of species of all kinds.

Bioindustries
Industries or companies working on or with life-forms.

Biosciences
All the sciences which work on or with life-forms: biology, medicine, molecular biology, cellular biology, chemical engineering, genetic engineering, biochemistry.

Biotechnology
Traditionally this was the use of micro-organisms in processes like fermentation. Today it means changing life-forms by techniques not used by nature, especially gene insertion.

Bio-Utopia
An imaginary perfect world created by improving on nature.

Blood plasma
The watery part of blood, including the hormones, salts and other substances it carries, but excluding blood cells.

BRCA1 and BRCA2
The two major genes carrying an inherited risk of breast cancer and – especially in BRCA1 – of ovarian cancer.

BSE (Bovine spongiform encephalopathy)
Known as 'Mad Cow Disease', this illness caused cattle to collapse and die. Blamed on meat from sheep infected with the similar disease scrapie, it has been thought to cause the fatal brain disease CJD (Creutzfeldt-Jakob Disease) in humans who eat infected meat.

BST

A milk-boosting GE hormone injected into cows. In Europe it is called bovine somatotrophin or recombinant bovine somatotrophin (rBST, rbST). The American name is bovine growth hormone (BGH) or recombinant bovine growth hormone (rBST, rbGH).

Carrier

Someone who has no symptoms of a disease or disability but carries the germs or the gene for a disability, infecting others or passing the disability on to the next generation.

Casein

A protein in milk, and the main protein in cheese. High in phosphate, it is easily digested by the gut enzymes of young mammals.

Cell culture

Growing cells in a laboratory.

Cells

The bricks which by themselves, or in colonies, make up all living things. Each is a mass of protein and has all the attributes of life, including the potential for reproduction. Your body is a cell colony of about a hundred thousand billion cells, all originating from the single cell of a fertilised human egg, which divided and subdivided. Plants, creatures and people have eukaryotic cells organised rather like an egg. The central nucleus holds the genetic code in its DNA; around that is cytoplasm, held in a membrane. The prokaryotic cells of bacteria have a looser structure and the DNA is coiled up in something called a nucleoid.

Chimera

Originally a mythic creature, half man, half beast. GE makes the creation of such a creature increasingly possible.

Chimeric

Chimeric is used in GE for a fusion of two 'elements' which

wouldn't occur in nature. So chimeric genes, combine 'elements' from two or more organisms.

Chromosome

In plants, creatures and humans chromosomes are thread-like structures, of DNA and genes, which broadly determine what an organism looks like and can do. Each chromosome is a twisted strand of DNA combined with ball-like proteins called histones to make a flexible 'necklace' which coils neatly into a tiny bundle: a piece of biological magic, for, stretched out straight, the DNA in one microscopic cell would extend 1.8 metres. When a cell divides, the DNA unwinds, copies itself and rewinds. Every cell in your body has the same twenty-two pairs of chromosomes, plus a pair of sex chromosomes (each pair consisting of one chromosome from each parent). Oddly, complex organisms may not have more chromosomes than simple ones: peas have seven pairs, potatoes twenty-four, but crayfish far outstrip us, with a cool one hundred pairs. Viruses and bacteria just have a length of DNA or RNA coiled up on itself to make one chromosome – simplicity that allows rapid change and adaptation.

Chromosome map

A chart showing the relative positions of genes along the length of the chromosomes.

Cloning

Making a genetically identical copy (a clone) of an organism or cell.

Codex

Short for Codex Alimentarius Commission: the body which sets international guidelines on such things as the permitted levels of chemicals in food.

Conjugation

The 'mating' of single-celled organisms (bacteria, etc.): genes transfer from cell to cell as they touch.

Convention on Biological Diversity
A legally binding agreement to conserve biodiversity, adopted in Nairobi in May 1992, signed by over 150 countries at the Rio Earth Summit, came into force on 29 December 1993.

Cytogenetics
Looks at the structure of cells related to genes and chromosomes.

Cytoplasm
A cell's chief substance, it contains the nucleus, and several minute functional structures. The female egg cell's cytoplasm is the basis of all the cells of an embryo.

Differentiation
The process by which, as cells divide to make an organism, they take on a particular role and form (as blood cells, skin, etc.).

DNA (deoxyribonucleic acid)
If you can say that you are definitely sober. DNA carries an organism's genetic code via the genes (a few viruses use RNA) and passes genetic information from one generation to the next. It's the famous 'double helix'. Imagine a zip fastener, in very flexible rubber, twisted into a spiral – several metres long but so narrow you'd need a strong microscope to see it. When a cell divides to make two cells, the DNA untwists, duplicates itself, and retwists.

DNA methylation
A natural process which may block the action of a gene.

DNA polymerase
An enzyme which strings nucleic acids together to make DNA.

DNAse
An enzyme that digests DNA.

Double helix
The name given to the twisting shape of DNA.

E. coli Escherichia coli
Bacteria much used in GE and usually found in the guts of mammals. Some are harmless, some cause food poisoning.

Ecosystem
A community of life-forms successfully interacting with each other and the environment.

Enzymes
Vital proteins like mini-robots which carry out tasks within an organism. Alone, or with co-workers (co-factors), enzymes make possible processes such as digestion, waste disposal and energy transfer. Genes determine which enzymes are made by cells, and what they do, within the cell or beyond it. But, to work well, each enzyme needs certain conditions: the right temperature, acid–alkaline balance, co-workers, or the absence of inhibitors. The wrong temperature, or chemical environment, can inhibit or kill them. If even one of your enzymes failed you could develop a metabolic disorder. So the impact of GE foods on gut enzymes could be important.

Epigenetic inheritance
The process by which acquired characteristics are inherited by succeeding generations (e.g. women who have suffered starvation have lower-birth-weight grandchildren).

Epistasis
Interaction between different genes, where one affects the activity of the other.

Eukaryote
See Cells.

Eugenics
Social engineering, possibly including sterilisation and gene manipulation, designed to improve the quality of the human race by promoting 'desirable' traits and eradicating 'undesirable' ones.

Ex situ
Off-site. See In Situ.

Gene
Genes are the physical units of inheritance which one generation passes on to the next. Despite great strides in genetics, scientists have only identified the gene sequences of a few extremely simple organisms; the roles and interactions of most genes remain unknown.

Gene amplification
Greatly increasing the number of copies of a particular gene.

Gene bank or seed bank
Temperature – and humidity-controlled storage for seeds, or other biological materials, for use in research and breeding programmes.

Gene mapping
A method of finding the relative positions of genes on the chromosome.

Gene pool
The genes and genetic components of one person, plant, animal, etc., or those within that family or species.

Gene replacement therapy
The use of GE to alter or replace genes causing hereditary disorders. Germline gene replacement therapy does this in the egg or the embryo; somatic cell gene replacement therapy inserts copies of a normal gene into the cells of an adult. This work is still experimental. Genes are interactive: removing a 'defective' gene, or inserting a 'better' gene, could upset vital gene interactions in ways we don't yet understand. Also, a gene which entails 'disadvantages' may also carry some 'advantages'.

Gene sequencing
Determining the order of the nucleotides in the DNA which together represent a gene.

Gene silencing
A process which shuts down the activity of particular genes.

Genetic code
The set of instructions carried in the genes that guides the creation of every part of the organism, how it maintains life and how it reproduces.

Genetic determinism or genetic reductionism
The theory that 'you are your genes', that each feature of an organism is pre-set; a 'one gene, one function' view which assumes that genes are stable and predictable. Most GE is based on this theory. But leading-edge biology shows that genes are reactive and interactive.

Genetic engineering (GE)
Altering the genes in a cell or organism by removing, inserting or recombining specific sequences of genes or DNA – usually from a totally different species with which normal breeding would be impossible. Animal genes can be put into plants, plant genes into animals and fish, human genes into either. The resulting organism is called transgenic. In nature, like only breeds with like. So transgenic breeding is not a natural extension of traditional breeding methods.

Genetic expression
A term used in molecular genetics to denote that the gene is active and does what it is encoded to do.

Genetic marker
A section of DNA which is easily found and acts as a reference point for finding genes near it.

Genetic monitoring
A method of checking for early signs of an inherited disorder or disease.

Genetics
A branch of biology which studies genes and heredity.

Genetic screening
Testing people for inherited defects, or abnormalities.

Genetic testing
Analysing someone's genetic material for signs of genetic disease or damage.

Genome
The whole of an organism's or individual's genetic material.

Genotype
The genetic make-up underlying a specific trait, or set of traits, in an individual or group. Or the genetic characteristics of an organism.

Germ cell
A reproductive cell – in humans a sperm or egg.

Germplasm
The genetic material transferred to offspring via a fertilised egg or seed.

GURTs
Genetic Use Restriction Technologies, the UN name for Terminator and Traitor technologies.

Herbicide
A chemical, or chemical mix, which destroys plants (a weed-killer).

Horizontal gene transfer
The transfer of genes to another organism, of the same or a different species, other than via pollination or breeding.

Hybrid
Usually a man-made cross between two plants of the same species but very different varieties. It may be done by pollination or by more artificial means, but it does not involve the transfer of specific genes used by GE.

Hybridoma
A cell made by fusing a cancer cell with one which produces antibodies.

Immune system
The interactive 'team' of cells which defend and heal the body.

Immunology
The study of the body's responses to challenges such as infections, allergens and cancers.

Insecticide
A chemical mix created to kill insects.

In situ ('on-site')
To conserve anything in situ is to ensure its survival in its natural 'home' or location. As opposed to ex situ ('off-site') conservation in a zoo, botanical garden or gene bank.

Intellectual property (IP)
Something which can belong to a specific person or organisation through a legal device such as a patent, copyright or trade mark.

Interrupted genes
Genes whose sequence is interrupted by uncoded passages.

In vitro, IVF and in vivo
'In vitro' means 'in glass', i.e. in a laboratory isolated from the whole organism. In IVF (in vitro fertilisation) a female egg is fertilised in a dish. Done within an organism, this is 'in vivo'.

Junk DNA.
See Uncoded DNA

Lecithin
An emulsifier mainly derived from soya beans used in chocolate and many other foods.

Lectins
Plant proteins which can protect plants against pests.

Luddite
Usually a term of abuse, implying someone who dislikes all technological change or 'progress'. After Ned Ludd, who opposed the eighteenth-century introduction of factory machinery.

Marker gene
Inserting genes into an organism is a hit-and-miss business. So the alien gene is combined with a marker gene which visibly affects the organism or can easily be traced. Where the marker gene can be found, the alien gene must be present too. Common markers are genes which resist antibiotics or alter the organism's colour.

Messenger RNA
See RNA.

Metabolism
All the physical and biochemical processes which keep an organism alive and in balance.

Metabolite
A chemical created in the process of metabolism.

Microbiology
The study of living organisms invisible to the naked eye.

Micro-organism or microbe
A life-form you can't see without a microscope.

Mitochondria
Tiny powerhouses, within cells, which generate energy for vital activities.

Mobile genetic element
A DNA sequence which can move from one part of the natural

gene sequence to another – without human aid. Also called a transposon or transposable genetic element.

Molecular genetics
The study of the molecular basis of the structure of genes and how they work.

Molecular probe
Usually a molecule of DNA or RNA, made radioactive or combined with a dye or enzyme, and used to find, identify or isolate genes.

Molecule
A very small particle, i.e. two or more atoms.

Monoculture
Agriculture using crops which are genetically the same or very similar.

Multigene
A family of similar genes, from a common ancestor, which occur several times, as a group, in the full length of an organism's DNA.

Mutagen
A physical or chemical agent (such as radiation, and some chemicals and viruses) that can damage the genetic code of an organism, such as a seed or embryo, causing abnormalities or cancers.

Mutation
An alteration to the genetic code. Normally, when cells divide, the gene patterns are copied so well that the DNA of the new cells matches the originals. Occasionally (or in response to mutagens) bits of DNA are lost or misplaced. The result is an organism with a difference. Changes to sperm, eggs or their equivalents (germline mutations) can be passed on to future generations. Mutations may improve, and contribute to evolution, or deform or disadvantage. See also Adaptive mutation.

Nucleotide

A chemical building block of DNA or RNA: one letter of the genetic code. Different nucleotides give the letters which, strung together, make up the code.

Nucleus

The 'core' of an animal or plant cell which holds most of the genetic material (genes, etc.).

Organism

Any life-form: plant, animal, bacterium, fungus or whatever.

Patent

Formerly a means to legal entitlement to exclusively control and profit from an invention. But laws have been rewritten so that patents can be taken out on GE processes which are so loosely defined that simply developing a technique for obtaining part of a living thing may enable someone to patent the living thing itself.

Pathogen

An organism which causes disease, i.e. a bacterium or virus.

Pesticide

A term embracing herbicides, insecticides and fungicides, but sometimes meaning just insecticides.

Pharming

Using animals, plants and other genetically engineered organisms to produce substances for medical use.

Phenotype

The physical characteristics of an organism determined by both its genetic make-up and environmental influences.

Plasmid

A circular molecule of DNA from a bacterium which can contain various genes. Plasmids can confer antibiotic resistance on a bacterium and can move from one bacterium to another.

Polygenic
A polygenic characteristic is one determined by the interaction of several genes.

Prokaryote
See Cells.

Promoter
The starting point, on a gene, for RNA transcription.

Proteins
The complex molecules which make up our muscles, tissues and organs, and also our hormones, enzymes and antibodies. To maintain them we need protein in our diet, from meat, cheese, pulses, etc.

Protein synthesis
Cells build proteins from strings of simpler units called amino acids. All proteins have about twenty amino acids in varying proportions, and some have a couple extra. The genetic code dictates the proportions and arrangement of the amino acids, and therefore the structure and function of each protein.

rBGH or rbGH
See BST.

Recombinant DNA
Artificially created DNA consisting of a section of DNA from one source joined to a section of DNA from another – often from a different species. A technique used in genetic engineering.

Recombination
A natural evolutionary mechanism by which new combinations of gene sequences are formed during cell replication.

Rio Earth Summit
The UN Conference on Environment and Development (UNCED) and related non-governmental organisations meetings, held in Rio de Janeiro, Brazil, in June 1992.

RNA (ribonucleic acid)
Essentially the same as DNA, consisting of sequences of nucleotides. Unlike DNA it has no uncoded sections. Different types of RNA do different jobs. For example, transfer RNA uses the 'recipe' carried by messenger RNA (mRNA), to assemble amino acids into the right protein. RNA is also the genetic material of some viruses.

Surfactant
Used in pesticides and detergents, this reduces the surface tension of liquids, letting them penetrate or foam better.

Tissue, or cell culture
A means of growing cells in a laboratory.

Toxin/toxic
A poison/poisonous.

Transcription
The natural process by which DNA is copied to form a complementary RNA sequence.

Transduction
A natural form of gene transfer among bacteria which is also used in genetic engineering, employing a bacteriophage.

Transformation
Successfully integrating 'alien' genetic material into the DNA of a cell, or cells.

Transgenic
An organism (plant, animal, etc.) is transgenic if some of its genes come from a different species. They could have been inserted into its germplasm, through genetic engineering, or the organism could be the clone, or offspring, of a genetically engineered organism.

Transposon
See Mobile genetic element.

Uncoded DNA or 'junk DNA'

A length of DNA which lacks the usual sequence of nucleotides. Its purpose is not yet understood by scientists.

Vector

A biological Trojan horse which smuggles in an alien of some kind. Bacteria and viruses are often used as vectors in GE, their invasive skills being used to carry new genes into the cells of other organisms. A disarmed version of *Agrobacterium tumefaciens*, which causes plant tumours, is a common vector in plant work.

Virus

A minute particle, far smaller than a bacterium, which invades and reproduces within a cell. Viruses are parasites, causing diseases of plants, animals and humans, such as colds, AIDS, hepatitis, and some cancers. They have a core of genetic material (DNA or RNA) coated in protein and can rapidly evolve – hence the different strains of influenza. Animal viruses seem increasingly able to infect humans, but the ultimate potential for this crossover is not yet known. Virus diseases cannot be treated with antibiotics; vaccines are the only protection.

Volunteer

A crop plant which has self-seeded at random.

Xenotransplants

Transplants of animal organs to humans. Human genes are now being experimentally inserted into animal reproductive cells in the hope of creating animals with organs which the human immune system won't reject. Such transplants would risk animal diseases being fatally transferred to humans.

Notes

1 Sowing the Storm

1 Michael Crichton, Introduction to *Jurassic Park*.
2 Dr Mae-Wan Ho, *Genetic Engineering: Dream or Nightmare?* Gateway Books, 1998.
3 D. MacKenzie, 'Mutant bacteria may escape from the mail', *New Scientist*, 4 April 1994.
4 Sheldon Krimsky, *Genetic Alchemy*, MIT Press, 1982.
5 James Lovelock, *Gaia: the practical science of planetary medicine*, Gaia Books, 1991.
6 Michael J. Reiss, Roger Staughan, *Improving Nature*, Cambridge University Press, 1996, p. 117.

2 Safety: Trust Me, I'm a Chemical Company

1 Quoted in the *New York Times* 25 October 1998.
2 J. A. Nordlee, *et al*, 'Identification of a Brazil-nut allergen in transgenic soya beans', *New England Journal of Medicine*, 334, 1996, pp. 688–92; Marion Nestle, 'Allergies to transgenic foods – questions of policy', *New England Journal of Medicine*, 334, 1996, pp. 726–8.
3 P. Spallone, *Generation Games: Genetic Engineering and the Future for Our Lives*, The Women's Press, 1992.

4 T. Inose, and K. Murata, 'Enhanced accumulation of toxic compound in yeast cells having high glycolytic activity: a case study in the safety of genetically engineered yeast', *International Journal of Food Science and Technology*, 30, 1995, pp. 141–6.

5 Written evidence submitted to the Science and Technology Committee of the House of Commons, reported on PA 11 8 March 1999.

6 Professor John B. Fagan, 'Assessing the Safety and Nutritional Quality of GE Foods', 12 1998.

7 Dr Ricarda Steinbrecher

8 Frank and Keller 13 1995, quoted in Mae-Wan Ho, *Genetic Engineering: Dream or Nightmare*.

9 'Special Safety Concerns of Transgenic Agriculture': a briefing for Michael Meacher, MP, Minister for the Environment, 1999.

10 *New Scientist*, 10 January 1999

11 *Genetic Engineering*

12 'Special safety concerns . . .'

13 Professor Joe Cummins, '35S Promoter (CaMV) in Calgene's Flavr Savr Tomato Creates Hazard' 15 June 1994.

14 The *Guardian*, 13 February 1999.

15 K. Popper, *Objective Knowledge*, OUP, 1979–81.

16 Professor Fagan, John B., 'The Failings of the Principle of Substantial Equivalence in the Regulation of Transgenic Foods'.

17 Ibid.

18 Op. cit.

19 Fagan, 'Assessing the Safety . . .'

4 Labelling: The Law With a Hole in the Middle

1 Professor Marion Nestle, PhD, MPH, 'Food Biotechnology: Labelling will benefit industry as well as consumers', *Nutrition Today*, Vol. 33, No. 1, January/February 1998.

2 Food and Drink Federation, *Consumers and Biotechnology*, FDF, London, 1995.
3 Commission of the European Communities/Directorate General XII (1994b), Biotechnology Work Programme, DGXII, Dir. E-I, Brussels.
4 Professor Marion Nestle, op.cit.
5 Monsanto report dated Autumn 1998.

5 *The Myth of Choice*

1 *Daily Telegraph*

6 *Farm and Country*

1 C. Crecchio, and G. Stotzky, 'Insecticidal Activity and Bio-degradation of the Toxin Baccillus Thuringiensis, subsp. kurstaki bound to humic acid in soil', *Soil Biology and Biochemistry*, 30, 1998, pp. 463–70.
2 Scottish Crop Research Institute, Dundee, published in *Molecular Breeding*, reported by James Miekle and Paul Brown, *Guardian*, 4 March 1999.
3 *Industry and Morals*
4 *Farmer's Weekly*, 5 March 1999.
5 Pesticide Action Network North America.
6 Marc Lappe, and Britt Balley, *Against the Grain*, Earthscan.
7 North West Coalition for Alternatives to Pesticides, *Journal of Pesticide Reform*, spring 1997.
8 Ibid.
9 Autumn 1997; website: http://www.ucsusa.org/Gene/F97.glyphosate.html.
10 Lappé/Bailey, op. cit.
11 *Crop and Soil Environment News*, USA, March 1997.
12 Marie Woolf, *Independent on Sunday*, 21 February 1999.
13 ACRE minutes – Quentin Gargan.
14 *Nature*, Vol. 396, 19 November 1998.

15 Quoted by J. Pretty in 'Feeding the World', *Genetics Forum*, Vol. 4, Issue 6, 1998.

16 *New York Times* Sunday magazine, 25 October 1998.

17 *Farmer's Weekly*, 6 November 1998.

18 C. Benbrook, 'Pest Management at the Crossroads', *Resistant Pest Management*, Vol. 8, No. 2, winter 1996.

19 Institut National de Recherche Agronomique (INRA), report June 1998.

20 Ho, *et al*, 'Gene Technology and Gene Ecology of Infectious Diseases', *Microbiology Ecology in Health and Disease*, Vol. 10, 1998, pp. 33–9.

7 BST: Madder Than Mad Cows?

1 *Biological Sciences Review*, Vol. 8, No. 1, pp. 15–17.

2 On BBC Radio 4's *Farming Today*, 9 June 1995. Quoted in D'Silva, Joyce, *BST – a distressing product*, Compassion in World Farming, p. 16.

3 Quoted by Emily Green in the *New Statesman*, February 1999.

4 Farm and Food Society submission to the Veterinary Products Committee, March 1997.

5 'Unlabeled Milk from Cows Treated with Biosynthetic Growth Hormones: A Case of Regulatory Abdication', *International Journal of Health Services*, Vol. 26, No. 1 (1996), pp. 173–85.

6 rBST (Nutrilac) 'Gaps Analysis' Report by rBST Internal Review Team, Health Protection Board, Health Canada (Canada health department).

7 *The Lancet*, 23 January 1999.

8 'US and Europe Row over GM Milk', *Independent*, 22 March 1999.

9 Cited in Health Canada, op. cit.

10 Hansen *et al*, op. cit.

11 Helman, 1995.

12 *Journal of the Royal Society of Medicine*, Vol. 85, December 1992.

13 Helman op. cit.

14 Submission to the Veterinary Products Committee, March 1997.

15 Hansen *et al*, op. cit.

16 Ibid.

17 Challacombe *et al*, 'Safety of milk from cows treated with bovine somatotropin', *The Lancet*, 344, 1994, pp. 815–16.

18 Erik Millstone, Erick Brunner, and Ian White, *Nature*.

19 Pell *et al*, 'Effects of a prolonged-release formulation of sometribove (n-Methionyl Bovine Somatotropin) on Jersey cows', *Journal of Dairy Sciences*, 75, 1992, pp. 3416–31.

20 D. S. Kronfeld, 'Health management in dairy herds treated with bovine somatotropin', *Journal of American Veterinary Medicine Association*, 204 (1), 1997, pp. 116–30.

21 Michael Hansen *et al*, 'Potential Public Health Impacts of the Use of Recombinant Bovine Somatotropin in Dairy Production', 19 September 1997.

22 Kronfeld, op. cit.

23 Hansen *et al*, op. cit.

24 Ibid.

25 Kronfeld, op. cit.

26 Hansen *et al*, op. cit.; Brady *et al*, 'Resistance development potential of antibiotic/antimicrobial residue levels designated "safe levels"' *Journal of Food Protection*, 56 (3), 1993, pp. 229–33.

27 Hansen *et al*, op. cit. Lazmezas *et al*, 1993; Prusiner, 1991.

28 Hansen *et al*, op. cit.

8 Animals: Human Triumphs That Shame

1 Vandana, Shiva, *Biopiracy: The Plunder of Nature and Knowledge*, Green Books, 1998.

2 'Animal Welfare Methodology and Criteria', *Rev. Sci. Tech.* 12, 13, 1994, pp. 277–302.
3 S.K. Walker, K.M. Hartwich, and R.F., Seamark, 'The production of unusually large offspring following embryo manipulation; concepts and challenges', *Theriogenology*, 45, 1996, pp. 111–20.
4 'Large Offspring Syndrome in Cattle and Sheep', Roslin Institute Annual Report 1997/8.
5 John Clark, 'Genetic Modification of Livestock', Roslin Institute Annual Report 1997/8.
6 A. Coleman, 'Production of proteins in the milk of transgenic livestock – problems, solutions and successes', *American Journal of Clinical Nutrition*, 63, 1996, S639–S645.

9 Medical Matters

1 R. Collins, *et al*, *Ethics of Clinical Trials*
2 The Council for Responsible Genetics (USA), 'Position Paper on Genetic Discrimination'
3 Ibid.
4 Loka Institute, *Genetic Discrimination: A Primer*, 1998. Alert no. 5:1, quoted in P. Wheale, R. von Schomberg, and P. Glasner, *The Social Management of Genetic Engineering*, 1998, p. 98.
5 Michael J. Reiss, and Roger Straughan, *Improving Nature*, p. 200, quoting P. Brown, and K. Kleiner, 'Patent row splits breast cancer researchers', *New Scientist*, 24 September 1994.
6 The Council for Responsible Genetics, op. cit.
7 Ibid.
8 Ibid.
9 *Wall Street Journal*, 2 May 1997.
10 Joseph Fletcher, *The Ethics of Genetic Control: Ending Reproduction Roulette*, Anchor Books, 1992, quoted in J., Rifkin, *Biotech Century*.

11 J. Platt, (1998) 'New Directions for organ transplantation', *Nature*, 392 (supp.), 1998, pp. 11–17.

12 Dr Mae-Wan Ho, *Genetic Engineering: Dream or Nightmare?*

13 J.S. Allen, 'Primates and new viruses', *Science*, 265, 1994, pp. 1, 345–6.

14 Pert Candace, *Molecules of Emotion: why you feel the way you feel*, Simon & Schuster, 1998.

15 Dr Gill Langley, and Joyce D'Silva, *Animal Organs in Humans: uncalculated risks and unanswered questions*, Compassion in World Farming and BUAV.

16 T.E. Starzi, *et al*, 'Baboon-to-human liver transplantation', *The Lancet*, 341 pp. 65–71.

17 Manfred Avidman, 'Creating, and marketing new forms of life' in: 1996.

18 The Council for Responsible Genetics (USA).

19 Human Genetics Advisory Commission and Human Fertilisation Embryology Authority, 'Cloning Issues in Reproduction, Science and Medicine: A Consultation Document', London, 1998.

10 Patents: Patently Wrong

1 Rural Advancement Foundation International (RAFI).

2 Quoted in RAFI, op. cit.

3 Vandana, Shiva, *Biopiracy: The Plunder of Nature and Knowledge*.

4 David Nason, 'Tickner warns over Aboriginal Gene Sampling', *The Australian*, 25 January 1994.

5 RAFI, 'Biopiracy Update: A Global Pandemic' September/October 1995.

6 Quoted in the RAFI report.

7 Richard, Hindmarsh, Geoffrey Lawrence, and Janet, Norton, *Altered Genes: Reconstructing Nature*, Allen & Unwin, 1998.

8 RAFI, 'Bioserfdom: Technology, Intellectual Property and

the Erosion of Farmers' Rights in the Industrialized World',
March/April 1997.

9 ibid.
10 ibid.
11 ibid.

11 *Terminator Technology: The Seeds of Strife*

1 RAFI Traitor Tech?
2 At a meeting on 30 September 1998 at an Auckland sem-
inar set up by Gene Pool, a local government-funded NGO,
in response to Auckland University lecturer Peter Wills's
attack on it.
3 American Seed Industry Association, Seed Industry
Announcements, News and White Papers section at website http://amseed.com/documents/, 22 January 1999, and
disseminated by GRAIN Los Banos (grain@baylink.
mozcom. com), the farming/bioindustry newsgroup.
4 Geri Guidetti, 'Seed Terminator and Mega-Merger Threat
to Freedom', the Ark Institute, June 1998, via website
http://www.arkinstitute.com/98/up0606.html.
5 Burson-Marsteller website, http://www.burson.marsteller.de.
6 RAFI,
7 Quoted in RAFI news release, 'Genetic Seed Sterilization
is "Holy Grail" of Ag Biotechnology Firms', 27 January
1999, website http://www.rafi.org/pr/release.
8 F. Gebhard, and K. Smalla, *Applied Environmental Biology*,
64, 1998, pp. 1550–9.
9 Monsanto, 'Report on Sustainable Development', 1997, p.
27, quoted in *Genetic Engineering and World Hunger*, the
Corner House, 1998.

12 *Reaping the Whirlwind*

1 HRH The Prince of Wales, 'The Seeds of Disaster', first
published in the *Daily Telegraph*.

2 First published in Rachel's *Environment and Health Weekly*, 586, 19 February 1998.

3 E.F. Schumacher, *Industry and Morals*.

4 Ibid.

5 James Lovelock, *Gaia*, Gaia Books, 1999.

6 Lynn Margolis, *The Symbiotic Planet*, Weidenfeld and Nicolson, 1999.

Selected References

A Brief Chronology of the Patent Debate of the North, http://www.idrc.ca/books/725/append.html, IDRC,

A Brief History of Biotechnology Risk Debates and Policies in the United States, Regal, P., Edmonds Institute, 1998,

A Case-Control Study of Non-Hodgkin Lymphoma and Exposure to Pesticides, Hardell, L., Erujsson, M., Cancer, 15 Mar, 1999, Vol. 85 No. 6,

A decomposition product of a contaminant implicated in l-tryptophan eosinophilia myalgia syndrome effects spinal cord neuronal death and survival through sterospecific, maturation and partly interleukin-1 dependent mechanisms, Brenneman, D.E. et al, J. of Pharmacology and Experimental Therapeutics, Vol. 266 (2), p.1029–35.

A Feeling for the Organism: a biography of Barbara McClintock,

A handful of food 'clusters' – alliances of producers and processors will dominate world food production in future – US farm group says., Reuters, 11 Feb, 1999,

A Mouse in Sheep's Clothing: The Challenge to the Patent Morality Criterion Posed by Dolly, Warren, A., E.I.P.R, 1998, Issue 12,

A project to promote familiarisation with and acceptance of crops project under Framework Prog.IV, European Commission, Paper OCS 8/96, Annex & Draft 19 Dec, 1995,

A review of the indirect effects of pesticides on birds, Campbell, L.H. et al, Joint Nature Conservation Committee Report No. 227,

ACNFP: Advisory Committee on Novel Foods and Processes, Ministry of Agriculture Fisheries and Food, 1999,

ACRE minutes extract 13.1.1999 re Monsanto maize, 13 Jan, 1999,

Action Alert: Maximum residue levels of Roundup in imported soya beans to increase, GeneEthics Network Australia, Mar, 1999,

Advertising Standards Authority Finds Against Nestle, Ferriman, A., British Medical Journal, 13 Feb, 1999, Vol. 318,

Advertising Standards Authority Slams Monsanto, Aldridge, J., Observer, 28 Feb, 1999,

Advisory Committee on Novel Foods and Processes Terms of Reference, http://www.maff.gov.uk/food/novel/nfrregn. htm, Maff, 1999,

Advisory Committee on Releases to the Environment Annual Report No.5: 1998, DETR, 1998,

Advisory Committee on Releases to the Environment: PGS oilseed rape, http://www.environment.detr.gov.uk/acre/pgs/index.htm,

Advisory Committee on Releases to the Environment: wildlife briefing, http://www.environment.detr.gov.uk/acre/wildlife/index.htm,

Affirmative action in cloning, Nature Genetics, 31 May, 1999,

Africa Splits over bar to plant patents., Masood, E., Nature, 11 Mar, 1999,

African Scientists Condemn Advertisement Campaign for Genetically Engineered Food: Call for European Support, www.psrast.org/afrscimo.htm, Gaia Foundation press release, 3 Aug, 1998,

After Dolly, meet Polly the therapeutic lamb, Hawkes, N., The Times, 19 Dec, 1998,

Against The Grain, Lappé, M., Bailey, B., Earthscan, 1999,

Agency Contradicted Own Experts in Approving Genetically

Engineered Foods, http://www.bio-integrity.org/FDADeception.html,

Agenda 21, http://www.icgeb.trieste.it/biosafety/bsf21.htm,

Agricultural Biotech faces Backlash in Europe, Science, 7 Aug, 1998, Vol. 281 No. 5378, 768–771.

Agricultural research for whom?, The Ecologist, 1996, Vol. 26 No 6,

Agriculture-environment new study backs up biotech fears, Inter Press Service Washington,

All Gene Tech foods should be labelled, GeneEthics Network Australia, 31 Jul, 1998,

All Monsanto's Men, Cohen, N., Observer, 21 Feb, 1999,

Allergenicity and tolerance to proteins from brazil nut (Bertholetia excela H.B.K), Melo, V et al, Food Agric. Immunol.,1994, Vol. 6, 185–195

Allergies to transgenic foods: Questions of policy, Nestle, M., The New England J. Of Medicine, 6–7, 1996, Vol. 334 (11),

Alliance for Bio-Integrity: Protecting the Right to Eat Genetically Untampered Food – Landmark Lawsuit Challenges FDA Policy on Genetically Engineered Food, Alliance for Bio-Integrity, 27 1998,

Altered Genes: reconstructing nature, Hindmarsh, R.L., G., Norton, J., Allen & Unwin, 1998,

Altered Salmon grow by leaps and bounds, MacKenzie, D., New Scientist, 6 Jan, 1996,

America's most under-reported news stories, Project Censored, 14 Mar, 1999,

Aminoglycoside resistance (including kanamycin) medical briefing paper.

An appraisal of the working practice of directive 90/220/EEC on the GM cures., Dobson, R., Independent, 23 Feb, 1999,

And now the Verminator, http://www.rafi.org/pr/release19.html, 24 Aug, 19989,

Animal organs in humans: uncalculated risks & unanswered questions, Langley, G., D'Silva, J., Compassion in World Farming, 1998,

Animal Research is Vital to Medicine, Botting, J.H., Morrison, A.R., Scientific American, Feb, 1997,

Annual report 94–95, Roslin institute, 1995,

Antibiotic resistance genes in transgenic plants, in particular ampicillin resistance in Bt-maize, Oekoinstitut Institute Freiberg On Behalf Of, Greenpeace Germany, 1997,

Antibiotic Resistance Genes, Collard, J.M.

Antibiotic resistance mechanisms, http://www.biosafety.ihe.be/AR/resistancedescrp.html,

Antimicrobial use in Livestock and the Problems of Bacterial Resistance in Humans, World Health Organisation briefing paper, 1997,

Applications Under Regulation (EC) No. 258/97 of the European Parliament and the Council, http://maffweb/food/novel/pq585att.htm, Advisory Committee on Novel Foods and Processes, 14 Apr, 1999,

Application for Monsanto Europe for consent to market maize genetically modified for glyphosate tolerance Ref 97/M3/2 – Re-evaluation in the light of further information (ACRE/99/P1) Re-evaluation in light of further information, ETR, Feb, 1999,

Appointments to the Medical and Scientific Panel and the Appraisal Panel for Human Suspected Adverse Reactions, MAFF, Mar, 1999,

Aspartame: adverse reactions escalating, Consumers Safety Network,

Assessing the risk of GMOs, Jewell, T., Stirling, A., Pesticides News, Mar, 1999, Vol. 43,

Assessing The Safety And Nutritional Quality Of Genetically Engineered Foods, Fagan, J., www.psagef.org/fasses.htm,

AstraZeneca and its genetic research: feeding the world or fuelling hunger?, Action Aid, 1999,

Australia to ship largest cargo of canola to Europe, Australian GeneEthics Network, 8 Jan, 1999,

Australia's first consensus conference: Canberra 9–11th March 99, GeneEthics Network Media release, 13 Mar, 1999,

Avis recueillis par les membres du comite de la prevention et de la precaution sur les risques lies a la dissemination des organismes genetiquement modifies, Ministere de l'Amenagement du Territoire et de l'Environement, 3 Dec, 997,

Baby Milk Action comments on European proposals to set limits for pesticide residues in baby milks and foods, Baby Milk Action internal papers, Nov, 1998,

Bacillus thuringiensis (Bt), Swadener, C., J. of Pesticide Reform, 1994, Vol. 4 No. 3.

Bacillus thuringiensis var kurstaki affects a beneficial insect, the cinnabar moth (Lepidoptera: Arctiidae), James, R.R. et al, J. Econ. Entomol, 1993, Vol. 86 No 2, 334–339.

Bacterial Gene Transfer by natural genetic transformation in the environment., Lorenz (Reviewed), M.G. et al, Microbiol Rev. 58, 1994, 563–602.

Bangladesh Monsanto Project Called Off, BBC World Service, 27 Jul, 1998,

Bank Takes Stand Against GMOs, Triodos Bank,

Basmati Rice Patent, http://www.rafi.org/genotypes/98040basm.html, Rural Advancement Foundation, Apr, 1998,

Be GM free is way to compete, Farmers Weekly, letter, 25 Dec, 1998,

Beasts Bring Home the Bacon, The Guardian, 18 Apr, 1999,

Bees spread genes from GM crops, Nuttall, N., The Times,, 15 Apr, 1999,

Ben & Jerry to Label rBGH free milk, Anderson, C., Associated Press, 1997,

Better Luck Next Time, Pearce, F., New Scientist, 1999,

Betting on Biodiversity: Why Genetic Engineering Will Not Feed the Hungry, Shiva, V. Research Foundation for Science, Technology & Ecology, India, 1998,

Biodiversity Jeopardised in Cartagena Biosafety Negotiations, Business Wire, 17 Feb, 1999,

Biodiversity Treaty: A 'Lose-Lose Proposition For US Consumers, Scientists and Industry, Miller, H., http://www.the-scientist.library.upenn.edu/yr1995/oct/comm951030.html, The Scientist, 12 Jun, 1995, Vol. 9. No.12, 13.

Biopesticide Fact Sheet: Bacillus thuringiensis CryIA(b) Delta-Endotoxin and the Genetic Material Necessary for its Production in Corn, Office Of Pesticide Programs, US Environmental Protection Agency, Mar, 1999,

Biopiracy: The Plunder Of Nature & Knowledge, Shiva, V., Green Books, 1998,

Biosafety Breaches in Australia, Cummins, J., Australian GeneEthics Network, 22 Jan, 1999,

Biosafety negotiations fail: trade and agro-business interests hijacked the process, says Friends of the Earth, Friends of the Earth Press release, 24 Feb, 1999,

Biosafety Pact Could Hit US Trade, Carter, J., Associated Press, 6 Feb, 1999,

Biosafety Protocol: key demands, German Environment and Development NGOs, Aug, 1998,

Biosafety Web pages of CGEB, http://www.icgeb.trieste.it/biosafety/bsfconc.htm,

Biotech Battlefield: Profits vs Public, Cimons, M., Jacob, P., Los Angles Times, 21 Feb, 1999,

Biotech experts to lose GM role, Waugh, P. The Independent, 12 Apr, 1999,

Biotech giant gets green light for GM crops: Government admits – they don't have to tell us anything, Friends of the Earth Press release, 5 Mar, 1999,

Biotech good giant wields power in Washington, Vidal, J., The Guardian, 18 Feb, 1999,

Biotech Industry Sees Big Threat to Modified Plants, Kilman, S., Wall Street Journal, 3 Mar, 1999,

Biotechnology and Animal Welfare: Summary of Animal Welfare Concerns, Jennings, M., Wrathall, J., RSPCA, Dec, 1997,

Biotechnology and Consumer Issues: where we stand, Monsanto, Apr, 1998.

Biotechnology and Milk: Benefit or Threat? An Analysis of

Issues Related to BGH/BST Use in the Dairy Industry, Hansen, M., Consumer Policy Institute, 1990.

Biotechnology and Natural Rubber – A Report on Work in Progress, http://www.rafi.org/communique/fltxt/19911. html, Jan, 1991,

Biotechnology and the European Public Concerted Action Group 1997, Nature No. 387, Mar, 1998, 845–47.

Biotechnology in Crops: Issues for the developing world, Spinney, L., www.oxfam.org.uk/policy/papers/gmfoods/ gmfoods.htm, Oxfam report, May, 1998,

Biotechnology in the Dairy, Mepham, B., Biological Sciences Review, Sep, 1998,

Biotechnology Myths, Altieri, M., www.purefood.org/ge/ biomyth.html,

Biotechnology News January 1999, National Farmers Union,

Biotechnology, Novartis,

Biotechnology, Weapons and Humanity, British Medical Association, 1999,

Biotechnology: Special issues 6 – Allergenicity, FAO, 1999,

Blair 'Frustrated' Over GM Food Debate, Press Association, 15 Feb, 1999,

Blinkered Science – Labs are full of researchers who can't see beyond the microscope, Monbiot, G., Guardian, 25 Feb, 1998,

'Blood' and 'Culture': Ethnic Conflict and the Authoritarian Right, The Corner House, Jan, 1999,

Blood Cell transplants are the key to saving young lives, Halle, M., The Daily Mail, 2 Jan, 1996,

BMA concern about terrifying side-effect of the fight against disease, Boseley, S., The Guardian, 22 Jan, 1999,

BMA warns on GE Weapons, Boseley, S., Guardian, 22 Feb, 1999,

Bonnie Baby, Cohen, P., New Scientist, 2 May, 1998.

Boom or Bust for Bt Crops?, Hagedorn, C., Crop and Soil Environmental News, Mar, 1998,

Booty and the beast – a creature part-pig and part-human bred to perform menial tasks, test drugs, and supply organ transplants., Langton, J., Sunday Telegraph, 19 Jul, 1998,

Borna virus suspected cause of neuropsychiatric disorders in Humans, Williams, B.,

Bovine Growth Hormone: Human Food Safety Evaluation, Juskevich, J., Guyer, C.G., Science, 24 Aug, 1990, Vol. 249, 875–84.

Bovine somatotropin – who's crying over spilt milk?, Morris, K., The Lancet, 23 Jan, 1999,

Bovine somatotropin and clinical mastitis epidemiological assessment for the welfare risk, Willeberg, P., Livestock Production Science, 1993, Vol. 36, 55–56.

Bovine Somatotropin, Verrall, J., Food And Farm Society: Special Report To Veterinary Products Committee, 8 Mar, 1997,

Boxed in by 'free trade' agreements the government is powerless to stop biotech giants putting GM foods on the market, Grey, J., The Guardian, 2 Mar, 1999,

Breaking the Chain, Antoniou, M., Living Earth, 15 Feb, 1999,

Breast Cancer and rBGH Milk, Rachel's Environment and Health Weekly, 8 May, 1998, No. 598,

Briefing on the rise of antibiotic resistance in Europe, http://www.cc.ruu.nl/ewi-enare/enare/index.html, European Network for Antimicrobial Resistance and Epidemiology,

Bringing the Food Chain Closer Together, Maff Press Release, 3 Sep, 1999,

British Advertising Standards Authority slams Monsanto, Aldridge, J., Observer, 28 Feb, 1998,

British Doctors Warn Modified Crops May Pose Health Risks, British Medical Association, 17 May, 1999,

British government internal concern about GM foods, Brown, P., The Guardian, 26 Feb, 1999,

British Water Utilities fear pollution by genetically manipulated crops, The Times, 5 Mar, 1999,

BST – A Distressing Product: an analysis of the health and welfare problems of dairy cows injected with BST, Compassion in World Farming, Aug, 1998,

Bt Cotton Fails to Control Bollworm, The Gene Exchange – A Public Voice On Biotechnology & Agriculture, www.ucsu-sa.org/Gene/W9.bt.html, Union of Concerned Scientists,

Bt Patent War Yields New Casualties, ISB News report, 4 Mar, 1999,

Build up of Bt toxins in soil, The Gene Exchange – A Public Voice On Biotechnology & Agriculture, www.ucsusa.org/publications/index/html, Union of Concerned Scientists, Fall, 1998.

Buildup of active BT toxins in soil, Union of Concerned Scientists, l/W, 1998,

Business booms for guides to biology's moral maze, Nature, 16 Oct, 1997, Vol. 389,

CA Calls for Immediate Action on GM Foods,, Consumers' Association, 11 Feb, 1999,

CA Methyl Bromide Victory, Pesticides Action Network, 22 Mar, 1999,

Call for a moratorium on xenotranplants, Nature, Correspondence, 1998, Vol. 391, 326.

Call for a moratorium on xenotransplants, Bach, F.H., Fineberg, H.V., Harvard Medical School, Nature (correspondence), 1998, Vol. 391,

Can Democracy Cope with Biotechnology?, Simpson, A., http://www.geneticsforum.org.uk/splice/democracy.htm, The Splice of Life, Dec, 1998, Vol. 5 Issue 2,

Can enhancement be distinguished from prevention in genetic medicine?, Juengst, E.T., J. Med. Phil., 1997, Vol. 22, 125–42.

Can risks from transgenic crop plants be estimated?, Williamson, M., Trends in Biotechnology, 1996, Vol. 14, 449–450.

Can we make supersalmon safe?, Mac Kenzie, D., New Scientist, 27 Jan, 1996,

Can we use experiments and models in predicting the invasiveness of genetically engineered organisms?, Kareiva, P., Parker, I.M., Pascual, M.P., Ecology, 1996, Vol. 77, 1651–1657.

Canada blocks move to regulate trade of 'Frankenfood', Shulgan, C., Ottawa Citizen, 26 Feb, 1999,

Canada Loses Market Due to GMOs, Resource News International, 22 Jan, 1999,

Canada loses entire EU OSR market thanks to GMOs, Resources News International 22 Jan, 1999,

Canada to reject Monsanto growth hormone – report, Reuters, Ottawa, 14 Jan, 1999,

Canada's GMOs, such as canola, remain tough to market in EU, Resources News International, 22 Jan, 1999,

Case study: food safety evaluation of transgenic potato. In Application of the Principles of Substantial Equivalence to the Safety Evaluation of Foods or Food Components from Plants Derived by Modern Biotechnology, Connor, A.J., World Health Organization, WHO/FNU/FOS/95.1, 1995, 23–35.

Cauliflower mosaic virus P35S promoter activity in E. coli., Assad, F.F. et al, Mol. Gen. Genet. 223, 1990, 517–20.

Centre for Genome Research web information, http://www.scottish-biomedical.com/genomics.htm, 1999.

China sets timetable for new patent copyright laws, World Intellectual Property Report, 15 Mar, 1999, Vol. 13 No. 3,

Ciba-Geigy Greenwash Snapshot No. 18. A case study in pesticide contamination and the potential hazards of biotechnology., Greenpeace,

Circulating concentrations of insulin-like growth factor-1 and risk of breast cancer., Hankinson, S.E. et al, The Lancet, 9 May, 1998, Vol. 351 No.9113, 1393–1396.

Circulating concentrations of insulin-like growth factor-1 and risk of breast cancer, Hankinson, S. et al, The Lancet, 9 May, 1998, Vol. 351,

Clinton lent on Blair to allow modified foods, Woolf, M., Independent on Sunday, 6 Sep, 1998,

Cloning Embryos for transplant, The Independent, 14 Dec, 1998,

Cloning for Medicine, Wilmut, I., Scientific American, Dec, 1998,

Cloning Issues in reproduction science and medicine, The Human Genetic Advisory Commission & Human Fertilisation and Embryology Authority, 1998,

Cloning Issues in Reproductive Medicine, Human Genetics Advisory Commission and Human Fertilisation and Embryology Authority, Dec, 1998,

Coalition of 41 health and consumer groups file petition calling on US FDA to pass EU-type ban on antibiotic use in cattle, http://www.cspinet.org/new/antibiotics.htm,

Code of Practice on the provision of information relating to genetically modified crops, NFU/UKASTA,

Code of Practice and Guidance on Human Genetic Testing Services Supplied Direct to the Public, Advisory Committee on Genetic Testing, 1997,

Comment on the Royal Society Peer Report on GM Potato, Cummins, J., 19 Mar, 1999,

Comments from the Cancer Prevention Coalition on IGF-1 and cancer based on article from Science magazine,January 23rd, and The Lancet May 9th, Epstein, S.

Commercialisation of Transgenic Plants: Potential Ecological Risks, Snow, A., Palma, P.M., BioScience, Feb, 1997.

Commodity Producers Try to Gut the Biosafety Protocol, Meyer, H., Feb, 1999.

Concern at GM food exposed, Brown, P. The Guardian, 26 1999.

Confidence Move on GM foods, BBC, 16 Feb, 1999,

Consumer attitudes to genetically modified foods: results of qualitative research, IGD, Institute of Grocery Distribution, Nov, 1997,

Consumers' Union comments on labelling of GEFs, Consumers' Union, 1998,

Consumers Policy Institute statement on the Canadian decision to ban rBGH, Hansen, M., Consumer Policy Institute, 15 Jan, 1999,

Consumers Union's Comments on Docket No. 92N-0139, Food Labelling; Foods Derived from New Plant Varieties, Hansen, M., Consumer Policy Institute, 29 Mar, 1999,

Convention on Biological Diversity, http://www.icgeb.trieste.it/biosafety/bsflib.htm,

Corn refuge spread Bt mutants, Cummins, J., briefing 1999,

Cost of Production in Dairy Herds in England, Kossaibati, M.A., Esslemont, R.J., The Veterinary Journal, 1997, 154, 41–51.

Costs of transgenic glufosinate resistance introgressed from Brassica napus into weedy Brassica rapa, Snow, A., Jorgensen, R., Abstract Of Paper From The Annual Meeting Of The Ecological Soc Of America, 6 Aug, 1998,

Cotton Growers Blame New Seed for Crop Losses, Augusta Chronicle, 25 Jan, 1999,

Cotton Picking Blues, Steinbrecher, R., The New Internationalist, No.293, 1997, p.22.

Could Transgenic Supercrops One Day Breed Superweeds?, Kling, J., Science, Oct, 1996, Vol. 274,

Creating, Patenting and Marketing of New Forms of Life, Davidman, M., http://www.solbraram.org/articles/clm505.html,

Crop segregation is possible – non-GM soy plant opens in U.S., Natural Law Party, 1 Mar, 1999,

Crop-weed hybridisation in radish (Raphanus sativus L): effects of distance and population size, Klinger, T. et al, Am. J. Bot., 1992, Vol. 79, 1431–1435.

Culling in Dairy Herds, Esslemont, R.J., Kossaibati, M.A., The Veterinary Record 11 Jan, 1997,

Currently Active GE Test Sites, http://www.environment.detr.gov.uk/acre/register, DETR, 21 Mar, 1999,

Dark Harvest of Suicide Seeds, Irish Times, 20 Feb, 1999,

Dead seeds, Mellon, M., The Gene Exchange – A Public Voice On Biotechnology & Agriculture, www.ucsusa.org/publications/index/html, Union of Concerned Scientists,

Deal Unlikely on Biotech Crops: US under fire for bid to 'torpedo' negotiations, Toronto Star, 24 Feb, 1999,

Declaration of A Heretic, Rifkin, J., Routledge and Kegan Paul, 1985,

Degradation of IGF-1 in the Adult Rat Gastrointestinal Tract is Limited by a Specific Antiserum or the Dietary Protein Casein, Xian, C.J. et al, J. of Endocrinology, 1 Aug, 1995, Vol. 146 No. 2, 215–225.

Democracy in Action: Genetically Engineered Food, Canberra Concensus Conference Report, http://www.abc.net.au/science, 19 Mar, 1999,

Detection of nptII (kanamycin resistance) genes in genomes of transgenic plants by marker-rescue transformation, Mol. Gen. Genet, 1998, Vol. 257, 606–613.

DETR Factsheet: Release of Genetically Modified Crops, DETR: Biotechnology Unit, 18 Mar, 1999,

Development of an immunoassay for the detection of glyphosate in water, Breuer, G.M., Berberich, S.L., 1997,

Development of Herbicide Resistance in Annual Ryegrass Populations in the Cropping Belt of Western Australia, Gill, D.S., Australian J. of Exp. Agriculture, 1995, Vol. 3, p. 67–72.

Diet and Body Build: Diet, Body Size, and Breast Cancer, Hunter, D.J., Epidemiological Reviews, 1993, Vol. 15 No 1, 110–132.

DNA shuffling to accelerate crop improvement. Press release, http://www.pioneer.com, 1999,

Do Infants need Nucleotide Supplemented Formula for Optimal Nutrition?, J. of Paediatric Gastroenterology and Nutrition, 1990, Vol. 11, 429–437.

Does medical mystery threaten biotech?, Raphals, P., Science, 1990, Vol. 249, p. 619.

Don't be scared of modified food – says US Ambassador, Rohatyn, F., The Independent, 20 Jan, 1999,

Don't bother to sue if GM foods do turn out to make you ill. You'll be wasting your time., Berlins, M., The Guardian, 24 Feb, 1999,

Down on the Farm: The Real BGH Story, Kastel, M., Rural Vermont – Rural Education Action Project, 1995,

Draft European Commission Directive on Foods for Special Medical Purposes: IBFAN briefing, Nov, 1998,

Drug Companies Merge: Astra and Zeneca combine, Feb, 1999,

Drug Firms Discuss Linking up to Pursue Disease-causing Genes, Bio-IPR, 4 Mar, 1999,

Drug Residues, Somogyi, A., World Health Organisation, World Health, Jul, 1985,

Du Pont Chambers Works 1987 Toxics Report, Greenpeace USA, 1988,

Duo bids to halt breeding of human-animal hybrids, Arthur, C., The Independent, 5 Apr, 1998,

Dupont agrees to buy Pioneer for $7.7 Bn, Wall Street Journal, Mar, 1998,

E-mail from Rick Roush to D. Bowes, http://gen.free.de/archives.html,

Earth Summit background: sustaining the future, http://www.un.org/ecosocdeve/geninfo/sustdev/es&5sust.htm

Effect of repeated low doses of biocides on the earthworm Apporrectodea caliginosa in laboratory culture, Springett, J.A., Gray, R.A.J., Soil Biology and Biochemistry Vol. 24 (12), p.1739–44.

Effect of selected forestry herbicides on ectomycorrhizal development and seedling growth of pine and white spruce under controlled and field environment, Sidhu, S.S., Chakravarty, P., European J. of For. Path., Vol.20, p. 77–94.

Effects of Genetically Engineered Microorganisms on Microbial Populations and Processes in Natural Habitats, Doyle, J.D. et al, Advances in Applied Microbiology, 1995, Vol. 40,

Effects Of Genetically-Engineered Endophyte On The Yield And Nutrient Content Of Corn, Hormick, S., www.geocities-.com/Athens/1527/btcorn.html, Summarised on web site., 1997,

Effects of Klebsiella planticola on soil biota and wheat growth in sandy soil, Holmes, M.T., Ingham, E.R. et al, Applied Soil Ecology, 1998, Vol. 326, 1–12.

Effects of the herbicide 2,4-D, glyphosate, hexazinone and triclopyr on the growth of three species of ectomycorhizal fungi, Estok, D. et al, Bulletin of Envir. Contam. Toxic., Vol. 42, p.835–39.

Effects of transgenic Bacillus thuringiensis corn-fed prey on mortality and development time of immature Chysoperla carnea (Neuroptera: Chrysopidae), Hilbeck, A. et al, Environmental Entomology, 1998, Vol. 27 No. 2, 480–487.

Emerging virus infection., Mahy, B.W.J., Virol Immunol. 48, 1997, 1–2.

EMS deaths:Is recombinant DNA technology involved?, Raphaels, P., Medical Post Toronto, 16 Nov, 1990,

End of the Germ Line, Edwards, R., http://www.newscientist.com/ns/980328/nseeds.html, New Scientist, 28 Mar, 1998,

Engineered genes in Wild Populations: Weed-Crop Hybrids in Raphaus sativus, Klinger, T., Ellstrand, N.C., Ecological Applications, 1994, Vol. 4 No. 1, 117–120.

Engineering Consent, The Corner House, Mar, 1998,

English Nature: position statement on genetically modified organisms, Nature Conservancy Council for England, Jul, 1998,

Enhanced Accumulation Of Toxic Compounds In Yeast Cells Having High Glycolytic Activity:A Case Study On The Safety Of GE Yeast, Inose, T., Murata, K., International J. of Food Science technology, 30, 1995, p.141–146.

Environmental & Economic Costs Associated with Nonindigenous Species in the United States, Pimentel, D. et al, www.cornell.edu/releases/Jan99/speciescosts.html, Cornell University, College of Agriculture & Life Sciences,

Environmental sustainability or commercial viability? The evolution of the EC regulation on genetically modified foods., European Environment 6: 48–54,

Eosinophilia-myalgia syndrome and tryptophan production: a cautionary tale, Mayeno, A. N., Gleich, G.J., Tibtech, Sep, 1994, Vol. 12,

EPA Approves Bromoxynil on Cotton, Pesticides Action North America Update Service, 1 Aug, 1998,

EPA Pesticide Factsheet 4/98, Bacillus thuringiensis Cry IA(b)-delta-endotoxins and the genetic material necessary for its production (Plasmid vector pclB 4431) in corn, OPPTS,

EPA reaches settlement with Monsanto over labelling violations of some Roundup products, US Environmental Protection Agency, 24 Mar, 1998,

Ethical analysis of food biotechnologies: an evaluative framework, Mepham, B., Chapter from 'Food Ethics', Routledge,

Ethical aspects of labelling foods derived from modern biotechnology. Opinion of the Group of Advisers on the Ethical Implications of Biotechnology, European Commission, CEC: Brussels, 5 May, 1995,

Ethics: there is a lot of it about, Crawshaw, S., The Independent on Sunday, 29 Nov, 1998,

EU closed to modified food, The Western Producer (Saskatchewan), 5 Feb, 1999,

EU Marketing Approvals, GeneWatch, 31 Dec, 1998,

EU parliament urges caution re safety of GMOs, NewsEdge Corporation, 22 Feb, 1999,

EU split delays overhaul of GMO policy, Cross, S. European Voice, 28 Feb, 1999,

Eugenics? Slipping down the slope, Shakespeare, T., http://www.geneticsforum.org.uk/splice/eugenics.htm, The Splice of Life, Dec, 1998, Vol. 5 Issue 2,

Europe's Firestorm Burns US Corn Farmers, Union of Concerned Scientists, Apr, 1999,

European Lepidoptera Potentially Vulnerable to Toxic GM Maize Pollen, 1999,

European Response To Genetically Modified Soybeans, Press Release, www.oilseeds.org/asa/news.htm, Nov, 1996,

Evaluation of antibiotic resistance markers in plant biotechnology, Monsanto,

Every Father's Fear, Palmer, A., The Sunday Telegraph, 19 Jul, 1998,

Evidence to the House of Lords on GM food risks, 29 Jan, 1999,

Evidence to the House of Lords Select Committee on Genetically Modified Foods, http://www.parliament.the-stationery-office.co.uk/pa/ld199899/ldselect/ldeu, Sep, 1998,

Evolution of resistance to Bacillus thuringiensis, Tabashnik, B.E., Annual Review of Entomology, 1994, Vol. 39, p. 47–49.

Experts worked for drug firm, Eggertson, L., Toronto Star, 21 Sep, 1998.

Exposed: Councils massive investment in Frankenstein food industry, Genetic Engineering Network, 1 Mar, 1999,

Expression and inheritance of kanamycin resistance in a large number of transgenic petunias generated by Agrobacterium-mediated transformations, Dolores, S.C., Gardener, R.C., Plant Mol. Biol., 1988, Vol. 11, 355–364.

Expression Of Antifreeze Proteins In Transgenic Plants, Hightower, R. et al, Plant Molecular Biology, 1991, Vol. 17, p.1013–21.

Expression of Cauliflower Mosaic Virus Gene I., Vlack, J. et al, Virology 179, 1990, 312–20.

Expression of insulin-like growth factor I and II inhuman smooth muscle tumours, Hoppener, J.W.M. et al, EMBO J., 1988, Vol. 7, 1379–1385.

Fact Sheet:BST, Compassion in World Farming,

Factor Influencing Drift Potential with Glyphosate, Hartzler, B., Briefing paper, 12 Dec, 1997,

Factors Influencing Drift Potential with Glyphosate, Hartzler, B., http://www.weeds.iastate.edu/mgmt/qtr97–4/glyphosatedroplets.htm, 12 Dec, 1997,

Family study aims to identify genetic cause of depression, Ahuja, A., The Times, 26 May, 1997,

Farm drugs face ban over superbug scare, Woolf, M., Independent on Sunday, 29 Nov, 1998,

Farmers' Rights: the crisis every Ugandan farmer needs to know about., Mundaka, W., Rural News – Integrated Rural Development Initiative, May, 1998, Issue 8,

Farming systems trial, www.enviroweb.org/publications/rodale/usrarc/fst.html, Rodale Institute, USA,

Fatal and near-fatal anaohylactic reactions to food in children and adolescents Sampson, H.A. et al, New England J. Of Med., 1992, Vol. 327, 380–384.

Fatal Flaws In Food Safety Assessment: Critique Of FAO/WHO Biotechology And Food Safety Report, Steinbrecher, R., Ho, M-W., www.psagef.org/fao96.htm, 1996,

FDA Approval of Flavr Savr Paves the Road for Genetically Modified Foods, http://www.essential.org/crg/consumer alert.html, Council for Responsible Genetics,

FDA Documents Show They Ignored GMO Safety Warnings from Their Own Scientists, Nottingham, S., Alliance for Bio-Integrity, 1999,

FDA Set to Approve Heart-Healthy Labels for (GM?) soya, Krebs, A.V., The Agribusiness Examiner, 9 Mar, 1999, Issue No. 24,

FDA warns dairy industry not to label milk Hormone-free, Schneider, K., New York Times, 8 Feb, 1994,

Feeding the world with sustainable farming or GMOs?, Pretty, J., 2 Splice, Aug, 1998, Vol. 4 Issue 6, p.4–5.

Fertility Doctor in 'human eggs for sale' row, Cooper, C., The Sunday Telegraph, 29 Nov, 1998,

Fields of Genes, Kleiner, K., New Scientist, 16 Aug, 1997,

Fifteen Ministers Demand GM Policy Change, Friends of the Earth Press release, 4 Mar, 1999,

Financial Interests of Authors in Scientific Journals: a pilot study of 14 publications, Krimsky, S. et al, Science and Environmental Ethics, Dec, 1996, Vol. 2, 395–410.

Fires Burn in Europe: Taking Stock of US Policy in the World Trade Organisation, Sprinkel, S., An Acres – Special Edition, 1999,

First Annual Report, Human Genetics Advisory Commission, Mar, 1998,

First Case of GMO Food Contamination, Keenan, L., www.essential-trading.co.uk/genetix.htm, Genetics Food Alert Press Release, 4 Feb, 1999,

First Cervical Cancer Vaccine – from dream to pipeline, World Health Organisation Press release, 19 Feb, 1999,

First Nationwide Interleukin-12 gene therapy trial announced, University of Pittsburgh Cancer Institute, 7 Aug, 1995,

Fishy Business?, www.geneticsforum.org.uk/, The Splice of Life, Dec, 1996, Vol. 3 No 3,

Five Years After Rio: Where do we Stand? http://www.un.org/ecosocdev/geninfo/sustdev/5years.htm, United Nations,

Flawed Monsanto data calls Irish sugar-beet trials into question, Genetic Concern (Ireland), 28 Feb, 1998,

Floodgates open to untested genetically modified foods, Phelps, B., GeneEthics Network Australia, 31 Mar, 1999.

Food Advisory Committee Terms of Reference, MAFF, 1999,

Food biotechnology: Labelling Will Benefit Industry as Well as Consumers, Nestle, M., Nutrition Today, Jan, 1998, Vol. 33 No. 1, 6–11.

Food for Our Future, Food and Drink Federation, 1995/7,

Food Intolerance and its impact on The Nation's Health, Graham, J. et al, York Nutritional Laboratory, Dec, 1998,

Food Supply Update: Seed Terminator and Mega-Merger Threat to Freedom, http://www.arkinstitute.com/98/up0606.htm, The Ark Institute, 5 Jun, 1998,

Foodfuture: Informing consumers about modern biotechnology, Food and Drink Federation, 1998,

Foreign (M13) DNA ingested by mice reaches peripheral leukocytes, spleen and liver via the intestinal mucosa and can be covalently linked to mouse DNA, Schubbert, R. et al, Proc. Nat. Acad. Sci. USA, 1997, Vol. 94, 961–966.

Foreign DNA sequences are received by wild-type strain of Aspergillus niger after co-culture with transgenic higher plants, Hoffmann, T. et al, Current Genetics, 1994, Vol. 27, 70–76.

Forest Cleansing: Racial Oppression in Scientific Nature Conservation, The Corner House: Briefing No. 13, Jan, 1999,

Formula Companies Miracle Cyre, Sterken, E., Update, Jun, 1992,

Formula for Disaster: an investigative report on genetically engineered bovine growth hormone in milk and the consequences for your health, Kamen, J., Penthouse Magazine, Mar, 1999,

Francophone African OAPI States are out-of-step with OAU and other African Countries, RAFI, 24 Feb, 1999,

Frequently asked questions concerning thalidomide, FDA Centre for Drug Evaluation and Research, USA,

Friend in need . . . The ladybird, an agricultural ally whose breeding potential may be reduced by GM crops, Miekle, J., Brown, P., The Guardian, 4 Mar, 1999,

Friends of the Earth Mailout (1996) 2 (8):1–3; (1997) 3 (1):4, Mar, 1998,

Friends of the Earth release leaked government document, Friends of the Earth Press release, 20 Mar, 1999,

From BSE to Genetically Engineered Modified Organisms: Science, Uncertainty and the Precautionary Principle, Shepherd, J., Greenpeace briefing, Jul, 1997, p. 28–29.

From Green to Gene Revolution: the environmental risks of genetically engineered crops, Steinbrecher, Ricarda, The Ecologist, 1996, Vol. 26, p. 273–282

From the Editor's Desk: Big & Bigger, The Gene Exchange – A Public Voice On Biotechnology & Agriculture, www.ucsu-sa.org/Gene/su98.big.html, Union of Concerned Scientists, 1998,

Functional Food Opportunities, Mullen, W., Rowett Research Services,

Further consultation document on implementing legislation:

EC regulation 1139/98 – EC regulation on GM soya and maize labelling, food labelling (amendment) (No. 2) regulations, MAFF, 1 Feb, 1999,

Further Consultation Document on Implementing legislation: EC Regulation 1139/98 – Food labelling (Amendment) (No 2) Regulations, MAFF, 1998,

FY96 Enforcement and Compliance Assurance Accomplishments Report, Environmental Protection Agency, USA, May, 1997,

Gaia: the practical science of planetary medicine, Lovelock, J., Gaia books, 1991,

Gastrointestinal Absorbtion of Recombinant Human Insulin-Like Growth Factor in Rats, Kimura, T. et al, J. of Pharmacology & Experimental Therapeutics, Nov, 1997, Vol. 283 No. 2, 611–18.

GATT and Agricultural Biodiversity, http://www.idrc.ca/books/725/chap4.html, IDRC, 1998,

Bioserfdom: Technology, Intellectual Property and the Erosion of Farmers' Rights in the Industrialised World, http://www.rafi.org/communique/fltxt/19972.html, RAFI, Mar, 1997,

GE – Breaking the Chain, Antoniou, M., Briefing paper,

GE – Flawed Monsanto Data Calls Irish Sugar-beet Trials into question., Genetic Concern Ireland, 28 Feb, 1999,

GE – Memorandum from 20 scientists, Genetech, 18 Feb, 1999,

GE – The corporate takeover of science, Monbiot, G., The Guardian, 19 Dec, 1998

GE Food – Safety Problems, Physicians & Scientists For Responsible Application Of Science & Technology http://www.psagef.org/indexgen.htm, 27 Mar, 1999,

GE Foods – Safety Problems, et al Physicians & Scientists For Responsible Application Of Science & Technology www.psrast.org/sitemap.htm, 1 Apr, 1999,

GE foods make front page news in Greek National Press and MM, E-mail communication from Dr C. Giannakenas, Univ. Hospital of Patras, 13 Feb, 1999,

GE Possesses Inherent Unpredictability, Physicians & Scientists For Responsible Application Of Science & Technology www.psrast.org/mianunpr.htm, 1 Apr, 1999,

GE: The corporate takeover of Science, Monbiot, G., The Guardian, 19 1998,

Gene crop charges, New Scientist, 4 Apr, 1999,

Gene Exchange, Union of Concerned Scientists, Fall 1998,

Gene Foods, Women's Environmental Network, 1998,

Gene Giants, Masters of the Universe?, www.rafi.org/communique/fltxt/19992.html, RAFI Communique, Mar, 1999,

Gene Map is on the Fast Track. Millions in Grants Speed up Project, Washington Post, 16 Mar, 1999,

Gene modified fish grows three times faster than normal, Hawkes, N., The Times, 26 May, 1998,

Gene Technology & Gene Ecology of Infectious Diseases, Ho, M-W. et al Microbial Ecology in Health & Disease, 1998, Vol. 10, p.33–59.

Gene Therapy Fights Frailty, Raloff, J., http://www.science news.org/sn-arc98/12-19-98/Fob1.htm, 19 Dec, 1998,

Gene therapy for enhancement, Miller, H.I. Lancet, 1994, Vol. 344, 316–7.

Gene Transfer and the Welfare of Farm Animals, O'Brien, T., Compassion in World Farming Trust,

Gene Watch Briefing No 1, Mar, 1998,

Genetic Approaches to Therapy for the Haemoglobinopathies: Gene Therapy, Antoniou, M., UKTS News Review, Mar, 1997,

Genetic Approaches to Therapy for the Haemoglobinopathies: The activation of Foetal Haemoglobin., Antoniou, M., UKTS News Review, Mar, 1997,

Genetic Approaches to Therapy for the Haemoglobinopathies: The Fundamentals, Antoniou, M., UKTS News Review, Mar, 1997,

Genetic Engineering and liability insurance, Swiss Re, Mar, 1999,

Genetic Engineering & World Hunger, Corner House Briefing No 10, Oct, 1998,

Genetic Engineering – Examples of Ecological Effects and Inherent Uncertainties, World Wide Fund for Nature, 1995,

Genetic Engineering and Biotechnology, EIRIS: Ethical Investment Research, Oct, 1998,

Genetic Engineering Can It Feed the World?, GeneWatch Briefing No 3,

Genetic Engineering Experiments on the Public, Montague, P. Third World Network,

Genetic Engineering in Agriculture and the Environment: assessing risks and benefits, Paoletti, M.G., Pimentel, D., BioScience, 1996, Vol. 46, p.665–671.

Genetic Engineering of Rice: Contribution to Sustainable Agriculture?, Meyer, H., Reiter, K., Third World Network Briefing Paper, 13 Oct, 1999,

Genetic Engineering Poses Inherent Unpredictability, http://www.psrast.org/mianunpr.htm, PSRAST, 1998,

Genetic Engineering: A review of developments in 1998, GeneWatch Briefing No. 5, Jan, 1999,

Genetic Engineering: Dream or Nightmare?, Ho, M-W., Gateway, 1998,

Genetic engineering: key issues, Soil association, 3 Nov, 1998,

Genetic Modification of crops: Lords give go ahead to new technology, House of Lords Press release, 21 Jan, 1999,

Genetic Seed Sterilisation is 'Holy Grail' for Agricultural Biotech Firms, www.rafi.org/pr/release26.html, RAFI Press Release,

Genetic Testing, Association of British Insurers Code of Practice, Dec, 1997,

Genetic Vaccines, Weiner, D.B., Kennedy, R.C., Scientific American, Jan, 1999,

Genetically Altered Food: Buyer beware, Fagan, J., USA Today, 6 Mar, 1999,

Genetically engineered Chickens, Union of Concerned Scientists, Fall, 1998,

Genetically engineered corn – no real benefits, Greenpeace briefing,

Genetically Engineered Crops – A Threat to Soil Fertility, Antoniou, M., Mar, 1999,

Genetically Engineered Crops and Food – The Case for a Moratorium, GeneWatch Briefing, Nov, 1998, No. 4,

Genetically Engineered Food – Canberra Consensus Conference Report, GeneEthics Network, 13 Mar, 1999,

Genetically Engineered Food – Safety Problems, Physicians and Scientists for Responsible Application of Science and Technology, 1999,

Genetically Engineered Food, Friends of the Earth briefing, Sep, 1998,

Genetically Engineered Foods a Serious Health Risk, Natural Law Party, 1998,

Genetically engineered oilseed rape (Agrevo/PGS), Fromwald, S., Strauss, S., Greenpeace International, May, 1998,

Genetically Engineered Oilseed Rape, Friends of the Earth briefing, 1998,

Genetically Engineered Oilseed Rape: Agricultural Savior or a New Form of Pollution?, GeneWatch Briefing No 2, May, 1998,

Genetically modified crops in the UK: your questions answered, Monsanto,

Genetically Modified crops spell trouble on the farm, Griffiths, M., Chartered Surveyor Monthly, /De, 1998,

Genetically modified food – Who's doing what?, http://www.connectotel.com/gmfood, Genetics Forum, 5 Mar, 1999,

Genetically Modified Foods, Jones, L., British Medical J., 27 Feb, 1999, Vol. 318, 581–584.

Genetically modified foods: adding to the debate – Special MPs' Briefing No 1, Diamond, E. et al, Friends Of The Earth, www.foe.co.uk, Mar, 1999, Vol.,

Genetically Modified Foods: Will Labelling Provide Choice?, GeneWatch Briefing, 1998, No. 1,

Genetically modified organism and the environment: coordination of government policy, Select Committee on the Environment Audit: 5th Report, May, 1999

Genetically modified plants for food use: statement 2/98, The Royal Society, Sep, 1998,

Genetically modified salmonella lacks ability to induce TNF-(alpha), Gene Therapy Weekly, 11 Jan, 1999,

GenPharm to Use Bull to Enter Market for Infant Formula, Chase, M., Wall Street Journal, 13 Jan, 1993,

Germ Warfare could Target Ethnic Groups, Arthur, C., The Independent, 22 Feb, 1999,

Germline therapy conference, http://www.nih.gov/od/orda/gtpcconc.htm, Jan, 1999,

Global agreements block precautions against trading manipulated food, Gray, J., Guardian, 2 Mar, 1999,

Global Biosafety Talk Collapse: Last Chance for International Safety Rules on Genetic Engineering threatened by Vested Interests, Women's Environmental Network, 23 Feb, 1999,

Global review of commercialisation of transgenic crops, James, C., ISAAA, Briefs No 8, Ithaca,, 1998,

Global Review of Field Testing and Commercialisation of Transgenic Plants, (1986 to 1995: the First Decade of Crop Biotechnology Commercialisation of Transgenic Plants, ISAA Briefs No. 1, ISAA Ithaca,

Global Status of Transgenic Crops in 1997. ASAAA briefs No. 5, Mikkelsen, T.R. et al, The International Service For The Acquisition Of Agri-Biotech Applications, Nature, 7 Mar, 1996, Vol. 380,

Global Trade and Biodiversity in Conflict, Gaia Foundation and GRAIN, May, 1998, Issue No 2,

Global Trade and Biodiversity in Conflict, Gaia Foundation and GRAIN, Apr, 1998, Issue No 1,

Global Water Supplies in Peril, UN Report Finds, J http://www.un.org/ecosocdev/geninfo/sustdev/waterpr.htm, United Nations,

Globalisation and Employment: New opportunities, real threats, Panos Briefing, PANOS, May, 1999, No. 33,

Glufosinate and genetic engineering, Jewell, T., Pesticides Trust, Nov, 1996,

Glyphosate Fact Sheet, Greenpeace International briefing, 1997,

Glyphosate Resistance in Annual Ryegrass, Pratley, J. et al, Proceedings of the 11th Conference, Grasslands Society of New South Wales, 1996,

Glyphosate, Part 1, Toxicology, Herbicide Factsheet, Cox, C., Northwest Coalition For Alternatives To Pesticides, J. of Pesticide Reform, 1995, Vol. 15 No 3,

Glyphosate, Part 2, Human Exposure and Ecological Effects, Herbicide Factsheet, Cox, C., Northwest Coalition For Alternatives To Pesticides, J. of Pesticide Reform, 1995, Vol. 15 No 4,

Glyphosate: environmental health criteria, Cox, C., J. of Pesticide Reform, 1996, Vol. 16 No. 4, p.15–16.

Glyphosate: Environmental Health Criteria 159, WHO, United Nations Environment Programme, International Labour Organisation, 1994,

GM could be used in up to 90% of processed food, says Gene-Watch, press release, 15 Feb, 1999,

GM could be used in up to 90% of processed foods, Genewatch, 15 Feb, 1999,

GM crops not for all, say US weed scientists, Baldwin, Ford Farmers Weekly, 5 Mar, 1999,

GM crops under wide attack – government to make statement at 15.30 GMT, BBC News, 16 Feb, 1999,

GM Crops: The Regulatory Process, ACRE,

GM Food Crisis: commercial planting is here already, Friends of the Earth briefing, 21 Apr, 1999,

GM food row splits Brit government, Guardian, 15 Feb, 1999,

GM foods – Current tests are inadequate protection, The Independent on Sunday, 21 Feb, 1999,

GM foods – revealed: false data misled farmers, Woolf, M., Independent on Sunday, 21 Feb, 1999,

GM foods – revealed: the secret report, Woolf, M., The Independent on Sunday, 21 Feb, 1999,

GM foods – statement by Jeff Rooker, Ministry of Agriculture Fisheries & Food Press Release, 17 Feb, 1999,

GM Foods – the price of disaster will not be paid by those responsible, Thornton, J., The Independent on Sunday, 28 Feb, 1999,

GM Foods – Watchdog's Silence on the guilty broke law, Lean, Geoffrey, Sunday Independent, 28 Feb, 1999,

GM Foods – safety and choice a priority says Jeff Rooker, MAFF Press Release, 2 Mar, 1999,

GM foods to be taken off menu in school, Ward, L., The Guardian, 25 Feb, 1999,

GM Foods: What's the hurry?, Kirby, A., BBC News, 17 Feb, 1999,

GM Labelling – Rooker puts new powers on the menu, MAFF, 18 Mar, 1999,

GM Oilseed rape results reveal poor performance, Natural Law Party, 3 Aug, 1998,

GM Trials warning, Farming News,

GM-Free Food Supply Under Threat, Christian Aid, 10 May, 1999,

GMOs enter food chain through livestock feed, The Independent, 24 Jan, 1999,

GMOs in Agriculture and Food: summary, Institut National de Recherche Agronomique, Jun, 1998,

GMOs lose American farmers international markets, NLP, 10 Jan, 1999,

GMOs Unlikely to Feed the World, Richardson, D., Farmers Weekly, 8 Jan, 1999,

GMOs: The Case for a Moratorium, Friends of the Earth briefing, 13 Oct, 1998,

Go Forth and Multiply, Coghlan, A., New Scientist, 25 Jul, 1998,

Government admits: They don't have to tell us anything., Friends of the Earth Press release, 5 Mar, 1999,

Government advice on genetic contamination challenged by new independent report, http://www.foe.co.uk/pubsinfo/infoteam/pressrel/1999/19990303, Friends of the Earth,

Government announces fuller evaluations of growing genetically modified crops, DETR, 21 Oct, 1998,

Government Commissions Secret GM-Health Report: Leaked Papers Show "Voluntary Moratorium" A Sham,

Government Inducements to Biotech Companies, The Guardian, 15 Feb, 1999,

Government operates a pollute now , pay later GM policy, Soil Association, 1999,

Government Welcomes the House of Lords Report on GM Crops, MAFF Press Release, 24 Mar, 1999,

Green MEP says greed has won out over food safety in GM debate, O'Sullivan, Kevin The Irish Times, 1 Mar, 1999,

Green parties of Europe call for a moratorium, Green Parties of Europe Joint press release, 1 Mar, 1999,

Green Parties of Europe call on their own Ministers to initiate Euro-wide GM Moratorium and Import Ban, Green Parties Press release, 1 Mar, 1999,

Greenpeace and Soil Association issue challenge to UK government to set organic target, Greenpeace & Soil Association, 17 Mar, 1999,

Greenpeace calls for national import bans as international talk on trade in genetic food fails to agree on safeguards, Greenpeace International press release, 24 Feb, 1999,

Greens and Growers Wide Apart on Biotech Food, Reuters, 22 Feb, 1999,

Growing New Organs, Mooney, D.J., Mikos, A.G., Scientific American,

Growth Enhancement in Transgenic Atlantic Salmon by use of an "all fish" Chimeric Growth Hormone Construct, Du, S.J et al, Biotechnology, 1992, Vol. 10 No 2, p. 176–181

Growth of artificially fed infant rats: effect of supplementation with insulin-like growth factor 1, Philipps, A.F., American J. of Physiology,, May, 1997, Vol. 272 No 5 Pt 2

Growth regulation and co-stimulation of human corectal cancer cell lines by insulin-like growth factor I,II and transforming growth factor alpha., Lahm, H. et al, Brit. J. of Cancer, 1992, Vol. 65 No. 3,

Guidance for Industry: Use of Antibiotic Resistance Marker Genes in Transgenic Plants – Draft Guidance, U.S. Food and Drug Administration Centre for Food Safety and Applied Nutrition, 4 Sep, 1998,

Gut reaction, Mac Kenzie, D., New Scientist, 30 Jan, 1999,

Gutachten Zur Wissenschaften Zielsetzung Und Dem Wissenschaftenlichen Sinn Des Freisetzungsexperimentes Mit Transgenen Petunien, Tappeser, B., Oeko-Institut e.V Freiburg, 1990,

Harm to Wildlife: implications of Cornell Monarch butterfly studies circulating comment, Institute for Agriculture and Trade Policy USA, 1999,

Health Canada Cover-up Alleged, Mc Ilroy, A., Toronto Globe & Mail, 17 Sep, 1998,

HGDP Internal Memos, http://www.rafi.org/pp/doble.html, Rural Advancement Foundation, 21 Jul, 1994,

HGDP's relationship with HUGO, http://www.rafi.org/pp/cavunes.html, Rural Advancement Foundation, 21 Sep, 1994,

Hi-tech canola causes stir in Sask, CBC, 23 Feb, 1999,

High Stakes in Genetic Accord Talks, Houlder, V., Financial Times, 15 Feb, 1999,

Hints of a language in junk DNA, Science, 1994, Vol. 266, 1320.

HM(ge), Novo's biosynthetic insulin, Nellermann Jorgensen, L. et al, MedView, Vol. III No 4,

Hobson's Choice, Hobson, W., Independent on Sunday, 20 Sep, 1998,

Horizontal Gene Transfer – New Evidence, Ho, M-W., NLP Briefing paper, 4 Dec, 1998,

Horizontal gene-transfer from a transgenic potato line to a bacterial pathogen (Erwinia-chrysanthemum) occurs, if at all, at an extremely low frequency., Schluter, K. et al, Bio/Technology, 1995, Vol. 13, 1094–1098.

House of Lords Report Evidence, http://www.parliament.the-stationery-office.co.uk/pa/1d199899/ldselect/. . .htm, 29 Jan, 1999,

House of Lords Select Committee on the European Communities – EC regulation of Genetic Modification in Agriculture. Session 1998–99: 2nd Report, The Stationery Office,

How a newborn baby could help to save a child's life, Laurance, J., The Times, 28 Dec, 1995,

How Can Biotechnology Benefit the Environment? The Report of the European Federation of Biotechnology Task Group on Public Perceptions of Biotechnology, http://www.bioportfolio.com/efb-conf.htm, The Green Alliance, 13 Jan, 1997,

How Should Genetic Engineering be Used in Medicine and Agriculture?, Antoniou, M., Briefing paper,

How the Terminator Terminates: an explanation for the non-scientists of the remarkable patent for killing second generation seeds of crop plants, Crouch, M. L., The Edmonds Institute, 1998,

HSE prosecutes Monsanto and Perryfields Holdings Limited following release of genetically modified crops, Health and Safety Executive, 17 Dec, 1998,

Human Genetics and noncommunicable diseases, WHO Factsheet, Jan, 1999, No 209,

Human genomic companies bankrolled by pharmaceutical giants, http://www.rafi.ca/mj/mjcompanies.html, RAFI, 1998,

Human germline gene modification: a dissent, Billings, P., Hubbard, R., Newman, S., Draft revised article, 17 Mar, 1999,

Human Insulin for second generation genetic engineering, Novo Nordisk, Identification of a brazil-nut allergen in transgenic soybeans, Nordlee, J. et al, New England Journal Of Medicine, 1996, Vol. 334 (11), p. 688–692

If Biological Diversity Has a Price, Who Sets It and Who Should Benefit?, Nature, Vol 359, 15 Oct, 1992,

Immunological reactions to DNA and RNA, Bowes, Dorothy

Impact of genetic manipulation on society and medicine, Motulsky, A.G., Science, 1983, Vol. 219, 135–40.

Importation Of Ciba-Geigy Bt Maize Is Scientifically Indefensible, Fagan, J., www.netlink.de/gen/BTcorn.htm,

Improving Nature: the science and ethics of genetic engineering, Reiss, M.J. Straughan, R., Cambridge University Press, 1999,

Incidence of clinical mastitis in dairy herds in England, Kossaibati, M.A. et al, The Veterinary Record, 12 Dec, 1998, 143, 649–653.

Incidence of production diseases and other health problems in a group of dairy herds in England, Esslemont, R.J., Kossaibati, M.A., The Veterinary Record, 16 Nov, 1996,

Incomplete knowledge of DNA, Physicians & Scientists For Responsible Application Of Science & Technology http://www.psrast.org/junk.dna.htm, 1 Apr, 1999,

Increasing Brain Tumour Rates: is there a link to Aspartame, Millstone, Erik Oct, 1996,

India's High Court Stops Field Trials of Biotech Cotton, Noronha, F., Environment News Service, 23 Feb, 1999,

Indigenous People Testify Before the National Academy of Sciences Committee on the Human Genome Diversity Project, http://www.rafi.org/pp/hgdpcomm.html, Rural Advancement Foundation, Oct, 1996,

Industry fails to win hearts and minds, Coghlan, A., New Scientist, Jun, 1993,

Infant threat from unlabelled foods, GeneEthics Network Australia, 29 Jul, 1998,

Infant threat from unlabelled Gene tech foods, GeneEthics Network Australia, 19 Mar, 1999,

Information about Intellectual Property Rights No. 1, Institute for Agriculture and Trade Policy,

Information note: genetically modified organisms, European Commission, 10 Jun, 1998,

Ingested foreign (phage M13) DNA survives transiently in the gastronintestinal tract and enters bloodstream of mice., Schubbert, R. et al, Mol.Gen. Genet, Vol. 242, 495–504.

Inquiry into work of GM food scientist, Connor, S., The Independent, 1999,

INRA (French Institut National de Recherche Agronimique) publishes report on GMOs supporting environmentalists arguments, Natural Law Party, Jun, 1998,

Insecticidal activity and biodegradation of the toxin Bacillus Thuringiensis subsp. kurstaki bound to humic acids from soil, Crecchio, C. Stotzky, G. Soil Biol. Biochem., 1998, Vol. 30, p. 463–70.

Insulin Manufacture and Formulation, Pickup, J., Williams, G., Chapter 31 of unidentified medical textbook,

Insulin-like growth factor-1 and new opportunities for cancer prevention, Holly, J. Lancet, 9 May, 1998, Vol. 351 No. 9113, 1373–1375.

Insulin-like Growth-Factor-Binding Protein 3 is Decreased in Early-Stage Operable Pre-Menopausal Breast Cancer, Bruning, P.F. et al, Internat. J. of Cancer, 1995, Vol. 62, 266–270.

Integration of foreign DNA and its consequences in mammalian systems., Doerfler, W. et al, Tibtech 15, 1997, 297–301.

Interactions between plant resistance genes, pest aphid populations and beneficial aphid predators, Birch, A.N.E. Scottish Crop Research Institute Annual Report, 1997, 66–72.

Interactions between resistance genes, pest aphid populations and beneficial aphid predators,, Birch, A.N.E. et al Scottish Crop Research Inst. Dundee, Annual Report, 1996/97 p. 68–72.

Internal Conflict: Adaptation and Reaction to Globalisation, Briefing No. 12, The Corner House,, Jan, 1999,

International Action on Toxic Chemicals and Hazardous Wastes, http://www.un.org/ecosocdev/geninfo/sustdev/toxic.htm, United Nations,

International Baby Food Action Network Newsletter, IBFAN, Jan, 1999, Vol. 1 No. 1,

International Biosafety: A Global Imperative, Regal, P., http://www.the-scientist.library.upenn.edu/yr1995/oct/comm-951030.html, The Scientist, 30 Oct, 1995, Vol. 9. No.21, 13.

International conference on emerging technologies for integrated pest management, North Carolina State University, Mar, 1999,

International scientists back shock findings of suppressed research into modified food, Gilliard, M., Guardian, 12 Feb, 1999,

International Talks break down without agreement because of intransigence by 6 grain exporting nations, WEN, 24 Feb, 1999,

Interview with Dr Vandana Shiva, Chamaraju, K., Deccan Herald (India), 28 Feb, 1999,

Intoxicating bacterium kills plants, UCSUSA, Union of Concerned Scientists, l/W, 1998,

Introducing IDDT, Insulin Dependent Diabetes Trust,

Insulin-like growth factor-1 and new opportunities for cancer prevention, Holly, J., The Lancet, Vol 351, No 9113, 9 May, 1998, p. 1372–75

It is a myth that world hunger is due to scarcity of food, Knight, D., www.psrast.org/nowohu.hmt, IPS Washington,

Italian Government Joins Dutch Challenge Against 'Life Patenting Directive', Oxford Analytica Executive Brief, 14 Dec, 1998,

Italian Government Joins Dutch Challenge Against 'Life Patenting Directive', 14 1999,

Jeopardising the Future? Genetic Engineering, Food and the Environment, Hansen, M., Halloran, J., Consumer Policy Institute, 29 Mar, 1999,

John Innes Research Centre Annual Report 97/89,

Joint FAO/WHO Expert Consultation on Biotechnology and Food Safety, http://www.fao.org/waicent/faoinfo/ecnomic/esn/biotech/safety.htm, Sep, 1996,

Jurassic Park, Crichton, M., Arrow, 1991,

Killer diseases making a comeback, says WHO, Mihill, C., The Guardian, 10 May, 1996,

Labelling Fact Sheet, MAFF, 18 Mar, 1999, Vol.,

Labelling of GM Soya and Maize, MAFF: Food Advisory Committee, 1999,

Labour day 1999 – is globalisation working, The Panos Institute, 26 Apr, 1999,

Labour government linked to biotech companies, Landale, J., 16 Feb, 1999,

Labour's links to the men doctoring food, Ingham, J., Rees, A., The Express, 27 Aug, 1998,

Land planted with GM crops may fall in value, Arthur, C. Independent, 12 Mar, 1999,

Land-Speed-Trials: Winners and Losers in the Biotechnology Race – Risks to Ecosystems, Lane, Michael F. http://www.a-cephale.org/bio-safety/l-s-t-index.html, 14 Mar, 1997,

Landmark Lawsuit Challenges FDA policy on Genetically Engineered Food, http://bio-integrity.org/lawsuit.html, Alliance for Bio-Integrity, 27 May, 1998,

Landmark Lawsuit Challenges FDA policy on Genetically Engineered Food, http://bio-integrity.org/lawsuit.html, Alliance for Bio-Integrity, 27 May, 1998,

Latest figures show factories still spewing out over 10,000 tonnes of cancer-causing chemicals., Friends of the Earth Press release, 11 May, 1999,

Lawsuit against FDA for not preventing use of antibiotics in cattle, http://www.hsus.org/programs/farm/antibiotic. html, Humane Society USA,

Leading geneticist urges GM caution: Steve Jones is concerned about GM crops, Kirby, Alex BBC News, 12 Apr, 1999,

Leading Global Seed Companies, Union of Concerned Scientists, l/W, 19989,

Leak reveals government GM PR offensive, Friends of the Earth Press release, May, 1999,

Legal Challenge filed with FDA to remove Monsanto's BGH from the market, The Centre for Food Safety and a dozen consumer groups, 15 Dec, 1998,

Legal Control lost over our food and health, Ehrlichman, J., The Guardian, 13 Apr, 1999,

Legal fight looms over patent bid on human/animal chimaeras, Dickson, David Nature, 2 Apr, 1998,

Les organismes génétiquement modifies (ogm): risques et perspectives, Ministére de l'Aménagement du Territoire et de l'Environnement, Jun, 1998,

Lets Make it Their Risk, Toynbee, P., The Guardian, 22 Feb, 1900,

Letter to the Editor, Collyer, R. et al, The Lancet, Vol 344, 17 Sep, 1994, 816.

Letter to the Editor, Griffiths, M., The Times, 4 Sep, 1998,

Little benefit to farmers from GM crops?, Farmers Weekly, 8 Nov, 1998,

Local government association calls for GE ban in Schools, 24 Feb, 1999,

Long term effect of GM crops serves as food for thought, Butler, D. et al Nature, Vol 398, 22 Apr, 1999, p.651–656.

Look what the Gene Dictators are growing just for you, Soil Association, 1998,

Lord Sainsbury announces public consultation on biosciences, Department of Trade and Industry, 18 Mar, 1998,

Lord Sainsbury to head biotech team, Independent, 12 Mar, 1999,

Low-Yielding Bt Cotton in Arkansas, Union of Concerned Scientists, Sep, 1998,

Luminal Stability of Insulin-like Growth Factors 1 & II in Developing Rat Gatrointestinal Tract, Rao, R.K. et al, J. of

Pediatric Gastroenterology & Nutrition, Vol 26, No 2, Feb, 1998, p.179–85.

M&S announces ban on GM ingredients, 15 Mar, 1999,

MAFF Report of the Committee on the Ethics of Genetic Modification and Food USE, 1993,

Maize is Maize: why we use gene technology, Novartis,

Major relief agency holds talk with troubled biotech multinational – who's helping whom?, Rural Advancement Foundation, 9 Mar, 1999,

Making big business mean good business: programme report for ethics in the workplace, Lord Haskins, RSA Journal, 4 Apr, 1998,

Making Crops Make More Starch, BBSRC Business, UK Biological Sciences Research Council, Jan, 1998,

Managing resistance to Bacillus thuringiensis: lessons from the diamondback moth (Lepidoptera: Plutellidae), Tabashnik, B.E. et al, J. Econ. Ent, 1991, Vol. 84 No 1, 49–55.

Manual for Assessing Ecological and Human Health Effects of Genetically Engineered Organisms. Part 1: Introductory Materials and supporting Text for Flowcharts, Scientists Working Group on Biosafety, Edmonds Institute, 1998,

Manual for Assessing Ecological and Human Health Effects of Genetically Engineered Organisms. Part 2: Flowcharts and Worksheets, Scientists Working Group on Biosafety, Edmonds Institute, 1998,

Meddling Minister [Lord Sainsbury], Eastham, P., Daily Mail, 9 Feb, 1999,

Medicines and Clinical Trials, Association of the British Pharmaceutical Industry: Media Briefing,

Memorandum from 20 scientist in support of Pusztai, 18 Feb, 1999,

Microbial utilisation of free and clay-bound insecticidal activity after incubation with microbes, Koskella, J., Stotzky, G., Applied and Environmental Microbiology 1997, Vol. 63 No. 9, 3561–3568.

Milk, rBGH and Cancer, www.geocities.com/Athens/1527/

rBGH/rach593.html, Rachel's Environment & Health Weekly. No.593, 9 Apr, 1998,

Milupa attacks over fatty acids – LCPs made from untested GE yeasts, Baby Milk Action, Update, Aug, 1995, Vol. 15,

Minister for the Environment [Brazil] gainst GMO crops, Gazeta Mercantil (Brazil), 23 Feb, 1999,

Ministers abdicate responsibility to protect organic farming from gene threat, The Soil Association, 21 May, 1999,

Minutes of meeting between the Rt Hon Michael Meacher, Minister for the Environment and Dr Mae-Wan Ho, 31 Jan, 1999,

Minutes of Meeting with Mae-Wan Ho & Michael Meacher, Ryan, A. Institute Of Science In Society, 31 Mar, 1999,

Misconceptions of GE, Altieri, M., http://www.nature.berkeley.edu/agroeco3,

Modification of protein content of soybean to improve seed quality, Nielsen, N.C., Advances in new crops, Timber Press, 1990,

Modulation of the Immune System by Human Milk and Infant Formula Containing Nucleotides, Pickering, L.K. Paediatrics, 1998, Vol. 101, 242–249.

Molecular mechanisms in retrovirus DNA integration., Asante-Appiah, E. et al Antiviral Research 36, 1997, 139–56.

Monarch Butterflies and herbicide resistant crops, Hartzler, B., http://www.weeds.iastate.edu,

Monarchs and their roots, Hartzler, B., Science, 8 Jan, 1999, Vol. 283: 171,

Money-Go-Round Peps Survey Part 1: Frankenstein walks with the eco-friendly brigade, Wright, M., The Daily Telegraph, 27 Feb, 1999,

Monocultures, Monopolies, Myths and the Masculinisation of Agriculture, Shiva, V., Aisling Quarterly,

Monsanto a checkered history, Tokar, B., The Ecologist, Sep, 1998, Vol. 28 No.5,

Monsanto admits 'unknowable' effects of GM technology, Natural Law Party, 30 Oct, 1998,

Monsanto advertisement samples, Sent to me by Monsanto, Mar, 1999,

Monsanto Agrees to Acquire Plant Breeding International Cambridge from Unilever, PRNewswire, 15 Jul, 1998,

Monsanto Greenwash Snapshot No. 19. A case study in Greenwash science., Greenpeace, 1992,

Monsanto in Court over GM Crop Safety, Friends of the Earth Press release, 17 Feb, 1999,

Monsanto investigator accused of trespassing, Weiss, Rick Washington Post, 2 May, 1999,

Monsanto is Behind AntiFarmer Legislation to Bill Discriminates Against Farmers, RAFI, http://www.rafi.org/pr/release28.html, Rural Advancement Foundation: Briefing paper, 7 Mar, 1998

Monsanto may face UK censure for GM food ads, Reuters, 1 Mar, 1999,

Monsanto pushes benefits of GM foods to the environment, O'Sullivan, Kevin The Irish Times, 1 Mar, 1999,

Monsanto rBGH information, http://www.monsanto.com/protiva/,

Monsanto reduces price of Roundup herbicides by $6 to $10/gallon, Monsanto press release, Sep, 1998,

Monsanto research, Monsanto, J. of Nutrition, Vol. 126, p.717–727.

Monsanto saw secret EU documents, Palast, G., Slavin, T., The Observer, 21 Feb, 1999,

Monsanto the Company that Gave the World PCBs, Snow, Susan K. http://www.204.176.47.38/timjam/monsanto.htm, 31 Oct, 1996,

Monsanto's Gene Police Harass Farmers, Weiss, R., Washington Post, 3 Feb, 1999,

Monsanto's Hormonal Milk Poses Serious Risk of Breast Cancer, Besides other Cancers, Warns Professor of Environmental Medicine at the University of Illinois School of Public Health, PRNewswire, 12 Jun, 1998,

Monsanto's Terminator 2, http://www.rafi.org/communique/
    fltxt/traitor.html, RAFI Communique,

Monsanto's Toxic Legacy, Deccan Herald, 6 Dec, 1998,

Monsanto's transgenic potatoes on the loose in Georgia (1996–
    1998): the need for an international Biosafety Protocol,
    Greenpeace, Aug, 1998,

Monsanto, BBC Money Programme, 1998,

Monsanto, DuPont decline comment on merger talks, Reuters,
    3 Mar, 1999,

Monsanto, IRRI, push pesticides on Thai farmers through Thai
    development NGO, Pesticide Action Network-Asia and the
    Pacific, 7 Apr, 1999,

Montreal Meeting of the Biodiversity Convention Must Move
    to Stop the GURT Hurt, RAFI Press Release, 18 Jun,
    1999,

Moore v. The Regents of the University of California et al
    Supreme Court of the State of California,

More T-DNA than meets the eye., Smith, V. Trends in Plant
    Science 3, 85, 1998,

Move to ban GM crops in Scotland, Hamilton, Sebastian Scot-
    land on Sunday, 21 Feb, 1999,

Movement of Landless Peasants (Brazil) destroy crops. (Trans-
    lation), Gazeta Mercantil, Brazil, 18 Feb, 1998,

Named and Shamed, New Scientist, 4 Apr, 1998, 4.

Need or Greed?, Panos Institute, Panos Media Briefing, Feb,
    1999, No. 30A (re-issue)

Neem – A therapeutic survey, Smith, L., http://www.neemaur-
    a.com/Misc/therapeuticoverview.htm, Therapeutic Botan-
    icals Inc,

Neem, a potentially valuable nectar and pollen resources for
    Indonesian beekers, Atmowidjojo, A.H., Erickson Jr., E.H.,
    USDA, 1998,

New Director General for the World Health Organisation,
    WHO, Jun, 1998,

New Evidence shows Prince right about GM food safety: the

truth about antibiotics and safety, Friends of the Earth Press release, 3 Jun, 1999,

New Gene for Retinitis Pigmentosa, Nature Genetics, Jun, 1999,

New Gene Therapy Fights Frailty, Raloff, J., Science News, 19 Dec, 1998,

New GM Labelling Laws Totally Inadequate, Friends of the Earth Press release, 18 Mar, 1998,

New Options with Roundup Ready Cotton, Hagedorn, C., Crop and Soil Environmental News, May, 1997,

New Patents for Terminator Seeds Threaten Farmers and Food Security, PANUPS, Pesticide Action Network Updates Service, 1 Feb, 1999,

New prenatal screening procedure raise spectre of more ''wrongful births' claims., Capen, K., Calif. Medical Assoc. J., 1995, Vol. 152, 734–737.

New Problems with Genetically Engineered crops, NLP Wessex, 5 Jul, 1999,

New Study Points to Inadequate Testing of Pesticides, Pesticides Action North America Update Service, 26 Mar, 1998,

New Trait Surfaces in Altered Plant, Associated Press, 3 Sep, 1998,

New Worries about moderate dose Bt Corn, Union of Concerned Scientists, May, 1999,

NFU GM food briefing, 1999,

NFU response to Joint Food Standards Group Review of the Food Labelling (Amendment) Regulations 1999 (for the labelling of GM soya and maize), 1998,

NFU response to The Office of Science and Technology Review of the Framework for Overseeing Developments in Biotechnology, 1998,

NGOs protest WIPO-WTO moves on UPOV at Bangkok, North South Monitor, 19 Mar, 1998,

Nick Brown welcomes radical reform, MAFF Press Release, 11 Mar, 1999.

NIH – Genetic Therapy Receives Broad Gene Therapy Patent, http://www.bioinfo.com/genether.html,

No cash for GM labels enforcement says trading standards, Friends of the Earth Press release, 1999, p. 23–24.

No Patents on Life, http://www.essential.org/crg/nopatents.html, The Council for Responsible Genetics, 18 Aug, 1997,

No Place to Hide from GM Crops: GM buffer zones will cover most of UK, Friends of the Earth Press release, May, 1999,

No Way Around Roundup – Monsanto seeds are designed to require more of the company's herbicide, Arax, M., Brokaw, J., www.purefood.org/mothjones.html, Mother Jones, Jan, 1997,

Non-target effects of Bt Corn Pollen on the Monarch butterfly (lepidoptera danaidae), Hansen, L.C., J.J. Obrycki, 1999,

North American Developments in Herbicide Tolerant Crops, Owen, M.D.K. http://www.weeds.iastate.edu/weednews/Brighton.htm, British Crop Protection Conference 1997, Paper,

Not Ready for Roundup: A Critique of Monsanto's Risk Evaluation, Greenpeace, 1997,

Notification of Oral Evidence, Press Notice No 11 of Session 1998–99, Science and Technology Committee, House of Commons, 25 Feb, 1999,

Novartis and Pioneer Obtain Evolution Technologies, BioWorld Today, 1999,

Novartis Bt-11 Maize, Novartis, Jun, 1998,

Novartis hit by data controversy, Gribben, R., Daily Telegraph, 18 Mar, 1998,

Novartis Seeds Expands Insect Management Programme; Bt Stewardship Incentive Rewards Farmers for Establishing Refuges, Novartis, 21 Sep, 1998,

Novartis' genetically engineered maize major threat to the environment and human and animal health, Greenpeace International, Feb, 1998,

Novo Nordisk's Little Book on Genetic Engineering, Novo Nordisk,

Now or never: serious new plans to save natural pest controls, Mellon, M., Rissler, J., Union of Concerned Scientists, 1998,

Nucleotides and misleading claims, newsletter, INFACT Canada, 1998,

Nutracuticals: poised for a healthy slice of the healthcare market, Brower, V., Nature Biotechnology, Vol. 16, p. 728–731

NZ University Adds Frog Genes to Salmon, Fitzsimons, J., Green Party (NZ) press release, 21 Feb, 1999,

Of Mice and Men, The Times, 16 Jun, 1997,

Official data reveals GM crop risks, Waugh, Paul The Independent, 16 Jun, 1998,

On the potential for Adverse Health Effects from the Consumption of Genetically Modified Maize (Zea Mays L), 21 Feb, 1997,

One gene in diamondback moth confers resistance to four Bt toxins, Tabashnik, B.E. et al, Proceedings of the National Academy of Sciences, 1997, Vol. 94, p.1640–4.

One Small Step for a Sheep, Coghlan, A., New Scientist, 1 Mar, 1997,

Opinion of the Scientific Committee for Pesticides on the Use of Genetically Modified Maize Lines Notified by Ciba-Geigy (opinion expressed on 9 December 1996), EU, The European Commission, 9 Dec, 1996,

Opinion on the Potentially Adverse Health Effects from the Consumption of Genetically Modified Maize (Zea Mays L), 21 Feb, 1997,

Orally administered IGF-1 increases intestinal mucosal growth in formula-fed neonatal pigs, Burrin, D.G.G. et al, American J. of Physiology, Vol 270, No 5, Part 2, May, 1996, Vol. 270 No.5 Pt 2 R1085–91.

Organic Agriculture, http://www.fao.org/unfao/bodies/COAG/COAG15/default.htm, FAO,

Organic Farming and Gene Transfer from Genetically Modified

Crops, Moyes, C.L. Dale, P.J., John Innes Centre, 1999,

Organic vs. Organic: The Corruption of a Label, Lilliston, B., Cummins, R., The Ecologist, Vol 28, No 4, y/A, 1998,

Origin and evolution of retroelements based upon the reverse transriptase sequences., Xiong, Y. et al, The Embo. Journal 9, 1990, 3363–72.

Ottawa accused of scuttling biotech deal, McIlroy, A., Globe and Mail (Canada), 26 Feb, 1999,

Ottawa Bans Growth Hormone, http://www., CBC TV Web-Post, 15 Jan, 1999,

Ottawa Refuses to Approve Bovine Growth Hormone, McIlroy, A., Globe and Mail (Canada), 20 Feb, 1999,

Ousted Scientists and the Damning research into food safety, Flynn, L., Gilliard, M., Rowell, A., Guardian, 12 Feb, 1999,

Outbreak of Meningitis is the worst for half a century, Laurance, J., Garner, C., The Independent, 10 Feb, 1999,

Outcry over danger foods, Rees, A., Ingham, J., The Express, 27 Aug, 1998,

Over Concentration of power in US food processors, AP News, Associated Press, 3 Mar, 1999,

Parliament [EU] urges caution re the safety of GMOs, NewEdge Corporation, 22 Feb, 1999,

Parliamentary Briefing:summary for the press, Natural Law Party, 9 Mar, 1999,

Patent Issued on Breast Cancer Protein, Women's Health Weekly, 8 Feb, 1999,

Patenting Genes, or "Just" Proteins?, http://www.rafi.org/pp/asquot.html, RAFI, 1994,

Patenting is Out of Control, http://www.rafi.org/msc/courting.html, Rural Advancement Foundation,

Patenting People, http://www.rafi.org/pp/, Rural Advancement Foundation,

Patenting, Piracy and Perverted Promises, Genetic Resources International (GRAIN), 1998,

Patents and Ordre Public, http://www.rafi.org/misc/bad-pats.jpg, Rural Advancement Foundation,

Patents Sought on Part-Human Creatures, Weiss, Rick Washington Post, 2 Apr, 1998,

Pathological and immunological effects of ingesting l-tryptophan and l-ethylidenebis (l-tryptophan) in Lewis rats, Love, L.A. et al, J. of Clinical Investigation, Mar, 1993, Vol. 91, 804–811.

PCBs – can the World's Sea Mammals survive them?, Cummins, J.E. The Ecologist, Sep, 1998, Vol. 28 No.5,

Pentachlorophenol – the chemical, Greenpeace USA briefing,

Perils Amidst the Promise: Ecological Risks of Transgenic Crops in a Global Market, Rissler, J., Mellon, M., Union of Concerned Scientists, 1993,

Pesticides in use, http://www.gks.com/library/biotech/monsanto.html, Pesticides Action North America, 1997,

Pesticide update 1997, Monsanto: Roundup, http://www.gks.com/library/biotech/monsanto.html, Pesticides Action North America, 1997,

Pests with a purpose, Kleiner, K., New Scientist, 21 Feb, 1998,

Pharmaceutical Companies Taking Contol over World Health Organisation, Van Meurs, R., Vrij Nederland (translated from), 21 Oct, 1989,

Pigs Grown with Human Genes, Eaton-Robb, P., Associated Press, 22 Feb, 1999,

Pioneer Enter $85M Crop Genetics Deal, BioWorld Today 1–5,

Pioneer Introduce 20 New Soybean Varieties for 1999, PRNewswire, 15 Dec, 1998,

Pioneer James Wilson Reflects on Gene Therapy's Hopes, Hype, Wilson, James http://www.the-scientist.library.upenn.edu/yr1996/jan/gene960122.html, The Scientist, 22 Jan, 1996, Vol. 10 No. 2,

Plagiarism or Protecting Public Health?, E. Millstone et al Nature, Vol.391, No.6499, 20 Oct, 1994, p.647–648.

Plant Breeders' Rights Threaten Farmers, http://www.rafi.org/genotypes/latest.html, RAFI Communique, 24 Feb, 1999,

Plant Breeders' Wrongs, http://www.rafi.org/pr/release20. html, Rural Advancement Foundation,

Plasma Insulin-like Growth Factor-1 (IGF-1) Concentrations in Human Breast Cancer, Peyrat, P. et al, European J. of Cancer, 1993, Vol. 29A No. 4, 492–497.

Plasma Insulin-Like Growth Factor-1 and Prostate Cancer Risk: a prospective study, Chan, J.M. et al, Science, 23 Jan, 1998, Vol. 279, 563–566.

Playing God in the Garden, Pollan, Michael The New York Times Sunday Magazine, 25 Oct, 1998.

PM Attacked on GM Crops, Waugh, Paul, Castle, Stephen Independent, 22 May, 1999,

Point of No Return, Editorial New Scientist, 1 Mar, 1997,

Poison Patent Alarms Aid Charity, Coughlin, A., New Scientist, 22 May, 1999,

Position Paper on Genetic Discrimination, http://www.essential.org/crg/gendisc.html, Council for Responsible Genetics, 18 Aug, 1997,

Post-Approval Blues: Flavr Savr Tomato – Squashed, The Gene Exchange – A Public Voice On Biotechnology & Agriculture, www.ucsusa.org/GENE/F97.agribusiness.html, Union of Concerned Scientists,

Potential Public Health Impacts of the Use of Recombinant Bovine Somatotropin in Dairy Production: prepared for a Scientific Review by the Joint Expert Committee on Food Additives, Hansen, M., et al, Consumers Union, Sep, 1997,

Precise Precaution versus Sloppy Science: a case study, Meyer, H., Bulletin for Science Technology and Society, Apr, 1999,

President Clinton Expands Federal Effort to Combat Invasive Species, www.doi.gov/news/990203.html, USDA press release, 3 Feb, 1999,

Press release by Steve Wilson & Jane Akre, www.foxBGHsuit.com/jasw0910.htm, 10 Sep, 1998,

Preventing pesticide related illness in Californian et al, Environmental Health Policy Programme Report, Berkeley,

Univ. California School of Public Health, California Policy Semi 1993,

Problems of germline therapy, Ewbank, J., Nature, 1998, Vol. 392, 645.

Produce-on-demand: what's good for US markets is good for world markets too, Nature Biotechnology, Vol 14, 1996, p. 802.

Production of human gastric lipase in the fission yeast., Smerdon, G. et al, Gene 165, 1995, 313–8.

Production of transgenic rabbits, sheep and pigs by microinjection, Hammer, R.E. et al, Nature, 1985, Vol. 315, p. 680–83.

ProMED Emergent Disease fact files, http://www.fas.org/promed,

ProMed emerging diseases data, http://www.fas.org/promed/about/index.html and links,

Promiscuity in transgenic plants, Bergelson, J. et al, Nature, 3 Sep, 1998, Vol. 395, 25.

Proposed Human Genome Diversity Project still plagued by controversy, Kreeger, K.Y., The Scientist, Vol 10 No 20, 1996, p.1–8.

Prospective appraisal of complaints of adverse reactions to foods in children during the first 3 years of life., Brooks, S.A. Pediatrics, 1987, Vol. 79, 683–688.

Protesters fear rise of genetically engineered superweed, Neale, G., Durisch, P., The Sunday Telegraph, 26 Apr, 1998,

Public Health implications of bovine somatotrophin use in dairying: discussion paper, Mepham, B., J. of Royal Society of Medicine, Vol.85, Dec, 1992, p.736–739.

Purple Loosestrife: Public Enemy No. 1 on Federal Lands, http://refuges.fws.gov/NWRSFiles/HabitatMgmt/PestMgmt/LoosestrifeProblem.html, ATTRA, Washington, 1997,

Quantum coherence and conscious experience, Ho, M-W., Kybernetes, 1997, Vol. 26 No. 3, 265–276.

Rachel's Environment and Health Weekly No. 538, On regulation, http://www.nirs.org/rehw/rehw538.txt, 20 Mar, 1997,

Rachel's Environment & Health Weekly, 27 Mar, 1997,

Rachel's Environment and Health Weekly: History of Precaution Part 1., 27 Mar, 1997,

Rachel's Environment and Health Weekly, 19 Feb, 1998,

Rachel's Environment and Health Weekly No. 598, 8 May, 1998,

RAFI Takes Terminator to COP IV in Bratislava, RAFI, http://www.rafi.org/genotypes/980602.html, Rural Advancement Foundation: Briefing paper, 2 Jun, 1998,

RBST (Nutrilac) Gaps Analysis Report by rBST (Nutrilac) Internal Review Team, Chopra, S. et al, www.nfu.ca/nfu/Gapsreport.html, Health Protection Branch, Health Canada, 21 Apr, 1999,

Re: The British Test: The Fall 1998 Research, Greenberg, Stan 5 Oct, 1998,

Reap what you sow, Coughlan, A., New Scientist, 10 Jul, 1999,

Recipe for Disaster, Bleifuss, J., www.purefood.org/recipe.html, In These Times, Chicago, Illinois, 11 Nov, 1996,

Recombination between viral RNA and transgenic plant transcripts, Green, A.E. Alison, R.F. Science, 1994, Vol. 263, 1423–1425.

Recommendations for developing and implementing resistance management plans for Bt-toxin-producing crops., Gould, F. et al, 1998,

Redefining Wealth, Onians, Dick RSA Journal, 4 Apr, 1998,

Rejection of Hormones in Milk Applauded by International Consumer Group, www.geocities.com/Athens/1527/rejrbgh.html, Consumers International press release, 3 Jul, 1997,

Release of Genetically Modified Crops, DETR Factsheet, 30 Nov, 1998,

Release of Genetically Modified Viruses, Cory, J.S., Reviews of Medical Virology, 1991, Vol. 1, p.79–88.

Repeat the Term: Governments at FAO's Gene Commission

fail to make RAFI, http://www.rafi.org/papers/op52.html, Rural Advancement Foundation: Briefing paper, Jul, 1999, Vol. 5 N . 2,

Report of the Biotechnology Working Group, National Farmers Union Council, Mar, 1998,

Report on animal health and animal welfare aspects of the use of bovine somatotropin, report of the Scientific Committee on Animal Health and Welfare, www.europa.eu.int/comm/ dg24/health/sc/scah/out21-en.html, 10 Mar, 1999,

Report on BST Grievance Hearings, 17 Sep, 1998,

Report on Late Onset Disorders, Advisory Committee on Genetic Testing, Sep, 1998,

Report on Riboflavin Derived from Genetically Modified (GM) Bacillus subtilis using Fermentation Technology, ACNFP Report,, MAFF, 1996,

Report on the Implications of Cloning for the Welfare of Farmed Livestock, Farm Animal Welfare Council, Dec, 1998,

Reporters Blow Whistle on News Station, www.foxBGHsuit.com/index2.htm,

Research News: promiscuous pollination, Dove, A Nature Biotechnology, Sep, 1998, Vol. 16, p. 805.

Research on bees and GM crops, New Scientist, 14 Aug, 1997,

Research Roundup: Franklin Hoke School of Medicine, USA, Almanac, 15 Jul, 1997, Vol. 44 No. 1,

Researcher Warns of Cancer Risk from rBGH (non-organic) Dairy Foods, www.holisticmed.com/gbh/prostate.html, Cancer Prevention Coalition,

Resistance to Antibiotics and other Antimicrobial Agents, House of Lords Select Committee on Science & Technology, 7th Report, 1998,

Resistance to Bt crops, California Farmer, Jan, 1999,

Resistance to toxins from Bacillus thuringiensis to B.thruingiensis susp. aizawai in the diamondback moth (lepidoptera: Plutellidae), Tabashnik, B.E., Appl. Environ. Microbiol., 1993 Vol. 59 No. 5, 1332–1335.

Resolving the DDT Dilemma: Protecting Human Health and Biodiversity, World Wildlife Fund,

Resources pointer No. 201, PANUPS, Pesticides Action North America Update Service, 24 Mar, 1999,

Restoring Public Confidence in Science is Vital to UK Economy says Byers, Press notice, Department of Trade and Industry, 21 Jan, 1999,

Return to 'Stone Age' pest management., Benbrook, C.M., Hansen, M., Remarks presented at EPA public meeting: 'Plant Pesticides Resistance Management', 21 Mar, 1997,

Revealed: Lord Sainsbury's interest in key gene patent, Flynn, L., The Guardian, 16 Feb, 1999,

Revolving Doors Monsanto and the Regulators, Ferrara, J., The Ecologist, Sep, 1998, Vol. 28 No.5,

Risk of Genes Escaping from Transgenic Crops, Williams, G., Williams, P., Hortideas, Apr, 1994, Vol. 14 No 4,

Risky Business, http://www.geneticsforum.org.uk/splice/mar98p.10.htm, Genetics Forum, 1998,

Roslin Institute Annual Report 95–96,

Roslin Institute Annual Report 96–97,

Roslin Institute Annual Report 97–98,

Round-up Problems, Cox, Caroline http://synthetic-pros.hypermart.net/aggand/roundup.htm, Northwest Coalition for Alternatives to Pesticides, 29 Apr, 1997,

Roundup Ready Sugar Beet: the crop the technology and the benefits, Monsanto,

Roundup: the world's biggest selling herbicide, Mendelson, J., The Ecologist, Vol. 28 No 5

RSPCA personal briefing on animals and genetic engineering, Mar, 1999,

Safety assessment for the consumption of food and feed products derived from insect-protected potato lines that contain the nptII selectable marker gene, Monsanto, undated,

Safety of Bovine Growth Hormone, Kronfeld, D., Science, Vol.251, 18 Jan, 1991, p.256–257.

Safety of Milk from Cows Treated with Bovine Somatotropin, Challacombe, D., Wheeler, E., The Lancet Vol 344, 17 Sep, 1994, p.815.

Safety of Milk from Cows Treated with Bovine Somatotropin, Mepham, B., The Lancet Vol 344, 17 Sep, 1994, p.1445–6.

Sales Boom in Pesticides: Herbicide-Resistant The Gene Exchange – A Public Voice On Biotechnology & Agriculture, www.ucsusa.org/Gene/F97, Union of Concerned Scientists, Sep, 1999,

Say it Ain't Soy, Monsanto, Bruno, K. www.purefood.org/aintsoy.html, Multinational Monitor, Jan, 1997, Vol. 18 No 1 & 2,

Say No to Genetically Engineered Foods, Pesticide Action Network Asia Pacific, Oct, 1998,

Schmeiser, P., www.btinternet.com/nlpwessex/Documents/contentsfall.htm, Western Producer, Nov, 1998,

Scientific Advisory System Inquiry (GM Foods), Ho, M-W. Saunders, P. et al Institute Of Science In Society, 28 Mar, 1999,

Scientific principles for ecologically based risk assessment of transgenic organisms, Regal, P.J., www.psrast.org/pjrisk.htm, Molecular Ecology, 1994, Vol.3, p.5–13.

Scientific Review Rejects the HGDP, http://www.rafi.org/pr/release07.html, Rural Advancement Foundation,

Scientists Clash over tests on modified potatoes, The Independent, 9 Mar, 1999,

Scientists' Warning about Genetically Engineered Food, Physicians and Scientists for Responsible Applications of Science and Technology, Feb, 1999,

SCIMAC position statement on commercial introduction of genetically modified crops, Supply Chain Initiative on Modified Agricultural Crops, Feb, 1999,

Second Annual Report, Advisory Committee on Genetic Testing, 1998,

Second thoughts about U.S. Patent No. 4,438,032, Burrows, B., Bull. Med. Eth., Jan, 1997,

Secret Deal will Ban GM crops until 2002, Woolf, Marie Sunday Independent, 14 Mar, 1999,

Seed Industry Consolidation: who owns whom?, http://www.rafi.org/communique/19983.html, Rural Advancement Foundation: Briefing paper, y/A, 19989,

Seed Industry Announcements and White Papers, AMSEED, http://www.amseed.com/documents/, American Seed Trade Association, 22 Jan, 1999,

Seed Sterilisation is "Holy Grail" of Ag Biotech Firms, RAFI, http://www.rafi.org/pr/release26.html, Rural Advancement Foundation: Briefing paper, 27 Jan, 1999,

Seeds of Discontent: Cotton Growers Say Strain Cuts Yields, Myerson, A.R., New York Times, 19 Nov, 1997,

Seeds of dissension, The Ottawa Citizen, 26 Feb, 1999,

Segregation of organic food, Prideaux, P., Private correspondence, 30 Feb, 1999,

Select Committee on European Communities Second Report: Appendix 4, 1999,

Selling Suicide: farming, false promises and genetic engineering in developing countries, Christian Aid, 1998,

Send in the Clones?, Tokar, B., Food & Water Journal, Spring 1997,

Setting Rules for the Biotechnology Trade, Pollack, A., The New York Times, 15 Feb, 1999,

Shock GM legal move by all-party MPs – politicians and MPs to sue government over seed fast tracking., Friends of the Earth Press release, 31 Mar, 1999,

Shoppers Unaware of Gene Changes, Burros, M., The New York Times, 20 Jul, 1998,

Sixteen untested foods to be approved (in Australia), Consumer Food Network, Sleuthing of Plant Genes Speeds Ahead of Schedule, Wood, M., http://www.ars.usda.gov/is/AR/archive/jan99/dopsis0199.htm, ARS News Service of USDA, 25 Jan, 1999,

Somatic v. Germline Therapy, http://www.u.arizona.edu/bpoepsel/somatic-germline.html,

Some Dangers of Hormones in Milk, www.enviroweb.org/pubs/rachel/rhwn382.htm, Rachel's Hazardous Waste News, No.382, 24 Mar, 1994,

Something strange is happening to our beans, http://www.enviroweb.org/shag/info/leaflets/bckgd.html,

Sovereignty or Hegemony? Africa and Security – Negotiating from Reality, RAFI, http://www.rafi.org/communique/fltxt/19973.html, Rural Advancement Foundation: Briefing paper, May, 1997,

Soya in artificial baby milks, Baby Milk Action briefing – draft, Mar, 1999,

Spain makes GE crop producers take insurance, GeneEthics Network (Bob Phelps), 19 Mar, 1999,

Spanish Farmers urge GM Food Moratorium, Brough, D., Reuters, 22 Mar, 1999,

Spare part baby clones to go ahead in weeks, Ballantyne, A., The Sunday Times, 29 Nov, 1998,

Special Issue on Monsanto, Cummins, Ronnie Food Bytes, 7 Dec, 1998,

Special Safety Concerns of Transgenic Agriculture and elated Issues: Briefing Paper for Minister of State for the Environment, The Rt Hon. Michael Meacher, Ho, Mae-Wan Institute of Science in Society, Apr, 1999,

Special Safety Concerns of Transgenic Agriculture and Related Issues, Ho, M-W., Institute Of Science In Society, 1999,

Species Jump: Human Ehrlichiosis – Mutant or Emergence?, Williams, B., http://www.doofus.org/mercatroid/ehrlichia.html,

Spontaneous Hybridisation between Oilseed Rape (Brassica napus) and Weedy B. campestris (Brassicaceae:A risk of Growing Genetically Modified Oilseed Rape, Joergensen, R.B., Andersen, B., American J. of Botany, Vol. 81, p. 1620–26

Starlings and Snails that Speak Nothing But Trouble, Gardener, Dan The Ottawa Citizen, 1 Mar, 1999,

State of the World 1997, Brown, L. et al, www.oxfam.org.uk/

policy/papers/gmfoods/gmfoods.htm, Worldwatch Institute Report, 1997,

Statement of Policy: Foods Derived from New Plant Varieties, Consumers' Union submission to the US Food and Drugs Authority, Aug, 1992,

Stimulation of intestinal epithelial cell proliferation in culture by growth factors in human and ruminant mammary secretions., Corps, A.N., Brown, K.D., Ju. of Endocrin., 1987, Vol. 113, 285–290.

Stop the Crops, Monbiot, G., The Guardian, 13 Feb, 1999,

Substantial Equivalence: A Licence to Kill?, Antoniou, Michael Nutritional Therapy Today, Vol. 7 No. 3,

Substantial Equivalence, Cummins, J., Web correspondnce, 7 Mar, 1999,

Superhumans, Taylor, R., New Scientist, 3 Oct, 1998,

Swedish study finds exposure to glyphosate and MCPA increases risk of non-Hodgkin's lymphoma, Friends of the Earth Press release,

T. DNA as a gene tag, Walden, R. et al Plant J., 1991, 281–8.

Terminator Seeds Grow Controversy, Phoenix Newspapers USA, 21 Feb, 1999.

Terminator Seeds Rejected by Global Network of Agricultural Experts, Shand, H., Mooney, P., http://www.rafi.org/pr/release23.html, Rural Advancement Foundation International, 2 Nov, 1998,

Terminator Technology and the Developing World, The Gene Exchange – A Public Voice on Biotechnology and Agriculture, www.ucsusa.org/publications/index/html, Union of Concerned Scientists,

Terminator Unleashed: patenting life, patenting death, Olsen, M.J., http://www.ratical.org/ratville/terminatorTech.html, Jun, 1998,

Terms of reference and membership of the genetics and insurance committee, DTI,

Thailand, the Jashmati trademark affair, IP Asia, Feb, 1999,

The Coming Plague, Garrett, Laurie 1994,

The Australian PBR Scandal: UPOV Meets a Scandal "Down Under" by Burying its Head in the Sand, http://www.rafi.org/communique/fltxt/19981.html, RAFI, Jan, 1998,

The Benefits and Ethics of Animal Research, Rowan, Andrew N. Scientific American, Feb, 1997,

The Biotech Century, Rifkin, J., Victor Gollanz, 1999,

The Biotechnology Bubble, Ho, M-W., The Ecologist, Vol 28 No 3, May, 1998,

The Bollworm Controversy – Monsanto's Bt Cotton in 1996, Hagedorn, C., www.ext.vt.edu/news/periodicals/cses/1997–01/1997–01-01.html, Crop and Soil Environmental News, Jan, 1997,

The buyer should beware of miracles of biotech, Irish Times, 22 Feb, 1999,

The Campaign Against Human Genetic Engineering, http://www.users.globalnet.co.uk/cahge/,

The Case Against Genetic Engineering, Wald, G., The Sciences, Sep, 1976,

The CAUSE newsletter, http://www.cdc.gov/ncidod/dbmd/cause/april97.htm, Apr, 1997, Vol. 1,

The Centre for Food Safety (CFS USA) – Projects – lawsuit against FDA, http://www.icta.org/projects/cfs/index.htm,

The Cloning of Dolly, Love, J., http://www.synapse.ndi-rect.co.uk/science/clone.html, Science Explained, Jan, 1998,

The Complete DNA Sequence of S. cerevisiae, http://geneome-www.stanford.edu/Saccharomyces/sequence-done.html, Stanford University, USA, Sep, 1997,

The composition of glyphosate-tolerant soybean seeds is equivalent to that of conventional soybeans., Padgegge, S.R. et al, Journal of Nutrition 126, 1996, 702–16.

The Crop that pumps iron, New Scientist, 6 Mar, 1999,

The Daily Telegraph (London), Clover, C., Irwin, A., 10 Jun, 1999,

The Danger of Virus-Resistant Crops, Cummins, J., http:// userwww.sfsu.edu/,

The Debate on Genetically Modified Organisms: Relevance for the South, www.oneworld.org/odi/briefing/1-99.html, Overseas Development Institute Briefing Paper, Jan, 1999,

The Dispersal of Maize Pollen, Emberlin, J., National Pollen Research Unit, Mar, 1999.

The Ecological Risks of Engineered Crops., Rissler, J., Mellon, M., MIT Press, 1996,

The effects of genetically engineered micro-organisms on soil food webs., Holmes, T.M., Ingham, E.R., Ecological Society Of America Bulletin, Abstracts of the 79th Annual ESA Meeting; Science and Public Policy, 7 Aug, 1994,

The Eighth Day, Batz, J., www.purefood.org/eighth.html, Riverfront Times, St Louis, 11 Dec, 1996,

The Emperor's Transgenic Clothes, Griffiths, M., Draft article, Jan, 1999,

The Engineer in the Garden, Genetics: from the idea of heredity to the creation of life, Tudge, C., Jonathan Cape, 1993,

The Environmental Risks of Transgenic Crops:an Agroecological Assessment, Altieri, M., Department of Environmental Science, Policy & Management, www.pmac.net/ miguel.htm, University of California,,

The evolutionary potential of crop pests, Gould, E. American Scientist, 1991, Vol. 79, 496–507.

The Facts of Life:Chemical & Pharmaceutical Companies see their Future in Biological Invention, Pilling, D., Financial Times, 9 Dec, 1998,

The failings of the principle of substantial equivalence in regulating transgenic foods., Fagan, J., GMF Market Intelligence, 2 Dec, 1996, Vol. 1 No. 2.

The feeding value of soybeans fed to rats, chickens, catfish and dairy cattle is not altered by genetic incorporation of glyphosate tolerance., Hammond, B.G. et al, Journal of Nutrition 1126(3), 1996, 717–26.

The flight of the Soya Bean, Cohen, P., New Scientist, 24 Apr, 1999,

The flood gates for unrestricted global trade in genetically modified food were thrown open last night after Mr Clinton's personal intervention., Ingham, J., Daily Express, 25 Feb, 1999,

The Food Labelling (Amendment) Regulations 1999 No.747, MAFF, Mar, 1999,

The Gene Giants: Masters of the Universe, http://www.rafi.org/communique/19992.html, Rural Advancement Foundation, ch/, 1999,

The Gene Hunters: Biotechnology and the Scramble for Seed, Juma, C., Princeton University Press, 1989,

The Greening Revolution, Tilman, D., Nature, 19 Nov, 1998, Vol. 396,

The Human Genome Diversity Project, www.niec.net/ipch/research/thehgdp.html, Indigenous People's Coalition Against Piracy, 1998,

The Human Tissue Trade, http://www.rafi.org/communique/fltxt/19971.html, Rural Advancement Foundation, 1997,

The Impact of Genetic Modification on Agriculture, Food and Health: An interim statement, British Medical Association, May, 1999,

The impact of Intellectual Property Rights on Sustainable Food Security and Farm Families Remains to be Felt, RAFI Communique, 20 May, 1998,

The Implications of Testing for Insurance, Human Genetics Advisory Commission, Dec, 1997,

The Insulin Debate, British Diabetic Association,

The Last Silver Bullet, Mellon, M., The Gene Exchange – A Public Voice On Biotechnology & Agriculture, www.ucsusa.org/cgi-bin/AT-ucssearch.cgi, Union of Concerned Scientists, 1996,

The Manipulation of Codex Alimentarius, Verrall, J., Report to the President of the European Commission, 1999,

The Medical Impact of the use of Antimicrobials in Food Animals: Report of a WHO meeting Berlin 13–17 October 1997, World Health Organisation,

The Monsanto Machine, St Clair, J., http://www.purefood.org/Monsanto/machine.cfm, In These Times, Chicago, Illinois, 7 Mar, 1999,

The Monsanto Monitor, http://www.purefood.org/Monsanto/monitor99may.cfm, A SEED Europe, 1 May, 1999,

The Monster Strikes Again, http://www.rafi.org/genotypes/980630mons.html, Rural Advancement Foundation,

The Motley Fool, US financial commentaries,

The Mystery in Your Milk, Akre, J., Wilson, S., http://www.foxBGHsuit.com.bgh7.htm,

The neurophsychiatric effects of aspartame in normal volunteers, Lapierre, K.A. et al, J. Clin. Pharmacol., May, 1990, Vol. 30 No.5, 454–60.

The Opportunity of Escape of Engineered Genes from Transgenic Crops, Hancock, J.F. et al, Hortscience, Dec, 1997, Vol. 31 No 7, p.1080–85.

The outdated basis of GE, Suurkula, J. et al, Physicians & Scientists For Responsible Application Of Science & Technology www.psrast.org/newgen.ht, 1 Apr, 1999,

The Parts of Life: Agricultural Biodiversity, Indigenous Knowledge,and the Role of the Third System, Mooney, P., Dag Hammarskjöld Foundation, Development Dialogue: Special Issue, Dec, 1997,

The patenting of human genomic material, http://www.rafi.ca/communique/19941.html, RAFI, Jan, 1994,

The persistence of glyphosate and its metabolite aminomethyl-phosphonic acid in some coastal British Columbia streams, EPS, Pacific Region,

The potato blight is back, www.grain.org/publications/oct952.htm, Seedling (Genetic Engineering Resources Action International),

The Potential Use of Gene Therapy in utero, UK Gene Therapy Advisory Committee Report,

The Precautionary Principle, www.psrast.org/precaut.htm,

Rachel's Environment and Health Weekly, 19 Feb, 1998, No 586,

The Presence of the Past, Sheldrake, R., Fontana, 1989,

The price of disaster will not be paid by those responsible, Thornton, J., Independent on Sunday, 28 Feb, 1999,

The Promise of Tissue Engineering, Mooney, D.J., Mikos, A.G., Scientific American, Apr, 1999,

The rBGH scandals, Monsanto dairies battle over free speech, Rosenfeld, P., www.geocities.com/Athens/1527/text4.html, The Times-Argus, 22 Feb, 1994,

The risk of Crop Transgene Spread, Mikkelsen, T.R. et al, Nature, 1996, Vol. 380, p.31.

The Scientific Advisory System: Genetically Modified Food, House of Commons enquiry, 25 Feb, 1999,

The Seeds of Wrath, Vidal, J., The Guardian, 19 Jun, 1999,

The Selection of Antibiotics – order information, Invogen web site, 1999,

The Social Management of Genetic Engineering, Wheale, P., Von Schomberg, R., Glasner, P., Ashgate, 1998,

The spread of plasmids as a function of adaptability, Tschape, H., FEMS Microbial Ecology, 23-, 1994, Vol. 15,

The Spud America Didn't Like, Green, Emily The New Statesman,

The Suicide Seeds, Time, 1 Feb, 1999,

The Symbiotic Planet: a new look at evolution, Margolis, L., Weidenfeld and Nicolson, 1999,

The Taming of Jim's Garden, The Voice of the Ukraine (translated), 5 Mar, 1999, No. 41 (2043),

The Terminator File, RAFI, http://www.rafi.org/papers/op53.html, Rural Advancement Foundation: Briefing paper, Aug, 1998, Vol. 5 No.3,

The Terminator Technology: New genetic technology aims to prevent farmers from saving seed, RAFI, http://www.rafi.org/communique/fltxt/19982.html, Rural Advancement Foundation: Briefing paper, Mar, 1998,

The Toxic Legacy in Breast Milk, http://www.oneworld.org/
    index.html,

The Unholy Alliance, Ho, M-W., Ecologist, Jul, 1997, Vol. 27
    No. 4,

The Use of Cauliflower Mosaic Virus 35S Promoter (CAMV)
    in Calgenes's Flavr Savr Tomatoes Creates Hazard, Cum-
    mins, J.,

The Violence of the Green Revolution:Third World Agricul-
    ture, Ecology and Politics, Shiva, V., Zed Books Ltd., 1991,

Third World Network: briefing paper, Meyer, H., 10 Feb, 1998,

Third World Opposes Genetically Modified Foods, Genetic
    Engineering Network, 28 Feb, 1999,

Third World Rejects GM and India halts trials, 1 Mar, 1999,

Third World Rejects GM, Lean, G., Independent on Sunday,
    28 Feb, 1999,

This I Believe and other essays, Schumacher, E.F., Green
    Books, 1997,

This is the real mad cow disease, Cobain, I., Daily Mail, 12
    Jun, 1999,

This strawberry tastes just like a strawberry, Monsanto adver-
    tisement, The Guardian, 4 Jul, 1998,

Three Year Ban Not Enough, Secret Paper Shows, Friends of
    the Earth press release, 15 Mar, 1999,

Threshold for GMO detection in food – Switzerland, BioLinX
    GmbH Biotech and Life Science Communications, Feb,
    1999,

Tolerant Rape not cure all, Leahy, S., Farmers' Weekly, 10
    Apr, 1998,

Too Early May Be Too Late, Traavik, T., Directorate of Nature
    Management, Jan, 1999,

Too Good to Go Wrong, Ellstrand, N., Greenpeace Science
    Briefing Paper, 1999,

Toxic Deception, Fagin, D., Lavelle, M., Carol Publishing
    Group, Rachel's Environment & Health Weekly, 10 Jul,
    1997,

Toxic Deception, Lewis, C., The Centre for Public Integrity, 6 Feb, 1997,

Toxicity in Bacillus thuringiensis CrylAb toxin to the predator Crysoperia carnea (Neroptera: Chrysopidae), Hillbeck, A. et al Environmental Entomology, Aug, 1998, Vol. 27 No. 4.,

Trade, Intellectual Property, Food and Biodiversity: Key issues and options for the 1999 review of Article 27.3 (b) of the TRIPS agreement, Tansey, G., 1998,

Traitor Tech: The Terminator's Wider Implications, www.rafi.org/Traitor/, RAFI Press Release, Mar, 1999,

Traitor Technology – Damaged Goods from the Gene Giants, www.rafi.org, RAFI Press Release, 29 Mar, 1999,

Transfer in marine sediments of the naturally occurring plasmid pRAS1 encoding multiple antibiotic resistance, Sandaa, R.A., Enger, O., Applied and Environmental Microbiol., 1994, Vol.60, 4243–4238.

Transformation of Acinetobacter sp. strain BD413 by transgenic sugar beet DNA, Gebhard, F. et al, Appl. Environ. Microbiol., 1998, Vol. 64, 1550–1554.

Transgenic pollen harms Monarch larvae, Nature, 20 May, 1999, Vol. 399, 214.

Trends in Animal Research, Mukerjee, M., Scientific American, Feb, 1997,

TRIPS Council moves slowly on review of life patenting exemption, ICTSD Internal files, 22 Feb, 1999,

Tryptophan summary, Fagan, J., 1998,

Turning mosquitoes into malaria fighters, Naik, G., Dow Jones News, 17 Jun, 1997,

Two sets of human-tropic pig retrovirus, Nature, 16 Oct, 1997, Vol. 389,

US the last evil empire? – the world's imperialist bully?, Fleming, T., The Independent, 7 Mar, 1999,

UK biosciences employment rising 20 per cent pa survey, Reuters, 1 Mar, 1999,

UK National Concensus Conference on Plant Biotechnology, 2 Nov, 1994,

UK Politics 'No deal over GM crops', BBC, 15 Mar, 1999,

UK seed merchant confirms huge commercial opportunity for non-GM foods, Independent, 20 Feb, 1999,

UK: Top researchers back suspended lab whistleblower scientist, Guardian, 13 Feb, 1999, Vol., umbilical-cord blood bank to be opened, Christie, B., The Sunday Times, 31 May, 1998,

UN Convention to regulate trade in hazardous pesticides, www.fao.org/news/1997/971108%2De.htm, FAO press release,

Uncontrolled genetic tests in Georgia, Greenpeace, 24 Aug, 1998,

Unlabelled Milk from Cows Treated with Biosynthetic Growth Hormone: a Case of Regulatory Abdication, Epstein, S. S., Int. J. of Health Services, 1996, Vol. 26 No.1, p. 173–85.

Unpalatable truths, New Scientist, 17 Apr, 1999,

Update on Risk Research – Process Counts, The Gene Exchange – A Public Voice On Biotechnology & Agriculture, www.uc-susa.org/publications/index/html, Union of Concerned Scientists, l/W, 1998,

Uptake of food-ingested foreign DNA, BioLin GmbH and Life Science Communications, Feb, 1999,

Urgent appeal to all governments to revoke the market approval of Monsanto RR soybean, Greenpeace briefing, 16 Oct, 1997,

US 'Observers' Lobby Against Trade Curbs on Biotechnology, Weiss, R., Gillis, J., Washington Post, 13 Feb, 1999,

US 'Wrecking' GM talks., Kirby, Alex http://news.bbc.co.uk/hi/english/world/newsid284000/284569.stm, BBC News website, 22 Feb, 1999,

US and China pull out stops for WTO deal, Walker, T., Fidler, S., Financial Times, 15 Feb, 1999,

US and OZ Stall Biosafety Protocol, New York Times, 26 Feb, 1999,

US Corporate link up with UK co-op rings alarm bells, NGIN press release, 1 Mar, 1999,

US criticised at international talks on biogenetic trade, Associated Press World News, 24 Feb, 1999,

US Funding of Human Biodiversity Collections Carries on Despite Contrary Scientific Advice, http://www.rafi.org/pr/release08.html, Rural Advancement Foundation,

US giant food processor starts to move away from GM soya, Natural Law Party, 10 Mar, 1999,

US loses huge market thanks to GMOs, Reuters, 3 Mar, 1999,

US Patent on New Genetic Technology Will Prevent Farmers from Saving Seed, RAFI, http://www.rafi.org/genotypes/980311seed.html, Rural Advancement Foundation: Briefing paper, 11 Mar, 1998,

US petition to label genetically modified foods, Green Alliance, 26 Feb, 1999,

US prepares $560M trade war on Europe, Arthur, C., Independent, 23 Mar, 1999,

US ruling aids opponent of patents on life forms, Weiss R., Washington Post, 17 Jun, 1999,

US Sabotages biosafety protocol (with help from a few friends), Lennard, J., The Guardian, 24 Feb, 1999,

US scurries to scuttle biotech trade curbs – fate of gene altered produce splits faction at Columbian conference, Florida Today, 14 Feb, 1999,

US seed merchant confirms huge opportunity for non-GM foods, Natural Law Party, 25 Feb, 1999,

US seeks to terminate negotiations on safeguards for trade in genetic foods, Greenpeace International press release, 22 Feb, 1999,

US Terminates Biosafety, Greenpeace press release, 22 Feb, 1999,

US warns EU not to impede farm trade over biotech, Reuters, Washington, 1998

US, Canada call for GMO Trade on WTO Agenda, Bridges Trade News Digest, 10 May, 1999, Vol. 3 No. 18,

Vaccine Development – Wisconsin Company helps develop Potatoes for Vaccine Experiment, Hepatitis Weekly, 18 Jan, 1999,

Verhandlungen der Gesellschaft fur Okologie, Meyer, H., Wolters, V., 1997,

Very Incomplete knowledge of DNA, http://www.psrast.org/junkdna.htm, PRAST, 1998,

Veterinary Products Committee Appendix Medicines Act 1968, MAFF, 1999

Victory for consumers, Hansen, M., Consumer's Union/Consumers Policy Institute Statement, 15 Jan, 1999,

Victory on Biopiracy, http://www.ozemail.com.au/hsca, Heritage Seed Curators Australia, 10 Nov, 1998,

Vote of confidence in approval system for GM foods, MAFF, 18 Feb, 1999,

Warning: Scientists risk official modification, BBC, 21 May, 1999,

Watchdog orders insurers to revise genetic test policy, The Daily Telegraph, 25 Oct, 1997,

We believe food should be grown with less pesticide, Monsanto advertisement, The Independent, 4 Jul, 1998,

Weed Ecology studies, http://www.res.bbsrc.ac.uk/cdm/research, Weed Ecology Group IACR Rothamstead,

Weeds Could Develop Resistance to Glyphosate, Rissler, J., http://www.purefood.org/glyphresis.html, Union of Concerned Scientists, 14 Feb, 1997,

Western Europe Drug Mergers, Oxford Analytica Executive Brief, 11 Dec, 1998,

What happened to putting the consumer first Mr Blair?, Macintyre, D., Independent, 15 Feb, 1999,

What is Biotechnology? Fact Sheet on Genetically Modified Foods & Crops, Tokar, B., www.purefood.org/ge/geFactSheet.htm,

What is Genetic Engineering: a simple introduction, http://www.psrast.org/whatisge.htm, PSRAST, 1998,

What is genetic engineering?, Steinbrecher, R., The Women's Environmental Network Trust, Jul, 1998,

What is Patently Offensive? Policy on 'Immoral' Inventions Troubles Legal, Medical Professional, Weiss, R., Washington Post, 11 May, 1998,

What is the FDA policy for Regulation of Genetically Engineered Foods?, www.essential.org/crg/consumeralert.html, The Council For Responsible Genetics,

What is Tissue Engineering?, Pittsburgh Tissue Engineering Initiative Inc Briefing Paper,

What is wrong with nature?, Steinbrecher, R., Resurgence, May, 1998.

What makes fruit companies tick?, Aitken, I., The Guardian, 9 Mar, 1999,

What to believe? A personal letter to you who are confused about Genetically Engineered (GE) foods., Suurkula, J., http://www.psrast.org/whatobel.htm, PSRAST,

What You May Not Know, Greger, M., http://arrs.envirolink.org/AnimaLife/spring95/BGH.html,

What's coming to market?, The Gene Exchange – A Public Voice On Biotechnology & Agriculture, www.ucsusa.org/Gene/w98.market.html, Union of Concerned Scientists,

What's wrong with nature?, Steinbrecher, Ricarda, Resurgence, May, 1998, No. 188,

WHO TB report shows global response to epidemic inadequate, World Health Organisation, Mar, 1999,

Why Soya is a Hidden Destroyer, Daily Mail, 12 Mar, 1999,

Why the UK baby milk law must be changed, Baby Milk Action Briefing Paper, Dec, 1997,

Why Transnational Corporations are Organising to 'Save the Global Environment', Finger, M., Kilcoyne, J., The Ecologist, Jul, 1997, Vol. 27,

Why we don't need GM foods., Tudge, C. et al, New Statesman, 19 Feb, 1999,

Will GM Crops deliver benefits to farmers?, http://www.btinternet.com/nlpwessex/Documents/gmagric.htm, NLP Wessex, 1998,

Will GM-foods mean less pesticide use?, Pesticides News, Mar, 1999, Vol. 43,

Wisconsin Company Helps Develop Potatoes for Vaccine Experiment, Hepatitis Weekly, 18 Jan, 1999,

Withdrawal of Pork Insulin, Insulin Dependent Diabetes Trust Newsletter, Jan, 1999, Issue No. 19,

World Food Output Dominated by Food Clusters, Reuters, 11 Mar, 1999,

World Hunger: Twelve Myths, Moore Lappe, F. et al, 1998,

World in Action, television programme, 12 Aug, 1998,

World Recoils at Monsanto's brave new crops, Lambrecht, B., Post-Dispatch Washington, 27 Dec, 1999,

World's largest retailer bans GM: Carrefour to Withdraw Gene Foods from Store Shelves, Dow Jones News, 14 Feb, 1999,

Worldwide conformity kills KIWIs' GM-free option, Sunday Star Times, NZ, 21 Mar, 1999,

WTO and the Environment, Bridges Weekly Trade News Digest, 15 Mar, 1999, Vol. 3,

You Did It! The European Biotechnology Directive at Last., Nott, R., http://www.lovellwhitedurrant.com/NewSite/PUBS/PharmaBio/Jan1999/101121−07.htm, 1998,

You too can make a perfect person, Rifkin, J., The Editor, 27 Jun, 1998,

Zeneca files anti-trust suit against Monsanto, Reuters, 28 Jul, 1998, 1997 Report on Sustainable Development including Environmental, Safety and Health Performance, Monsanto, Mar, 1998,